Pelican Books

Mothers Alone

Dennis Marsden was born in Huddersfield in 1933 and was educated at a grammar school and Cambridge University. He has worked at the Institute of Community Studies and taught at a secondary modern school; during this period he also lived at Toynbee Hall in London, helping with the Poor Man's Lawyer and working with deprived families. After a brief spell at Salford Royal College of Advanced Technology, where he studied the problems of redeveloping slum areas, he moved in 1965 to Essex University to take part in a national survey of poverty; *Mothers Alone* grew out of his preliminary studies for this survey.

Dennis Marsden is now a lecturer at Essex University. His publications include *Education and the Working Class*, and *Working Class Community* (both in collaboration with B. Jackson and available in Pelicans), a Fabian pamphlet, *Politicians, Equality and Comprehensives*, and an autobiographical chapter in *Breakthrough* (ed. R. Goldman).

For Daniel, Sarah, and Ben

Contents

Acknowledgements

My main debt is to the 116 mothers who so movingly discussed their problems with me. I also wish to thank the Joseph Rowntree Memorial Trust who are financing the larger poverty research project of which the present study is part. I hope they will feel that my research builds usefully on the great Rowntree tradition. The Trust is, of course, in no way responsible for any of the views expressed here.

That I wrote the book is entirely due to Peter Townsend, who first suggested that I should study fatherless families in poverty, and who has provided much valuable editorial comment on the various drafts. I would be pleased to think the book now shares something of his vision.

I am indebted to the other members of the poverty research team, above all for the illumination of the numerous discussions involved in setting up the national survey. Brian Abel-Smith read my drafts at every stage, providing shrewd advice particularly about knotty points of social security. At Essex, Adrian Sinfield has presented me with a steady stream of ideas. From his research and from that of Hilary Land and John Veit Wilson I have borrowed much. Sheila Benson and Marie Brown have also kindly read preliminary drafts.

The managers and staff of 'Seaston' and 'Northborough' N.A.B. offices gave of their time in drawing and contacting the mothers in my sample, and also in providing comprehensive statistics for the group of mothers to whom letters were sent. I regret that it was decided by the authorities that issues of confidentiality ruled out any further discussion with local staff, from which my research would undoubtedly have gained.

I have also received advice, sometimes of salutory toughness, from Brian Jackson, and from Margaret Wynn who is the pioneer in the campaign for the rights of fatherless families. At various times Joan Busfield, Lotte Cox, Harry Day, Colin Gibson, Michael Humphrey, Tony Lynes, John McKenzie, Mike Miller, Marie Oxtoby, Martin Rein, Ernest Rudd, Renate Simpson, Dorothy Smith, and Jonathan Stein have kindly given advice or read and commented on sections of the manuscript.

I am grateful to Marion Haberhauer and Wendy Morgan for their patience and skill in preparing typed drafts from my scripts.

Finally I would like to thank my wife, Pat, for her continuing interest and help in the project.

Wivenhoe
February 1969

Preface to the Pelican Edition

The core of this Pelican edition of *Mothers Alone* is still the evidence from the survey of unsupported mothers on national assistance which I carried out in 1965 and 1966. But I have taken advantage of republication to completely rewrite the analysis in the concluding chapters on 'help from the community', so as to incorporate valuable new material on homelessness, illegitimacy, and separations, and the workings of the Supplementary Benefits Commission. I have also streamlined the rest of the text by some reordering and rewriting, and by the removal of most of the tables of figures to an appendix.

My main aim has been to say more forcefully now what I originally said in 1968. I feel that the elements of grief and loss in these mothers' descriptions of their lives will not date, and there has been no more recent detailed study to improve our knowledge of the living standards of unsupported mothers. Nor, I would argue, have there yet been any fundamental changes in provisions or attitudes which would substantially improve the mothers' position in society.

Hopefully, perhaps by the time this edition is published, the recommendations of the Finer Committee on One-Parent Families will render obsolete my criticisms of the present social security provisions. Yet even so, the record of our slow and halting steps towards recognizing the needs of this varied and stigmatized section of the population, and towards devising and providing for them an equitable and flexible system of support, will retain permanent lessons.

I would like to acknowledge the continuing support of Peter Townsend, Adrian Sinfield, and Margaret Wynn in the revision of this edition. I am also indebted to Colin Bell for helpful references on the family, and to Michael Hill for a new light on administrative 'discretion'.

Wivenhoe
October 1971

Introduction

This book is about the lives and living standards of mothers alone; about unmarried, separated, divorced, and widowed mothers and their children. Our society defends the institution of marriage by stigmatizing some of these mothers as less worthy than others: for example, although some are legally entitled to pensions, or to maintenance from their children's fathers, others are entitled to nothing. But in this book I call all these mothers 'mothers alone' or 'unsupported mothers', and their families 'fatherless families', to stress that however they came to their present situation they now have needs and problems in common.

Mothers alone suffer the double deprivations of fatherlessness* and poverty. They are often lonely and socially isolated in their task of bringing up their children without adequate emotional support from their children's fathers or from the community. And, above all, fatherless families are likely to be poor because women are in a subordinate position in marriage and in society. Maintenance payments from the children's fathers are often inadequate; and on average a woman can earn only half as much as a man, while a mother who works will have the additional problems of seeing that her children are adequately cared for.

Society does offer limited financial security to mothers who are alone, in recognition of their value as mothers. They are allowed to stay at home to look after their children, supported by national assistance (or supplementary benefit, or 'social security', as it is now called).[1] With this allowance from the state, and not working or working only part-time, many mothers can be financially less badly-off than if they had to support themselves and their families solely on their small full-time earnings. But their

---

*For want of a composite word, throughout this book I have sometimes used 'fatherlessness' to include also the mother's lack of a husband.

standard of living on national assistance would still be only half that of the average two-child family in the community.[2] In fact, in 1966 in England and Wales, out of the 349,360 mothers with their 596,670 dependent children who were in fatherless families, more than one in three received national assistance.[3] And it has been estimated more recently that of mothers alone who have no pension two thirds must now be dependent on supplementary benefit.[4]

These figures for dependence on the state reveal that, in a time of increasing prosperity, mothers alone are failing to share fully in the overall rise in living standards.

This small survey of mothers alone is intended to stimulate public debate about the problems of fatherlessness and about how we treat one group among the poor who are dependent on the state. In 1965 and 1966 I interviewed 116 mothers alone who were drawing national assistance in two areas, which have been given the fictitious names of Northborough and Seaston. I wanted to see how the mothers faced their common problems: the mothers were poor in a society with rising living standards; they were unsupported and living alone when most mothers were married and lived with their husbands; they were women in an economy geared to men's work; they were dependants of the state in a society which put a premium on independence, thrift and self-help; they were clients without rights facing a powerful bureaucracy, the National Assistance Board, whose workings were secret; they were poor and had children when rents were high and children were unwelcome; and they were mostly suppliants for maintenance from their children's fathers, in a legal system designed by men and geared to the needs of the middle classes.

I wanted to know what these mothers could afford to buy, and I wanted to ask a question which is, curiously, seldom asked of the poor – how poor did they feel? The deprivations of fatherlessness and poverty are intermeshed, and how the mothers feel will depend not only on their incomes but on their whole social situation. I wanted also to see whether national assistance was properly designed to cover the range of social situations to be found among fatherless families.

What is poverty today?

In a way which this book will explore, these dependent mothers might be said to be living in 'poverty', and the state subsistence level is a sort of 'poverty line'. For although conventional measures of poverty have attempted to compare the living standards of the poor with some hypothetical minimum subsistence level, it seems likely that poor people themselves will compare their living standards with those of relatives, friends or neighbours; so that the amount of cash a person needs for physical well-being, for social activities, and in general to keep up morale will depend intimately on prevailing levels of spending in the community.[5] The state subsistence level should be a 'poverty line' in the sense that it should express a political decision by the community on what share of our increasing wealth ought to go to the poor.[6] In other words, the level should indicate the community's view on what standard of living is the minimum to be tolerated in a society as wealthy as ours.

Research like the present survey is necessary because unfortunately the general public, and even the administrators and M.P.s who are periodically involved in re-setting the levels of allowances, can know remarkably little about how these levels are arrived at, how the money is supposed to be spent and how in fact it is spent. There has been very little detailed discussion and virtually no published research which would readily permit us to look at the living standards of particular disadvantaged groups in the population.[7] There remain large question marks about what should be counted as 'income' in such comparisons, and about the extent to which different groups among the population benefit from hidden incomes such as gifts from relatives, from so-called 'fringe benefits' (meals, pension schemes, housing, etc., subsidized by employers), from welfare benefits, and from the use of the National Health Service. To collect this sort of information on poverty today, we planned a comprehensive national survey of the incomes and resources of all types of households in the United Kingdom, and one of the preliminary pilot studies[8] was the present survey of fatherless families.

Who are the fatherless?

This survey was also intended to illuminate the variety of social situations covered by the term 'fatherlessness'. For although the term is being used in this book to stress that the families have common problems, it must not be taken to imply that fatherless families are all alike in other ways. Rather, the reality of fatherlessness for mother and children is much less clear-cut and less linked with the mother's marital status than we usually take it to be.

What is a fatherless family? The distinction between 'complete' and 'fatherless' families is blurred because there is no common agreement in our society about how a man who is a father (and a husband) should behave. We might suggest that ideally a father is the principal wage earner, he provides sexual fulfilment for his wife and emotional support for her and the children, he has been traditionally the focal point of authority and decision-making, and he is an embodiment of stability and industry for his children. But many fathers would not fit this description. The role of father is changing, and, assisted perhaps by women's liberation, it will no doubt change more. And at any time there are wide variations between different social groups in the way fathers behave. A man who lives at home with his family may be grossly inadequate in some respects, so that his wife and family suffer the deprivations we tend to associate with the fatherless or husbandless family. Servicemen's and commercial travellers' families, children whose fathers are in hospital or in prison, and children at boarding schools might be counted fatherless (and some of their mothers husbandless) for much of the time. By contrast, in families where the father has gone, someone else may take over his role, wholly or in part, for example as the mother's lover or as a 'second father' to the children.

Clearly fatherlessness is not one situation but a whole spectrum of possible relationships and sets of circumstances. Such variety presents very serious problems if we are trying to devise a scheme of social security for fatherless families which will deal with all these situations simply and equitably. We need a clear perception of who the fatherless are.

The present research – a group of mothers on national assistance

Previous research on fatherless families had been concerned only with mothers of one marital status, or who were unsupported for one reason, for example widows or prisoners' wives.[9] A sample of mothers on national assistance had the double advantage that it permitted a study of mothers living on the poverty line, but also among the mothers were women of differing marital status who were unsupported for a variety of reasons. Obviously mothers on national assistance are a selective group, the victims of misfortunes and failures of formal and informal support: an examination of why mothers come to be on assistance is an integral part of the present study. Yet such a large proportion (60 per cent or more) of mothers alone become dependent on the state at some time[10] that it is hard to argue that the group of mothers on national assistance is, as a whole, very untypical. The names of 116 mothers were obtained with the help of the National Assistance Board, who contacted for me initially 215 mothers in two areas and who furnished statistics covering this larger group, but whose responsibility for the survey ends there.[11]

The two contrasting districts of Northborough and Seaston were chosen to provide some check on possible variations in local conditions and in the administrative practices of the N.A.B., the courts, and other organizations with which the fatherless families had dealings. Northborough is a relatively prosperous northern industrial town of 130,000, where a woman can earn as much as £15 a week as a mender or weaver in the textile mills. West Indians and Pakistanis now work in the textile and chemical industries, and immigrant families account for almost a quarter of all births in the town, among them a proportion of the illegitimate births so that a few immigrant unmarried mothers appear in this survey. Seaston is a southern market town of 60,000 near large camps of British and American forces. Several Seaston factories employ women at piece-rates, but the few concerns in the area which pay wages comparable with those of a man are in seasonal trades such as canning. On the other hand, agriculture around Seaston is a convenient source of casual earnings for women field-workers, who can take their small children along with them. These two areas probably present less serious housing problems for fatherless families than London, which like other large cities tends to draw young unmarried mothers seeking anonymity.

The mothers whom I eventually interviewed were mostly working-class, aged between twenty and forty, although there were also middle-class and older and younger mothers among them. And they were indeed living in a variety of family arrangements. On average they had two dependent children. But they included a sixteen-year-old unmarried mother with her baby living at home with her parents, a fifty-year-old widow with two teenage children and a male lodger, and a separated mother aged forty-three who had eleven children by six different men and who lived with one of her daughters and the daughter's two illegitimate children.

Yet it was striking that on the whole the families tended to be differentiated most clearly by their positions on the age and child-rearing cycle. Thus the unmarried mothers tended to be younger with young children, while in contrast widows tended to be older with older dependent children. Separated and divorced mothers tended to be intermediate, being, as it were, old enough to have married, but not yet married long enough to become widowed.[12] This range of family types challenges us to see fatherlessness and dependence as evolving and changing over time, albeit linked by the common fertility and child-rearing cycle.

The families also revealed a range of relationships not only with the children's fathers but with other men or with kin who performed aspects of the father's role.

Without further introduction than the initial letter asking permission to visit and explain the survey, I called on mothers at home and often interviewed them then and there, for the only deadline was the return of the children from school; there was no man to consult and plan for. As nearly as possible I tried to make the interview a conversation, feeling that this would be flexible in allowing mothers to explore and describe situations which were complex in detail and emotion. The average interview lasted two and a quarter hours, and I spent more time with the larger families (up to five and a quarter hours in one instance) because they tended to have more severe problems and more complex social histories, and least time with the unmarried mothers, among them six West Indians with whom I had difficulty in discussing the emotional aspects of their situation. After the interview I recorded for transcription the mother's version of her experiences, as far as I could remember in the words she had used.

It was apparent from the mothers' willingness or reluctance to be interviewed, and from their reactions to me in the interview, that they saw me in a number of different roles and, consciously or unconsciously, angled the presentation of their experiences for my benefit. It appeared that those who replied were more likely to feel 'worthy', to have broken completely with their children's fathers and to hold less unfavourable views of the N.A.B. Thus, the widows responded well, but unmarried mothers and separated wives with small families, who might feel the greatest stigma or whose relationship with their children's father might be in a delicate state of balance, were not so willing to be interviewed. The mothers of large families replied most readily, apparently because they were in more desperate need of help. The largest group of mothers, about a third, said they wanted to 'help others', while the next largest seemed to have replied automatically to an official-looking document, perhaps to show they had nothing to conceal. Some mothers greeted me eagerly, and very often they wanted not a single interview but a continuing helpful relationship. They hoped I was a social worker to solve their problems, a source of cash or influence with the authorities, a potential lodger, someone to give advice and discipline the children, a relief from the tedium of an entirely female social circle, or, more nebulously and nearer my real role, someone who would publish 'the truth' of their situation to the wider society.

Some women replied very late, and others not at all, although I was able to trace some of the non-respondents via their friends and they agreed to be interviewed. These were often women who had had the least happy relationships with officials. They saw me with more trepidation as an N.A.B. 'snooper', as a confidence trickster, a potential seducer, or a disapproving member of the tax-paying public. Thus among the very interesting group of mothers whom I describe later in this book as the 'underclass' scarcely any responded directly and I had to trace them through a chain of social contacts.

Those mothers who moved frequently could not receive my letters. Others who failed to reply, or who replied as much as three *months* late, had piles of letters awaiting reply behind the clock on the mantelpiece, or in a drawer, where mine had waited until they could summon up the energy to drop the card into a letter-box. A further small number of women were proudly independent and unwilling to make any further gesture which might seem like a request for help. It is also doubtful whether women whose relationship with their children's father was in a delicate balance replied at all readily. And finally there were those who valued their privacy: 'It's like that play, have you heard of it, by Pirandello, *Naked*, I feel naked after I've spoken to you.'

To preserve the confidentiality of the interviews I use no names in this book, for even false names would permit a linking together of pieces of information from different parts of the book to build up identifiable individual portraits.

Interpreting what the mothers said

A survey based on 116 interviews from two areas, with mothers describing their experiences to a stranger, is open to a number of doubts as to how far these stories are reliable, typical, and a suitable basis for generalization. Apart from the restriction on numbers, I was not able to interview the children's fathers or the N.A.B. officials with whom the mothers had had dealings. I discuss these questions again in other parts of the book, and in an appendix,[13] but it is also necessary to say something here about the claims being made for this research and the process of interpreting the evidence.

To produce a representative sample to bring out all the

nuances of situation of all types of fatherless families in the various regions of the country would require initially approaches to about 100,000 households of all kinds, randomly selected from the general population. A survey on this scale would have been far beyond the resources of a private research team, but it would also have been premature in the existing state of our knowledge, and inappropriate for the kinds of insights we were seeking. Large surveys achieve their statistical respectability only with very crudely or easily measured quantities, and at the cost of a loss of fine detail and insight. In the present survey I wanted to illuminate the human situations of poverty and fatherlessness, and while the range of situations among 116 interviews was obviously not complete, it was remarkably broad and sufficient for my purpose. The use of quotations from the mothers' speech is not merely a device to sugar the pill of statistics: the mothers' accounts come nearer to conveying the quality of the experience of fatherlessness.

I have felt more free to generalize from the present survey when several conditions are fulfilled. The first is where the mothers' experiences rest upon some identifiable aspects of the social or economic structure which are common over a wide area of society. Thus, the mothers not only had a common income level from national assistance, but that income level was laid down nationally. The law, the administrative structures of the N.A.B., and (with exceptions which I note) the basic structures of the family may all be said to be fairly similar in other parts of the country too. The second condition is that the stories, drawn from mothers who usually did not know one another, should be mutually consistent. And the third is that they should square with any available national statistics or independent published descriptions.

With regard to the 'subjectivity' of mothers' accounts, I am not seeking the reader's indulgence and credulity, so much as inviting him to engage in interpreting what the mothers said. Sometimes, indeed, we are not interested in objective fact but in the way the mother perceives her side of a relationship with the children's father, say, or with an official. Similarly, while the mothers' tendency to re-interpret past and present experiences in terms of each other makes the task of accurate objective description difficult, at another level this interweaving of past and present is itself a major theme of the research. Similarly what might crudely be called 'bias' in the interviewing situation was often really a valuable source of evidence. A perception of the roles into which I was being pushed became a way of understanding the mothers' fears, hopes, and needs.

I deliberately invited mothers to recall specific experiences rather than to express general opinions not anchored to any particular incident. And inevitably in what follows some interviews will be given more importance than others. This is not just a matter of numbers, although some experiences will be more typical statistically of the whole group. But there are mothers who have had key experiences – some kind of crisis or an encounter with an official, perhaps – which are more revealing of their whole situation. (For example, we may learn more about the class structure from someone who has been forced to think about class differences because of a move from one social class to another through education: or alternatively there is the analogy with the anthropologist who illuminates social structure by the analysis of one key episode.) Not only have some mothers had intrinsically more revealing experiences, but some are also more perceptive than others, more capable of crystallizing and describing their experiences in words, and more willing to talk to an interviewer. The eliciting of interviews, the selection of material by the mother and by the researcher, and the process of interpretation seem to me to be essentially more subjective and skilled processes than sociology sometimes allows. An excessive use of statistical techniques could therefore mislead as to the essential nature of a case-study approach. However, there is a place for numbers, and I have tried to include in the text the numbers of individuals or incidents upon which my descriptions are based, even at the risk of some tedium to the reader and of charges of attempting to give the text a spurious air of science.

Because the research was originally carried out in 1965–6, there is a possibility that with changing levels of state support the living standards of mothers on supplementary benefits relative to the rest of the community will today have improved on the position described here. Between 1966 and 1969, for example, more fatherless families became dependent as supplementary benefit scale rates rose by 8 per cent more than the retail price index (which, however, does not relate to the spending patterns of low income groups).[14] But the improvement is debatable: one of the lessons we are too slow to learn is the remarkable persistence of inequalities. The contemporary situation can only be discovered by thorough, continuing research, which is still not being undertaken.

I believe that, unfortunately, until there are major changes in public attitudes and in the structure of social security for mothers alone, the description of their lives presented in this book will remain only too up-to-date.

Part One *Poverty*

CHAPTER ONE

The Incomes of Fatherless Families

The opening chapters are concerned with describing poverty, beginning with objective measures of incomes, and standards of housing, and moving on to the more difficult questions of how mothers choose to spend their money and how they feel about their standards of living. For readers who are not at home with figures the main, necessarily statistical, findings of this first chapter on incomes and the next chapter on homes will be found summarized at the ends of the chapters.

Of the data which can be obtained in one interview, the total weekly incomes of these fatherless families provide the best single indicator of living standards. Here the definition of weekly income has been broadened to include averages of lump sums and the cash values of goods received.[1] No single measurement can be adequate, for living standards have a number of different dimensions: levels of amenity in the home and the possession of, or access to, certain labour-saving devices contribute. And if the life chances of the family, their build-up of social capital, are also to be assessed, the use of certain free or subsidized services, particularly education, should be taken into account. But a single income measure has the advantage that it permits partial comparisons both among the fatherless and with the rest of society.

While this measure is satisfactory for three quarters of the families, it must be stressed that for up to a quarter income was likely to fluctuate when mothers, or children who were paying board, started or stopped work, or for other reasons. Some kind of averaging of incomes over a longer period would give a truer picture of living standards.

The incomes received by these families in the form of cash were to some extent tied to the national assistance basic scale rate, which in fact represented a level of approximately half the cash income of the average two-child family in the community. However, national assistance allowances were means-tested on a narrow range of cash resources, and families dependent on assistance were permitted to receive cash incomes from some sources, for example pensions and casual earnings, which were partly or wholly ignored by the National Assistance Board (N.A.B.). Moreover, it was still possible in certain circumstances for a fatherless family on assistance to receive in kind or even in cash considerable income from non-dependent members of the same household, or from others. In addition there were various welfare benefits. We wished to know whether such incomes when added together raised some of the families very far above the national assistance basic scale, and which types and sources of income were most important.

The total incomes of fatherless families

The average 'total' income of the families (from all sources, including goods, expressed as the cash equivalent) was £9 6s. od. a week, or £485 a year, to keep a woman and two children, paying £2 a week rent. The smallest income was £4 13s. 6d. a week for a sixteen-year-old unmarried mother of a six-month-old baby, boarding with her parents; the largest, £20 a week for a divorced mother, the householder in a family with one working child, four dependent children, two foster children, and a married daughter with her husband and children, who paid board.

For ease of comparison between families of various sizes and compositions in different households, the incomes have been expressed as percentages of the national assistance basic scale rate: the families at the same percentage of the scale should then have approximately the same level of living.[2] On average the mothers had an income in cash[3] of 105 per cent of scale rate, that is, only a little above the basic level. When incomes from all other sources were taken into account, the mothers' average total income was still only 123 per cent of scale rate. Thus, additional incomes in cash and kind (other than those assessed for their national assistance allowance) did not bring them very far above the national assistance scale rate.

There are no comparable figures of total incomes from all sources available for average and richer families in the community: but families at all levels receive 'hidden' incomes apart from cash, and it may be that richer families receive larger amounts in these ways.[4] It seems likely that fatherless families, far from making up their deficiency of income from such 'hidden' sources, may fall further behind the general population if total incomes are compared.

The cash and total incomes of fatherless families varied over a wide range (Appendix Table 2). According to the principle of a minimum income no fatherless family on assistance would receive in cash less than 100 per cent of the scale rate, yet 8 per cent of the families had an income of less than 90 per cent of scale rate. On the other hand, 3 per cent of the families had cash incomes of over 150 per cent of scale rate. So in practice, national assistance, the state subsistence level, by no means represented a uniform level for all assistance recipients. Nor was it for these families a minimum below which none could fall.

To a limited extent, mothers of different marital status had different incomes. The average widowed mother had a total income slightly larger than the average for all mothers (Appendix Table 3), while unmarried mothers were slightly worse off than average. Some of the difference can be accounted for by the N.A.B. Regulation which permitted widowed mothers to keep the first 7s. 6d. per child out of their widowed mother's allowances. But this is not the whole reason, and these averages conceal significant features in the spread of incomes. Compared with other mothers none of the widows had high or *very* low incomes. But among other mothers were to be found both relatively large and very small incomes. Those divorced and separated mothers whose dependent children were illegitimate had *total* incomes of 106 per cent of national assistance, and as a group they were much the poorest.

Further light can be thrown on these overall variations in income, and variations between mothers of different marital status, by looking at the different types and sources of income.

Types of income

Incomes could be grouped into categories, by type of method of receipt (Appendix Table 4). The mother's regular receipts in cash were by far the most significant incomes in her standard of living. Regular and dependable cash (for example from national assistance, pensions, family allowances, husbands' maintenance payments, earnings, and boarders) amounted to, on average, four times the receipts from all other sources. Private incomes in kind, and 'tied' income (allocated by the giver for a specific purpose such as TV rental) made the next most substantial contribution, and included a great many small items. Occasional state and local authority payments and benefits (such as maternity or school uniform grants) were negligible when averaged weekly, although this is not to deny the importance of lump sum payments in times of need. Finally, although undeclared earnings and incomes from the children's fathers or other men were a major source of worry to the N.A.B., the undeclared incomes revealed in these interviews were negligible. However we must remember that the mothers who felt that they had something to conceal may have been reluctant to talk to me about it, or even to be interviewed at all.

Thus, regular cash incomes fixed the overall living standard of these families, and accounted for some of the variation between mothers, while other incomes tended to make relatively marginal differences.

Regular cash incomes

All the mothers drew assistance, and the majority depended primarily on it. Had the mothers been entirely dependent on assistance (that is, with no earnings, pensions, maintenance, etc.) the average allowance would have been £8 15s. a week, and the actual average payment was £6 1s. This is much larger than the average national assistance payment to all types of recipient, which was £2 6s. 3d. per week at this time.

The mothers' assistance allowances varied according to incomes from other sources deductible for national assistance purposes. Widows derived most of their regular cash income from sources other than national assistance, mainly from their pensions, while the unmarried mothers had most from assistance. The separated and divorced mothers' incomes from assistance varied according to the support received from their husbands.

Maintenance and voluntary payments

The most significant feature of these cash incomes was the low level of support from living fathers. For the divorced, separated, and unmarried mothers, possession of a court order which was paid fully and regularly would have given a mother independence, or at least a useful foundation upon which to build by working. Thus, at the time of this survey, a magistrates' court[5] could have awarded ' innocent' wives a maximum of £7 10s. for themselves, and regardless of the mother's 'guilt' each child living with her could have been awarded £2 10s. from the legal or natur al father. Illegitimate children could also be awarded £2 10s. On this basis, the mothers on assistance were entitled to maximum magistrates' awards totalling £1,057 10s. per week from 142 possible orders (some families included children of more than one father). If these maximum court orders had been made and paid in full, fifty-nine of the legally 'innocent' separated and divorced mothers would have been living at a standard above assistance rates and would not have needed assistance. However the awards made by magistrates totalled only £217 weekly, from only seventy-three orders. Orders could be signed over to the N.A.B. and only twenty-seven orders were retained by the mothers. On these the actual income received directly by the mothers must have totalled less than £88, that is £3 5s. each on average, per week. Voluntary payments totalled only £17 per week for all mothers.

So, in fact, the mothers interviewed were receiving direct less than one tenth of the maximum support possible under magistrates' court awards. And such low incomes from the fathers are typical of all fatherless families on assistance.[6]

Widows' pensions

All but two of the widows received a pension at the rate of £4 for the mother, plus £2 (including family allowance) for each child.

This brought their incomes close to, but not yet above, national assistance rates when rent was taken into account.

Incomes from non-dependants in the same household

The next largest influence on the living standards of a number of the mothers was whether they had income from a non-dependent member of their household. Mothers who were householders might receive from their working children more money than it cost to keep them. Mothers themselves boarding with their parents might pay less in board than the parents spent on them. Or occasionally the balance of the exchange might go the other way. The 1948 National Assistance Act finally ended the duty of relatives, under the old poor law, to support those in the same household who became dependent on the state, so the N.A.B. Regulations applied to such situations were merely a standard formula which, on both legal and practical grounds, could not and did not attempt to assess the true value of the exchange. However, in practice, the situation was more complex because the N.A.B. sometimes took notice of, or appeared to assume, exchanges and made deductions which according to my calculations were larger than the limits set in the published Regulations.[7]

There were thirty-eight mothers who were householders with one or more non-dependants, almost all of them working children, and I estimated that the mothers profited on average by 26s. a week.[8] There were fifteen mothers who were themselves boarders, and I estimated that they were subsidized at the rate of 22s. a week, taking into account lighting, heating, and rent. Additions or deductions by the N.A.B., according to their formula or individual officers' discretion, reduced the average profits for householder mothers to 11s. net, and the average subsidy for boarding mothers to just over 18s. net. However, both householder and boarder incomes varied widely. Boarders' net subsidy ranged from nothing to as much as £4. And eight of the householders probably made a net loss, in one instance of £3 14s., while the largest profit was £3 6s.

No claims can be made for any great accuracy of these figures, but they do represent a closer approximation to the real situation than the N.A.B. could practicably make. The variations emphasize that, according to the arrangement made between individuals, the family on national assistance may receive a large concealed subsidy or alternatively may experience a considerable drain on its resources from other members of the household.

Most of the householder incomes were from working children. In one form of exchange, frequent among Northborough families where children were more often expected to repay their parents for the years of dependence, the young worker handed over his entire wage and in return was given spending money, bus fares, lunch money, or packed meals. Clothing was also bought, or money for clothing was given to the child.

For example, one daughter got £3 8s. 8d. wages, which she handed over to her mother. She received back 10s. for pocket money, out of which she paid for her youth club and her bus fares to the club. She had another 10s. which she split, 2s. 6d. for insurance and 7s. 6d. for savings stamps for clothes. But when she was within striking distance of buying an item her mother put the rest towards it. In addition she had 10d. a day for bus fares and 2s. 6d. a day for lunches. She also had sweets bought for her, and very occasionally was given half the price of a record.

Such arrangements varied from family to family, amounts being paid out in a number of separate small sums. Keeping a child on this basis was thought to be more profitable to the parent, and the child was permitted to move over to 'keeping himself' (that is, paying a figure for board) as a mark of status and when the time came to save up for marriage.

The alternative arrangement for the child paying board was common in Seaston, and in Northborough children were said to be boarding sooner and sooner, as mothers lost the battle with teenage marketing pressures. Mothers said they were thankful if the child was self-supporting and not actually a burden financially.

Apart from these householder incomes from independent children, fifteen dependent school children were earning. Five of them gave their mothers money, two of them more than ten shillings. Eight children had less than ten shillings. This money, whether given to the mother or kept by the child, marginally eased the pressures on the family budget.

Arrangements for mothers who boarded with relatives varied more. Young mothers living at home were likely to get fairly heavy subsidies. One separated wife, who paid only £3 board for herself and two children, said, 'That wouldn't cover half the food we eat even.' A young unmarried mother paid £2 and for this she got everything including her young baby's food, a 10s. clothing club paid, money for nights out and the occasional packet of cigarettes. Her father remarked drily, 'She gets good value for her £2.'

In other houses there was an unpredictable, unsystematic intermingling of finances. An unmarried mother said, 'My mother helps me out. If she sees I'm short she gives me a bit, if she sees we haven't any butter or anything like that.' Money was paid towards the fish and chips, the coal bill, and the gas bill, and support for the fatherless family absorbed all the relative's extra earnings. Arrangements were not even as clear as this in some instances, for mothers either couldn't or wouldn't work out their expense on household items. As one separated wife said, 'I do pay a little, but I've no idea how much it would be. I pay a few pounds. I pay the coalman sometimes, or the light bill, but I wouldn't like to say how much it is. It's just a few pounds when I feel I can manage. We all muck in together. We live as a family.' It was almost bad taste to attempt to calculate the benefit. The unfortunate member contributed what she could, but enjoyed the standard of living of the rest. This, however, depended on there being several earners in the receiving household who could carry the dependent member. A danger in some families with only one earner appeared to be that the mother was in effect being forced to live at a higher dietary level than she could afford if she was to pay for what the family ate.

Apart from this variety of arrangements between individuals, the N.A.B. practices in making allowances or deductions sometimes brought a greater gain or loss to the mother. Younger mothers living with parents and already receiving a subsidy were still entitled to a rent allowance from the N.A.B. And sometimes mothers who were householders were able to profit from N.A.B.

Regulations: a woman receiving £4 10s. from her brother only had ten shillings stopped from her allowance on that account. But the same standard ten shillings might also be stopped in instances where the mother was supporting a teenage son who should have been working but had no income. Very great loss to the mother might occur if her allowance was reduced because the non-dependent boarder was a man assumed by the N.A.B. to be having sexual intercourse with her: a woman said she received £3 from a man with whom she was cohabiting but was stopped almost £5, and so (taking into account his food) found herself almost £4 worse off than if she had lived alone. Women in this situation of suspected cohabitation invariably came from among the unmarried, separated, or divorced mothers.

Incomes from work

The earnings of twenty-nine mothers who worked were small, the average being £2 8s. 6d. or just below the maximum above which earnings were wholly deductible. Ten mothers earned above the maximum, but only seven received over £3, and only one had £6. The mothers who worked tended to be older, the widowed or divorced women with older children.

Education maintenance grants

Out of four mothers who were eligible for education maintenance grants, worth over £1 a week per child, only one was receiving such a grant. These grants were not deductible from the assistance allowance, and together with this allowance would have brought the money for a sixteen-year-old Seaston child at school up to £3 14s. 6d., which was at least competitive with what the mother might expect to receive from a working child, particularly if the child at school took free dinners.

Variations in regular cash income between mothers of different marital status

We can now explain some of the differences in cash income noted earlier between mothers of different marital status. Apart from the N.A.B. Regulation which permitted a widow to keep some of her widowed mother's allowance, widows never suffered from deductions by the N.A.B. for suspected cohabitation. Because they were older and had more working children, the widows drew householder income relatively more often than any other group. Moreover, widows seldom had very young children, so that a larger proportion could work part-time.

By contrast, the low incomes of mothers whose dependent children were all illegitimate (including some divorced and separated mothers) could be attributed to unfavourable assessments of the size of their allowance by the N.A.B., their lack of householder or boarder income, and the fact that the mothers did not go out to work because their children were very young.

On the other hand, the widows did not receive the relatively large boarder subsidies which went to a few very young separated or unmarried mothers living with their parents. But these larger subsidies were probably of short duration only, and would decrease when the mothers set up home on their own.

Regular cash incomes and dependence on assistance

These findings about cash incomes reveal the mothers' degree of dependence on assistance, which may be measured as the amount a mother would have to earn to achieve independence of assistance and maintain a similar living standard. The standard of income attainable on national assistance is the basic scale rate plus the £2 part-time earnings the mother would be allowed to keep. Earnings required for independence at the same living standard must then be the difference between this amount and mothers' resources from family allowances, pensions, and court orders or voluntary payments, taking into account gains or losses from boarder or household incomes (Appendix Table 5).

Only a quarter of the mothers needed to earn less than £6 a week. A variety of factors helped these families towards independence: they had small rents, small families, and possessed other income. Eleven, or almost half of them, were widowed, eight of those widows needing to earn between £3 and £4 to become independent. These mothers may be less able-bodied or for other reasons less capable of work.

Half the families would have had to earn at least £8 a week to match assistance rates. A quarter needed to earn almost £10 a week, and there were two mothers who would have had to earn over £14 a week, merely to maintain the same level of income as assistance could provide. These estimates have not taken into account insurance stamps for the divorced and the unmarried, income tax (the divorced can claim no married person's allowance and so pay more tax); nor any loss of free school meals and clothing grants as their income rises, or expenses incurred in baby-minding (sometimes as much as £2 a week), fares to work or extra money on meals eaten out. Such items might add £2 or £3 to the earnings required for independence.

So, even ignoring the difficulties entailed for mothers working full-time, assistance was probably an economically superior alternative to work for half to three quarters of the mothers interviewed.

Incomes other than regular cash

The remaining incomes received by the fatherless families did not influence dependence on assistance very markedly, because they were small, irregular, not dependable, given in kind, or not assessed for the assistance allowance. Nevertheless at these low income levels their value to the mother's morale probably far outweighed their size, and there were occasionally families where incomes other than regular cash made a sizeable difference to living standards.

Other incomes from relatives

Twenty-eight mothers had had some cash help from their parents or (in several instances) brothers or sisters who did not live in the same household. But possibly national assistance was an alternative to living off relatives: it gave mothers independence of the family, and cut down the flow of money and gifts which might otherwise have taken place.

Mothers were uneasy about these amounts, fearing that they might be deducted from the allowance by the N.A.B. The total number of such amounts may therefore have been underestimated. Thus, one separated wife said, 'My mother pays my rates. Well, she doesn't pay my rates really, she says to me, "You save up your money for the rates and when the time comes, I'll give you that amount as a gift. That's not paying your rates, is it? That's a gift from me."' There was, perhaps, rather more delicacy in not giving cash but trying to pay a bill or provide a service. Probably because of this uncertainty only four mothers had weekly amounts of ten shillings or more in actual cash, the average being less than five shillings.

Gifts of money for specific purposes, or gifts of furniture or clothing, were more widespread. Thirty-five mothers had some kind of help worth more than five shillings a week from within the family: of these three had an income worth over £2 per week, six had incomes worth over £1 per week, and twenty-six had incomes over five shillings. Over forty other women received smaller amounts. These figures are minimum amounts, for the value of some of these exhanges could not be established with any accuracy.

At one extreme, relatives had bought houses for mothers and their families to live in. At the other, a brother who lived nearby fed the dog of one of the fatherless families with an occasional tin of dog food. In other families help came in gifts of coal, paint, cigarettes, or food. One unmarried mother had had six weeks living with her parents free of charge during the last year. The parents of a separated wife kept her children in sweets, pocket money, and clothes, bought fish and chips, fed the family at the weekend, gave her cigarettes, paid her TV licence and gave her the set, bought coal, and so on. Some relatives who came on visits brought food for themselves and a bit over. One widow practically lived at her mother's, saving on heating and lighting, and eating free vegetables from the garden which her brother cultivated for the two women. Two thirds of the families received substantial gifts at birthday and Christmas times, and it was often understood that these would be essentials such as clothing, rather than toys. A great deal of help had been given with furniture. One unmarried mother, for instance, had had a kitchen table and chairs, a studio couch and easy chairs, and a bedroom suite, all from relatives. A separated wife said, 'My mother will buy something new just so she can give me what she doesn't want.' Relatives also helped with holidays.

Individual items which could be picked out show which sort of help was most frequent. Thirty-nine families received new clothing regularly. Next came pocket money to the children, from twenty-three grandparents and from other relatives, including the children's fathers. In one instance the children received in all sixteen shillings. Twenty-three mothers said they also benefited because they or their children received a substantial proportion of their meals from relatives. Nineteen mothers were helped by their families (including boarding children) with payments for TV licences, and ten were helped with weekly TV payments (not counting those boarding mothers who had free access to a TV set belonging to a relative). Mothers with slot TV received very substantial rebates, of up to 30s. a month in one instance. In a household where there were other non-dependants slot TV was also useful to the mother because it shifted the burden of payment from her to the earners in the family. Nineteen mothers received cigarettes from relatives. Sixteen families had subsidies from relatives with holidays, ranging from gifts of money to the renting of caravans and chalets.

Help from outside the family

There was less help by payment of bills or gifts from sources outside the family, although this may in part reflect mothers' reluctance to disclose help which sometimes came from men-friends. Forty-one mothers received some help. One had the equivalent of almost £4 if school fees were taken into account. However, there was only one other mother receiving more than £1. Thirteen received less than 10s. and the remainder less than 5s. on average. Again there was help with furniture and with secondhand clothing, eighteen of the families having recently received clothing from the W.V.S. and ten new clothing from friends. Twelve of the families had been helped with holidays, mostly through an arrangement between the N.A.B. and a charity, but also directly, the children being selected by their schools, or through doctors. Eight had been helped by friends to have a holiday.

Only three mothers had ever had substantial incomes from charities. One mother had been wholly maintained by a charity and another had received a regular supplement to her pension in the past. Another mother was still receiving very substantial help from a charity. Families had received food and furniture from the N.S.P.C.C., parcels at Christmas time from other charities, the odd bag of coal from a church charity, a few vouchers from the British Legion at some time in the past, and so on. But the activities of charities were minuscule in the face of the total problem.

Other incomes from official sources

The largest income from official sources apart from assistance was derived from free school meals. Fifty-four families had children taking free school meals, which could be worth up to £1 a week. However, of the children who would have been eligible for free meals only two thirds received them.

Mothers on national assistance with pre-school children should have received one pint of milk free per day per child under five. Pregnant women on assistance were also entitled to a pint of milk for themselves. Unfortunately I did not make an adequate check of whether all mothers were receiving their free milk until the later stages of the interviewing, when several mothers were discovered who had not had their tokens (there was also a tendency to conceal further illegitimate pregnancies from the authorities, so that tokens were not taken up for such pregnancies). There appeared to be a similar failure of the N.A.B. to distribute tokens for free orange juice, although there was some doubt about whether mothers valued this particular benefit. [9]

Two widows had not received the death grant for their husbands. And maternity benefit was payable only to mothers who had, or whose husbands had, sufficient insurance contributions. Thus while eighteen mothers had received some kind of grant at the birth of a child (within the previous two years), two of these had received less than the full maternity grant to which they would have been entitled on full contributions, and three mothers who had had babies received nothing at all. [10]

Undeclared income revealed by the survey

At the time of the interviews I discovered six mothers whose earnings, either in part or wholly, were not disclosed to the National Assistance Board. On average 27s. a week was not disclosed, the largest sums being £3 10s. and £2, and the smallest 10s. Six other mothers had had work in the recent past without declaring their earnings but the benefit over the period of time covered by our questions was less than 10s. per week. Earning in this way was usually a temporary and even desperate measure taken to relieve a financial crisis and soon stopped or discovered. The sums would not have been entirely deductible had they been declared.

Two mothers were definitely receiving regular income from the children's fathers unknown to the N.A.B. A small number of mothers, five, probably had income from a number of men-friends, but this was an area which the interviews could not probe, and any information was received not from the mother herself but from acquaintances also included in the sample.

The pattern of incomes other than regular cash

These smaller incomes proved to have a distribution different from that described for regular cash incomes. The separated, with on average 34s., divorced with 31s. and unmarried mothers with 22s., all received more income in this way than the widows, who had on average 18s.

However, these extra incomes went chiefly to a fairly small number of the separated and divorced. In all, nineteen mothers were being helped substantially by a relative, usually the mother's parents. All but four of these mothers did not live with the relative concerned, so the extended family was an important source of help, but only to a number of younger separated and divorced women. The widows and the mothers of illegitimate children, including the West Indians, tended to lack such help from friendly relatives close by.

So, piecing together cash incomes and incomes from other sources the widows tended to receive their money from the state or from workers in the household, while a group of the younger unmarried, separated, and divorced mothers were helped considerably by parents with whom they lived or who lived nearby. But there was a group of mothers of illegitimate children, including unmarried, separated, and divorced women, who had help from none of these sources.

A note on capital resources

The fatherless families had scarcely any capital. Only four mothers had any savings, and they were spending them at an average of 28s. a week (included in the above calculations). One mother had over £500 after her husband's recent death, but three more who had been working before they came on assistance had less than £100. Ten mothers had houses of varying quality and at widely different stages of purchase: but those who were still buying must find the capital repayments out of their current incomes, a forced saving. Approximately half the mothers had insurances, but only one of these was anything more than a small 'burial' or 'education' policy. Only three mothers had drawn insurances of any value within the last two years, and these were spent on the children (again this has been included in the incomes described above). At least ten mothers had lost insurances through arrears mounting up when the insurance man failed to call.

This lack of capital explains why the lump sums and other gifts, which made such a small change in the mother's living standards when averaged out over time, nevertheless had such a great impact on mothers' morale. The mothers had no capital out of which to buy the goods, nor, at these low income levels, could they save even small amounts.

Summary

National assistance proved not to represent a uniform level of income, or a minimum below which no family could sink. The average total income of these fatherless families from all sources was 123 per cent of the national assistance scale rate, or just over

£9 a week to keep a mother with two children paying a rent of £2 a week, and of this four fifths was in regular cash from various sources. But 8 per cent of the families had cash incomes below 90 per cent of the scale. Regular incomes in cash were most important; support from relatives in lump sums, income in kind, or earmarked income came next; and only negligible undeclared incomes from earnings or the children's fathers were revealed by this survey.

Widows were found to be least poor among the families, while the mothers who had only illegitimate dependants had the smallest incomes of all. Widows also drew the least proportion of their income from national assistance, and in that sense were less dependent. A major cause of dependence was lack of support from the children's fathers. Measured in terms of the earnings required to attain independence by working while matching assistance incomes, assistance was probably economically preferable to work for half to three quarters of these mothers.

The variations in mothers' incomes could be attributed to several main factors or influences. First, widowed mothers received formally, in the National Assistance Regulations, slightly preferential treatment of their pensions, as compared with women who had support from their husbands. Second, it was found that informally, through the exercise of N.A.B. officers' 'discretionary powers', certain other women were given low allowances, and these women tended to be mothers who in any case are held low in public esteem, the mothers of illegitimate children: they were more likely to be suspected of cohabitation, and to have their allowances lowered on that ground. Third, because the mothers of different marital status were at different stages of family life, proportionately more of the widows had support from non-dependent children and could work parttime. Fourth, to some extent independently of marital status, help from the extended family was more frequently given to *young* mothers who had been 'readopted', usually by their parents.

CHAPTER TWO

The Home

The level of comfort in their homes was an important dimension of the living standards of these fatherless families, which proved to be to some extent independent of their incomes. This chapter will apply various measures to show how the families compare with the community in possession of the conventional sanitary necessities, adequate space and furniture, and access to labour-saving devices. But it must be stressed that because of the way the interviews were obtained none of the families interviewed was currently homeless, and highly mobile families who might be in the worst housing were under-represented: thus the housing problems of fatherless families on assistance are probably understated.[1]

Amenities

Forty-six of the families interviewed (40 per cent) did not have the exclusive use of cold and hot water taps, W.C., and fixed bath (the four standard amenities checked in the census), a proportion slightly higher than that for the two regions studied and the average for the whole country.[2] Twelve families shared an outside W.C., and nine an inside W.C., sometimes with over a dozen people. Twenty-six families had no fixed bath, while ten families shared the use of a bath with other families. And twenty-nine had no hot water supply, but had to heat all their water on a stove or fire.

The housing standard proved to be buttressed by the unusually high proportion of families living in council dwellings, which at 57 per cent (sixty-two families) was over double the average for the localities.[3] These council dwellings were on the whole good, and were never very bad. Prefabricated council houses

even had built-in refrigerators, which few families could otherwise aspire to. The best houses were owner-occupied suburban
semi-detached houses worth £3,000 or £4,000 at current prices,
with fitted kitchens and through lounges, one of them having
central heating. However, owner-occupied houses were variable
in standard and three of the twelve had poor amenities. Private
houses rented from relatives, while they sometimes lacked
amenities could be successfully renovated and made cosy. This
leaves the very bad housing concentrated almost exclusively in
accommodation rented privately, but not from relations: out of
forty-two private tenancies only eight had all the standard
amenities.[4] This distribution, of course, is not peculiar to fatherless families, but represents the state of the housing market
generally. Fatherless families of certain types were disadvantaged
in that they had to find accommodation in the worst sector of
housing, the privately rented market.

Since tenancies were unevenly distributed with respect to
marital status, the standard of housing varied markedly between
the widowed, divorced, separated, and unmarried mothers.
None of the widows lived in privately rented accommodation,
so that their housing was up to average standard. But almost
two thirds of the unmarried mothers (including five out of the
six West Indians), and a little under half of the separated and
divorced mothers were in bad accommodation, nearly all
privately rented from non-relatives.[5]

In the worst instance, a separated wife with three children had
taken a cottage owned by the mill so that she could be near her
work, for a minimal rent of eleven shillings. The cottage was two
hundred years old. It had stone floors with no damp-course, and
floor coverings soon rotted away. The back room which was dug
into the hillside was uninhabitable and dangerous; its stone flag
roof, supported on rotting beams, was likely to fall in. Upstairs
the first bedroom was divided from the staircase by a waist-high
partition, and the second bedroom could only be reached by
crossing the first. The outside W.C. was fully 100 yards away, so
that it could not be used at night, and the mother said, 'That's
about the worst thing, because you've got to use chambers all the
time, and it isn't only the little boy, I'm running after all of them,

and I think when it's like that you're conscious of it all the time.'
Her rent was controlled, but there were other houses nearly as
bad, and for one of these a family paid £4 10s. rent. Even a
caravan could be superior to this.

As well as having the most adequate accommodation, mothers
in council property came off best in terms of repairs. The state of
repair of owner-occupied property depended on how long the
mother had been on assistance and the original condition of the
house when she had become dependent: without extra resources
few repairs could be done by these mothers whose national assistance allowance was effectively lowered by the amount of the
mortgage capital repayment.

Often, private landlords would not do repairs without a
directive from the sanitary authorities; the mothers had insufficient security of tenure or self-confidence to make demands,
nor could they afford to have the necessary work done by themselves. An unmarried mother, who remained the last statutory
tenant in a row of houses which had been sold, had never had
electricity – the house was lit by gas – the doors were unpainted,
and the front room ceiling was falling in. Another unmarried
mother, whose man-friend helped her to make improvements to
her rented accommodation, had her rent raised and then she was
evicted.

Mothers living in their husband's house could be in a similar
situation if their husband did not choose to do repairs because he
wanted them out of the house and could not evict them. Thus, in
a road of well-kept houses, the door of the home of a separated
wife was conspicuously shabby, unpainted, and with light shin-
ing through the cracks in the wood panels.

Mothers in the very worst accommodation were likely to pay
more for their housing, because very few of them were statutory
tenants. The average housing costs were just over £2, which as a
proportion of the mother's income was more than double the
national average. Housing costs were higher for all types of
houses in Seaston. And in both Northborough and Seaston the
proportion of income spent on housing was highest for rented
rooms, and lowest for houses rented from relatives. None of the
Northborough mothers paid over 50s., and they could get the

use of most of a house or a whole house for £2 or less, while a single room could be rented for 30s. By contrast, in Seaston the top council house rents rose to almost £3, two very poor privately rented houses were costing £4 10s., and single rooms cost from £2 10s. upwards. A Seaston mother living in what was virtually a single room was paying £3 10s. Sometimes a housing charge in multi-occupied dwellings was concealed in high bills for heating or electricity which should have been paid by another flat (the N.A.B. would not pay such concealed charges).

When rents reach such high levels, the prospect of independence for mothers in the worst accommodation are small.

Overcrowding

Lack of space was also a problem for a high proportion of these fatherless families. By an objective measure,[6] one in five families needed at least two bedrooms more than they had and a further one in three families lacked one bedroom, making over half the families overcrowded to some degree. This compares with the Plowden Report's findings (using the same standard) that only one in twenty households with primary school children, and one in ten of all households, are overcrowded.[7]

Almost three quarters of those in privately rented accommodation, but only a quarter of those in council dwellings and owner-occupied houses, were overcrowded; so that overcrowding, like lack of amenities, was linked with marital status. Three quarters of the unmarried and half the separated and divorced mothers were overcrowded, compared with a quarter of the widows. The worst overcrowding, therefore, usually occurred among unmarried mothers in privately rented rooms.

One unmarried mother lived with her five children in the small front bedroom of an old working-class terrace house. Most rented rooms were in multi-occupied dwellings, and in one such house, which was three hundred years old, a divorced woman with an illegitimate child lived, cooked, and slept in a long narrow room like a cave. There were only two small windows high on one wall and at two o'clock in the afternoon the room had to be lit by electric light. The woman had become so apathetic that she did not even bother to draw the curtains. The outer windows of the house were broken, the holes crudely blocked with cloth and cardboard and the passageways and staircases were whitewashed like farm outbuildings. In two other houses the rooms were divided by tatty blankets hung from string, but often rooms were so small that partitioning was impossible. Another unmarried mother lived in a space not much more than three times the area of a double bed, which was occupied by her bed, her child's cot, a couple of small tables, a chair, and a large wardrobe on which were piled her only possessions, two suitcases. Her stove was on the landing, shared with another two households, and to dry washing she had to go down three flights of stairs. Yet she was lucky in having a hot water supply, for in most of the multi-occupied houses the shared bathroom was out of order. Each room contained a family, and mothers found it difficult to say how many other people lived in the house. Rent from one house such as this was estimated at over £30 a week.

Lack of beds

Sometimes linked with the lack of bedrooms was a lack of beds. Comparing groups, only the widows all had enough beds for the needs of their families. Altogether, two out of five of all the families were sleeping in such a way that at least one person lacked adequate bed-space (defined as a separate bed for children of opposite sex, or children over ten, and not more than two children to a double bed). In one in ten families there was a shortage of bed-space for at least two people: thus, one unmarried mother slept in a single bed with a two-year-old child and a baby. The lack of bed-spaces was linked with lack of space in the accommodation itself in twelve instances. For example, in the worst situation a mother and fourteen-year-old son shared a narrow bed because there was not enough room for two beds (there was not even enough space for a wardrobe, and freshly ironed clothes were neatly piled on chairs by the bed). In three families mothers were worried that with members of the family of opposite sex sharing beds the arrangement was 'not nice', as they put it. In thirteen families which were larger, or had enuretic children, the shortage of bed-spaces was really a shortage of bedding: one mother had two double beds, a single bed, a camp bed, and a cot; but she had to sleep with two children while another two slept top to tail in a single bed, owing to the lack of bedding.

Household appliances and furniture

Lack of beds was but one example of the families' lack of furniture and possessions. A check was made on mothers' ownership of, or access to, TV sets, washing machines, refrigerators, and telephones. Compared with all families in urban Britain fewer of these fatherless families had these particular appliances, possibly with the sole exception of TV (Appendix Table 6). Shortages were concentrated particularly among the unmarried mothers.

The fact that 84 per cent of the mothers had TV indicates that it was considered virtually essential in their lives. However only sixty of these mothers had to pay for their sets, the remainder who had access to a set being mothers who lived with relatives. Mothers who had to pay were helped with weekly payments and licences by relatives, although a third had no licence because they said they could not afford one. The unmarried and separated were more often without access to a set, only one widow being without TV. And of the mothers who owned sets only one was unmarried.

A lower than average proportion of mothers had washing machines although almost all the families would have liked one and a straight comparison with national figures of ownership probably understates the shortage among the fatherless if, as seems likely, families with children more often buy washing machines. The fatherless families also had fewer refrigerators than the national average, and for both washing machines and refrigerators the unmarried mothers came off worst. Only five mothers had telephones, a proportion well below the national average, and none of the mothers had a car. Use of cookers and wardrobes was also checked. Nine mothers, none of them widows, had defective cookers; and thirty-eight mothers, among them only three widows, had no storage space or only inadequate space for clothing: for example, one mother had only hooks on the doors and a suitcase for her family's clothing.

These statistics cannot convey the enormous range in the quantity and quality of the furnishings in these homes. One divorced woman's front room was bare of carpet and the interview had to be conducted with the two of us sitting side by side on the small sofa which was the room's only furniture. In another house the stairs facing the door had once had lino on them, but now only fragments clinging to the protruding nail-heads remained. In the living room, walls, and ceiling were sooty black. Over the mantelpiece the wallpaper was torn and some of the plaster was chipped away. Two chairs in the room had crude covers on, but a sofa and the other chairs, once moquette, were now worn shiny black and greasy with margarine and flies on them. In other houses, springs and frames protruded from holes in furniture, and tiny rooms were dominated by old pianos and huge Victorian mahogany pieces, inherited from parents and put there to fill up a space. Incongruously, one house was crammed with items from three-piece suites, a complete suite downstairs and two sofas and some chairs upstairs, for, of all furniture, suites were the most easily obtainable. In many houses the only new furniture was the rented TV. Several families lacked even a table from which to eat, and took their meals off the end of the draining board or balanced on their knees. There was a shortage of lamp shades and light bulbs, and a lot of small repair jobs waiting to be done. One separated wife had broken her sink: 'An accident or anything like that, I'm stuck. It's the little things like that when you realize how difficult life is, £4 might not sound a lot to you, it didn't to me, but now it seems out of this world. I haven't a hope of saving that up.'

By contrast, in a few houses furnishings were lavish. One widow's front room was newly decorated, newly furnished, and newly carpeted out of her husband's insurance. Another had a new three-piece suite costing £256. A divorced mother's house was like a colour photograph from a women's magazine. Families with approximately the same money income lived in environments which were dramatically different.

Weekly payments for furniture

The actual ownership of furniture or appliances which were available did not necessarily influence the families' living standards directly. If a TV set belonged to a parent with whom the mother lived, or a set of furniture came with her rented rooms, she could still use it. However, it did matter a great deal if families were having to buy furniture out of their small incomes, because assistance allowances were not meant to cover this. Expenditure on furniture could effectively reduce the families' living standard below the subsistence level.

Weekly payments for furniture to some extent reflected the figures of access or ownership just described. The widows and divorcees had steady weekly payments of about 10s. (excluding TV costs), while of the unmarried mothers, two thirds had no payments because they lived in furnished rooms or with relatives. The separated wives, however, varied widely in their payments, half of them making no weekly payments, but the remainder averaging nearly £1, the highest figure being 55s. a week.

Broadly speaking, the widows and the divorced mothers had a substantial amount of furniture, although they needed replacements or improvements to their stock. Some separated wives, too, were still in the marital home and had little need to buy furniture. But those making high payments were recently separated from their husbands and were desperately trying to make a new home. Other separated wives and unmarried mothers, who lived in furnished rooms or with parents, had yet to face the problems of getting a home together. Some of the mothers living with parents would be lucky, and when they set up home on their own they would take with them items such as beds and chairs which they were using at home. But for others, with no capital and a subsistence income, a decent home would be built up only at the expense of an adequate diet and clothing. Lack of furniture was equivalent to an enormous debt which must sometime be paid.

Summary

The housing standard of these fatherless families was only a little inferior to the national average; a fact partly due to under-representation of housing problems on this survey, but also explained by the high proportion of mothers in council dwellings, 57 per cent, which was double the local proportion. However, no fewer than two thirds of the unmarried mothers and half the separated and divorced wives, but no widows, were in the worst housing which was privately rented from non-relatives. Such property was also in the worst state of repair, and cost the most to rent. The families had proportionately double the housing costs of the average household in the country.

Half the families were overcrowded judged by shortage of bedrooms, the worst conditions again occurring among unmarried mothers, in privately rented rooms. Two out of five of the families lacked adequate beds. And, with the possible exception of TV, which was regarded as a necessity, the families had fewer household appliances than the average. They also lacked, for example, cookers and wardrobes. In these comparisons the unmarried mothers came out worst, and the widows least badly.

Furniture needs were to some extent geared to the marriage and home-building cycle. Thus, few of the separated wives were spending a great deal on H.P. for furniture, the widows and some divorced and separated wives already had a stock, while the unmarried mothers living with parents or in furnished rooms would have to face the problem in the future. There was a danger that expenditure on furniture would take money which should have been spent on food and clothing.

CHAPTER THREE
Spending on 'Necessities' and 'Luxuries'

In asking what further deprivations these fatherless families experienced, we have to face the question: what are necessities? At one time public assistance was given entirely in the form of vouchers so that only 'necessities' could be obtained. But people have psychological and social needs related to the society in which they live. And in an increasingly sophisticated society it becomes difficult to decide which items, or how much expenditure on certain services, are essential for the maintenance of an individual's well-being. This chapter will illustrate the difficulty of dividing expenditure into essential and non-essential or luxury spending.

The problem of estimating whether the families lacked food is typical of the difficulties encountered in measuring poverty. It would be possible, according to nutritionists, to buy an adequate diet for around one shilling a day, provided that a person is prepared to eat unfamiliar and unpalatable foods. But in practice the pattern of eating which prevails in the community, an individual's own preferences and cooking skills, and the various other calls on income, determine whether or not an adequate diet can be achieved on a given allowance. And even a diet which is adequate nutritionally may be boring or dispiriting if it includes none of the small treats a family are used to.

No really comprehensive assessment of the nation's diet has yet been attempted,[1] and the present survey can say little about actual malnutrition. If everyone in these fatherless families had drunk an appropriate share of the milk bought, nobody would have been suffering from malnutrition, for the average consumption was half a pint per head per day.[2] In fact, although this was difficult to measure, it seemed very unlikely that all the mothers got their share.

But rather than attempting the complex task of studying malnutrition, I was looking for signs of social deprivation in the form of any major departures from ordinary food customs or restrictions in diet.

The mother's food

Certain mothers probably did not get a satisfactory diet, because they ate either too little or the wrong food. One in ten mothers maintained, in spite of detailed questioning, that they had eaten literally no solid food on the day before the interview. A further check showed this was a fairly frequent occurrence, and they (and probably others) regularly had days when they did not eat, or had no cooked meal. Half the mothers never ate breakfast, which seems not unusual for women. But in addition to those who had not eaten during the previous day, a further nineteen missed both breakfast and the midday meal. One divorced woman, who had eaten literally nothing the previous day, said,

I put my mind to it and try and think about something else. And I drink a lot of coffee. It makes me feel sick and I get a bit tired, but I still can't sleep when I go to bed. I haven't enough you see. Usually the middle of the week I have to start thinking about what we're going to have for weekend. My appetite's gone now. I think with being short of food for so long and not eating much my appetite's just dwindled down.

The credibility of such statements was supported by the women's gaunt appearance. A separated wife said, 'The doctor said I'm getting thinner and thinner, and that soon he won't be able to see me coming into the surgery!'

By contrast a second group of mothers said they had a badly balanced diet and were putting on weight. Some felt the urge to eat: 'The doctor says you nibble to take your mind off things.' But they could not afford diets with much protein. A separated wife, who for her lunch the day before had eaten the scraps from her children's breakfast plates, said,

I eat all right, but all I ever eat is bread. I'm just eating toast after toast, and the doctor says he should tell me to diet, but it's no good because what can I diet. I can't eat any other sort of things. I can't afford chickens and things like that, and eggs. And if I cut down on bread I get a headache and I get desperately hungry.

Altogether, between a quarter and a third of the mothers were missing out meals every day, or were regularly eating very little or the wrong sort of food.

These patterns of eating were moulded by past hardships and the influence of relationships within the family as much as by the present budget. In a sense mothers were sometimes economizing on their own food more than the size of their income dictated. For instance, a separated wife who lived on a bun and several biscuits a day said,

My son says I'm suffering from malnutrition. You've seen these photographs of these people who get malnutrition and their stomachs come out. Well, I'm like that. It was all those years living with my husband being afraid to eat when he said I was only a housekeeper. [She had refused sexual intercourse with her husband.] I used to go for days sometimes without food, and I trained myself to manage. You can do. You can live on drink alone if you try. Then, you see, in the hostel [for the homeless] I hadn't got much money and I thought if I went carefully on my food I'd be able to get built up and David [her son] wouldn't go short of anything. At first I had to go without, but now it's my own fault. I can't face a cooked meal. I've never had a cooked meal for three years. I cook a meal for them, but I couldn't touch it myself. [She threw open the cupboard doors of her gloomy little parlour and revealed a huge hoard of food, tins of beef slices, chicken breasts, tinned fruits.] I always buy something. I think it's a habit left over from the war. I couldn't touch it myself. My stomach's shrunk.

The stress reaction to living on a low income was not commonly as severe as this, which bordered on anorexia, but it seemed to be shared in some degree by many other women who had been on assistance a long time.

This mother's hoarding of food for her child highlights a general anxiety that the children should not suffer, and a determination that in the eyes of neighbours, school teachers, and former husbands (and interviewers) the children must be seen not to suffer. A separated wife said, 'In the school holidays I sometimes stand there and cook a full dinner for them and tell them to go in the kitchen and get it, and when they say, "Where's yours?", I say I'm on a diet.' Another woman said, 'I'd rather the children had the food than I did. It seems to satisfy me more. *They* don't go short, I do.' Of three mothers who had had special national assistance discretionary allowances for food because they were ill, only one had spent it on food for herself. Another said, 'Well, I ask you. How could I sit down with a piece of chicken when the kids are wanting things.' A separated wife recalled, 'It's like the old saying, "In a poor family the mother gets nowt."'

In any case, with no husbands at home and the children at school or too young to want a large cooked meal, women had little incentive to cook. As one said, 'I think there's nothing so uninteresting as putting on a saucepan of taters for one.' Perhaps it was the absence of the need to cook for the children which was most crucial in lowering the mother's diet, and those most vulnerable were the unmarried mothers with young babies who had never before had a home of their own or had to cook for themselves.

The children's food and school meals

The children fared rather better, both through their mothers' efforts and from school meals and milk. Only in seven families had the children had no breakfast. And of school-age children only forty, or 15 per cent, came home for meals.[3] In at least a third of the families school meals were the staple diet of children who had no cooked meals at home.

The importance of school meals was underlined by mothers' difficulties when the schools were closed for the weekend or holidays. On the day of the interview one mother was trying to keep her children in bed so they would need no breakfast and would be less hungry for lunch. Another said that on the Sunday before I called they had only had bread and soup, on credit. At weekends and in school holidays when more milk should have been bought to make up for the lack of school milk the tendency in larger families was to buy less, for at such times there were extra calls for small expenditures on outings. The mothers with the largest families were liable either to run into debt at these times or to call heavily on the resources of relatives, sending the children round to eat with them. Families often had least money at the weekend because income from national assistance, pensions, family allowances, and court orders was all paid at the beginning of the week. Thus the absence of school meals was felt more keenly because it coincided unfortunately with a low point in family resources, and in effect the children's standard of living dropped sharply.

In these circumstances it is vital that access to free school meals should be unrestricted for these families. Yet one third of all the children eligible did not take them, and it appeared that some families paid for the meals, while in others children came home rather than face the stigma of taking free dinners. Both mothers and children rationalized their feelings, so that the influence of stigma is difficult to estimate, but probably one in six children failed to obtain free school meals for this reason.[3] One mother said, 'Stella could have free school dinners but she won't, so I pay for those. I shouldn't want to go myself.' Another said of her daughter, 'She cries when she goes back at the beginning of term and has to get a new ticket.' Mothers of younger children managed to trick them into thinking the dinners were paid for, and with an understanding teacher embarrassment in class need not arise, but only one mother said she had a special arrangement to conceal the non-payment for meals.[4] Three mothers did not know there were free meals: either they had applied in the past when the means test was higher, or no one had told them. Six mothers, who had incomes from relatives or alternative sources considered it 'not worth bothering about' or 'greedy' to try to get free school meals as well.

Children who did not take free school meals came from smaller families. Eleven mothers said they cooked a dinner at home so that their children would have adequate food or so that they could be together as much as possible. Cooking for the children was also an incentive to eat something themselves. There were elements of pride and anxiety here which prevented the mother from taking advantage of the free school meals but the children did not suffer. However, in some families the children themselves decided not to take school meals and these children, possibly 5 per cent of the total, were liable to get less food if they did not stay for school dinners. They preferred bread and jam at home – and this was what they got. They were used to a relatively restricted diet at home and found it difficult to cope with the unaccustomed foodstuffs and the social situation of school dinners.

Thus, for these families the school meals service was a qualified success. It was important for many, and of those whom it did not reach, few children appeared to suffer. Yet access could be improved. And the service is now under increasing political attack.

Restriction of diet

Apart from the actual quantities of food consumed, there was further evidence, from data for the whole family, of an overall restriction of diet and lack of variety. A tenth of the families had spent nothing on fresh meat during the previous week and indeed seldom or never had any, as against the average expenditure for all households of 23s.[5] One in six never had a Sunday roast, and a further one in four had one only once a month or less frequently; some families had a joint only when they got the gas rebate. A third of the families had spent nothing on butter. One mother said, 'The only time we have any butter in this house is when they have these free samples that come round.' One in ten families had bought no fresh fruit the previous week, and a further one in five were not able to buy fruit regularly. A separated wife said she bought bananas: 'If the grocer's got some with black skins, they're cheaper than the others. I don't let them see the skins and we make them into banana sandwiches.' These families really were not able to buy the meat, butter, and fruit they would like. If a family wanted to eat well, other items must be sacrificed.

While some items could not be bought at all others had to be reduced in quantity. A mother said, 'Do you know what I'd like to see in our kitchen. I'd like to see a basin full of eggs. If I had the money I'd go out and buy four dozen eggs all at once, and I'd look at them. Oh, ours were thrilled to bits on Sunday when they had an egg for their breakfast, they thought they'd really got something.' Another woman said, 'Crumbs, I feel hard up for necessities. I'm not asking for luxuries, I'm not asking for cars and washers. I mean it's no good looking at a tin of salmon. It's baked beans for us, and you don't get a terrifically varied diet.' Other women said that they never had puddings, just custard, small tins of beans instead of big tins, fewer biscuits, and few of the many new varieties of breakfast cereals that the children asked for.

Whether a fairly restricted diet was found boring depended very much on local custom and the mother's standard of living in the past. A separated wife said, 'Some days I look in the cupboard and I don't fancy anything, and I think, "I wish I had something nice," so I don't eat anything.' Those who had been on assistance for a long time found their capacity even to imagine a better diet dulled: 'I could go round the shop blindfold and take the same things off the shelf every time.' These mothers, brought up in a society of ready-prepared, if expensive, convenience foods lacked the traditional skills required for getting the best out of the cheaper foods and cuts of meat which were all they could now afford.

Yet often it was apparent that families lived on a diet moulded as much by restrictions in the past as by present stringencies. They were eating the kinds of food they were used to. Indeed the diet of a whole region could be so shaped. In Northborough fresh meat was felt to be an extravagance in itself, the right of male manual workers only. Many people still called margarine 'butter', and butter 'best butter' (the margarine consumption for the area is three times the national average). These cultural restrictions on diet tended to cut down feelings of deprivation with regard to food.

Clothing

In a similar way, although clothing was also clearly a problem for many families it was difficult to set a firm standard of adequacy and to measure by how much the average expenditure of a family fell short of that standard. Again it seemed that the mothers might not be as well-provided as the children. The national average expenditure per household on women's outer clothing, hats, gloves, and haberdashery was over 13s. per week. Yet at least half the mothers interviewed said they now never made any major purchases of clothing for themselves. Instead they often relied on gifts of secondhand clothing from relatives and friends. One separated wife said everything she was wearing at the time of the interview was given to her by a neighbour. Another said, 'I must look like everybody else's wife, the number of coats I've been given.' Only forty-five mothers, less than half, had a coat which they had bought themselves, often years ago. Mothers who had been on assistance for a long time had come to rely on gifts of clothing or secondhand clothes to such an extent that one said, 'I should like to go and buy something new, but I should never be able to wear it. I should never feel comfortable in new things.' Clothes were personal, and mothers felt guilty about spending money on themselves in preference to the children.

All the children had some new clothes. But in almost one third of the families most of the children's clothes were bought by relatives or passed on. The few badly or incongruously dressed children whom I saw during the interviews were wearing clothing from the W.V.S. Several little girls were wearing thin party dresses playing outdoors in winter, and one girl on a council estate was in jodphurs! Usually such clothes were kept for wearing near home and the children had best clothes to go to school in. It was not possible to check the truth of mothers' frequent assertions that their children were *better* dressed at school than average. But if they were, this must often have been as a result of gifts or at the expense of the mother's own appearance or diet.

Reliance on gifts had a number of aspects. Mothers of small, young families said they could get more than enough clothes given. But the problem of clothing was greater for larger families, for boys of all ages, and especially for teenage boys and girls to whom secondhand clothing was offensive. It was hard to get footwear. In nineteen families there was at least one child without adequate footwear; that is, a child had no shoes or shoes too big or small, only a pair of wellingtons or cheap moulded plastic sandals, or footwear inappropriate for the time of year, for example, summer sandals in the middle of winter. In ten families children had been off school because they lacked clothing or shoes.

Families dependent on gifts were badly hit by the increasing school demands for uniform; not grammar school uniform, because few of these children went to such schools, but secondary modern and even primary school uniform. One unmarried mother said, 'It's only a secondary modern school, but they're so strict with the boys, and those children that turn up in jeans, the headmaster has them out and ridicules them.' Five children who went to secondary school where uniform was required did not wear it. A separated wife said of her daughter's primary school, 'They don't have to have uniform for that school, but I've heard our Brenda talking about another girl in the class and she was saying how she was wearing this scruffy skirt that she'd had so long. Children notice things like that.' Some secondary schools imposed conditions that children going on trips must wear the uniform.

If a child at secondary modern school was pulled up by the teachers there was a chance that the mother would get an education clothing grant. But these were not easy to obtain, nor were they adequate for the full range of clothing required and they were only given once every two years. The education grants were meant to provide clothing and shoes only for school: thus families had been told that school shoes were not to be worn at home or in the street, although the children had no others. Although mothers were under pressure from the primary schools and their own children to obtain primary school uniforms, no education grant was payable.

A reliance on clothes that someone else had worn, or the necessity to make clothes last longer because of shortage of money, meant that these families suffered in comparison with the general population by having unfashionable clothes. Children could not have an anorak as well as a mackintosh; they could not have 'twist' dresses or straight dresses when they were in season; they could not have shoes with pointed toes. One mother said:

He wants these pointed toes, but I say he's got to have some shoes that last. I buy him a pair of them pointed ones, and within three weeks he wants another pair, so this last time I've got him some round-toed ones, some of them Tuf ones. I was determined he'd have something that would last. I tell him these fashions are for people who live on the Riviera.

Even quite young children whom advertisers now call the 'pre-teens' were fashion-conscious – and conscious that they themselves were not in fashion.

Along with clothing might be included spectacles, for here similar considerations of fashion operated. Recipients of national assistance are entitled to free N.H.S. prescriptions and spectacles (but only those with the very cheapest, often unpleasing frames) and free dental care. However, four mothers needed new spectacles but could not afford them and said they would not have N.H.S. ones. One said, 'These give me a headache. I was supposed to go in 1962, but I don't want these sort again. The children tell me to go. They say these are old-fashioned. They say, "You're a square," but I can't afford.' Seven mothers had spectacles bought by a friend or relative. Eight reported that their children would not wear N.H.S. spectacles, 'because everybody knows what they are', so that the child went without or in one instance the mother had to pay for private ones.

It was probably in clothing that gifts to these families made the greatest impact. As a consequence, families which could not rely on gifts were worse clothed than the general population, and their clothing was also inferior to that of others on assistance.

Fuel

Fuel costs, too, were a problem for some families. Assistance rates are the same for winter and summer, and, except in relation to the number of individuals in the household, take no account of the size of the dwelling. Mothers who were householders said they spent on average 30s., slightly more than the national average household with children. The figure may have been exaggerated, but most families had young children and the mothers did not work, so that they spent more on fuel. There were enormous variations in fuel costs for large centrally heated houses and single rooms with only a paraffin heater. Some mothers said they lit the fire late, or lived only in one room to save expense: 'In winter I forget I've a dining-room, I just close that door.' An unmarried mother, paying concealed rent through a meter fixed at a very high charge, had had to lie in bed during the day with her clothes on to keep warm. A separated wife had had to steal coke at midnight from a mill yard.

Some families evened out fuel costs by buying clothing in summer and fuel in winter on the same weekly club payment. Only thirteen mothers, six of them widows, could afford to buy coal in bulk, and the remaining mothers, with only small resources, found it difficult to get a coalman who would deliver only one or two bags. As a result eight mothers were using small, expensive bags of coal.

Rebates on gas and electricity were often large, running up to £8, because families tended to use an over-charging meter as a money box. The great interest in rebates was a further sign of the mothers' difficulty in raising small lump sums.

Spending on other needs

So far, only conventionally approved basic 'necessities' have been described, but mothers also chose to spend their money (or they would have liked to spend it) on items such as television, which were not essential for physical subsistence, yet which were evidently necessary for their psychological well-being or for social reasons.

A family without TV felt really deprived. Mothers spoke of their children wanting TV so that they could talk about the same programmes as their friends. A mother without TV lost her children for substantial parts of the day to other households who had a set. Those with TV were defensive, but determined. They felt the N.A.B. frowned on their expense, but, 'I told them, "I pay for it, you don't." It's hard enough having to make ends meet without having to go without everything.' Mothers said, 'It's my only hobby,' and 'I'm entitled to a bit of something.' Television or a washing machine became a symbolic reward for other deprivations.

Just over half the mothers smoked, the same as the national proportion of women smokers in this age range.[6] One said, 'That's one thing that's come out of this. I never used to smoke, but I've tried to give it up and I can't, and I get so crabby.' Some mothers said they smoked 'Freemans' (other people's cigarettes), or they were given occasional packets by relatives. But gifts seldom amounted to more than ten or twenty a week, so that most of the smoking was at the expense of other items. One third of the mothers smoked 70 or more cigarettes per week, and of these, five smoked 120 or more, and one smoked 210 cigarettes a week. A separated wife said, 'What I smoke I don't eat. I can't afford to do both, and I only have one meal a day.' Whatever qualifications must be made in view of mothers' nervous condition and the stress they were undergoing, it was evident that some mothers were going short, sometimes seriously short, of other things in order to smoke.

Among other regular expenses which might be considered not strictly necessary for the families' physical well-being, twenty families had pets which cost money to feed. One mother said, 'We had a dog, but it was too expensive. I feel so guilty. The children don't mention him, but sometimes they get his photo out and then the tears run down their faces.' The average expenditure on the twenty pets was 5s. per week. But there were eight which cost 7s. or more, and one cost 15s. There were other families who insisted their pets lived off scraps and leftovers: 'When we're without she's without, except the neighbours are good to her. Honestly to see them waste their dinners, it makes me angry. And the things they've brought for her, one of them brought her a casserole of stew, but without being funny I could have sneaked it myself.' These pets were company, and sometimes, for a mother who was the only adult in the house, a reassurance that she was not defenceless. But more than this, they were members of the household who could not be lightly cut off when poverty came to the family.

A substantial number of mothers and children had wanted a holiday, like schoolmates and other families nearby, yet they could not afford one. Lack of a holiday was not always seen as a loss. Some of the mothers came from families where there had never been money for holidays, and they had never had one either as children or later when they were married: 'What you've never had you never miss.' Mothers with larger families felt it would be too much of a strain. One said, 'To tell you the truth, I'd rather not go, it's such hard work for me, and then in the evenings, not having another adult, it's so boring.' One mother had turned down a holiday she was offered by the N.A.B. Nevertheless, the small proportion of families who had holidays was evidence of deprivation. In half the families nobody had had a holiday in the previous year, and in only one fifth had the whole family been away. In three families the mother had been away for her health, but not the children, while in four families the children had been away but not the mother. In twelve of the remaining families only one child had been away, and in the remaining families two or more children. The previous chapter showed that thirty-six families, or almost one third, received help with holidays from relatives, friends, and charities. In holidays, as in other matters, the families had to rely very largely on outside help if they were to behave like the rest of the community.

Other expenditure was more closely linked with participation in the wider family or community. Relatively few mothers went out frequently. Less than a third went to pubs at all: only eleven mothers had been to pubs alone or with another woman in the last fortnight; four mothers said they went to a pub or club with a relative and seventeen had been with a man-friend – they were treated and rarely had to buy drinks. Again contrary to a popular stereotype of the poor, only four had been to bingo. Ten went to the pictures alone and four went with a woman friend. Three had been dancing. Three were members of social clubs. In fact, sixty-nine mothers, 60 per cent, had not been out on any evening during the previous fortnight, which probably meant they never went out in the evening, for those who went out at all had a regular outing. Only seven mothers had been out more than twice in the evening in the previous fortnight, approximately one fifth had been out twice, and another fifth once.

Yet although these figures are low they do not differ markedly from comparable working-class marriages, and it appears significant that mothers found it difficult to say whether they were kept in by lack of money or by their social situation – the lack of somewhere to go and someone to go with.[7]

Housekeeping on a low income

A great deal of interest has always focused on whether deprivation of the kind described here arises because low-income families mis-manage their resources. We have seen that these mothers didn't spent their money on beer and bingo, and in a situation of stress they smoked if no less, then no more than the average in the community. Nevertheless, their budgeting showed wide variations, not all suited to living on a low income.

Some mothers had always been used to budgeting and others appeared to find it no real strain, although they might deplore the necessity of having to keep a tight rein on themselves all the time. One woman said, 'Your mind gets like a cash register after a while and as you go round the supermarket you add up as you go through. It's awful in a way.' Some were conscious of their spending right down to the last shilling: 'If it's a penny cheaper, I go there. Even if it's only a halfpenny. My friend says, "Why, it's only a halfpenny!" I say, "A halfpenny's a lot to me."' There were a few who put their money in a series of little envelopes, for gas, laundry, the Co-op order, milk, TV, H.P., the greengrocer, electricity, rates, mortgage, coal, and insurance. Some developed little systems of saving: 'You have to take a penny out of your purse and put it back and think, "If I save enough of those I'll have a pound."' One mother said, 'If I go shopping, and I get something a bit cheaper than it should be, I pretend I've spent the money and put it away.' Another said, 'What I have, I have a little tin, and I put 2s. or 2s. 6d. or sometimes 5s. and that's for my furniture, or if the children want anything, and whatever happens I never touch that. Sometimes I kid myself that I've put something in, but I know I haven't.' Another woman had had £7 in savings on the day her husband left, and she kept this amount untouched.

This kind of saving, in lots of different small amounts, is fairly normal in working-class homes, as the popularity of a slot TV testifies. Few would have agreed with a mother who said that she enjoyed housekeeping more now, and yet there was a sense in which many of these actions assumed a ritual and expressive character beyond their value as thrift. They enabled the mothers who practised them to develop some feeling of control over their situation, and it was apparent that while they complained some of these mothers derived a grim satisfaction from measuring up to the task in hand.

What might be called 'splash' budgeting was common to a wider group of mothers. Richard Hoggart regards 'the splash' as a fundamental feature of working-class life:

Most working-class people . . . only want the little more that allows a few frills . . . The extras for adults may be only occasional and quite small in apparent importance – fish and chips for supper in mid-week, for instance. But they add variety or colour or some gaiety to life; they are among the freely-springing things in a life which is largely an imposed routine, the routine of clocking-in-and-out, or of the family's meals, washing and repairs. Where the routine or work is rarely changed and is almost entirely imposed from outside, the attitude towards free and personal acts takes on a special complexion.[8]

The analogy between the conditions of life described by Hoggart and life on assistance is close; and the latter being more drab, perhaps the pressures to have a splash are the more urgent.

The mothers on assistance could not keep up the steady skimp and scrape, the constant vigilance. As one said, 'Sometimes you feel that if you didn't buy anything extra you'd go mad.' Usually if these mothers were tempted into buying something they could not afford it was clothing for the children ('You can't do both, you can't eat and dress'), or something for the house. They knew they would regret buying, but felt that this was the only way, buy first and think later. It was a kind of emotional release, which kept them in touch with the pleasures of ordinary living. The spending of many families was governed by the fact that the rent was paid fortnightly, so there could be a splash every other week, or the fact that there were four holiday weeks when rent was not due (the N.A.B. average the rent out in the allowance over the year). Other splashes came with the gas or electricity rebate, or drawing the Co-operative dividend. These were the only times when mothers found the 'extra' pound or two to buy some items.

A small number of mothers patently had difficulty in managing their incomes. Two had their rents paid directly to the local authority. One described how she paid for her gas:

I pay fifteen shillings to a pound a week, that's if it's not duds. Well, you put curtain rings in. You can buy twenty curtain rings for tenpence in town, or a washer. Or I've even cut out tops of cans, or filed down halfpennies. The last time the meter man came I said, 'How much is there?' He said, 'You've two shillings.' 'Two shillings!' I said. He says, 'Yes', and I'd got two shillings; he'd given me back all my duds and there was about thirty bobs' worth!

Several other mothers were not saving to pay rates or fuel bills which they half hoped the N.A.B. were going to pay (the N.A.B. would not) or they were getting deeper and deeper into club debts.[9] One mother said, 'I've always got it in the back of my mind to get out of paying for clubs, but all the time I get further in, because it's things you've got to have.' Another said, 'If I stopped to write down every little thing I have to pay I'd never get anything. You've just got to stick your neck out and then pay for it the week after.' One mother was supposed to pay five different clubs in all: £1 on Monday for clothing, 30s. Tuesdays for toys, £2 once a fortnight on Thursday for a vacuum cleaner, 10s. on Friday for clothing, and 5s. on Saturday for some mats.

High payments like these, and the consequent financial difficulties, could only be temporary, for they would probably end with repossession of the goods. Mothers in this situation tended to be the separated wives who were just setting up homes and whose status was more transitional than other groups. The unmarried had yet to come to these problems; the divorced and widowed whose families had been fatherless for longer had sometimes passed through this stage.

There were further influences of background on spending behaviour. Some middle-class mothers and a certain group of the working class did not buy secondhand clothing, nor did they 'believe in' hire purchase, or clubs. One mother said debts and credit-buying were 'her one fear'. Another woman who had run up a small bill for clothing said the bill was a millstone. A mother who had no TV, no washer, no H.P., no clothing clubs, said 'We've not been used to that (H.P.) in our family. None of us have ever had it, and I don't believe in it.' Some mothers also did not like jumble sales, for similar reasons. One said, 'I don't know if it's pride or not, but that's one thing my mother never did. It's funny how you copy, isn't it?' Another said, 'I'm always frightened there'll be somebody I know, and I don't seem to be the type either, because when you get there, well, I spend all my time watching the others. You'll see them, and they'll all rush in and dive in. I wouldn't be able to do that.'

It was evident that these attitudes would prevent mothers from getting into debt. But where items of furniture or clothing were needed these mothers would have to go short if they could count on no other resources than assistance. Overall, it was very difficult to see whether the mother's particular methods of housekeeping made much difference to the family's standard of living. The ability to buy coal in bulk, rather than in small bags, payments for clothing in cash rather than clubs, adequate standards of diet, and so on, were time and again found to be not marks of superior thrift so much as indications of greater income or outside help, or smaller needs.

These first three chapters have attempted to make an objective comparison between the situation of fatherless families and the average standard of living, income, and amenity in the community. In spite of the difficulty of defining and measuring needs and collecting information about the mothers' spending patterns, this exploration has produced clear evidence that a proportion of the families were suffering material deprivation. A tenth to a quarter were short of food, and without substantial gifts of clothing from relatives one third to a half would have been badly dressed. The previous chapter showed that many of the unmarried mothers and some of the separated and the divorced lacked furniture and household appliances, and were short of space and amenities in the home.

Even for these accepted necessities, and more so when we

go beyond them, in deciding what constitutes *deprivation* the mothers' subjective preferences for certain types of spending or activity have had to be taken into account. This chapter has looked at individual items, to some extent artificially abstracted from the total context of the mothers' lives. It is now time to try to fit these separate items together and form an overall picture of the way in which material deprivation was affecting the mothers' morale and social relationships.

CHAPTER FOUR

On Feeling Poor: The Social Context of Poverty

One way of assessing the adequacy of national assistance at this time is to ask, how poor did the mothers feel? Poor people's feelings about their material standards should be among the factors to be weighed in determining what the state minimum income level should be. Yet drawing the state 'poverty line' by finding a level of benefits at which none of the recipients feels poor would be impracticable, because people's feelings of deprivation do not derive solely from their immediate material circumstances.

What the mothers said about feeling poor was evidently coloured by the experience of fatherlessness and by their whole social situation. Their feelings of deprivation were based very often on some kind of comparison, not the same comparison for each mother, and not always a comparison with other people.[1] One of the purposes of this chapter is to ask what sorts of comparisons mothers were making when they said how poor they felt, who they were comparing themselves with. But beyond this we have to try to understand what else the mothers were saying when they talked about poverty.

In poverty or hard up?

Mothers found the word poverty insulting. A separated wife said sarcastically, in reply to a calculated question whether she considered she was in poverty,

Well, thanks very much. I've been labelled destitute by the National Assistance, but I don't think I consider myself in poverty yet. That's a horrible word. You think of little children with no shoes and only thin dresses and no fire. I don't think there's anybody like that in these days. If there is it's their own fault.

'Poverty' for these mothers retained some of its grosser meaning in terms of a lack of fundamental necessities, especially the visible ones of clothing and furniture. But the word obviously carried a stigma, and the mothers preferred to talk of being 'hard up'.

When a mother said she was 'comfortable' or 'poor' she balanced a number of perhaps conflicting emotions, and indeed some mothers made contradictory statements about their feelings at different stages of the interview. Mothers who did not volunteer an overall subjective assessment of their situation were asked, 'Do you feel hard up?' One third said they felt 'hard up all the time', 'terribly poor', or said that they were 'not living, just existing' (Appendix Table 7). Another third said they were hard up 'sometimes', 'occasionally', or regularly at some period of the week. But the remaining third said they were not hard up; they were 'comfortable', or at least they 'managed'. A majority of the unmarried felt hard up, but most of the widows said they felt comfortable.

These statements must be interpreted very cautiously, for although as many as two thirds of the mothers were prepared to say they were poor, perhaps the proportion should have been even higher because there were various pressures which tended to influence them against revealing deprivation. They differed greatly in their willingness to discuss hardship. Some were eager to talk. Thus when one mother was asked by her young daughter whether there was salad cream for tea, the mother turned to me with a kind of triumph and said histrionically, 'Salad cream! *We* can't have salad cream. That's a luxury, that is.' She and other women brought out one instance after another of how difficult their lives had become on national assistance, in order to drive home the point, 'You don't *live* on national assistance, you just exist.' These mothers in a sense embraced the suggestion that they were deprived, as a criticism of their children's fathers and the N.A.B. They aligned themselves with the poor against a hostile community.

However, a substantial number of mothers who were obviously experiencing shortages were very reluctant to say anything about their standard of living which might indicate dissatisfaction. An alternative attempt to get mothers to estimate whether they were poor by asking if they needed extra money also proved inconclusive. The response was often, 'It's not for me to say.' One woman said, 'You arrange your money according to how much you've got, don't you.' Another said, 'You can't expect to be greedy. I often say, be thankful.' It was noticeable that mothers hesitated about what they were 'allowed' to want, wondered could they have TV, a holiday, could they save for a rainy day or for Christmas or birthdays, could they have H.P., could they smoke, and so on. If these mothers gave any estimate at all of how much money they needed, they would ask for £1 or 30s. They were not looking for money to bring them up to any kind of average level, but merely wished for a slight easing of the present stringencies.

To confess that they would like more money was for them tantamount to asking for charity. An admission of deprivation was a confession of personal inadequacy, and of a failure as a mother to measure up to the housekeeping job posed by the income the state provided: it was a confession that the children were deprived, and even disloyal to them, for they were in a measure responsible for the mother's dependence. Thus, in marked contrast to those who aligned themselves with the poor, these mothers identified with the non-poor in seeing the condition of the poor as blameworthy and a sign of personal failure.

So, not surprisingly an attempt to relate mothers' feelings directly to their objective material circumstances was not very successful. The lack of possessions or poor housing might have been influential, since the group feeling poorest were the unmarried, who had the poorest homes. And of the mothers who said they felt comfortable or that they managed, relatively few had very low incomes, most of them living at 130 per cent of the N.A.B. rate or over. But the association between feeling hard up and income was not at all close or consistent. A third of the mothers with the highest incomes said they felt hard up, usually all the time; while a small number of mothers with the lowest incomes said they did not feel hard up. It was striking how some mothers who mentioned deprivations in small or even large matters denied feeling poor. Yet mothers who in many material respects were manifestly well-off nevertheless, when they made an overall judgement of their situation, said they felt poor.

The overriding influences on how mothers felt appeared to derive from outside their immediate material situation. However, there was no evidence that mothers were comparing themselves with society on a national scale: their comparisons were much more personal and local.

Memories

It was clear that at least two thirds of the mothers were very strongly influenced in their attitudes by their own living standards in the past. In fact mothers' standards of living on national assistance could represent a considerable improvement on anything they had known in their married lives. Of the Seaston mothers who had been married, only one in six said they were now very much worse off than when they were married. A further one in six said they were no worse off, while one in three said they were better off than when they were married. During her marriage one divorced woman had had to live for three days on nettles from the garden, and at other times on what she could collect by returning her husband's empty beer bottles. Another divorced woman said,

> I used to have to take the pram from one pub to another to see if he was in there, to get money for the dinner. We always had the 'cruelty man' and the police up there because we never had no food for the children. You know, sir, this is the first few years I've had enough to eat, since I been on National Assistance.

Other women compared unfavourably the uncertainties of budgeting during marriage with the regular income they received from the N.A.B.

An improved standard of living after separation might merely reflect the former husband's selfishness in keeping his earnings to himself. But as we shall see later, there is the very important and more fundamental difficulty for social security planning here, that because many men are paid at rates below national assistance levels separation can bring a financial improvement for the family. In this sense, depending on the point of view, either low wages or our social security system constitute an incentive to family breakdown.

Women who had worked, or whose husbands had been good workers, were more liable to feel hard up. One unmarried mother said, 'Really, I'm not hard up at all compared with some people. But it's hit me so hard because I'm used to having plenty of money and savings to fall back on. I feel lost now without them.' There were also some mothers who compared the present with the situation as it might have been. Had one woman's husband not died, she would by now have furnished her living room completely, and she said,

Some people looking at me in this house must think I'm pretty well off, but they don't know how often I've been desperate and sat down here and cried. It's not going in other people's houses that depresses me most, but sitting in this house day after day, week after week, looking round and never seeing anything new.

Other women tended to feel they might have been better off had they managed to stay with their husbands, and feelings of financial deprivation mingled inextricably with longing for the husband himself.

There were further ways in which feelings about present living standards might be influenced by the past. Women who had been dependent on assistance or a state pension for many years welcomed the slow improvement in subsistence living standards brought by rises in national assistance scales, widows' pensions, and other benefits. A widow said, 'When I got your letter I said to my mother, it would have been a good thing if you'd come a few years back when I was badly off. I feel as though I'm one of the better off ones now.' And some mothers had had periods of their lives when they had dropped to a very low level of living. Such a period was during the interval before mothers had found out about assistance, when they had depended on relatives or savings. For other women, who had deserted, or been evicted by, their husbands, starting from scratch to get a home together had proved the most severe strain, and they described how they had lived off orange box furniture and cooked by a coal fire at that time.

Comparisons with kin and neighbours

A third of the mothers spoke of relatives and another third mentioned friends or neighbours as being better off and making them feel poor themselves. One mother said of her brother's home, 'To me his house is a luxury house. It may not be to them, but to me it is, and at times you just lose heart.' Mothers who had friends with expensive tastes might recognize that they were not badly off in absolute terms, but yet feel poor. One woman, who envied her friends their cars and houses, said of her feelings, 'But that's not *poverty*, that's personal humiliation.'

The standard of living in the neighbourhood could have a very considerable influence on the mother's sense of well-being. A widow had an average income for this group and was among the very best-provided in terms of furniture, yet she still felt poor.

You see, the National Assistance woman tells me when I go for anything that we're not really badly off, and really when I look at myself I'm not. It's not as though we're pinching and scraping. She says that there are some families that really need the money, where they've got husbands that are only bringing in £8 a week. Only the trouble here is that all the women go out to work, and it's nothing for them to get £20 a week housekeeping. They all seem to be able to buy things.

Two of the mothers had been persuaded by salesmen to buy expensive vacuum cleaners because, 'They've all got them round here,' yet one of the mothers had no carpets to clean and the cleaner had been unused for months. Another woman said,

It's the little things that aggravate you. I used to have some curtains for many years, and those curtains used to get on my nerves, the colours of them, until finally I started scratching and saving, and putting a bit on one side, and I used to say to myself, 'That's my curtain money, and I'm not touching that for anything.' And finally, I got them curtains that I've got now. And when I'd put them up, I thought, 'Right, my curtains are as good as anybody's curtains in this street.'

However, many of these fatherless families lived on very poor estates and had friends or neighbours who were not markedly better off. So a mother could easily find someone in the vicinity who was manifestly poorer than she was. One mother had virtually no furniture yet she was not the poorest in her terrace.

There's this family two doors on and the father's living with them and three kids. *We* give *them* stuff. I have to because when our Glenys is out the back eating anything they come hanging round looking at her, and I can't bear to see them looking like that.

My impression was that mothers tended to select such situations from their present experience to back up an assessment of standards which had its origins in a comparison with the past.

The cycle of deprivation over time

The mothers' sense of deprivation relative to the community was heightened because they did not get their incomes at the same time as most other families. National assistance allowances for these families were paid on Monday (or for widows on Tuesday), and also court payments were likely to be made at the beginning of the week. So unless they had wages of their own or from children, mothers tended to be short of money at the weekends. This was the time when most other families received wages and the time the mothers had been used to receiving money when they or their husbands were working. The fatherless families were therefore out of tune both with the life of the community and with their former pattern of spending. These mothers saw their neighbours setting off and returning laden with shopping at the weekend, but could not join in.

The feeling that they had 'got to' shop at the weekend remained strong, except for mothers who took a certain delight in symbolically rearranging their spending habits and making sacrifices. So mothers often compared themselves unfavourably with the community in this respect if nothing else: 'Anybody, even if she's got a husband and a wage coming in, she always just has to manage on Thursday and Friday on what there is in the cupboard, but when it's Saturday and Sunday you've got to have something a bit more special.' There were good practical reasons for wanting the money at the weekends. The children who had school meals all week were at home, needing extra food and asking for money for the baths or pictures, or a trip to the seaside. On estates there were clubmen, milkmen, coalmen, and other tradesmen who called on Friday evening as part of the rhythm of estate life. With immediate pressing needs earlier in the week mothers found difficulty in maintaining a sense of proportion about priorities in the budget.

Altogether, almost half the mothers said they would prefer to be paid on Friday, although some suggested that the N.A.B. deliberately paid them on a Monday to make them save![2] Several mothers had made arrangements to draw the money on Friday, one officially with the N.A.B., although this was later stopped as contrary to Regulations, another in an unofficial arrangement with the local post-mistress. One mother worked mainly because she felt she had to have the bulk of her money on Friday. A sign of straitened circumstances was that although the mothers wished to have money at the weekend, only one could afford to save until then. Several mothers lent money to neighbours at the beginning of the week, so that they would be able to borrow at the weekend when the neighbours were more affluent.

The situation might be illustrated by Figure 1. The expenditure cycle for fatherless families is out of phase with that of the average family by approximately three days. The distance between the two curves is a very rough indication of the relative deprivation of the fatherless families. By adjusting the time of

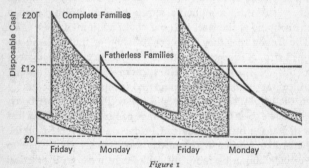

Figure 1

Suggested pattern of weekly fluctuations in disposable incomes of fatherless and complete families.

payment of the national assistance allowance to Friday the extreme difference between the curves at the end of the week could be avoided, and feelings of relative deprivation possibly be reduced. From the community's point of view misunderstandings about the relative 'affluence' of these families at the beginning of the week might also be less likely to arise.

There were also seasonal cycles of relative deprivation. At Christmas expenditure by the fatherless families could not go up to match the increasing spending of others. One of the more isolated mothers said, 'No, I won't be going anywhere for Christmas. I've got no friends. There'll be just me and him (her son) stuck in the front room. I go in there with the boy and we have a bit of a game or something.' She had been to ask the N.A.B. if there were not some extra grant 'to make it feel a bit more like Christmas'.[3] Another isolated mother said,

I hate Christmas coming. I dread it, because every time you go out you seem to be spending and spending, and I don't like them to miss anything. I like them to have all the trimmings. I tell you what. I hope you never have to do the same with your children as I've had to do with mine. Tell them that Father Christmas hasn't got any toys for our house this year. That's what I've had to do. And I've had to wait until Marks and Spencers have had their sales and then I've had to buy a doll for them and say that Father Christmas has remembered after all.

Not only did the children not have toys, but,

You see all these children from Corporation Homes and different works and it's in the *Reporter* every week that they're going to this trip and that trip, and they're going to the pantomime. And ours are always on at me, 'Why can't we go to a party?' Nobody thinks about such as mine as their mothers are separated.

Another mother was interviewed on the morning of the first day of school after Christmas, and she said, 'I'm dreading them going back to school this morning and people will be asking, "What did you get? What did you get?"' Mothers who did not have Christmas with relatives were faced with the dilemma of ignoring Christmas altogether and feeling guilty; as one said, 'I felt rotten about that. It was Christmas and I didn't know it.' Or they planned so far ahead that, 'It seems like one long Christmas.' Or they went into debt 'up to the eyeballs', as one mother put it. The size of the Christmas festivities was limited by mothers' attitudes to credit buying.

Whitsuntide was a comparable festival for rather fewer mothers in Northborough when traditionally there are church 'walks' and the 'scholars' from Sunday School parade in their new clothes and go round to visit the neighbours to show their clothes and receive small presents of money. Support for these traditions was very patchy, but strong on the council estates. One Northborough mother insisted, 'They *will* be rigged out at Whitsuntide. Other children have it, so they will.' For mothers like this one, feelings of deprivation may have led them to adhere more closely to these customs which other, better-off families were less determined to support.

Thus in spite of their relative isolation some mothers still felt the weekly cycle of income and expenditure of complete families and the pull of community festivals. Their sense of exclusion or the feelings of being out of tune with the wider society in these respects increased their feelings of deprivation.

Poverty and the children

These stories of the seasons underline a major theme: in a complex and not always consistent way, the mother's feelings of deprivation were entwined with her feelings for her children.

Young children were a tie, but they were often thought a compensation for all hardships, including the absence of the father. An unmarried mother said of her baby son, 'He's my riches. I'd rather have him than all the money in the world.' Again and again this feeling was expressed, 'We may not be wealthy, but we've plenty of love.' It was evident that ultimately having children could soften the harshness of comparisons of living standards with childless couples who were manifestly much better off financially.

But although children were sometimes seen as a compensation for hardships, over a third of the mothers said they were most sharply pierced by feelings of deprivation *through* their children:

the comparison group was the children's friends. For while the mothers themselves had developed various defences against feeling poor, the children were at once more in touch with society and less knowledgeable about the family income and prospects. The children were less isolated socially from the community, for they had to go to school every day. Mothers wanted to give their children what others had, and there were in fact things which had to be bought or paid for if a child was to participate fully with his friends and in school activities. The multiplicity of small items was difficult to measure, but mothers spoke of their children not having enough fireworks on bonfire night, not having a decent party dress, not being able to go to the Saturday matinee at the cinema, or to the swimming baths. A separated wife said, 'It's not the *big* things, you want to put this down, it's the *little* things that aggravate you. Like the ice-cream van. Every night that ice-cream van comes and stops right outside my window, and there are these (the children) looking out of the window at it.' Children who could not take their threepence to Sunday school did not get a stamp. Those who could not afford uniform were not members of the Cubs or Brownies. Those without bikes could not go on runs with their friends during the evenings or at weekends or on holiday. Shortage of money and poor furniture meant that mothers were reluctant to let their children bring friends round to tea, and the children themselves were less often invited out. In many ways, none perhaps in themselves significant, poor children were marked off from their friends.

Few children received no pocket money, although in fourteen families they received it from relatives rather than the mother. On average the children received pocket money or sweets worth probably 1s. 6d. or 2s. per week. Yet to mothers anxiously concerned that they should not be deprived, they still seemed worse off than their contemporaries (which may have been so, for a national survey of pocket money gave the figure of 3s. 9d. for the average 8–15 year-old in 1966[4]).

Exclusion through lack of money also pervaded school activities. In addition to the embarrassments of free school meals and uniform, children had problems in getting the full range of clothes for P.E., sports, and science. It appeared that very few of the children even went on school trips, and certainly not on the continental holidays which grow more popular every year. Nine mothers confessed to difficulty in finding even the small amounts of money for sewing and cookery lessons. A separated wife said, 'Some of the things they make up there – salads, they've got to take everything, cucumber and lettuce and cheese they've got to take. I've seen me spend 8s. 6d. sometimes on cookery.' Girls who could not take money for cookery were put on cleaning and washing up. One mother said, 'They used to beg and plead to me for money for cookery lessons, but if I hadn't it, if I was really desperate, they wouldn't go.' One girl said, 'What will the other girls think. They'll think I'm a pauper.'

The demands from school were growing. Children instead of making a class cake now made a cake each, and there were cakes for Christmas and cakes for Mothering Sunday. Infants and juniors as well as senior girls now cooked. There were requests for donations to the school fund or to a charity. Children were asked to bring a bulb for nature study or to buy the school photograph. In all, the mothers felt, 'When the teachers ask children to come home and get so much money, I don't think they realize some can't afford it.' Occasionally mothers mentioned understanding teachers; one who devised a system whereby a child need not reveal non-payment for school dinners, or a headmaster who frequently paid for a girl's cookery class himself, but these appeared to be exceptions. The fatherless families tried to keep up, but from what mothers said they often failed, and as a consequence the children were marked off from their schoolmates in many small ways.

School aspirations

These children did relatively badly at school. Of the 150 over selection age, only fifteen, or 10 per cent, had passed the selection tests, although there were over 23 per cent of selective school places for Northborough and Seaston averaged together.[5]

These findings run contrary to one stereotype of the effects of fatherlessness, where the loss of the father is claimed to improve ambition. A vivid illustration of the rejection of the idea that the children might be deprived was provided by the response to an article I wrote depicting the problems of the school child living on national assistance in an increasingly affluent society.[6] The evidence seems clear that on the whole fatherless children on national assistance do less well at school, but the suggestion was violently challenged in most of the dozen letters I received, in response to the article, from mothers quoting the instance of their own children who had gone to grammar school and reached university. They felt about my article, and will no doubt feel about this book, that the revelations of hardship and suggestions of handicap had stigmatized and condemned them. Their children's success shows that we must not underestimate the spur provided to a minority of mothers and children by the challenge of fatherlessness. Yet they are a minority.

On the other hand, the lack of school success of the children in this survey may overstate the effect of poverty on school performance. Fatherlessness itself may affect school performance.[7] Also, these were working-class children already at a disadvantage in a school system which selects and grades children often from the age of seven: the whole system is basically unresponsive and fails to acknowledge the gifts and provide for the needs of such children.[8] Nevertheless, it seems probable that poverty may have played some part in the children's lack of success.

Before the selection test some mothers were less inclined to encourage their children because they feared the expense of grammar school. A divorced mother said, 'I wasn't bothered about her passing the 11-plus because I knew it was an impossibility. I knew she couldn't go, even if she'd passed. I know they give you a grant, but it doesn't cover everything. It was out of the question.' Another woman said, 'I'm worried to death now in case she *does* pass the 11-plus. She'll have to have school uniform and she's got to have clothes for games and sports equipment, and I don't know where it would come from.' The fear that you had 'got to have money at the back of you for anything like that' also applied to the 13-plus, and indeed to other courses of action entailing extensive training. Mothers had not known about maintenance grants, and said how they looked forward to the time when the child would bring in a good wage. There was also a little evidence that poverty affected the child's aspirations. After selection, several of the few children who passed had left, even before taking O-levels, to begin earning. A gifted girl, who had been picked out by her headmaster in class for her ability in French, came to him and asked if she could drop the subject. 'She couldn't see the point in doing it because it wasn't any use, there was never any chance of her going to France and speaking French.' A friend of the headmaster offered to pay for the girl to go on the school trip to Paris, but she still required £7 spending money, which the N.A.B. refused to provide: 'They just laughed. They said, "You want it for *spending* money!"'

At the level of aspirations poverty could have influenced the children's chances, whether it acted directly or whether it merely served as a final justification for mistrust of the grammar schools and all they represented. It was also possible that, if teachers did not have full knowledge of the situation, absences from school, the awkwardness of school meals and cookery, failure to go on school trips, and unorthodoxy of dress, might just tip the balance between a child going into a high or low stream. Thus, children already deprived had their life chances further diminished by being excluded from the full benefit of education.

The family cycle

Because children were a hope for the future or a present financial burden, a worry or an economic support, mothers' feelings of deprivation were linked with the stages of the family cycle. As young children became less of a tie, hope began to stir in the more ambitious mothers who intended to take up a career. And for some of the older mothers the burden was beginning to lighten as their children began to earn a full wage, and this relative affluence was visible in front rooms only recently furnished and decorated by working sons who wanted somewhere decent to bring their girl-friends.

As children grew older they were more able to see their full situation, and they might not make as many requests on their mother. But on the other hand, the wants of older children tended to widen. They came under the influence of advertising directed at teenagers and felt the competition of other teenagers who had a comparatively large amount of money to spend. There was enormous pressure to keep up with fashion and to know all the pop records. This was one reason why children were being allowed sooner the housekeeping arrangement known as 'boarding' by which they keep a larger share of their earnings. Yet there was inevitably an interval, which was growing longer as advertising stretched down towards the group now called the 'pre-teens', when the burden of filling a child's wants was great and it fell very largely on the mother's national assistance allowance. Children are entering puberty earlier and the school leaving age is shortly to be raised. The problem of catering for sexually mature but dependent adults is growing for all families, but particularly for the fatherless. [9] So the mother's feelings of hardship through her children are likely to be prolonged and to become more acute as these trends proceed.

The maturity of the children was not the end of the story, for after a brief spell of work they would want to marry and leave home, and the mother's standard of living could drop again. A divorced woman who had been on assistance for seventeen years said,

I'm worried about what will happen when they all leave me. I didn't care at all at first when my husband left me. I thought, 'Let him go, I've got my children. When they grow up they'll be working.' I used to look forward to it like a dream, and then when my eldest girl got working it was like heaven. But then, a bit later on, you realize that your children, they aren't your own really. You can't keep them at home for ever, and I think deep down inside, I'd like them to stay the same, I wouldn't want them to get married, I'd like them to stop here with me. But you can't make them do that, can you? But I won't live on my own. It worries me at night-time. I can't sleep. When I'm in bed and I should be sleeping, I'm thinking what will happen to me when they've all gone. You see I can't go back to how I was before. I don't want my daughter to get married because I can't do without her wage. As we've been these last few years we've been able to, what I call, live properly. We've been able to keep a good table. There's many a time before when we've had beans on toast for a meal, but I don't want to go back to that now. I couldn't go back to that now.

Thus as the children grew and family fortunes changed, so the mother's feelings of deprivation and aspirations underwent a series of fluctuations and shifts. These backward and forward glances go far to explain why mothers' feelings of deprivation did not correspond as closely as might be expected with their present living standards.

Nevertheless, whatever the subtleties of the situation, it is worth recalling at this point the stark finding that two thirds of the mothers said they were poor or very poor.

Throughout these chapters on material deprivation, we have constantly been drawn into glancing aside at the mothers' social lives, and at the way in which the experience of poverty is moulded by relationships. But, as the discussion of the children's schooling has hinted, relationships are themselves stunted by poverty. It will now be clear that in order to assess the full effects of present social policies and to devise more appropriate schemes we must learn much more about the mothers' lives and relationships. Accordingly, the next section will focus directly on the experience of fatherlessness.

Part Two *Fatherlessness*

CHAPTER FIVE

Broken Marriages

The first marriages of seventy-six[1] of the mothers had ended in divorce or separation, and these mothers described marriage breakdown with different degrees of insight and sophistication. Some were apparently choosing from a number of possible explanations the one they found most satisfying, while others could find – or would volunteer – no explanation at all. For various reasons it seems unlikely that we can regard the mothers' accounts as providing a full and balanced description of the 'true' reasons why their marriages broke down. But, carefully interpreted, the accounts do reveal how the mothers had adjusted to the broken marriage, and also throw light on why husbands now gave them so little support and why a proportion of the women were in such poor accommodation.

Before presenting any detailed descriptions from the mothers of how these marriages ended, it will be as well to raise some general problems posed by the study of marriage breakdown. For in spite of – or even because of – the great public interest in broken marriages we still know remarkably little about the causes of individual breakdowns or even the total incidence of broken marriages.

The incidence of broken marriages

Misconceptions about the incidence of marriage breakdown arise because we can collect statistics only on marriages which are ended legally, either through divorce or legal separation. But in addition to divorces and separations there will also be marriages which have ended informally, so that no record exists of their ending. Only a very delicate, perhaps even impractical, study of the 'epidemiology' of marriage breakdown in the community would give us really accurate information. Probably the incidence of marriages broken from all causes is now 10 to 15 per cent.

In these circumstances divorce and separation statistics are a treacherous index of marriage breakdown, yet society has been obsessed by the divorce statistics alone as an indication that marriages were becoming increasingly unstable. It is true that divorce figures have risen greatly over the past hundred years or so in which divorce has been permitted outside the aristocracy. From a mere handful of upper-class divorces in 1857, the annual rate of petitions (not all of them successful) was running at 61,216 by 1969.[2] But much of this rise could be accounted for by the increasing *availability* of divorce. And there has also been a switch from separation to divorce, with the result that the numbers of legal separations have increased much less markedly in this century and stood in 1969 at 32,433 petitions to magistrates' courts.

In short, we might suppose that in the past there were many more marriages which were 'empty shells' where no affection remained, and many more informal separations; how many we do not know. As the length of time which a marriage might last became greater through early marriage and increased life expectation of the partners, there was more risk that the marriage would break through separation or divorce rather than death. So an increasing proportion of spouses may have decided to live apart; increasingly they have turned to the law to end their marriage in legal separation or divorce; and increasingly they have chosen to divorce rather than to separate. Up to the late 1950s, then, it could be argued that the statistics might reveal mainly changing modes of signalizing the end of dead marriages rather than a drastic increase in marital instability.

However, Chester has now analysed the trends in marriage breakdown between 1959 and 1969.[3] These show a rise in the annual divorce rate, per 1,000 married, of 100 per cent; and an estimated rise in the numbers of breakdowns coming to public notice (that is, through separations also) of 65 per cent. He suggests that, 'Although the rates and numbers of unrecorded breakdowns are unknown, and may be diminishing, it is concluded that breakdown is probably increasing in volume among contemporary marriages. On the basis of speculative estimates it is also suggested that perhaps one sixth to one quarter of contemporary marriages may ultimately experience some form of breakdown.' He believes that changes in social structure since the war have fostered a more permissive approach to personal behaviour, which became apparent from 1955 onwards, and that 'relatively high rates of marriage breakdown will henceforth be an integral feature of social experience.' This would mean a divorce rate of 10 to $12\frac{1}{2}$ per cent, $1\frac{1}{2}$ to $2\frac{1}{2}$ per cent of permanent separations, and a further 5 to 10 per cent of 'empty shell' marriages.

Yet this need not mean a breakdown of the institution of marriage and the family. Comparative evidence from other societies shows that the family system can continue even with high rates of instability for individual marriages.

Exploring the causes of individual marriage breakdowns

Within the overall pattern of marriage breakdown, the individual causes of breakdown will vary over time and from marriage to marriage. Can we see any patterns? In fact, the relationship between a couple's behaviour in marriage and the breakdown of that marriage has proved unusually difficult to explore, for a number of reasons.

A major difficulty is that there is no standard of 'normal' marriage with which to compare broken marriages. Previous research workers have often, wrongly, tended to regard any deviation from happy, democratic, companionable marriage as a sign of maladjustment, likely to lead to breakdown.[4] Yet conflict and disagreement may be a fruitful and indeed essential stage of adjustment. And community pressures and economic and legal barriers may work to keep even unhappy and unstable marriages in being, so that conflict between a couple is accommodated without the marriage breaking down. Alternatively, marriages can be very stable, indeed perhaps more stable, where a couple do not demand happiness, sharing, or sexual fulfilment, but expect to carry out their matching tasks separately and to pass most of their time in different activities, each with their own kin or groups of friends of the same sex.[5] A rise in the divorce rate may thus represent an increase in people's expectations and demands on the marriage relationship. Moreover, the types of behaviour which may lead to conflict or unhappiness differ within and between groups and societies: for example, physical violence and intense sexual jealousy are regarded as normal in some cultures (associated with the *machismo* of some Latin countries), and are probably relatively more common, and therefore less remarked, among sections of the British working class than among the middle class.

Included in these cultural and class variations in marital difficulties must be the whole style of marriage breakdown. The broad distinction drawn in a recent American study between middle- and working-class marriage breakdown probably holds in some measure for England:

> The less articulate people of the lower class are, in large part, propelled down the road to separation and divorce by physical acts and bad behaviour: people of the middle class are propelled by earnest talk, unveiling, and truth-telling.[6]

Thus, a feature of the present research was the lack of discussion between the partners.

The variability in styles of marriage means that we have to try to see a couple's relationship in their own terms. And where a long marriage was manifestly unsuccessful or unhappy, rather than turning immediately to psychological explanations of one or others partner's 'need to be punished' it is important to ask what societal pressures held the couple together, and what opportunities or external pulls enabled or caused them to separate when they finally did.

Interpreting marriage complaints

The attempt to get at the couple's own view of their marriage raises some problems for the present survey, because, as in other research, we are here given only the wives' one-sided accounts of marriage breakdown, and especially complaints against the husbands which can seldom be objectively validated.

Several studies have clearly demonstrated that couples do not agree about the nature and causes of their disagreements. Slater and Woodside commented that after interviewing both husband and wife they had 'learned once and for all that no judgements, whatever the apparent facts, can be made on a marital conflict until both sides have been heard'.[7] Locke found that a group of divorcing couples disagreed more than a control group of the happily married even over factual matters such as the date of their marriage.[8] It is at best only a partial solution to say (with previous research workers in this field)[9] that the very subjectivity of the wife's reaction is what interests us, for inevitably we want to be able to treat some of the things the wife tells us as fact. Using interview techniques only, there is no solution to this problem.

In fact one research worker, Goode, has suggested that the complaints which divorced wives make against their husbands are probably mainly true, because men, who in our culture have a greater range of permitted interests and activities outside marriage, tire of the marriage first.[10] But, says Goode, the husband adopts a 'divorce strategy' to drive his wife away and thus avoids, consciously or unconsciously, the guilt and stigma of openly breaking up the marriage by desertion, although the blame for breaking the marriage should be his. Goode also points out that the wife in our society, should she desire divorce, must use different weapons, sulking, nagging, or refusal of intercourse: as a consequence a classification of complaints must appear to place the blame on the husband, simply because his behaviour is more public.

This analysis is questionable on a number of grounds. It seems likely that wives who take the initiative in ending the marriage, by desertion or eviction, will more often blame their husbands because they themselves need a reason, or excuse, for ending the marriage: indeed perhaps wives may not take the initiative unless they have a suitable explanation – in terms of the husband's bad behaviour – of why they had to act. Alternatively, case studies of marriage problems, quoted by Pincus and Dicks, have shown to what a marked extent even quite brutal behaviour on the husband's part may be a reaction to subtle provocation by the wife, and the tensions generated in marriage are sometimes sufficient to bring mental illness.[11] Finally, Goode himself takes a male viewpoint in underestimating the influence on divorce of women's frustrations in the home: while he virtually assumes that all divorced women have complaints against their husbands, which, as we shall now see, is not true.

The marriages in outline

It must be stressed that the mothers interviewed were not wholly typical of women whose marriages break down. Most of the marriages were working-class, nine out of ten of the husbands having been manual workers. Also these working-class mothers dependent on assistance tended to have remained unmarried longer than the average divorcee, possibly because they had more children: when they divorced only two of the couples had no children, whereas one third of all divorcing couples are childless.

Most of the mothers had married young, a third below twenty and nine out of ten below twenty-five. Also, a fifth had married in the late 1930s or during the last war. Young or war marriages like these are known to show a high rate of divorce in the general population. Three fifths of the marriages had lasted *legally* for ten years or more (the same as the national divorcing population) and the average length of the marriages was twelve years.[12] However, the average length of time the couples had lived together was really much shorter, only eight years up to the most recent separation.

In outline, the picture presented by these mothers was overwhelmingly of one or other partner much more committed to the marriage: very seldom did the final separation come about by anything approaching mutual argreement. Thus, according to the wives, in twenty-one marriages the wife herself left the husband, and in twenty-two the husband was forced to leave by the wife, sometimes when she obtained a legal separation or divorce (Appendix Table 8). These wives who left or evicted their husbands nearly always blamed them for offensive or intolerable behaviour, almost half complaining of physical violence or sexual assaults (Appendix Table 8). By contrast, in the remaining thirty-three marriages where the husband was said to have deserted, it was remarkable how deserting husbands were much less often blamed by their wives, only two wives complaining of violence or sexual assault.

This pattern was mirrored by the information on temporary desertions before the final break. In half the marriages, most often where he finally deserted, the husband had frequently been away for shortspells; while in a third of the marriages much less often where the husband deserted, the wives had deserted before, but on one or two occasions only. Complaints about the husband's failure to support the family financially or by providing a home during marriage were also more frequent among wives who left or evicted their husbands. By contrast, three quarters of the wives whose husbands had deserted them, even for another woman, made *no* firm complaint about their husband's behaviour during marriage. Thus, the general picture of marriage breakdown was of one partner having to escape from, or to precipitate the end of, the marriage against the wishes of the other.

If we can place some reliance on what the wives said, the pattern of marriage breakdown and the figures of non-support begin to explain why a proportion of the women now had poor homes and some of them had become dependent on national assistance. If the family income had been low during marriage, few goods would have been bought, and wives who left their husbands appear more likely to have housing problems and to lack goods from the marital home. And if over half the wives had not been adequately supported by their husbands even during marriage, what chance was there of their getting maintenance after the husband and wife had ceased to live together?

A major question which hangs over these marriages must be: what is the influence upon the stability of marriage of national assistance rates which afford the separated wife a higher standard of living than her husband's wage or generosity will permit in marriage? The influence of economic difficulty in these desertions became intermingled with more personal considerations. But if there is occasion for a separation, then the conjunction of assistance provision for the wife, as against the husband's low wage, may be an added incentive to marriage breakdown. And husbands may more easily desert wives whom they know will not suffer economically. Restraining factors, however, are lack of knowledge of assistance and difficulty of access, both of which are discussed in a later chapter.

Wives who left or evicted their husbands

Sometimes a marriage appeared to founder on a multitude of disagreements, sometimes on one major issue. The behaviour complained of could be slow to develop or quick, continuing or intermittent; the couples remained together up to the end, separated several or many times; the wife, the husband, or both went away at intervals. But in all this, most wives who left or evicted their husbands complained that the husband had either behaved with a complete lack of consideration or had attempted to exercise a degree of authority which was intolerable. The wife felt her husband's behaviour had been such as to deny her identity and rights as a person. The situations ranged from cultural mis-matches to nightmare relationships which sharply raise the question whether some husbands or wives can be described as mentally ill. Basic clashes were visible in the handling of money, in physical violence, in the question of the wife's personal freedom, and in sex.

Cultural mis-matching could stem from an accident. A young London grammar school girl, working in Devon to escape from her unhappy home, had very quickly married a glamorous but, as she now felt, uneducated fisherman:

He would have made a good husband for somebody, but not for me. He was one of those men who had old-fashioned views on marriage. He thought that when he'd paid for the licence you ceased to be a person, you were just a wife, you were just his. What really sickened me, I had those two children, and then in arguments he let it out that he'd given me two children and that was the way of keeping me in and keeping me satisfied. He hadn't had a good education like me. He doesn't think it's important, education. I'm glad I left him because his idea for my son was that he should go to sea, and I didn't want him to do that, I wanted him to work with his brain. My husband used to hold it up against me if I wanted to talk to him about anything other than washing the dishes, or if I expressed an opinion. If he had an opinion that was *our* opinion, if you understand me. It was just a question of personality.

Such men were proud, suspicious, authoritarian, like one old stereotype of the working man; and by the wife's account they were deadly dull and even frightening to live with. These marriages resulted in a clash of two distinct styles of living, or ideologies. Repeated pregnancies were enslavement and marriage breakdown represented emancipation for the wife. Marriage with the fisherman had not lasted long, for the wife had valued what she felt to be her independence and with outright opposition to her husband open warfare had threatened to develop. But there appeared to be every chance that the husband could have made a good marriage with a woman from a background similar to his own.

However the same could not be said so confidently of other husbands. Another separated wife described her marriage, which lasted nine years:

It ought to have broken up in the first week. He started knocking me about. There were other women as well. And the drink! I knew that he drank before we got married, but nothing like that. He used to come home blind drunk at four o'clock in the morning, and he didn't care what he did when he was drunk. Anything that I'd got, he smashed it all up, and he broke all the windows. And he just didn't care how he was. He used to wet the beds and mess in the beds when he was like that. And when David was only little he used to kick him out of his bed so he could get in there and do it.

There were descriptions in similar vein of other violent husbands: 'He wouldn't just argue with you, he'd go demented. And he got that look in his eye, really wild. I don't think he knew what he was doing.' With allowance for exaggeration by the wife and her own part in provoking the husband, the question remains: was this more than a simple conflict of cultural expectations or personalities?

Complaints of non-support covered a number of different

situations. The fisherman could not fish in winter and was too independent to take orders from a land-foreman in any other type of work, so to her horror his wife had to collect national assistance. There were men who did not work regularly for other unknown reasons, twelve of them petty criminals who had had spells in gaol: their wives thought them work-shy. Ten husbands had been regular servicemen, several of them, according to their wives, attracted to service life specifically by its security. During their forces service their wives automatically received an allowance, but upon demob these men were unable to adapt to civilian life. They ceased to support their wives adequately, and virtually forced them to desert. A wife said:

At first I used to get his meals, but in the end I never used to get anything. It got so that I got just an egg or a tin of beans for my breakfast for myself, and I had all my meals in the canteen, and then if he asked where his meal was, I'd say, 'You're not getting any until you go out to work and bring in some money.' He didn't come from a very good family. They didn't encourage him to go out to work. I think he had his meals up at his mother's.

Even where there were small children the marriage was sometimes kept going by the wife working. Some wives said they had bought all the furniture and even worked to keep their husbands.

There were further situations amounting to non-support. Husbands might work regularly and yet spend so much on themselves, drinking and gambling, that there was not enough for the housekeeping. Or even though they paid housekeeping they could be, according to their wives, monumentally improvident; they freely spent the rest of their money and tried to get back as much as possible from what was left out of the housekeeping or family allowance. A house-proud wife married to a man who thought little of home comforts described her attempts to build up a home as like a game of snakes and ladders: 'We'd get a radiogram. We'd paid 81 guineas on it and we'd paid it off because that was the time he was working. Well, I came back one day and the radiogram had gone! He'd sold it for £17! Anything he'd sell, just anything to get money and make a loss on it.' There was about these stories almost an air of sabotage, the husband kicking against the web of domesticity his wife was trying to weave around him.

A few men would not give their wives any money: much more than in the average marriage they were using money as a form of social control. They refused to allow their wives to work, and one separated wife said she had to take her husband to court for maintenance even while they were living together: 'He used to give me thirty shillings at the weekends to buy in, but anything else I had to ask him for. I could never get any money in my hand. If I wanted a loaf of bread even, I had to ask him for a shilling.' By contrast with the improvident husbands, who wanted to hand over all budgeting worries and responsibilities to the wife, these other husbands suffered acutely from an inability to share.

The frequency with which mothers spontaneously mentioned sexual problems will understate the extent of such difficulties. Disagreements over sex may have sources elsewhere in the marriage relationship, but once present they can become issues in themselves. In at least a third of the marriages the wives said their husbands had gone out with a number of other women, although still using home as a base. The wife of a sailor said, 'He'd been used to having a wife in every port, and when he came home he wanted a port in every street!' These were only the instances actually known to the wives, and they do not include husbands who eventually deserted with 'the other woman'.

A much more serious problem for about a quarter of the wives was the husband's acute sexual jealousy, which was part of his attempt to control the wife's social life. A separated wife said, 'It was laughable really, if you could have laughed at the time. If the electricity man had been, you should have heard him! He'd say, "You look as if you've been dragged through a hedge this morning," and the electricity man was a little feller with one eye and one leg shorter than the other! But my husband thought I had to have nobody but just him. No relatives, no nothing.' Another man insisted on examining his wife's underwear every time she had been out without him; another insisted his wife must always take the children with her if she went out, another locked up his wife's clothes, another accused the doctor of interfering sexually with his wife. Sometimes husbands' suspicions may have been well grounded – one wife admitted to having a man-friend – but it was a matter of degree. And among these husbands were five who had made sexual assaults on children. The husband's sexual suspicions led to social restrictions which became intolerable to the wife.

In eight, or one out of ten, marriages, this sexual jealousy was associated with what the wife considered to be violent sexual assaults. A divorced woman said:

It's terrible to be afraid of somebody like that and hate them. I would have murdered him if only I thought I could get away with it, and that it wouldn't harm the children. I often sat there at night and thought I'd like to wring his neck, and I think he would have murdered me too, if he could have got away with it. And he was very jealous. He was always on about me going with other fellers, but he would never let me be. Nobody would believe how he was. I wanted to sleep apart and I used to go upstairs to sleep with the kids, but he used to come and drag the kids out and hit them until I went downstairs to sleep with him. [In the later stages of the marriage the husband had made the wife move all the furniture which she had bought upstairs mean-while living himself off tea-chests and orange boxes on the ground floor]. It was degrading, I don't know anything as degrading as to be with a man and sleep with him and not want him. He used to have blue eyes and remind me of a snake.

Typically these were the older working-class women who, per-haps, had initially been afraid of sex, and whose husbands may have been too urgent or clumsy in their sexual approaches. A woman described how:

On the wedding night he unleashed himself on me, and I thought to myself at the time, I thought , 'Dear God, have I got this to cope with,' and I knew then that I couldn't love him. So that's why I let the children come along, I thought I'd have something to love. But in the end it got so bad that I had to get out or get into a coffin, because he just wouldn't leave me alone. He was a sex maniac. The doctor said if I'd stopped with him another twelve months I'd have been wanting flowers. I've told my daughter little things about him, you know, since she's grown up, and she's said to me after she's got married, 'You know Mum, you didn't love my dad, because, well,

I go a lot with Bill [her husband] but it hasn't turned me against him.' So I said to her, 'Well, perhaps you're right, love, but you didn't marry Bill to get away from home.'

He was just like an animal or something. If he saw a bit of me when I was like changing in front of him, or if I was having a bath, he always used to sit on the side of the bath and devour me. I used to say, 'Oh go and get a book or something. Don't sit there like that.' It was as though he was nicked, and he'd say, 'I've a *right* to sit there and watch you, and look at you like that. You're my wife, I've a right to do what I want with you.' [One night when she was trying to have a bath by herself he returned unexpectedly.] He said, 'Are you having a bath? Let me in.' And I could hear his mate saying, 'What's the matter with you man, she's only having a bath', and my husband was saying, 'She's no right to have a bath without me there.' Well, he brayed and he kicked at the door, I thought he was going to knock it down. And when he came in he said, 'That's the last bath you have without me there,' and by gum, it was too!

But were these encounters something more than a prudish wife cringing from a sensual husband? The health of these wives suffered through worry or too frequent childbirth. The separated wives in particular had larger families than they had wanted. Several wives had had to be sterilized, and more would have liked to be, had their doctors cooperated.

Physical assaults on the wife had taken place when she was pregnant, and several wives had miscarriages. Perhaps these attacks during pregnancy were brought on by the frustrations of social and sexual life occasioned by the wife's condition. Yet there was also evidence that violence was directed towards the unborn child. A woman's husband told her to get rid of her baby or he would 'knock it out of her'. Other husbands were openly jealous of the children, and this resentment may have been linked with sexual difficulties. One husband had been forced to leave home because the N.S.P.C.C. said they must take his children into care if his cruelty continued. His wife said,

I'd sit and wonder and wonder at night time wondering if I were to blame because I was always saying no to him about sex. But it's nothing is it, sex? I can't see it. They blow it up and blow it up these days on T V as though it's everything, and it's the smallest part of your life is sex. Well, it's over, and five minutes later you're asleep.

But on the telly they're coming towards them and their mouths are hanging open. It's disgusting I think. I don't mind a bit of a kiss and a cuddle, but I never wanted anything more. But perhaps it means more to a man, doesn't it? Do you think it does? But you see what could I do? I didn't want any more children. Oh it was awful, every time I went with him I was frightened I might have a baby.

The final bitter twist which brought the tension to a literally murderous pitch was that these urgent husbands with frigid wives were too suspicious to permit the use of the female contraceptives which might have alleviated the wives' fears and allowed them to enjoy sex.

How the marriages ended

The marriages where the husband's behaviour was found most offensive had often lasted longest; and indeed it took time for a degree of violence or dominance to build up. Some women had tolerated a great deal more violence than others, when a determined stand might have gained the day. Cultural expectations and personal needs differed, between those wives who 'liked a man to be a man' and felt it was 'natural' for a man to have several affairs, and those who wanted an equal partnership and whose ethical code forbade any sex outside marriage. A psychological explanation would say that wives who tolerated offensive behaviour were 'submissive' women married to 'dominating' men. But this is to some extent tautologous, and ignores a range of important explanations why the marriages had not ended.

The wife's lack of freedom to leave cannot be overstressed as an influence in prolonging marriage. Wives with children were economically dependent on their husbands. They did not know about alternative income from national assistance, nor would it have been easy to find other accommodation.[13] They feared that if they left they might lose custody of the children. There was also the practical point that much of the furniture in the home might really be the wife's property, bought with her money, and the difficulty of getting away from home with the furniture proved almost insurmountable when the husband objected, for the police would offer little help in cases of domestic disputes. A mother of six recalled the time during her first pregnancy when her husband beat her for criticizing his drinking and going with other women:

That time I went home to my mother, and she told me, she said, 'Now you want to make a clean break. If he's like that now, he'll be like that for good. You can't make no difference.' But you see every time I left him he'd come round talking and wanting me back, and I'd go back to him. And then, of course, when I went back to him I'd find out I was pregnant again, so I wouldn't want to leave him because of the baby.

In other larger families a moment of decision had arisen early when the wife had only one or two children and the husband had proved unfaithful, but, once past, that moment could not be regained as the family, and with it the mother's dependence, grew.

The desire that the children should still have a father as they grew older was not much mentioned in the light of later events, but it had evidently motivated some wives long past the point where the husband ceased to fill the role effectively. One separated wife said,

You keep sticking it out and sticking it out, in the hope that it will get a bit better, and you say you're doing it for the children's sake, but I realized in the end it wasn't doing them any good. It was upsetting them. The boy was afraid to ask his father direct questions, he always had to ask me first.

To a lesser extent, perhaps, similar considerations must have kept unhappy husbands at home. Men who did not get on with their wives could still feel a deep bond with their children. Working in a secure job, locally, with a house to live in and a network of friends, men would not readily break up the marriage.

Personal and community attitudes towards broken marriage were also influential in keeping couples together. One woman's mother was, 'One o'th'owd stock. She thought that when you got married you had to stop with 'em whatever they did to you.' On one occasion when this wife had tried to leave her husband she was told by her mother, '"You go back to him and don't you leave him no more."' Sometimes it was the church or probation officer who brought the couple together again after separations of anything up to five years. A woman, whose husband regularly staged suicide attempts, said:

He was up there in the hospital and he was enjoying himself, and every time I opened the door a vicar or a parson or a welfare officer or somebody was coming on at me. or the probation officer was on at me to have him back. If they'd left me alone I was all right. This terrible pain in my head it would go down, perhaps, if I had a day by myself I'd get settled down. But then another of them would come. The vicar, and could he have a word with me? He'd come in shaking his head, did I remember my marriage vows?

Where the husband was recognized as mentally ill and was receiving treatment the full weight of reconciliation machinery had come to bear on wives little able to withstand additional pressure. Apart from the moral pressures against divorce and separation there were the difficulties, to be discussed later, of gaining legal evidence in order that a wife who left home might claim maintenance for herself and the children.

In these circumstances the end of the marriage was not brought about by a gradual process of talk and progressively firmer decisions. In all but six of the forty-three marriages ended by the wife there had suddenly occurred a crisis or an opportunity. The two were not distinct: a crisis such as the discovery of her husband's V.D. clinic card might bring at last the resolve to separate, with the opportunity of legal evidence and an offer of accommodation from a relative. Crises were varied, but in all of them a new element entered the situation which brought an access of energy or resolve to the wife. Eleven marriages ended with the wife discovering evidence against her husband, for example finding him with another woman, or by the husband contracting V.D. or being involved in a court case of indecent assault. Eight marriages ended with a fight, physical assault or rape of the wife, sometimes associated with her pregnancy. In seven marriages the wife who had previously been self-supporting became pregnant and had to go home to her relatives because her husband was giving her no money.

Six marriages ended only through a crisis which brought the intervention of an outside agency to effect separation. In three marriages where there was cruelty to the children the N.S.P.C.C. intervened and said the husband must go. A separated wife had for many years concealed her husband's brutality to herself and the children, keeping the children off school when they had been bruised; but one day she inadvertently allowed the eldest child to go when a medical inspection took place, the N.S.P.C.C. were called in, and the husband was evicted. Two more families were threatened with eviction for rent arrears, and the solution was eviction of the husband by the council.[14] One wife discovered her husband's incest with the teenage daughters, and the husband was gaoled.

In a further five families the sole new element in the situation which served to split the marriage was the opportunity of accommodation. And indeed, in thirteen of the twenty-one instances where the wife deserted, she was enabled to do so by the offer of accommodation from her family, who thus played a key part in ending the marriage. One separated wife's parents took her in to live with them, then bought a new house and rented her their old one cheaply, fully furnished. The moves away from home had to be planned in deadly secret. One woman said,

I'd never seen him drunk, but that night when I left him he was really bad. He came and tried to knock my mother's door in. We had to have police protection for days. When we moved again we never told a soul.

In eight of the twenty-two marriages where the husband was evicted the wife's family also helped by providing moral support and advice to clinch the decision, and even by helping physically. One woman had carefully arranged for the tenancy of the house to be put in her name and then was able to call on the police to put her husband out. But later the same day he came back and the police refused to help again:

So he said, 'Well, who's going to put me out then?' And my brother had always said, 'Just let me get my hands on him and he won't play about like that any more,' but I always told him not to. And I said to my mother [who had arrived in the interval], 'Do you want to go somewhere for me?' I said, 'Will you go up and get our Dick, and tell him to collect a few of his pals on the way as well.'

Seen from this point of view, wives with kin are more likely to separate. Perhaps in some instances the wives and husbands would have tried harder to make marriages work had there been no such possibility of escape. Or even if the marriages had continued unhappy they would not have broken. However, it must be remembered that support from kin could also keep a financially shaky marriage in being, so that the final balance of the influence of kin upon marriage breakdown is very difficult to draw up.

Marriages where the wife deserted and those where she evicted her husband have been discussed together because the final manner of breakdown was to a large extent dependent on accidental or extraneous circumstances, such as which spouse had the tenancy of the house, and the intervention of external agencies. Unless the wife was lucky, or, seeing troubled times ahead, had insisted on getting the home in her name, she was likely to find herself unable to evict her husband. Only if she got a legal separation or a divorce could she keep him out. But in six instances the housing authority had helped, either by evicting the husband while the wife went to live with relatives for a short spell, or by quickly changing the tenancy during the husband's temporary desertion, so that he could not come back.[14]

This is the moment to return to Goode's suggestion that usually the husband desires divorce and consciously or unconsciously adopts a strategy to make his wife go away. In fact these interviews very seldom bore this out, except in some instances where the husband did not support his wife. Husbands may be unaware of or indifferent to the effect of their behaviour, or unable to control it, and behaviour offensive to the wife may actually be designed not to drive her away but to effect greater control over her. But Goode's suggestion cannot be tested without taking into account such apparently mundane matters as which spouse is the tenant, and the various pressures and tensions from outside the marriage.

The discussion has also shown how the living standards of wives who had left or evicted their husbands were influenced by a complex chain of circumstances. It was by no means certain that there would be any household possessions if the wife was not supported or could not work during marriage. But if there was a marital home to salvage, whether the wife was able to take some furniture with her or whether she could evict her husband and retain the furniture often depended on help from her family or some external agency.

Deserting husbands

The thirty-three wives of deserting husbands had few complaints against them. The wives themselves had seldom deserted, but the husbands had deserted frequently before the final separation. Thus the marriages presented a picture of wives much happier and more settled than their spouses. One divorced woman said, 'He used to scrub the floor for me, and then when I came back he'd say, "Hallo, darling, I've been thinking of you among the pots and pans." He was a really nice gentleman.' A separated wife said, 'He's an absolute poppet. Even now I can't find it in me to dislike him. And all his friends, everybody he's ever known, even people who didn't like him have said he was a jolly good chap and a nice fellow. He's so kind.' When these husbands deserted, the wives were at a loss to find an explanation which was not damaging to their self-esteem.[15]

In some instances the wife's own behaviour may have caused the desertion. One wife, according to an acquaintance of hers, was pregnant by a soldier; and six wives reported their husbands had contested paternity of a child (although this could be a device for avoiding paying maintenance). A separated wife admitted, 'I suppose I was a bit the frigid type. Well, when somebody's been away for six weeks and then comes back and he only wants one thing and you've been coping with the children for six weeks it's a bit difficult to drop everything. I suppose it was my fault in a way because I used to try to get back at him through sex. I think I drove him away because I wouldn't sleep with him.' There were other half-suppressed admissions that sex had been a failure for the husband. A few deserting husbands appear to have been impotent and unable to sustain the marriage for that reason.

A feature of these desertions which had caused the wives a deal of heart-searching and a loss of morale was that at least a third of the husbands had gone off with 'the other woman'. A divorced woman said, 'He just got tired of me. He said he fancied a mistress.' A separated wife had had a paralysing illness. Others felt uneasily that they had 'let themselves go' or had perhaps been poor housekeepers. But on the whole these were not very palatable explanations to the wife who preferred, not inconsistently, to look for other factors such as job failure, inequalities of education, too many children, or housing troubles. She was also very much inclined to ponder her husband's character for possible 'weakness'.

The husband's desertion was the more inconclusive because there was seldom, to the wife's mind, any open crisis, any formal leave-taking, or pronounced 'cooling-off' period in the relationship. The departure *seemed* sudden and inexplicable to the wife, and often, as she described it, there really was a dramatic disappearance or alternatively an extended but unexplained petering out. Soon after coming out of the forces one woman's husband

just said goodbye one morning and set off and never came back, and that evening I found out because my sister-in-law and her sister came up and she said to me, 'What have you been doing with our Wilf?' and I said, 'Nothing, why?' and she said he was down at their house and he was crying, so I said, 'Shall I go down and see him?' But he wouldn't see me and always after that he used to run away.

Another husband tried to poison his wife, was forgiven, but disappeared suddenly three weeks later after buying her an enormous box of chocolates. A separated wife had a letter from her husband saying, 'By the time you get this I will be in another world. This is too much.' She did not see him for four years, then he contacted her again, but again disappeared. A fourth said:

I didn't know he was leaving. We hadn't had a row or nothing. He had a day off work, and he went up home to see his mother, then he came back in, it was tea-time, and I was making the kid's tea. He didn't say a word. He got his suitcases out, and he packed all his clothes. He didn't say anything and then he made for the door. And he said, 'Well, are you going to try and stop me?' And I said, 'No, I'm not, but if you go that's the last you'll see of me; you're not coming back no more. If you want to go, go.' But I left my door unlatched for two years after that in case he came back.

Sometimes it was discovered later that there had been a crisis in the husband's affairs, or that he had had a new opportunity to leave. But the wife could seldom provide this kind of explanation. Equally inexplicably from the wife's point of view, other husbands went to work away, returning less and less often until the visits stopped altogether. The only connecting link was that in six of these desertions the man was a regular soldier recently demobbed. But there were civilians who deserted in this way too.

Several marriages ended so casually that it was difficult to say whether they *had* ended, or who deserted. One serviceman's wife began married life living with her mother for six weeks. Then the couple got a one-roomed flat and her husband was gaoled for stealing food. Out of gaol he lived with her for six months in another flat but deserted and she went to her mother's to have a baby. Reconciled, the couple went to live with a friend, but separated again when the husband started going out with another girl. The wife commented, 'Well, nobody deserted anybody else, it was mutual really.' She thought of bad housing and her husband's poor wage as contributing most to the failure. A housing change could be the occasion for the husband to go; one southerner brought his wife and numerous family up to a council house in Northborough for which he had exchanged the tenancy, and then went south again himself, effectively marooning his dependants.

Making allowances for the wives' idealization of husbands they had not wanted to lose, I am inclined to think that the wives' lack of complaint about their husbands' behaviour has a basis of truth. Compared with husbands in marriages where the wife said she was forced to initiate the separation, these deserting husbands had probably behaved in a less overtly offensive way, although they may still have been more subtly inconsiderate and lacking in affection.

Support from the husband after marriage breakdown

If we can place a similar reliance on other details supplied by the wife, these deserting husbands are more likely to have supported their wives during marriage (Appendix Table 8). Thus there is more chance that the marital home is furnished, and unless the husband disappears entirely there may be a better prospect, other things being equal, that deserting husbands will support their wives after separation.

The marriages studied were too few and too highly selected for this suggestion to be followed up in any detail: only one third of the husbands had paid anything at all to their wives, and the whereabouts of at least half of the remainder were unknown. But thirteen out of thirty-three deserting husbands, or over one third, had paid maintenance comparatively generously; as compared with six out of twenty-two divorced or evicted husbands, and only four out of twenty-one deserted husbands paying minimal amounts. These figures show a slight trend in the suggested direction and, in particular, reveal that a woman who deserted her husband was very unlikely to receive maintenance.

Alternative or further explanations of marriage breakdown

Whether a wife looked beyond her husband's immediate behaviour for deeper causes of marriage breakdown depended on her degree of sophistication and insight, or simply on how much she knew of his background. Her search for an explanation was apparently also guided by the circumstances of her marriage and how it had ended, and this could be seen most clearly in explanations involving mental illness. Mental illness of the husband is not really a further explanation of marriage breakdown, for to say that the husband was 'mentally ill' is perhaps merely to label certain behaviour as not fitting the cultural situation. Seven, or just under one tenth of the husbands, had been diagnosed by a doctor as mentally ill. But a further one in four of the husbands whose wives had initiated the separation or divorce were suspected of mental illness by their wives, a suspicion which appeared to announce the alienation of the wife's affection, and the feeling that the situation was beyond her control. In contrast, half of the husbands who deserted were suspected by their wives not of mental illness but of some kind of 'immaturity' or 'personality defect' for which the wives had been prepared to make allowances. Often these suggestions of 'immaturity' transferred blame from the husband to his kin or some impersonal force such as heredity.

Resentment focusing on the kin who provided accommodation for the deserter may explain why some wives referred to their husbands as 'mothers' boys', implying a psychological dependence and character immaturity or weakness. Sometimes the wife said that the father's early childhood had also explained a lot for her. One said, 'It wasn't his own father and he had a very unhappy life. He had a terrible childhood. He was never wanted and I used to excuse a lot for that reason.' The husband's illegitimacy or stories of rejection as a child also allowed some women to distance their own resentment. One wife of a man who had fathered at least eight children by four different women explained his behaviour in this way:

It was reliving his childhood. His mother had him but he was brought up by her sister, and a year afterwards his mother went away, and in this little village, when he grew up to be fifteen and sixteen, he used to think all the others was talking about him and I think when he felt like that he thought he'd get his own back on women for what his mother had done to him. If we'd had a row, he'd get ready and go out with his mates and have a few drinks and then he'd be thinking, 'How can I get back at her', and he'd look round and see a woman or a young girl and he'd think, 'That's it.' Really he was looking for a motherly affection. He was all right until I started having the babies and getting big so I couldn't go out with him, but then when I had 'em and they used to be crawling round me and crying he couldn't bear it. He'd shout, 'Get away from her, leave her in peace!' But that wasn't it. He was jealous, he couldn't share me with them, he couldn't stand me loving them as well as him. I think that's why I've tried to be lenient with him.

Other women described husbands as 'spoilt' by their mothers. A further suggestion about the husband's background was that husbands who frequently deserted might come from families where desertions were common. One husband was one of nine children, 'And every time his father put his mother in the family way he used to bugger off. That's why I threw him out when I did. He weren't going to follow in his father's footsteps.' Several women said the marriages of the husband's brothers and sisters were also unstable. These instances all had the general theme, that marriage breakdown or fatherlessness runs in families and may be somehow self-perpetuating and more common in a particular sub-culture.

Certain mothers were also inclined to look to their own childhood or the circumstances surrounding their marriage for an explanation of their plight. Most vividly, poverty and lack of affection in childhood were seen as links in the chain leading to a too-hasty and subsequently broken marriage. One woman recalled,

My father's done time for me (i.e. been to jail for cruelty) in Scotland. To think, we lived six years in one room, one room in an old tenement building. Well, we eat, lived and slep' in it, and it was crawling with rats. I was sent away six months of every year; I was never at home. And when I was I used to get knocked all over. Yet he never lifted a finger to my sister. He was always throwing it at me that I ought to have been a boy. When I was little I was always clothed by the parish in them horrible hairy jumpers, I can remember them yet, and a liberty bodice and hobnailed boots. And if there was trouble at home they'd always say, 'Send the big'un away,' and that was what they called me, 'the big 'un'.

I'd never have got married if I'd had a better home life, but my father used to knock me for six every Saturday night when he'd been out drinking. I'd have married anybody. I indulged in sex before marriage because I tried to get pregnant. My dad wouldn't hear of marriage. Then one Saturday, my dad was pummelling me about, so I said, 'Why can't you let me go? Why can't I get married?' I said I'd marry anybody, eighteen or eighty, 'I'll marry anybody, I don't care who it is.' And Charlie was there and he never said anything that night, but a day or two later, I'd not thought any more about it, my dad said, 'When's the wedding then?' And I said, 'What wedding,' I said, 'Come off it, you're joking!' He said, 'No I've had an offer for you.' I said, 'Oh, it can't come too soon. Will my birthday do?' He said, 'You don't know who it is.' I said, 'I don't want to know, I don't care.' It could have been Old Father Time as far as I was concerned. It could have been the old boy next door and he was eighty odd! He said, 'Well, it's young Charlie,' so I said, 'Good,' and that was it.

Key aspects of this story were mirrored in other reminiscences of childhoods which wives saw as leading up to hasty marriage. Such experiences may have caused broken marriages, or merely in some way provided a comforting explanation for the women. But the following suggestions might be worth testing. The eldest child of a poor family may more often have to bear the greatest strain, through violence from parents or responsibility for supporting the family; or this child may most frequently be the one who is sent away to an institution. Eldest children may consequently have a poorer chance of making a successful marriage. Alternatively, it may be the 'scapegoat' in the family who has more chance of duplicating an unhappy childhood in unhappy marriage. Broken homes are often singled out as causes of social problems, but the more vivid instances from the present survey involved childhood with a brutal father or step-father, or with mothers described as over-demanding or dominating.

Three wives who had been pregnant when they married or had an illegitimate child, and who had married the child's father, saw themselves as victims of family pressures which accounted for both pregnancy and marriage. One who married, when eight months pregnant, a man who had to get special leave from gaol said, 'I thought, oh well, if I married him, I'd be on the right side with my mother.'

In a similar way some women looked for explanations of their troubles to other social circumstances surrounding their marriage. A fifth of these marriages were contracted during the war. One mother said, 'You can't really remember what it was like at the time, but it was awful, and all my mates were getting engaged and I thought if I didn't hurry up I was going to be the only one left, so I thought to myself, "I'll marry the first one that asks me."' In this particular marriage the couple scarcely lived together, and the husband spent the first fortnight of married life with another woman, according to his wife. Wives described how during the war the normal precautionary courtship had not seemed important, or was impossible. They had attempted to clutch at security and happiness, and had sometimes married men whom they had known for, effectively, less than a week. There were also women whose lives had been disrupted by other social upheavals. One came from Hungary in 1956 with her parents, who then returned; she said, 'I married for just security. We both felt sorry for each other. I'd only known him for six months. I realize now that it was not long enough.' Another came from East Germany one June and was married in the December of the same year. She said bitterly,

I couldn't speak no English and it's like my doctor say, I was diddled into it. My husband told me all sorts of lies, like he was the same age as me, twenty-one, when he wasn't, he was twelve years older. The only English word I know was the word for good. It's too easy getting married; they marry you even if you don't speak English if you pay your 7/6d.

Coming from an unhappy or unfavourable background themselves, some wives thought they had been more likely to marry a man of similar origin because each would recognize in the other the same needs. In addition they suggested that certain occupations such as nursing and the Forces attracted people eager to get away from unhappy homes, and that this partly accounted for the high rate of marriage breakdown among service personnel. Not counting war service and national service, twenty-one, or almost a third, of the husbands had been in the Forces. There are, of course, other possible explanations for this high proportion, such as the disturbed condition of service life, and the fact that Seaston was near some army camps.

The confirmation of suggestions of family and social influences is beyond the scope of the present study. The wife's adoption of one or other of these views was probably influenced by the marriage relationship, and may even have worked to prolong or shorten the marriage. The strand of fatalism which ran through some of these explanations was also interwoven with the wife's approach to building up a fresh life for herself: women apt to think of themselves as the victim of circumstances were not generally optimistic in facing the future.

The shifting sands of subjectivity prevent any firm reliance being placed on individual accounts of marriage conflict. But there is sufficient evidence in this chapter for an overall picture of marriage breakdown as a number of different 'careers' which depend on the husband's behaviour, the degree of support he gives his wife in marriage, the manner in which the marriage ended, and a number of accidental or external factors, such as help from kin. Upon the particular path she had followed will depend the wife's change of living standard and, as we shall see in a later chapter, her morale.

CHAPTER SIX

Illegitimate Births

Almost half the mothers interviewed had had illegitimate children. There were twenty-six unmarried mothers, together with twenty-six separated and divorced, and two widowed, women who had had an illegitimate child at some time. The unmarried mothers and the ten formerly married mothers with illegitimate children only, proved to have the lowest incomes and the fewest possessions of any of the fatherless families. This chapter begins the inquiry into why this should be so. We ask how far the birth of an illegitimate child was a similar experience for all unmarried mothers, and whether any analogies can be drawn between illegitimate births to the unmarried and to the formerly married.

It is not suggested that this group of mothers is very representative of the national situation. Nationally, for example 40 per cent of illegitimate children are born into stable two-parent homes. The sample is weighted towards illegitimacy because, of all unsupported mothers, those with illegitimate children are most likely to experience poverty. Nationally one in nine illegitimate children is born to a married woman living apart from the child's father, whereas for the group of mothers interviewed the proportion was nearer half. And while nationally 63,000, or 7.2 per cent, of all live births in this country are illegitimate, almost one third of the children of these mothers on assistance were born out of wedlock (the proportion is boosted by a small number of large families where the children are mainly or all illegitimate).[1]

Nevertheless, differences in the marital situations of the unsupported mothers, and in the ages of those who were unmarried at first conception, do roughly span the national situation and enable us to get a sense of the variety of experiences which we usually lump together as illegitimate births. Among the unmarried mothers interviewed for the present survey (including the West Indians), fourteen had conceived their first child before the age of twenty, but the remaining twelve mothers first conceived in their twenties or later, and this underlines the often overlooked fact that illegitimacy is not exclusively or even mainly a problem of unmarried teenagers. Teenagers have about one third of all the illegitimate births and their contribution to illegitimacy is increasing, but the most vulnerable group of unmarried women is the twenty-five to twenty-nine range where the proportion of women having illegitimate children is three times that among teenagers.

The causes of illegitimacy

There is very little good evidence on the causes of illegitimacy, and what there is points confusingly to illegitimacy having a number of different, sometimes multiple causes, rooted in the society in which a mother is born, her personal circumstances, and her psychological make-up. In particular the psychoanalytical 'explanations' of illegitimacy, in terms of the mother's need to have a baby or to be revenged on her parents,[2] simply are not verifiable or predictive, although they have unfortunately proved very seductive to the social work profession.

The overall rates of extramarital conception, the proportions of the pregnant who marry (and so do not become unmarried mothers), and the speed with which they marry have been shown to be interdependent and to vary systematically between different societies.[3] For example, in the Caribbean (where six of the mothers on the present survey were born) 70 per cent of the children were born out of wedlock, but the proportion of the population married rises with age until it approximates to that in other societies.[4] Explanations of why individual women bear illegitimate children have changed remarkably over the last half-century.[5] It is now thought that the youngest unmarried mothers, at least, will be not very different from the general population at risk.[6] A recent trend is for an increasing number of middle-class girls to have and to keep illegitimate babies, although middle-class girls who keep their babies tend to slip down the social scale.[7] The effect of the new abortion laws and increasing availability of the pill have not yet been fully assessed,[8] but in 1968 illegitimacy reached its highest peak since the war, at 8.5 per 100 births, and has thereafter declined, but very slowly.

Probably the most thorough and sophisticated study of unmarried mothers which we have to date, by Clarke Vincent,[9] stresses that all our ideas about unmarried mothers are likely to be false because they are based on the untypical groups of mothers who come into contact with social agencies: workers in these agencies sometimes 'need' theories of causation to remove from their shoulders some of the fearful responsibility of making decisions about, say, adoption, and this is one way in which stereotypes develop. Thus the high incidence of broken homes found in certain studies neglects that fact that a similarly high proportion of *all* children have their homes broken by death or separation of parents; as a result the studies may 'represent primarily a description of the kinds of individuals who seek help from welfare agencies and charity institutions'. Similarly, Vincent notes that the proportion of unmarried mothers coming from homes which can be described as 'mother-dominated' may be no higher than the proportion of such homes in the general population. Unmarried mothers who describe unhappy home backgrounds may do so because they are more likely to *feel* their childhood was unhappy, looking for a cause of their present troubles.

In short, illegitimacy like broken marriage has proved extremely difficult to investigate, and the present small survey can add little to our knowledge of its causes. Rather, this chapter will be interested in the consequences of the birth for the mother's morale and living standard. The unmarried mothers, English-born and West Indian, will be described first.

Unmarried mothers and dependence on assistance (Appendix Table 9)

The unmarried mothers revealed clearly the link between family size and dependence on assistance. Eight young unmarried mothers with only one child were probably temporarily dependent: two married during the period covered by the interviewing, and there were others (including one of the six West Indians) who seemed likely to go off assistance soon, either through marriage or return to work. In order to work the mother must have help with child-minding from the family or some outside agency. Thus, the five remaining West Indian mothers, when they had their first and second children, had been dependent for only short spells and had then gone back to work, supported by an extensive but unofficial and probably largely illegal child-minding network.

On average the unmarried mothers had fewer than two children. But once a mother had two or more illegitimate children her chance of marriage probably dropped sharply, and, unless she had considerable family and voluntary financial support, national assistance became economically and practically preferable. Nine white mothers and five out of the six West Indians had reached this situation: the West Indians came on to assistance permanently when they had three children. These five West Indians had an average of four children each (one third of all the illegitimate children born to unmarried mothers on the sample). Only one English-born unmarried mother had more than three children.

Four older English-born mothers stood out from this pattern because they had only one child, much older than the rest. Three of them had been on assistance ever since the child was born. These four, and two older mothers with several children, were the only women encountered who had as yet kept their illegitimate children for any length of time.

Relationships with parents

As we have seen, the high proportion of English-born mothers who report poor relationships with the home, or broken homes, may point only to a cause of dependency rather than a cause of illegitimacy, for mothers without help from kin are more likely to become dependent.[10] There may be different factors at work in the lives of women who had their babies while in their teens, twenties and thirties.

Of nine English-born mothers who had their first child in

their teens, five came from homes broken in their childhood, while a further three described very unhappy home backgrounds. Certain groups may have a greater tolerance of premarital intercourse with the risk of an illegitimate child, and of illegitimacy itself. Several of the younger girls said that all their friends had become pregnant at about the same time, or claimed that their families were 'broad-minded'.

Of seven English-born mothers who had their child in their twenties, two came from broken homes, the father of another had been imprisoned for cruelty to her, and a fourth, with a mentally ill mother, had herself been in mental hospital both before and after the illegitimate birth: altogether five of these seven said they had been extremely unhappy as children.

The remaining four English-born mothers had their only child at the age of thirty or later, and none came from homes broken in childhood. Two continued to live with their mothers (who were present at the interview) and the other two had lived alone in the family home since their parents had died. The two who were interviewed alone felt they had been forced to stay at home, one to look after aged and ailing parents, the other to look after a blind father and mentally ill mother. The second said:

My mother would never let me out. She nearly drove me mad. The only time I got away was when I was in the Air Force. That was the happiest time of my life, that four years, and I did get engaged to a feller but my mother stopped that. I'll never forgive her for that. I think that the trouble really was my mother. When she went [to mental hospital] I just went out and enjoyed myself. I went wild.

She conceived a child almost immediately, and the other woman conceived a child almost as soon as her parents died. There is an echo here of the French writer, Colette, who conceived a child extramaritally within a month of her dominating mother's death.

The theme of the marriage chance, blocked by the woman's mother, recurred in a number of interviews. It was sadly symbolized in one dingy flatlet by an expensive-looking tea-set, displayed on the sideboard but never used, which the mother said had been intended as a present for her wedding. Even if the stories are inventions or exaggerations, they indicate the degree of resentment against the women's mothers.

The evidence from these very small numbers hints that women who have their children later in life may either have been rendered vulnerable by 'dominating' mothers or, on the other hand, kept on a tight rein by their mothers because they really were ill-equipped for life alone; the situation could appear in either light. Alternatively, the births to older women might have resulted from the despairing indiscretions of those who felt destined to be left on the shelf. The shock of the birth had been very great, and three of these older women had no longer been able to face social relationships with workmates and neighbours. They had withdrawn from life outside the home, and they lived very intensively through their children.

Relationships with the children's fathers

With certain exceptions, relationships between English-born mothers and the children's fathers had been fairly short and casual and had now stopped. Particularly among the younger mothers there had apparently been no intention of marrying the father when sexual intercourse took place, and two girls who actually married the fathers after birth had done so with reluctance, for neither of the fathers had seemed a very good marriage prospect. One of the girls who subsequently married said:

I didn't really want to get married. Well, he's not the sort of lad you can see settling down really to get married. He's always been one to go off with his mates a lot. That's why he was in the Army. And I wanted to make sure I was having a baby, and then I didn't want him to have to marry me. I wanted him to marry me because he wanted to. And then after the baby was born we had a row and we split up, and I've only seen him about twice since then. But now he's written to me, and says that he wants to marry me, so we might get married after Christmas. I want to get a house and get some furniture together and get it all established before he comes out.

Choice may be freer for younger mothers where kin and the community bring less pressure to bear on them to marry, and it has been shown that marriages made out of choice after delay, rather than under pressure, are more likely to last.[11]

In four common-law marriages the mother, during her

twenties, had borne at least two children by the same man and had lived with him for one to three years. Probably the men were already married but the mothers admitted that the little they knew was unreliable. However, although the men had been violent and poor supporters of their families, when they deserted the mothers were desolate. There was still a chance that two of these common-law marriages might be resumed.

Three middle-class women, a nurse and two secretaries, had also had their child in their middle twenties, apparently as a result of a failure in contraceptive techniques. They had safely had sexual experience with a number of men previously, and were inclined to believe that all unmarried mothers must be promiscuous. One said,

These people who tell me that they've only been with one man and they've had an illegitimate child, I just don't believe them. Even if it was no good with that man, the girl will try again just to see what it's like. You don't want to feel you're missing out on anything.

The first time she had intercourse it proved uninteresting, but, 'I started going out with somebody else and I gave in to him and that was quite different, and after that I was away!'

Education may have been the critical factor in preventing an illegitimate birth at an earlier age. The relationship with the child's father had been short, with little emotional commitment on either side, and there were consequently many difficulties in continuing it or getting support for the child. Of all the unmarried mothers, these women showed the greatest concern for secrecy.[12] Two styled themselves 'Mrs', one had changed her name so that it was the same as the child's, and all three had changed their address, two living in caravans for privacy.

Only the older unmarried mothers, who tended also to have had their children later in life, were likely to claim that they had been 'engaged' when they conceived, although the assertion may have been calculated to save face. These older mothers had been timid, and had had few men-friends. They felt they were tricked by their children's fathers, three of whom were older, local men, in two instances workmates still unmarried, and this had increased the shock and the shame of the birth. A woman who had had her child at the age of forty said,

Nothing like that had ever happened in our family before. I suppose there must be others like me, but I didn't know any. I begged and begged him to marry me, but he just said that he didn't think we'd be happy together, and went off and left me. It wouldn't have been so bad, but he was single he said, that's what makes it so bad, it's not like the usual one where it's a married man. He even went so far as to get the licence, so I don't know what changed his mind.

The mothers tended to picture the fathers as weak, vacillating men, 'confirmed bachelors'. But the three fathers who lived locally did still minimally support and very occasionally see their children.

In general, little was known about the fathers of these children of English-born mothers, but ten, or more than a third of the total twenty-eight, were said to be soldiers. We recall that Seaston is near some army camps, although there were also soldier fathers in Northborough. Other fathers were an Italian sailor, a Pakistani shop-keeper, and itinerant Irish or Scottish labourers, but not, for this group of unmarried white mothers, any West Indians.

Adoption

A decreasing minority of about one quarter of illegitimate children are adopted. Information about the possibility of adoption of these children was scanty and unreliable, for a mother might be reluctant to recall that she had even considered adoption. Sometimes when a relative was present there would be a clash of evidence, and relatives appeared very likely to suffer violent swings of feeling: several mothers remarked how illegitimate children had become favourites, one mother suggesting that this could be a kind of over-compensation, bred out of the grandparents' guilt because they had once pressed for adoption.

Probably there was more pressure for adoption from social workers or parents where the mother was younger with few resources and might be thought still to have a good chance of marriage. By contrast, older mothers who had more capital were pressed to keep their babies. One mother who was thirty when she had her child recalled her attempt to have the baby adopted:

It was ever such a cold day, and I remember the baby was howling, poor little mite. I took him up to this place near Baker Street and there was this pokey little room, and the woman asked me all these questions, how I was feeding him, and she told me to think it over. She advised me against it. She said, if I'd got a little home of my own I'd be able to struggle through, but I didn't see it.

Far from showing concern to take the child, according to another older mother, a social worker had seemed filled with the idea that she must shoulder the consequences of having her illegitimate baby:

She [the social worker] came up to the hospital and she screamed and yelled at the nurses, how I wasn't married, and I'd told her particularly how I wanted everything confidential. She told them how I'd no money, and she said the baby couldn't be fostered for nothing, it would cost me £6. The result was the hospital wouldn't even let me leave him overnight. I wanted to leave him there so that I could get home and get a few things ready. I wish now I'd kicked that women down the stairs.

There was still a possibility that some of the children of younger mothers would be adopted, for none of them had as yet kept their illegitimate children for any length of time. It was noticeable among those mothers who had that they regarded their children both as a punishment for their 'sins' and as a compensation for an unhappy childhood, someone to love for themselves. One was scandalized even at the possibility of adoption: 'I couldn't have left him behind, my baby! It would have been like leaving part of myself behind.'

West Indian unmarried mothers

In contrast to the English-born mothers, among the West Indians there were mothers still friendly with their children's fathers. Two West Indian mothers had been supported in the past, although now they had been abandoned, but three mothers were still being supported by fathers who visited regularly. They had exceptionally large families, and the key to understanding this may be the difference in social structure between the Caribbean and Northborough.

Describing the consensual unions common in the Caribbean Goode says,

The average girl has little chance at marriage, early or late, unless she is willing to gamble that a more permanent union will grow from one relationship or another ... Motherhood lowers the girl's value in the market, but if she does not produce a child for the man with whom she is living, or with whom she has a liaison, her chance of a stable union is low. The decision to marry ... is his rather than hers, and she gains more from marriage than he does ... Meanwhile, however, a woman may have children by several men, and may leave some or all of them with her parents or relatives when entering a new union – a practice often resulting in the 'grandmother' family.[13]

Thus, while illegitimacy is very common, it appears that marriage remains an ideal which is postponed primarily through economic circumstances. In Northborough similar unions were being set up. One mother said, 'You English people not understanding. Like having four children but not going with a lot of different men. I *live* with Madalyn and Arthur's father.' Even if the couple had not lived together, the father had visited regularly and paid towards the support of his child. These unmarried West Indian mothers could not readily get contraceptive advice, and, as their families grew larger, one of two things might occur. In a stable relationship, it became advantageous for the mother to stay on assistance. Marriage came to involve an economic loss and as a mother, with four children by the same father, said, 'To be quite honest with you we could be married, but what's the use. He don't get enough wage. He only just get enough to keep himself and keep the children.' So stably united couples became less likely to marry. Alternatively, if a union broke down, the mother could not pass children back to relatives who would look after them while she worked and tried her luck in a new relationship, for her parents were in the West Indies. One girl was trying to ship her children back to her mother, at £40 a passage, but this was a slow process. Usually as a mother had more and more children she was forced to keep them and her chance of marriage fell.

The other influences on West Indian mothers must not be ignored. West Indian immigrants have adapted considerably to

British society, and illegitimacy rates are very much below those in the Caribbean. Moreover these West Indian mothers were young and away from home for the first time, perhaps with few contacts with kin or friends. Nevertheless, it still looked as though the births often occurred as part of a stable relationship which was a conventional preliminary to marriage.

This was the only evidence from the present survey of the development of a situation analogous to that of the American Negro family. With the possible exception of these few West Indians, the mothers were not members of a whole culture where the father with poor education and job opportunities is only loosely attached to the home and many children are illegitimate. There is no firm evidence from the present survey of the extent to which these few West Indian mothers in Northborough may be representative and the forerunners of a developing pattern. But my impression is that they represent only a minority of instances, where the effects of cultural expectations brought from the West Indies have been reinforced by personal isolation and lack of integration with Northborough's West Indian community.

Changes of living standards

The economic consequences of an illegitimate birth differed vastly among the unmarried mothers. In addition to having the child to feed, the unmarried mother suffered a temporary or permanent loss of earning power, depending on whether she decided and was able to work again. Of fourteen mothers living at home six had to leave, and of twelve living in lodgings another six left. Of all the unmarried mothers, the four who had their children late in life were least affected by housing, all continuing to live in the same house. The West Indian mothers, too, seem to have been relatively little affected at first, since they were already in furnished lodgings and frequently moved, but later on further children brought severe overcrowding. It proved difficult for all the homeless mothers with young babies to find accommodation, but the effective loss of support was much the greatest for those who left home.

Mothers had different amounts of savings at the birth, depending on how long they had worked and how well paid they had been. The teenagers had no savings, nor had the West Indians. But the middle-class mothers had had savings running into hundreds of pounds, and so also had the mothers who were in their thirties when their child was born.

Thus, as with broken marriages, it was possible to see among the unmarried a number of distinct 'careers', which markedly influenced changes of living standard, levels of living on assistance, and, in a few instances, attitudes of mind.

Illegitimate births to separated, divorced and widowed women

Almost two thirds of the twenty-eight separated, divorced, and widowed women who had had illegitimate children compared very closely in their present or past situation with the unmarried mothers just described. Eight women, including the two widows, had once been unmarried mothers themselves, three of them marrying the child's father. Ten mothers, the poorest group, had at the time of the interview illegitimate dependants only: two had never had legitimate children, and five husbands had custody of the children of the marriage, while another three women had illegitimate children late in life and their legitimate children were no longer dependent.

None of these illegitimate births to formerly married women had occurred while the husband and wife were living together. In addition to the births before marriage, eighteen women, or almost two thirds, had their babies after they and their husbands had ceased to live together, although almost always while they were still married. Although some of these illegitimate births provided evidence for divorce cases brought by the husband, only in two instances, the wives maintained, was the child born of a relationship which had speeded the marriage breakdown.

Some of the wives who had illegitimate children after separating from their husbands seemed to be responding to an unhappy, broken, or brutal marriage much as unmarried mothers may have been influenced by their early life. Or, alternatively, these stories were reminiscent of the sudden release of the older un-married mothers from their forced seclusion. One wife said:

> I think it was with being penned in all those years. When I did go out I went wild. I had about four drinks and I didn't know if I was coming or going. I think if he hadn't had a car to take me home I'd have finished up just lying in the gutter. I wouldn't have known where I was, and when I got home I just bawled and bawled, I was so pent up, all those years, and he couldn't stop me. It could have been anybody really that I met. I was lucky that it was somebody good like Bill, because he's a steady lad.

The pregnancy was not always the immediate aftermath of mar-riage breakdown. Sometimes it was the long, continuing strain and loneliness of bringing up the children without a father which had weakened a mother's defences. Another separated wife said:

> It didn't seem like I could get round somehow. And there was this feller, he'd always been pestering me. I used to know him with going down on the bus to me mother's and he was always asking me to go out with him. I only went out with him this once. I don't know any-thing about him. He disappeared after that. I don't know whether he was married or single. But it was just, I think it was just having a bit of affection, having somebody to talk to.

Three women had babies when they tried to set up a home alone again after living with their parents. So often these relationships with men were short and almost inadvertent. Only three mothers were waiting, possibly hopelessly, for a divorce so that they could marry the child's father. Otherwise marriage was hardly men-tioned, or was rejected by the mother herself who said that her feelings were too unsettled.

It appeared unlikely that most of these mothers would have further illegitimate children after these 'crisis' births, and only seven, a much lower proportion than the unmarried mothers, had two or more illegitimate children. But one had had eight illegitimate children by five fathers, another had had five by five fathers, and another at least four by four fathers. One may have been a prostitute, although if so she was remarkably unsuccessful. The others had passed through life apparently clutching at straws, constantly hopeful that the latest relationship would flourish and the man would help them out, always regarding themselves as unlucky or let down. A separated wife went over her illegitimate pregnancies commenting feebly, 'That was a big mistake that was', 'That was a dark night', 'He was a soldier', or 'Once bitten twice shy'. The mother of eight, who had separated from her husband when he contracted VD, said she had 'never had the time' to go in for a divorce:

One thing led to another, and I took a chap on to have somebody to help me because it was real rough, and I just wanted to have somebody to help me bring the children up, because in them days, the 'Guardians', the food ticket you used to have, it didn't run to best butter and it didn't run out to a nice bit of jam, and you couldn't get any furniture. But anyway I was unlucky with that feller, he died. And then when he'd gone, still for the same reason to get somebody to help me to bring the kids up I took on somebody else, and I was unlucky with him, I got let down with him. But what can you do when you've got all them children? I didn't give up then. And after that, not anything wrong like, I got somebody else, but he didn't really turn out right. I thought he would help me, but somehow it seemed as though he didn't want any responsibility. He was a great big feller as well, six foot one and seventeen stone. But he would never take the plunge and come and live with me. He used to have his own room down at Bank Bottom. I saw him more often than not; he used to come down every day and I'd see him at weekends. He was a smart set-up feller good appearance and manner, just like a detective – in fact they've asked him to be in the police force. But in the end somebody else came his way. But it's with having his children really that I've got right down to rock bottom.

She was surprised that I should ask about contraception, and felt that you had to be 'in real trouble' to go to the clinic.

In character these families were like two others, an unmarried mother who had four children by three fathers, and another woman who had been divorced once, widowed once, and then married again only to separate. All these families had in common the mother's succession of unsatisfactory relationships with men, which seemed to follow on her own lack of an adequate father, but may also be seen as a reflection of the unsupported mother's difficulty in finding another father for her children once the first father had gone. Yet these mothers appeared to be not merely 'unlucky' but to have a definite propensity for *choosing* the wrong man. Thus, a woman who had been divorced from her first husband then married a patently ailing man who soon died. She then married another, shabby-looking man, who had an incestuous relationship with his twelve-year-old daughter, tried to live off his wife's teenage daughter's earnings, and then deserted to have an illegitimate child by a fifteen-year-old girl. It looks from such instances as these that the difficulties of fatherless families occasionally spread out into a complex web of maladjustment.

All these families had had children in care, and where children were older a proportion were diagnosed as backward. In two of the families the daughters also had illegitimate children. All the older children were beyond control, if indeed they were still at home, and in two families these children had an awe-inspiring record of 'accident proneness'. These multiple-father families had problems out of all proportion to their size. But probably the most significant point to make is that *such families were very few in number*.

Of the remaining English-born mothers with more than one illegitimate child, two were being drawn into West Indian society, one with three children in a consensual union, the other with two pregnancies by different West Indian fathers. This latter woman seemed to know only West Indians and separated, divorced, or unmarried white women with illegitimate half-caste children.

Again, relatively little was known about the fathers of these illegitimate children beyond their country of origin or occupation. Three were West Indians, and a third of all the fathers were soldiers. Only two of the fathers could definitely be placed in the middle class. It seemed that the men most likely to support their children were older men with local roots, or the West Indians, who were said not to object to other men's children.

Changes of living standard among the formerly married

On the whole the economic consequences of the birth of an illegitimate child to a separated or divorced woman were less severe. At worst she might initially have had no settled home and no children by her marriage, so that she was plunged into the situation of the unmarried mother. But most often she already had children and a home of her own which she did not lose. She was already on assistance, so the birth tipped the balance between temporary and permanent or short- and long-term dependence, without much changing her standard of living. This may have been the reason why there was little talk of having these children adopted. The finding that, of all families, divorced and separated women with illegitimate children only were the worst off, proved to have no single explanation in the mother's history, But half these wives had initially left their husbands, while the remainder had never been supported during marriage, so that they all came from among the poorer broken marriages.

CHAPTER SEVEN

New Relationships with Kin and Community

Adjustment to fatherlessness cannot be discussed in isolation from the altered social situation into which the families were plunged. There were immediate practical problems of getting an income and somewhere to live: one third of the families had to find a new home and a half had no furniture or very little. And with these problems the families received a great deal of help from kin. But often the mothers felt they stood in an altered relationship with kin and community. Feelings of ostracism and a sense of stigma may have stemmed in part from self-doubt, yet it looked as though the mothers' perceptions were also firmly grounded in real changes in the behaviour of others towards them and their children.

At the time of the interviews the living standards of thirty-two families, or over a quarter, were considerably raised by help from parents. Fifteen families still lived with parents, and others who lived nearby were helped. One separated wife said, 'My mother's the only one who keeps me here. I could have moved away many a time. I think to myself how easy it would be just to let the children go into homes and go off myself. What a good time I could have.' Not counting mothers who had never left home, almost a quarter of the families had lived with the mother's parent at some time during fatherlessness, four had lived with brothers and sisters and ten had lived with another relative. Several women had been entirely maintained by parents, for months at a time, and in addition two middle-class fathers had footed divorce bills of hundreds of pounds. Apart from the expense, there had been great inconvenience to relatives in overcrowding. A working-class family took their daughter and her children to live with them and then bought a new house for themselves, leaving the daughter to rent the old one from them fully furnished. At the time of the interviews some overcrowding persisted, and a separated wife slept with her sister, the room being so overcrowded that the youngest child had to sleep in a carry-cot on the dressing table; this woman's mother and father said jokingly they were thinking of leaving home because they now had only a single bed in the tiny room formerly occupied by the sister. There were also instances where the birth of an illegitimate child to one of the daughters made worse the conditions of overcrowding already existing. In other families, after the mother left to build up a home for herself, the parents had hastened to fill her unfurnished rooms with furniture, some of it their own. 'You see what worries them is that they can't bear to think that I'm living in poverty. That's what sickens them most,' said a mother whose parents had bought her a washing machine, sideboard, beds, chest of drawers, wardrobe, and carpets. Even a number of years after the fatherless families had ceased to live with kin, the standard of furnishing was often dependent on such help.

Relationships with the mother's kin – 'readoption'

On the whole the mothers who received help were younger, for twenty mothers, usually older (and including half the widows) had no parents alive, and the parents of a further fourteen were said to be old, feeble, and poor. Thus the older women received less help unless they had married daughters of their own, and even then they were themselves the family head from whom it was more natural to receive: only seven mothers had much help from married children.

Apart from being, on the whole, younger, the mothers who were helped by their parents tended to be unmarried, and so had never left home, or to be separated or divorced after only a short marriage and could more easily be taken back as daughters. 'Re-adoption' was marked in some instances by a sharp switch of attitudes. Parents did their best while they believed the wife could be happy, or while she still wanted to try to make the marriage work. Some fathers of unhappy wives had forbidden discussion of marital problems on the grounds that 'that's nowt to do with us', and it was difficult to help wives whose husbands spent most of their money on drink. But when the wife had made a determined appeal, the change in attitudes of her parents could be swift. A separated wife said:

I think my father was rather hard, he took the line, she's made her bed, she must lie on it, and I never told them about how the marriage was going, but in the end, I'd got nothing for the baby, and I was seven months pregnant, and I couldn't see myself ever getting anything, so I wrote to my mother, and when my father came in that night she showed him the letter and he said he'd catch the next train. We brought away just what we could carry.

An older woman could more easily develop a close relationship with her mother if her father was dead, so that the two could set up house or at least spend much of the time together: for example, two widows, mother and daughter, spent alternate days at one another's houses, always eating together and being visited jointly by other members of the family. Other women who had become very tightly bound in to the parental household again were acting as housekeepers, either to parents who both worked or in families where the mother was dead, so that the daughter became 'a second mother', as one put it.

Some of the more frequent 'readoption' or 'father substitution' situations might be represented diagrammatically by Figure 2. The financial advantages of living with parents were offset by considerable drawbacks. If the grandparents were both alive, the fatherless children gained a father substitute, but there was a real danger that the grandmother would effectively take the mother's role from her, especially if the latter went out to work all day, and if, falling back from an unsuccessful marriage, she lacked self-confidence and was prepared to adopt once again her role as daughter. For instance, a separated wife found that when she did set up house alone again her small daughter made innumerable objections to sleeping there, pretending she was afraid of the bunk beds, and succeeded in spending most of the time at her grandmother's: 'She'll say to me, "She's not me Nan, she's my other Mum!" In some ways she's closer to my mother than she is to me.' In another interview a separated wife's parents took no pains to disguise the fact that they regarded her as a failure. Her

Family of Origin*	Family of Reproduction** (broken)	Readoption

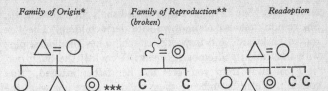

***

After only a short spell of marriage or unmarried motherhood, the young mother (who was a younger daughter) goes back with her young children to the home of her own mother and father, where her unmarried brothers and sisters are still living. She becomes, once again, her mother's daughter, rather than a wife and mother. She loses her maternal role, especially if she is out at work all day, and her children become in effect her mother's children. Tensions arise over her answerability to her parents, and over who controls the children.

Family of Origin	Family of Reproduction (broken)	Readoption or Substitution

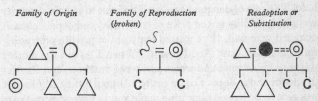

After a long spell of marriage, the older mother (who was the only, or older, daughter) goes back with her children to the home of her father and brothers, her own mother now being dead. She retains her maternal role, but becomes a substitute wife/housekeeper to her father, and a substitute mother/housekeeper to her younger brothers. Her father, and brothers become very possessive, jealous of her ex-husband, and unwilling to permit a reconciliation with him or to allow her to set up a separate home again with her children.

Family of Reproduction	Family of Reproduction (broken)	Father Substitution

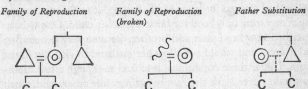

After a long spell of marriage, the older mother takes in to live with her as a lodger her unmarried brother (or he comes to visit very regularly). He becomes the decision maker and a source of financial support for her, and he becomes a substitute father for her children.

    *The family of origin is the family into which the mother was born.
    **The family of reproduction is the family in which she produced her children.
    *** Symbol representing the unsupported mother in all these kinship diagrams.

Figure 2
Some examples of 'readoption' or father substitution[1]

father said, 'She lives here with us and she's got no overheads. She couldn't manage on her own with them children.' The wife rocked backwards and forwards, clutching her shoulders, pink with frustration and embarrassment. 'I could!' she burst out, 'if I got away from you lot!' But her father insisted, 'You couldn't. We've brought up them children more nor what she has.' The wife shouted, 'Shut up,' and her mother intervened to say, 'You see, young people and old people don't get on. We get on each other's nerves a bit and you can't bottle it up all the time.' Quarrels over the children were probably a healthy reaction, a sign that the daughter was not prepared to adopt too readily or permanently her subordinate position in the household. The role of daughter was itself difficult to sustain. Security was achieved only at the price of conformity and dependence. A divorced wife said, 'I've wasted ten years of my life pretending to be someone else.' Another said, 'When I go out my mother wants to know what and where and when and how, and I've got to answer and it doesn't come easily.' Although they admitted it was nice to be looked after for a while and to have someone care again, the time came when the mother must break free if she was not to become a permanent family pensioner. Where a woman had become housekeeper – and indeed in several instances the mothers' dependent position was being exploited by their families – it was even more difficult to break away. An unmarried mother had worked for years as a housekeeper to her mother and sister, receiving only food for herself and her child. One woman described how her father and brothers became very demanding and jealous, and would not allow her husband to visit her in the house. Under these conditions, it looked as though a few mothers would never leave the family again, while others said, albeit thankfully, that they had left only because they were forced out by overcrowding or because another member of the family needed the grandmother's help.

There were several reasons why fatherless families did not receive more help from parents who were still alive and active. Twenty-one mothers were estranged from their parents and indeed most of their other relatives. The unhappy family relationships which preceded illegitimate births and broken marriages had seldom been healed by the mother's changed situation. During some marriages women had been isolated from their kin by their husbands' unsociable behaviour. One separated wife recalled:

My mother used to help when she came. She knew there was something wrong. She'd say, 'Come on, get out. You've sat in this house till you're t'colour o't'walls,' but she was coming one day and my husband was round the back and he said, so she could hear, 'Is that old so and so here again,' and do you know, she never set foot in this house after that. You see Jim was so awful with them when he was here. He used to insult them. It was as if we hadn't to have any visitors.

Even women who had thought they had good relations with their kin had discovered that the bond would not withstand the social stigma when they separated from their husbands. A separated wife said, 'When I was little my mother was always one for scandalizing, you know what I mean. But as soon as it happened to me she doesn't want to know about it, she keeps out of the way.'

Thus, the mother's predicament forced her relatives to 'take sides', and while a proportion were emphatically on her side and helped her considerably, a number had previously been estranged, or preferred not to be closely involved in any social embarrassment. They did not support the father instead – only one wife reported that her kin sided with her husband – but they avoided the mother herself.

A similar re-alignment appeared to have taken place, with more drastic effects, among the woman's brothers and sisters, although in three instances an unmarried brother had become a substitute father for the children, one lodging with his sister and the other two eating their main meals with the family. It looked as though more help may have been given initially. There was considerable confusion about how much help these mothers on national assistance were allowed to receive, which may have cut down what was given to her. And while the parents were alive and helping it looked as though other kin would give less. But there were other explanations of reduced help, based on the changed social situation. A too great preference from her parents seemed likely to create jealousies among the mother's kin. A woman with two sisters said her mother sometimes helped her with gifts, but, 'She'll say, "Now don't you go telling the other two."' In-laws, too, were felt to be less sympathetic to the claims of fatherless families, and were said to have discouraged gifts to them. A divorced mother said of her daughter, 'She sometimes gives me a back-hander, five or six shillings, but her hubby hasn't to see.'

Gifts and financial transactions were probably only one sign, if a revealing one, of a woman's changed situation with her kin. However, except for a vague sense of unease, mothers were not inclined to analyse relationships with brothers, sisters, and in-laws. Whether mothers' expectations of help had risen, or contacts had actually declined, mothers said they went round less in the evenings to see relatives, and if they did go out together it was not the same. A separated wife said, 'Sometimes my sister, her husband waits on at a night club, and she'll say, "Now come up. We've got a turn on and some bingo and you'll enjoy yourself." But when I go I always feel the odd one out.' Far from enjoying themselves on such occasions, the ex-wives were all too aware of the empty space at the table. Without a man the mother no longer fitted into patterns of behaviour in the family nor could new patterns easily evolve.

There had also been a change in relationships with kin as a result of changes in income and dependence on national assistance. Few mothers were very happy in the role of family pensioners, and the mother's dependent position and her low income had sometimes brought constraints even in the normal exchange of small gifts between relatives. The needs of the fatherless family were so manifest, and the questions of how much to give became so difficult, that the issue was sometimes evaded and nothing was given. A separated wife said that since her separation her children had, for the first time, not received a single Christmas present from her kin. The lack of help soon led to accusations of snobbery against relatives. Loss of the father made the family a misfit, and differences in living standards meant that social awkwardness could more readily harden into permanent estrangement.

The husband's kin

Very few separated and divorced women now had any contact with their husband's kin, and there were only three instances of the mother receiving substantial help from them. At the time of the parting the kin had aligned themselves against the wife, even to the extent in several families that the marriage breakdown was an issue for fights between small cousins in the school play-ground. Alternatively, finding themselves unable or unwilling to take sides, the husband's relatives avoided the wife, and the wife, on her side, decided that they were acting queerly and didn't want to get involved: 'I just gave it up with them. I let everything drop; it's the best way. If I saw them I'd go the other way quick.' Her resentment against her husband tended to be re-directed against his mother, with whom the husband was some-times living, or who was held in some more oblique way to be responsible for his conduct. One wife said,

I think his mother put him up to it. He left me once before, but his father made him come back. His father said, 'You've made your bed. Now you can lay on it.' But then, when my baby was eleven weeks old, his father died. His father died on August 29th and on the 5th of September he left me.

Also wives resented the behaviour of the husband's relatives who were thought to have known about 'the other woman' and to have fostered the relationship, or to be concealing the hus-band's whereabouts. In the two or three instances where the hus-band's parents had sent money or his brothers and sisters had behaved kindly towards her, the wife seemed apt to interpret this as guilt. Thus one wife said of her sister-in-law, with whom she exchanged Christmas presents, 'She feels ever so guilty about me marrying her brother. They all feel guilty. Nobody would decide on Christmas till I'd decided where I was going.' Such feelings were not a good basis for a continuing relationship, and it seemed significant that in the only instances of close contacts with the husbands' kin separation was very recent.

Scarcely anything was known about the kin of unmarried fathers, except in those instances where the mother and father were young and the families had lived close together; then hostility was generated by the fact of the birth, each family tending to feel the other's offspring was at fault. Moreover, where paternity was an issue, open recognition by the father's kin was impossible.

Nor, at the time of the interview, did the widows have any important contacts with their husbands' kin. Peter Marris's research[2] showed that initially there was help, but with the husband dead the chief link with his kin was gone, and contacts gradually fell away. For the widows interviewed during the present survey, this process was already complete.

Fatherlessness and the community

To a much smaller extent, fatherless families had received help from friends and the local community. One mother's social contacts could almost be mapped through the furniture in her living room (just as the string of washing overhead represented her family tree in gifts of clothing). She had bought very cheaply from a workmate a three-piece suite, a table had been passed on by a neighbour who was moving, she had bought a gas washer from another workmate for 5s., and had been given an old radio set, a pram, a Victorian crib, and a high chair by someone else who was moving. This kind of furniture was inferior to that provided by kin, but it was invaluable to mothers whose kin could not or would not help.

However, a majority spoke of changes in their relationships with friends and neighbours, who seemed to stigmatize the family in some way, tending to isolate it from such help. In their complaints, mothers could be seen coming to terms with their own feelings. Unmarried mothers felt they were regarded as sexually loose, and widows that they were pitied, and cast a blight on any company they were in; while separated and divorced wives complained of elements of both these reactions from the community.

For the unmarried the stigma was felt most by the older women. The younger mothers seemed much less worried, less given to self-blame and a sense of sin against society, although this might not be due to a change in the climate of public opinion so much as a lack of the long years' experience of bringing up illegitimate children which the older mothers had been through.

The problem of the widows who were grieving for their husbands was the pity of others which was expressed in avoidance or censoriousness. One widow said,

With my husband dying, I bought a black coat, and I put the pink coat away. Well, I never needed it for a year with being in mourning, but then last summer it was a nice day and I brought this coat out. Well, do you know, three people stopped me to ask me where it had come from, and they said, 'Oh, there you are, all dressed up.' It's as though you shouldn't dress up when you're a widow.

Another said, 'People look at you in a funny way, because if you're down in the dumps they're all telling you to buck up and not be so miserable and not let yourself go, and then if you do buck up and leave your cares behind you, they say, "Oh look at her, she doesn't give a damn."' This narrow equilibrium has been well described by Peter Marris as a delicate balance between not grieving enough – and so never being free of the experience – and grieving too much and losing touch with life and hope for the future. Marris suggests that one of the primary functions of kin and friends in such a situation is to gently tell the widow when she has grieved enough and to remind her of her family responsibilities.

The experience of separated and divorced wives was compounded of both sexual stigma and pity. It would be wrong to give the impression that all these separated and divorced mothers felt stigmatized. There were women secure in their self-esteem who scarcely worried about their status. Older women too felt more secure from accusations of sexual promiscuity, so that probably only those women who regarded themselves as likely to remarry worried about the way people regarded them. At worst, however, I got the impression in talking to some mothers that for them the street was full of eyes. One said, 'My neighbours watch me like a hawk, yes, from behind the curtains. There might be somebody there now, but I've told all of them round here, they can come in any time of the day or night and see what I'm doing.' Apart from the feeling that neighbours were watching out for men, especially where the custody of the children was an issue, mothers confessed to fears that if they went out to enjoy themselves they might be reported to the N. S. P. C. C. or their husbands for child neglect: 'You always have it in the back of your mind that people will say that you're not capable of looking after your kids and then they'll get took off you.'

Typically this largely working-class group spoke of relationships with neighbours, rather than with friends, because they had never had very many social activities which they and their husbands shared with other couples. They had to learn to fit in with the local community in a different way. The first, and for some the most difficult, problem these mothers had faced was to explain to others a marriage breakdown which they could scarcely explain to themselves. A separated wife said that at first,

The only time I felt happy was when I was lying in bed. That way I didn't have to spend anything. I didn't have to fork out for our meals or light, and I didn't have to meet people, people weren't looking at me and wondering. It was an odd sensation, but I felt that in bed I was away from people's eyes and questions and I was most contented there.

Another wife said, 'People ask you why your husband left, and you say you don't know, and they think you must be simple or something.' Another said, 'When your back's turned they say there must have been some reason why he left you. Smug, that's what they are, to think they've still got their husbands.' The woman whose husband had committed incest with her daughters was herself stoned by the neighbours. Moving to a new district brought new explanations: 'They weren't saying, "*How's* your husband?" They were saying, "*Where's* your husband?"' Equally difficult to bear were the neighbours who wanted to express pity. 'People used to say, "Whatever will you do? However will you manage?"' Some wives felt that like the widows they were treading a tight-rope between on the one hand not letting standards and morale slip, and on the other appearing not to care about their husband. Two wives who moved to a new area preferred to pass themselves off as widows.[3]

The children sometimes suffered from a similar ostracism,

although mothers were seldom sure of what went on at school. A separated wife said,

You know what children are, when she was at school at first they used to say to her, 'You haven't got a dad, and you haven't got a father,' and she used to worry about it, and she got in the end so she wouldn't go. I had to get the teachers to tell the class that she had got a father

Such insults to a child already feeling insecure through the loss of one parent may several times have tipped the balance and brought on symptoms of 'school phobia'.

Working-class fatherless families also faced problems of fitting into the structure of a neighbourhood life geared to homes with an authoritarian father. The husbandless woman was aware that the lives of her friends moved to a routine regulated by the departure and arrival home of the husband. A divorced woman said of her married neighbours,

They say they've got to do so and so for their husbands when they come. I think, 'Oh, I wish that had been me!' And then you know how you do, you nag a bit and you say you wonder what mood he'll be in, but I tell 'em I wouldn't care what sort of a mood he was in as long as he was there.

Sometimes the neighbours themselves felt marriage as a constraint and envied, or said they envied, the husbandless woman:

I think some of the younger ones are jealous. Well, I think, when you're married, after a bit you get a bit bored. They say to me, 'You've got a life of your own and you can do what you want to do.' But I wish I could change with them.

Who envied whom in this situation depended very much on the marriage experience. But either way the feeling of difference was there.

The absence of a man in the home destroyed the balance of the family's relationships with neighbours, and had two undesirable consequences from the wife's point of view. It became more difficult for her to repulse neighbours whom she regarded as 'nosey'; and neighbours 'took liberties' in other ways. Thus there were complaints that neighbours came in without knocking, stopped gossiping too long, borrowed things, asked questions about the cost of new things on the washing-line, bought expensive clothes for a child with a deliberate eye to recouping some of the cost by selling to the fatherless family, took short cuts through the garden, set fire to a dustbin outside the back door to make a bit more room in it, or parked children for the afternoon in the knowledge that there was no evening meal to prepare. Mothers were convinced that none of this would have happened if they had had a man in the house. One separated wife recalled:

I'd bought some little flowering trees, and I put them in the back garden. Well do you know, the feller two doors along (God rest his soul, he died two weeks ago), we hadn't been in so long, and he came and he dug my trees and he put them in his garden. And my son says to me, 'Hey, there's a feller digging in our back garden.' 'Oh', I said 'I'll come and see in a minute.' And by the time I'd come, these trees were off, and I couldn't get them back. He said, 'Them trees belonged to that woman who lived in that house before you did, and she promised them to me.' That's how you are, they put on you.

Mothers also felt that without a man in the house they had more trouble with the neighbours over their children, and three mothers said they had actually had to fight neighbours before they could re-establish the status they had before the father went away.

We were all outside and the neighbours shouted, 'You've got a stick in your hand Annie,' and I said, 'I don't need a stick, I can manage without.' He hit me so I hit him back. Oh, if I could only get away from this place I'd be the happiest woman walking on this earth!

Another said, 'I was the sort of woman, if anybody came and told me my children had done wrong, I'd go behind the door and cry, and I'd smack my children. Now I wouldn't care what they told me. I'd tell them to go to yond shop!' Fatherless families lacked the woman's ultimate threat of, 'I'll send our Stanley round to you.' To regain their position in some of the communities where they lived mothers and children now had to be that bit tougher than the neighbours.

Mothers may also have withdrawn from visiting and being visited because they found painful those situations where disparities of living standard became too obvious. One mother said, 'If you've been in a nice home where everything's all nice and you come back in here you feel down. That's why I don't like having people in very often.' And another said, 'I'm always ashamed to see anybody come here because I know they've all got carpets on their floors, and Hoovers. That's why I don't invite anybody.' The normal borrowing relationships among neighbours were disrupted because fatherless families lacked resources to lend or were over-concerned that their loans should be returned.

Middle-class mothers

The situation of the few middle-class mothers differed in that they spoke more often of the problem of new relationships with friends whom they and their husbands had formerly known together. There were fewer local tensions, but the mothers experienced with friends the sort of re-alignment or avoidance which has been described for kin. A separated wife said, 'Where the people next door and the ones further on go to a dance as a foursome, when my husband was here we used to go as a sixsome.' Apart from the question of loyalties to one or other of the couple, there was the practical point that the basis of these friendships had been in shared activities like dancing or parties which demanded that the sexes should be evenly balanced, and even that all the couples should be married. A divorced woman said, 'I do get invited to the odd party by married couples, but where you find the odd man of a certain age is welcome, the odd woman of a certain age is very odd indeed.' There were complaints of former women friends becoming very possessive about their husband, and 'clutching him' to them. If couples did come round together, the husbands were said to feel out of it: 'It's not the same as if they could have a talk to my husband, male conversation.'

These awkwardnesses meant that some couples had dropped away altogether, so that the mother was not even invited to all-women's activities in the evening, such as a woman's keep-fit class. Or, alternatively, relationships which had formerly involved couples in outings together in the evenings or at week-ends shifted or were restricted to other activities involving women only, during the day. One wife recognized clearly the split which had taken place: 'As far as what I call my daily life is concerned, that's just the same, life with "the girls", coffee mornings. But I don't fit in at all in the evening life in a social way. Where I used to get asked out to parties with my husband, I go out with my girl-friends or boy-friends, get the best of both worlds I call it.' It was very rarely, however, that mothers could regard the new arrangement as an improvement.

The women in the worst situation were those who had former-ly been comparatively well-off. The activities in which their friends took part cost more money than they could afford. And while to a considerable extent friends could cushion the shock of a sudden drop in income, the situation was tension-ridden. One woman said she aged ten years in the past three since her husband deserted:

I feel it's a Jekyll and Hyde sort of existence. When I've been with my friends and I come back here, I feel as if I've put on a disguise. And my speech has deteriorated, and my son's too. We find that sometimes when we're in the house we put on a bit of Seaston slang. My friends have remarked on it, and the teachers at my son's school have remarked that he doesn't speak quite as nicely.

As another woman put it, 'Really, I'm a bit of an Aunt Sally to my friends. They think, "Poor old Jean", and they bring me all sorts of things and I should be grateful, but I'm not. I hate them for it. After a few years you get all churned up about it.' This woman was at first extremely offended at being contacted for an interview and began by being very abusive, but confessed later that this was a façade she always put up to prevent people expressing pity for her. A position of permanent indebtedness was far from comfortable.

Relationships with men

A major restriction on mothers' prospects of remarriage was the lack of suitable places or social contexts where women could meet and get to know men of their own age without the sur-veillance and gossip of neighbours. And mothers feared that so much stigma attached to their position that the men they did meet would have an unfavourable attitude, seeing them as actively looking for a partner in sex outside marriage. Most of these impressions were gained from visiting tradesmen or other callers, and may indeed have resulted from a very narrow selection of contacts with men. There were stories of men who had suggested that a bill might be forgotten if the woman was 'nice' to them, of a milkman who always sought to take hold of a woman's hand, a coalman and a clubman who became too 'friendly' and wouldn't go away, a vacuum cleaner salesman who came round every night for a week on finding out that a woman was alone. A divorced woman said,

You get it all the time round here, mate. They make you laugh. There's one came round selling stockings. He said he'd give me two dozen pairs if I'd let him put a pair on, and I said, 'You're joking!' Anyway I said come in and I was talking to him and gave him a cup of tea. I said, 'Look, you're married and you're away, aren't you, away from home a lot?' I said, 'Does your wife get door-to-door tradesmen?' And he said, yes, he supposed she did and I said, 'How do you know they're not saying the same thing to her?' And he was offended at that. He said, 'I was only trying it on with you because I knew you were divorced, and not having a husband I thought you'd be missing it.' And I said, 'Don't make me sick!' I said. 'It's men like you who get a woman like me in the bad!'

The few mothers who had been dancing or who had otherwise met men socially outside the home, in a pub or at bingo, all said that a change came over the man when he found out their marital status, so that after a while they learned to keep it secret or at least a matter of doubt: 'They say to me, "Are you married?" And I say, "Yes, three times, and I've got three children by each husband!"' There was the feeling that in courtship the divorced, separated, or unmarried woman must be extra careful, or the man would take advantage of her.

We're very good at sizing the men up, whether they're married or not. We look at their handkerchiefs when they take them out, and if they've a handkerchief that's nicely pressed, then we know they're probably married, or else they've got a thoughtful mum and we find out which it is. But if their shirts are dirty and their handkerchiefs are all crumpled, you know they're on their own.

The mothers tended to have a very poor view of men, and were highly sceptical that anyone would approach them with a genuine intention of marriage.

Links between the fatherless – the underclass

The net result of these strains was that at least one in five of the mothers appeared to have no outside friends whatsoever, and for a further proportion social life was severely restricted. One woman said she went to blood donor sessions because this was the only time she got anyone else to make her a cup of tea. It was not just that mothers needed to make special efforts to start up new relationships; they must work hard even to keep those friends they formerly had.

In these circumstances the mothers turned to one another for companionship. In both Northborough and Seaston – where I interviewed probably one in ten and one in three respectively of all the fatherless families – there were couples or small groups of mothers who used to meet regularly for a chat or even to stay with one another. Because of the thicker spread of interviews in Seaston, I was able to trace mothers who had not replied by following up friendships, and this has the effect of making the groupings look tighter. Yet, even so, it seems striking that when I drew a chart of which mothers knew, or knew of, one another, almost half of those interviewed were connected, and in addition there were several pairs of mothers and two groups of four and six; this in a population of 70,000.

So strong was the common bond of fatherlessness that it could unite women of quite dissimilar tastes and behaviour. A divorced woman told me, with a reluctant fascination, of her relationships with an unmarried mother who regularly had children by different fathers. 'She says, "If I were your age, I'd have a rattling good time with the men," but I don't know what she means. It's funny, I often say to her, "Doris, why am I a friend of yours, because really we've got nothing in common."' Mothers had struck up acquaintances while out shopping, or collecting children from school. The concentration of fatherless families on certain housing estates, in certain poorer areas of the town, in the houses of several notorious landlords, and even in the same house, accounted for many of the contacts.

A small minority of mothers who made up the more cohesive groups were held together by the ostracism of local society and by a common interest in, and a sort of rivalry for, the largest pools of unmarried men, in Seaston the Army, in Northborough the West Indians or groups of young workmen imported by the local chemical works. In Seaston a set of mothers (ten of whom were interviewed) with free time during the day frequented several cafes in a run-down area of the town. One said, 'All the unmarried mothers go in there. In fact some of them go in there so often they've had their kids took off them.' In the evenings they met soldiers in the pubs. But the links between the mothers were more complex than this. Two unmarried mothers lived together in the same house and one had looked after the other's child when she went into hospital: they were going to share a chicken for Christmas. One of them was given clothes by a separated wife, who also had a soldier's illegitimate child. She had stayed, when first turned out of home, with another unmarried mother. Apart from company and advice, these mothers were able to give one another help which they could obtain in no other way.

In a similar group in Northborough all the illegitimate children were half-caste. At an interview with a separated wife there were two other women present, another separated wife with three half-caste children, and an unmarried mother with two coloured children. From them I learned of another mother with four half-caste children. These women often spent the day down in the West Indian quarter of the town. They lived on the roughest estate, but even so they were shut off from the surrounding community. The woman I was interviewing said, 'I feel all caved in. I don't know any married people, not happily married, except the coloured ones. The only ones I know are all separated.' Her conversation was filled with stories of beatings and fights. That day they were 'laying out' for somebody who kept watch on them and informed the police or the National Assistance Board if they were away from home, or if they had any West Indian visitors: 'We'll do for her.

If I catch her today, she won't be fit to be seen by the time I've finished with her.' They told the story of an acquaintance whose children they used to look after:

She used to go out and leave the kids till midnight. This night we went down and all the neighbours were out, and the baby, well the nurse daren't pick it up because it was so thin. And the milk in the bottle was all stale, and the teat was all hard, so I brought the bottle up home and sterilized it and made a feed for the baby, but it was too hungry, it couldn't feed, it was so weak.

A West Indian drove up to the house, and brought in a bottle wrapped up in tissue paper, Lucozade for another of the mothers who was in hospital.

If we can talk of an 'underclass' in terms of groups cut off from society, then these groups of mothers in Northborough and Seaston belong to one. They felt trapped and desperate, and they had ceased to look to society for their standards, seeking comfort where they could find it. Because they were excluded from conventional courtships, they turned to the men in the community least likely to marry: a number of the women possibly had small earnings from prostitution, but, if they had, the earnings were not reflected in any increased comfort in their living surroundings. The mothers helped one another because there was no one else to help them, and at the back of their minds was always the spectre that some day their nerve might crack and they would abandon their children, as some of their friends had done. Yet at best this kind of society offered a more enjoyable, if more hazardous, existence than that of the more isolated mothers.

We must not leave the impression that these groups were representative of all fatherless families. Possibly as many as one in six mothers could be said to belong to this kind of society. But from its fringes were links spreading out to other mothers, more stably rooted. It seemed that the 'underclass' was a kind of well into which the mothers slipped as they lost their hold in the local community.

CHAPTER EIGHT

The Meaning of Fatherlessness to Mother and Children

For a fifth of the families less than one year had elapsed since they became fatherless, for another fifth over ten years, while the remainder had been fatherless for some intermediate spell. Bringing up to date the account of how mothers and children adjusted to fatherlessness does not involve a shift of focus, for the mothers, in talking about their broken marriages, illegitimate children, and relationships with kin and community have already given pointers to their feelings. Adjustments had different meanings for mother and child. The mother had to try to understand the broken relationship, and possibly in facing the future she might consider remarriage. But for the child interest centres also on longer-term effects, on the possibilities of delinquency, unmarried motherhood, or unhappy marriage. Although many of the children were still young, we can look at the developing relationships within the family to see if these were suggestive of future difficulties.

With such a spread over time and variety of situations, relationships were caught at different stages. In two thirds of the families, including of course the widows, the fathers were never seen. But in the remaining third, the father of a child was still seen occasionally, and even – in fourteen instances – weekly or more often. Of the mothers who still met the fathers at all, nineteen were divorced or separated: ten had visits from their husbands or ex-husbands and nine were still in touch with the father of an illegitimate child. A further three wives went to see a child who lived with the husband; three West Indian unmarried mothers and one white divorcee had unions with the West Indian fathers of their children; I discovered that two unmarried mothers soon married their child's father, and a third met the father when he paid the paternity order each week.

In addition to these continuing relationships with the fathers, probably fifteen of the families could in some sense be said to have 'substitute' fathers or husbands, a relative, a lodger, a neighbour, or a man-friend. So while the majority of the families were fatherless in every sense, for over one third the impact of fatherlessness was modified in some way by contacts with the father or another man.

The mother's emotional involvement with the father

The mother's emotional bonds with the father did not snap cleanly with the parting. Almost half the mothers, many of whom had completely lost touch with the father, had a sense of longing for him. A separated wife did not at first wish to be interviewed because, 'Put it this way, it opens up old wounds.' Her husband had gone working away and his visits tailed off and then stopped. But

I suppose really I'm still in love with him. Those few times he came down he was really nice. And my husband, he's the devilish type you know, he pulls your leg a bit. I wouldn't get married again. I think too much of the husband I've got.

She had not lived with him for four years. Another woman took violent exception to our introductory letter's use of the word 'fatherless', although she had been divorced many years. She wrote indignantly in reply:

I don't know where you get the idea my children are fatherless just because he couldn't stay and do his job right close does not mean my children are fatherless I will see you. but don't come with that attitude.

Another separated wife still kept all her possessions packed three years after moving into a new home, reluctant to give her present position any permanence. It was evident that a sizeable minority of women persisted, in spite of evidence to the contrary and sometimes for many years, in thinking that they would somehow be re-united with their children's father.

The descriptions of broken marriages and illegitimate births suggest that these were women for whom the final parting had been principally the husband's, or children's father's, decision or primarily of his making, one-sided, unexpected, and therefore somehow premature.[1] This group included most of those whose husbands (legal or common-law) had deserted. But also there were women who felt their hand had been forced when they divorced their husbands not for violence but for associations with other women or for persistent non-support. Older unmarried mothers who claimed they had been engaged also suffered lasting disturbances when the relationship ended. Analogies with widowhood, where by contrast there was definitely not the remotest possibility of renewing the relationship with the husband, must not be carried too far. Yet there was a striking similarity shown in the attitudes to death by some widows whose husbands had died suddenly or after long spells away in hospital.[2] They too had difficulty in accepting that their husbands were gone. A young widow described the feeling:

They wanted me to go and identify the body, but I couldn't bring myself, and then before the funeral I would have gone to see him, but my brother-in-law told me not to. I think if I had gone to see him I would have realized better that he was dead. I couldn't accept it. I used to think he was coming back. People die when you want them to die, I suppose. I used to sit and think and try to remember something that I'd got angry with him about, but I couldn't remember anything. I thought if there was one thing I could have turned against him it would have been a relief.

As with the broken marriages there was somehow a 'failure to take leave', the ending of a relationship which was for the wife still in full flower. And where the children's father suddenly disappeared or deserted, his spiritual 'death' for the wife left an aftermath strikingly like bereavement. If some of these deserted mothers appeared to have a remarkable capacity for self-delusion, it must be remembered that their husbands were often described as likeable men who had never injured them; and to accept that the husband had gone was to bow to dependence on national assistance. These mothers were given to self-doubt, apt to feel they had failed in some way. They wondered what they could have done that they had left undone, or what gesture of affection they might have made before the parting.

Unless they could see the children's fathers as blameworthy, they blamed themselves.

For most women, longing for the father – or longing for a husband, it was sometimes difficult to say which it was – would probably dwindle away. A mother, long since separated, said, 'It's funny to think of him. I sometimes pass him and wonder how I had all them children by him. I pass him like a stranger.' But there were also several women whose initial shock and longing had turned over the years into a kind of frozen outrage; there was about such households an atmosphere of *Great Expectations*.

A third of the mothers immediately or quickly felt hatred for the children's father, sometimes not on their own account but for the sake of the children whose chances in life they felt had been injured. One wife took a knife with her when she went searching for her husband. Two others had in-patient treatment for paranoid delusions since their husbands had left. One said: 'I hate every man. I just want one man to try it on me. I'd get my revenge back on them. I don't know where I'd hit him, I feel so bitter inside.' Several of these mothers even speculated about the possibility of forced labour camps for husbands who left their wives and children in a situation of shame and financial insecurity. A separated wife said,

I can laugh at it, but it's not fair. He tells all his mates down in the pub he's seen the 'struggle and strife'. I saw him last week and he said, 'I'm not going to give you a penny you know.' And I said, 'I hope you never pay. I hope you get sent to gaol.' If only you could get back at them in some way, that's the trouble.

The women's feeling of impotence contributed greatly to their resentment.

The remaining one in six mothers frankly confessed that the overriding feeling had been relief when they had broken with their children's father. A divorced wife said, 'When he went out of the door it was as if a chain dropped off me,' and another said ironically, 'I don't miss him, he was never here to miss.' A woman whose husband had been a poor supporter said after the divorce, 'It was lovely to come home and know that you'd got a home and that you'd get your money and could lay it out as you wanted.' Nor were all the widows grief-stricken: for something like half, the death had not been a major upheaval, and several had even found it a release. One said, 'I know it sounds a rotten thing to say, but I was a bit shocked at first, when I heard the news about him, but after that I was relieved really, because he's never been any good to me.' It was difficult to believe that some of these mothers had been married, so little regret did they show.

Most mothers, however, even those glad to be rid of their husbands, seemed to have moments of loneliness, brought on by thinking what might have been, or from sheer change of habit if nothing more. They missed a man to decorate, to do the garden, to mend fuses. Weekends, Saturday mornings, Sunday mornings when children were seen out with their fathers, tea-time when the other fathers came home, the sight of a young couple holding hands, their own children playing 'mothers and fathers', family shows on television, shopping for furniture, were all likely to raise a lump in the throat or even bring tears. And for those with young children evenings were a trying time. Mothers felt they lacked somebody to talk to about adult matters, sex, the neighbours. They saved up their household chores like ironing for the evening. Above all television was a great comfort: several who had been without TV for only a short time said they had felt as if they would go mad, and one said, 'I tell my mate I'm married to that thing now my husband's gone!'

The mother's health

The break with the father had often caused a deterioration in the mother's health. Altogether, thirty mothers, or over a quarter, said they had suffered from 'nervous breakdowns', and at least thirteen, or one in nine, had made suicide attempts. A separated wife said:

I had a sort of nervous breakdown for about six months. I didn't know what I was doing. I was so bad, I was wandering about drugged with phenobarbitone, I nearly got one of the children run over by a bus. I've had the lot, depression, suicide. I was so bad they wanted to put me in a home and let the children go away. But I was afraid that if I went away I'd never come back, and I don't think I would have done.

A minority of the breakdowns could be clearly connected with the added difficulties of a low income. One wife said,

I didn't really mean to kill myself. I think I just tried to frighten the children. It was one of those days when I'd got no money at all and they were all on at me crying for food and could they have money for this and could they have money for that, and I kept trying to explain to them that they just couldn't and they were fighting and running in and out and all I seemed to be able to hear was, 'Mummy, mummy!' so I went to the cupboard and I took these tablets.

However, although injury to health might result from later difficulties, it looked as if much of the past and continuing distress sprang from grief, and where there had been some sort of crisis it had usually occurred soon after the death or parting.

At the time of the interview, half the mothers still suffered from bouts of depression. A quarter complained of tiredness. A tenth were on pills, usually tranquillizers, and another tenth had been on pills in the past. Mothers who took pills were 'addicted' in the sense that they could not get through without them: as one said, 'They're my walking-stick.' During the interviews, grief, nervousness, listlessness, and ill-health were still all too visible. One mother rocked herself back and forth with arms crossed in front of her, her hands clutching her shoulders, another endlessly drew a silk handkerchief between her fingers, another bit and bit the skin of her fingers until they bled. A divorced woman yawned repeatedly and confessed that because she couldn't sleep at night she usually spent each afternoon sitting on a hard stool with her head pillowed in her arms on the kitchen table. A separated wife had for five years been afraid to go out of the house. She said,

I just feel like I've got right down to rock bottom and my head's in a whirl. It's as though the inside of my head, it's all tired. I could just cut my head off and put it over there and give it a rest.

A few mothers' health was also indirectly affected because of the difficulty of leaving the children to go into hospital. A separated wife said,

Ever since I had Janice I've had these veins in me legs, varicose veins, and I ought to get them shifted. These last few months they've been aching. I don't know where to put my legs sometimes. And then I keep losing blood you know, when I shouldn't do. There's something inside that needs doing. And some nights I'll have the most awful pain when I turn over in bed. But you see I had a little talk with the children and said perhaps they could go into a Home while I went in the Infirmary, but they started crying, so I haven't mentioned it again.

Going to hospital, or going to the doctor, might also involve stopping work, which the mothers were reluctant to do.

Such symptoms, and general feelings of apathy and tiredness, partly account for the very few outings which mothers made in the evenings for entertainment. No systematic check was made on their daily routine, but at least nine mentioned that they went to bed at nine o'clock in the evening or earlier. These mothers themselves could not distinguish between feeling tired, illness, or sheer boredom: the response to fatherlessness was compounded of all three.

The children's involvement with their father

Over and above her own problems the mother sometimes had to help the children to cope with the grief and confusion arising out of separation. The mother's own attitude to the father must have been a powerful influence on the child, and it was evident that she tended to attribute to the children feelings like her own. Yet from what she said, the children's reactions to the loss of the father were by no means simply a reflection of hers. Depending on her feelings and the age of the children, disturbing tensions could arise.

Tensions were most pronounced in the minority of families where the father had continued to visit frequently after separation or divorce. If the mother still had a lingering affection for him she fostered the children's loyalties and memories and supported his visits. But where, as usually happened, resentment built up between the parents, all too easily the father's visits or contacts with the children became a battle for their affections. Young children soon forgot even violence and neglect and were puzzled and distressed that the father could not stay. Happy visits when he was able to indulge their wants contrasted with the pinching and scraping and bad temper which were too often the result of the mother's financial position. One separated wife said in disgust, pointing to a toy friction car her husband had bought the children on their last outing,

Whenever he takes them out he buys them things. Look at that, 6/11d.! I think to myself, God, what I could do with that. I think he's trying to get them off me, he's trying to win them over, that's why he makes such a fuss of them. He's making up to them now, but when he lived here he never took them out, and he always liked them in bed when he came home from work. Yet now, he can't see enough of them.

The father promised or represented to the older children more freedom, and they used his gifts and promises to score against the mother, threatening to go to live with him. In one interview the child's divided loyalties were all too obvious. She very much resented my questions to her mother, made faces behind my back until her mother threatened to hit her, and said, 'What's he doing here then? I'll tell my father about him.' Her mother became very angry, 'It's because your father's gone away and he's not doing his job supporting us that we've got to take money off the National Assistance, and he's coming round to find out about it.' The argument developed, the daughter stoutly defending her father. It seemed that both the parents and the children at times played upon the dramatic tensions inherent in this situation. The three mothers whose children remained in the father's custody described similar conflicts, but from the other side.

In the light of these difficulties it was easy to understand why only one of the fathers who now visited had been coming for as long as five years. The usual story appeared to be that visits which began well had tailed off. One husband

used to come to see them every week, but then he dropped off and I used to have them all ready dressed for him to take out and he'd never come. Next time he came our David got out of the way and wouldn't go with him, so when he realized I wasn't going back to him he said, 'What's the use.' It's better that way really, we know where we are instead of being torn between two.

Repeated contacts with the father only served to dramatize and exacerbate the conflict of affection, and by active discouragement – or by an equally eloquent display of 'neutrality' when the child appealed to her for a decision about writing to or seeing the father – the mother worked to bring the relationship to an end.

In most of the families, where the father was seen much less often or not at all, the problems differed with the age of the children. Those with whom mothers had the greatest difficulty were a few aged from five to twelve when the separation or death occurred. The widows' children were reported as grieving most, and several appeared as dangerously withdrawn and over-balanced by grief. In six families, including two widows, mothers had felt that their children blamed them. A separated wife said, 'They said a lot to hurt me. My daughter said, "We've got to get rid of mummy, and then daddy will come back to live."' A widow said,

I think inwardly she blames me, and she's took it out on me. She told me once, 'I don't want you.' The schoolteachers say they can't get through to her, and I'm not surprised, because I can't either. She seems backward, she doesn't try. Funny ways she got. When she goes to bed at night she never tells you. I'll just miss her and I'll go to her room and she's in bed. And she's gone back more to her baby ways. She bothers more with her dolls now.

This mother was considering whether to send her daughter away to a Home, so uncomfortable had the relationship grown. The resentment was increased by the mother's inability to provide any longer the treats and spending money the child had been used to. And sometimes the child's resentment stemmed from the threat of the mother's new man-friend. A situation of this kind multiplied the mother's own difficulty in coming to terms with her own feelings. However, although such instances were striking, they proved to be a very small minority.

Older children had seen something of what was happening, and knew that the fathers had gone for good. It seemed that if they were to continue living with their mother they had to believe she was in the right and they staunchly upheld her. Only when they were married and away from home a few had resumed contact with their fathers and seemed to take a more evenly balanced view of the situation.

The most common situation was where the children were too young to understand – probably a quarter of the families – or young enough to be satisfied by the mother's explanations so that as yet no problem was recognized. Mothers differed widely in their approach. Many had still to face the problem, and for various reasons of shame, or a misreading of the child's emotional defences, or lack of the right words, had avoided the explanations altogether. A divorced woman had told her son that his father, whom he had never seen, was dead: 'And he said, "Was he poorly before that?" and I said, yes. It makes you feel awful saying things like that, but what can you do?' Unmarried mothers tended to worry over what they would tell their children: 'I don't want him to think I was one of these old scrambags in the street and went with anybody. That's what I worry about most, what he'll think of himself when he grows up.' These children who had not been told had still to come to terms with the situation, although it seemed possible that sometimes they must know more than they or their mothers were prepared to admit.

With the aid of the mother, the child might develop an idealized or blackened picture of the father, usually the former because the mother wanted the child to approach adult life without adverse preconceptions. But in a few households the child was told nothing. The remoteness of the father was caught in a divorced woman's account of the first meeting one Christmas between her ex-husband and his teenage son:

One of the lads came through and said, 'Hey there's a right funny feller at the back door,' so they let him in and who should it be but my husband, blind drunk he was, the great daft thing, and I didn't know what to say. So I thought, well perhaps he'd like to see Jimmy, and I sent for him to come in, but he never said hello nor nothing, that was the way he was, you see. He wasn't interested. So when he'd gone Jimmy said, 'Who was that bloke?' And I said, 'That was your father.' And he said he didn't like him.

The child whose father is alive always has the possibility of testing the image against reality, but this may not be a salutory experience, as the above encounter shows.

This variety of experiences of fatherlessness may account for the relatively small amount of immediate disturbance shown by the children. At the widest estimate in only a quarter of the families were any kinds of emotional stress apparent, such as nightmares, hysteria, or very withdrawn behaviour. Violent partings in several instances had brought on attacks of temporary enuresis. But in the main the immediate impact of separation or death was cushioned in various ways.

It has been shown that the children did badly at school.[3] However, from the mothers themselves there was conflicting evidence about how the children's school performance might be sensitive to family problems. Mothers were apt to point to school experience after the parting as an indication of the child's disturbance. One mother recalled,

Jane would sit there and really she'd be miles away, from the expression on her face, so sometimes the teacher used to give her a clip, but then one day she asked her what she was thinking about, and Jane said, 'I was wondering whether my daddy will be coming home for Christmas.' And the old teacher said that it really made her heart bleed.

Yet there were other stories of earlier bad performance at school due to the father's *presence*. In this field of school results, where the mother knew so little anyway, it appeared that often her stories of the children's struggles were oblique expressions of her own feelings about the father, and justifications of her behaviour.

Mother and children

The more serious problems, such as the seventeen families who had a child or children in trouble with the police or referred to the Child Guidance Clinic as delinquent, might arise through the developing pattern of relations within the fatherless families as much as through grief or the child's conflict of allegiances and self-blame for the loss of the father. It is also of great interest to find out what sort of training for adult life the family was providing. Unfortunately, we have no information about complete families with which to compare our results, but over half the mothers, mainly with older children, felt the lack of a father was a serious problem because of the direction in which family relationships had developed.

These working-class mothers usually had the very clearly defined idea that the family structure should be based on an authoritarian masculine father, with their own function being to comfort and show affection. Many complained of their inability to fill both roles at once, particularly the difficulty of maintaining authority while remaining at the same time loving.[4] A separated wife said,

I've always been affectionate. I like to have a cuddle, that's the trouble with being on your own. I have to be mother and father to them. You've nobody behind you. You haven't that last threat, you can't say, 'Wait till your daddy comes back.' You have to be a bit hard. Before I was always one to give a bit of leeway, but now I've gone the other way.

Hovering between two extremes, mothers either worried that the children were getting too much discipline so that they felt unloved and were naughty or whiney to gain attention, or they thought they were being too soft and the children took advantage of them. The two conflicting attitudes could be seen in the matter of work and pocket money, some mothers refusing to let their children work, others insisting that the children earn every penny of what they spent, and on the whole the trend was towards protectiveness. Several mothers described themselves as a split personality, or a Jekyll and Hyde, where they could play either part more or less adequately, but not both at once. Even if they were able to combine the two roles, they worried that their control over the children would still lack some of the flexibility of a complete family, for a child with only one parent had no court of appeal. Part of this sense of difficulty in being a parent was attributable to there being no *adult* present who would help the mother to decide how she should behave, and no 'audience' other than the children.

Mothers worried about the lack of an ideal of masculinity for their children. Fathers, they felt, would teach boys male pursuits, such as sport and woodwork. A widow said, 'Poor little things. They sometimes say to me, "Come out and play football mummy." Well, I've no more idea how to play football than the man in the moon.' Mothers were less worried about girls having a father, the feeling being that a girl, while she might worship her father, didn't need him as much as she needed a mother. But they did worry about the more remote future, wondering whether their daughters would be afraid of men and would not marry happily, or alternatively worrying that their daughters too easily took to any men who showed them attention.

The lack of a husband promoted other tensions in child-rearing. Some of the unmarried mothers and others who were isolated knew very little about bringing up children and could not get information from the usual source, their mothers or other women relatives. Even mothers with good relationships with their own kin felt they tended to worry more. A widow said, 'If one of them doesn't feel well on a night time, if I had a husband I'd be able to talk it over with him, and he'd say "Oh, it's all right. If he's no better, we'll get the doctor in the morning," but now I sit up all night with them, and I've nobody to comfort me.' These mothers were conscious that they fussed their children and felt that they were being over-protective.

If the family did not gain a substitute father or husband, the nuclear family itself adapted to the strain in other ways. In nine families one child became, in effect, a substitute parent. Usually this was the eldest son. A separated wife said of her son, 'Billy's the father to the youngest ones. If I say to them, "Now we need a haircut", Billy will look at them and say, "Saturday dinner time, that's the deadline", and it *will* be cut by Saturday dinner time!' A widow's son had a nervous breakdown at the age of fifteen, his mother thought because he was trying to take over his father's responsibilities. These sons took over to varying extents the roles of confidant, chief bread-winner, or disciplinarian. In two instances, however, it was the eldest daughter who took over the authoritarian role when the mother's health or confidence broke down; these two mothers both spent a great deal of time in bed ill. One said, 'If I have any trouble here, she's the only one I can turn to. If there's owt wrong I ask my daughter to come down and she comes and tells 'em off.' It was almost as if the daughter took over the father's role, or at least took over the mother's role when she abdicated it. Failing a real father or authority figure, his place could be occupied almost mystically. A separated wife said,

I've always built up Grandad Phillips. I've always tried to tell the kids stories about him, and make it out that he was looking after them. Our Donna believes he is. When it's a bright starry night, she looks out and picks out the brightest star she can find and she thinks that's Grandad Phillips looking down on her, watching over her.

In ninety of the families, or about three quarters – that is, the ones where the children were old enough for the question of the mother's control to arise – it was possible to see two contrasting types of development. The first trend was that in twenty-nine families, or about a third, the mother felt herself only narrowly in command. And in a further twelve of the larger families there was something like anarchy, with the mother ineffectual: this group included the multi-father families. Elements contributing to the anarchy appeared to be the sheer size of the family, the greater length of fatherlessness, the mother's debilitated condition, her confused relationships with other men, and possibly the pattern of child-rearing (although I saw very little of the last). Not all these children whose mothers reported they were out of control were yet old enough to have committed any serious offences, but the mothers felt it was only a matter of time before they did. Even three-year-olds were giving difficulty. Large families put an enormous strain on the mother, particularly where the children were older and the mother's health was poor. In one family the children were fighting with knives and pokers, and the mother said, 'I had to separate them with a broom, but to tell you the truth I got the broom, well, I got it where I shouldn't and I got all bruises across the top of my leg.' For every mother who failed completely to maintain control there were two who kept it only by using considerable violence. One middle-class mother said, 'I'm a believer in a jolly good whack with a stick. I have trouble with the girls too. I'm sorry to say that last Saturday I gave Tina a punch in the face, I really did, I lost my temper. She resents me dreadfully and I resent her.'

The social stigma attaching to these families may lead to the children being more likely to be labelled by the community as delinquent, and it also appeared to result in the families being placed in housing areas more likely to have juvenile delinquent gangs. Perhaps for this reason mothers were hypersensitive to signs of delinquency, and this was part of a whole complex of forebodings about the children's future development. A divorced woman said, 'I've talked while I'm black in the face, while I can hardly talk any more, about right and wrong.' A separated wife said, 'There was a time when I looked forward to them growing up, but I can't say now. I can't say how they'll turn out.'

Punishment of the children tended to be harsh in these families, owing to the fear that once control had been lost it could never be regained. Comparatively small incidents, a lie or the taking of a little money, provoked a reaction out of all proportion. A separated wife said of her small daughter, 'She took two shillings out of my purse and the woman next door had to pull me off her. I raised blood on her legs.' Several mothers had themselves reported their children to the Probation Officer for minor offences of the type probably committed by a majority of working-class children living in that area. The hope was that the Probation Officer would provide a steadying male influence. But the mother's extreme concern about delinquency appeared very likely to produce the behaviour she dreaded, and the mother thus played a direct part in having her child labelled delinquent.[5]

The other main trend in family relationships was that by contrast, in a further twenty families – out of the ninety with older children – mothers and children were said to be 'closer'. These were families where there were daughters, where the father could more easily be viewed as 'in the wrong', or where the situation demanded no conflict of allegiance and the mother's relationships with other men did not threaten the children's security or divide their loyalties. Mothers said they looked upon daughters and sons more like sisters and brothers. 'When I got my divorce,' said one, 'they bought me a present, and

Brenda said, "You've got no husband to look after you now, so *we'll* look after you." ' There were other small gestures, almost formal recognitions by the children of their new charge.

Such a strengthening of family ties is probably seen as children grow up in complete families. Occasionally, however, mothers expressed worries lest the relationship was becoming *too* close, particularly where the sons were involved. Closeness here appeared to be a response to feelings of insecurity, the children fearing they would lose their mothers, the mothers afraid their health or resolve would fail. Children were over-anxious when their mother was late back from a friend's house, or over-solicitous about her health. One mother said,

They've always been lone wolves, my boys. I don't know what it is, they've got a lot of energy that they've got nowhere to channel it into. I went to see one of them chaps at the Clinic (Child Guidance) and that's what he said. But they don't want to leave me, they'd rather be hanging round me. The eldest one, it's as though what he'd really like is him and me by ourselves to be together.

There were also instances where the mother's friendships outside home had withered away, so that she was living out her life more intensely through the children. A few mothers said they had never been out in the evening for as many as ten or more years, and had no friend they could go to in the day. One said, 'I'd just as soon sit at home. I'm in a rut. But then, it's not a bad rut, is it.' Nine mothers in these close families slept with an older child for company, one with a nineteen-year-old girl, another with a fourteen-year-old boy. Closeness of family ties and the children's nervousness about their mothers may partly account for five instances where children developed school phobia.

Poverty and the quality of relationships

Poverty sometimes increased mothers' troubles with their children. As we have seen, the mothers tried to give their children what they expected, even to the extent of great personal sacrifice. They went short of food; and one mother, unable to pay for her daughter's wedding, had given the daughter her three-piece suite and left herself with furniture fit only for the rubbish heap. But in spite of such sacrifices it seemed that mothers were not always able to fulfil their children's expectations. Where there was friction in the family the shortage of money served as a focus and irritant in family quarrels. One mother said wearily, 'Family life in the home is different. My children are different. If I could get them what they're used to having, it would be different altogether. People say money isn't everything, money isn't happiness. But it goes a long way.' Another said, 'They want this and they want that, and David is so resentful if they can't get it.' Mothers with delinquent children felt this was partly because the children were dissatisfied with their lot compared with other children. In a few instances, the mother's self-sacrifice had led to her demanding gratitude from her children, and had heightened her perceptions of ingratitude where perhaps there was only children's heedlessness. A divorced woman who did not want her daughters to marry said, 'They're not grateful. You can't make them grateful. It's somehow not clicked with them. They can't see that I count at all.' Children under such pressures, far from being grateful, seemed likely to become hostile and bitter, fighting for independence.

Even where family relationships were harmonious, for the working child living with the family on assistance could create a situation of tension. If the wage was swallowed up by the family's needs, the working child had less money than his friends. A number of sons, and four daughters who had later had illegitimate babies, were said to have left home early because they were dissatisfied with having to give up their wage. If the working child chose to stay at home and attempt to retain his or her wage, the visible difference between the child's standard of living and that of the rest of the family was difficult to sustain. It seemed likely that children in poor families would tend to marry early. The whole delicate balance of duties, obligation, expectations, and rewards, normal to and derived from a more affluent society, was seriously disturbed in families undergoing hardship, and it was not too much to say that shortage of money was contributing to the early break-up of the family.[6]

Further disruptions of family life

Fatherlessness brought in its train a host of further disruptions of family life, some of which were in themselves sufficient to cause severe emotional disturbance in the child. For instance, loss of the father often entailed temporary loss of the mother too. One mother described her daughter's reaction after a long separation.

My little girl's all mixed up about me. She said to me the other day, 'You're not my real mummy, are you.' When I first got them back she used to say when I put them to bed, 'Give us a kiss! Give us another! Give us another!' On and on like that, 'You won't go away will you?' And she didn't like going to school either. She'd say, 'Oh Mum, I don't like this school. We go twice as long to this school. I think about you all the time and I think so hard it gives me a headache and then I can't do my work.' When she comes home from school she's looking through the window when she comes down the path, to make sure I've not gone away.

This child had nightmares and was under sedation. Altogether, in the past a child or children had been away from the mother in twenty-three instances because of her health and in fifteen instances because of the child's health. There were a further twenty-five separations caused through children going into care,[7] through housing difficulties, because the husband took the child for a while, or because the child went to an approved school. At the time of the survey eleven children were still separated from their mothers for similar reasons.

In general mothers were reluctant to part with their children even for pressing operations, so the number of separations understated the extent of the families' difficulties over health and housing. However, a very few mothers from the largest families complained that they had made unsuccessful attempts to have the children put in Homes, so that they could have a rest for a week or two. For these and other women a holiday away from the children remained something to dream about. It seemed that more help from Child Care Departments might have reduced the risk of the mother's health breaking down completely.

The children were apt to suffer for the mother's ill-health even if the family did not split up. For instance, in sixteen families older children had been kept away from school to look after the mother: 'The School Board Man came round to see where they were. He wasn't too bad. He got a bit cross one morning. He said, what would I do if I hadn't got these, and I said to him, I shouldn't be here if I hadn't had them.' Mothers said the attendance officers had been unable to do anything about this. School children were kept off in preference to working children, so that a wage would not be lost.

Thus, the lack of a husband or father may also produce adverse results indirectly through the chain of difficulties for the mother which his absence creates.

Marriage or remarriage

What sort of solution did the mother's marriage or remarriage offer for the problems of the fatherless family? It is known that rates of remarriage among certain of the widowed and divorced are comparatively high. For example, on average a divorced woman under twenty-five years old will remarry within three years, and a widow of the same age within six years. However, the chances of remarriage drop sharply in a woman's early thirties,[8] and the women in the present survey differed from the average in having children. Moreover, a third of these mothers were still legally married and had yet to face the difficulties of divorce. In fact, at the time of the survey only a quarter of the mothers had a steady man-friend (including the fathers of illegitimate children) while half said they never even met any men. So that although very few of the families were likely to be completed by the return of the father, only a minority appeared to be in a situation where remarriage was a possibility. The decision even to look for a husband required the balancing of a number of conflicting pressures, and there were other impediments to finding a suitable man.

The mother's need to receive and give affection, her financial difficulties and problems in bringing up the children alone, and the social discomforts of the fatherless family could all constitute pressures towards remarriage. Goode has suggested that the lack of any institutionalized position in society for the mother with no husband functions effectively to deter her from remaining unmarried.[9] Kin and friends appeared to act with the separated and divorced mothers somewhat as they have been said to behave towards widows,[10] urging them after a while to forget the children's father and think of finding someone new. A separated wife said, 'My mother and father and sisters, they say to me, "You'll meet somebody else, you'll have a better time."' Another separated wife felt, 'I need that push, somebody to push me to get a divorce. I haven't got a mum to lean on, you see. I've come to the conclusion that women who go straight on to get a divorce are the ones who go to live with mum.' In several families kin or friends had arranged meetings between the mother and a man thought likely to make a suitable new husband. Possibly the one mother in six who persisted in her attachment to a long-departed husband could more easily do so because there was no strong network of kin and friends to urge a new relationship upon her.

Obstacles to remarriage

However, the pressures towards remarriage were accompanied by changes in social relationships which made remarriage more difficult. For various reasons the children were usually hostile to remarriage. Sometimes they were still strongly bound to their father. Alternatively, in his absence the family had changed to give the children a closer bond with their mothers which they would be jealous to relinquish, or a degree of independence which they valued. In nine families children, usually teenagers, had been hostile to their mother's man-friend, and two mothers had been advised by their doctors to get rid of their men-friends because of the nervous strain of such conflicts. A divorced mother said, 'With us being so close and with them drawing so close around me, I daren't really start courting, because anybody that came would have to be all right. He'd have to pass them before he could get to me.' So, more often, it seemed likely that the children deterred mothers from even beginning a courtship, forming a barrier around her.

Mothers lacked suitable places to meet men and mistrusted the motives and attitudes of those they did meet. A further difficulty was felt to be the restricted range of choice. Mothers thought that the 'marrying' kind of men in the age group must already have married. Unmarried men who were willing to marry women with children were suspected of merely looking for a mother figure. Once-married men who showed eagerness to remarry were suspected of calculating on a ready-made home. Some signs of restricted choice could be seen in the age gaps between women and their men-friends, the couple's ages differing in half the instances by five years or more, and in a quarter by ten years or more. There was often a suggestion of dissatisfaction with a current man-friend as being too immature, too old, or too ill; and even while courting, these mothers were looking over the man's shoulder to see if they could find someone better. Their sense of the rarity of a man who would combine all the qualities they required was expressed in the phrase 'a good man' or a 'kind man' (occasionally a 'soft man'). This implies, apart from a lack of excitement, a condescension and sacrifice on the man's part which showed that the mothers did not rate their marriage prospects very highly.

Even supposing the right man could be found there might remain a considerable financial disincentive to remarriage, especially where the women had a large family or a high rent, for upon marriage she would have to give up her national assistance allowance. One mother said, 'It would be no good me marrying an ordinary working man earning £15 a week. I want somebody to pull me out of this rut.' Another said she had written to Paul Getty, satirically proposing marriage. Women who were better off financially on national assistance than they had ever been with their husbands knew that marriage could bring an overall financial loss. But more than this it would bring loss of control of the money.

Remarriage, in fact, would mean a loss of independence in more than money matters. Women spoke of fears of being tied to a man who might turn out to be mean, brutal, unreliable, or mentally ill, or simply of the difficulty of once again being unable to please only themselves. Their first marriage had alerted them to the wife's subordinate role, and if they were to marry again, then the man must be worth it. Thus, although there did appear to be genuine practical difficulties to courtship and remarriage, it was also probable that the mothers, grown more choosy, tended to exaggerate them. After all, many unmarried girls would make similar complaints about men's intentions. Complaints about stigma seemed in part to reflect the mother's worries about her own sexuality and whether she was again open to sexual advances. The feeling that opportunities for meeting and choice were restricted may have been an indication that the mother had decided to cut her losses after one marriage and was opting out of the search.

Balancing pressures for and against remarriage

Confusion as to whether she was able and willing to remarry appeared in the mother's difficulty in defining her marital status. Older women were more likely to feel definitely that they were married, but younger women said they felt married only when with the children and single apart from them. A widow said, 'I'm neither one thing nor the other. I'm a mother, and when you put down your occupation, you put down housewife, but I'm not a wife any more.' Another woman defined her feelings of difference by noticing that she put on cosmetics during the day, unlike most married women she knew.

Social pressures demanded that mothers with children should wear a ring, so that taking the ring off signalized a definitive resolve in these circumstances, and usually indicated that a woman was once again seeking marriage or had definitely ended her first marriage. All the widows and almost all the separated wives wore rings, but only two thirds of the divorced and unmarried mothers did. Retaining a ring could be a sign of loyalty to the husband, but was also a mark of indecision: a woman said, 'I feel married and yet single. In another point, I know I'm free to go after another man if I see one, but I still wear a wedding ring.' Other women said they used their ring as a protection against 'wolves'. It allowed them to talk to a man and size him up before he got any idea that they were open to advances. Several women remarked that they had tried taking their ring off, but felt 'naked' without it. A divorced wife who did not wear a ring said it was a 'hypocrite', and she remarried shortly after the interview. It was easy to see why several of the younger unmarried mothers repeated the superstition that it was 'unlucky' to wear a wedding ring as their justification for not doing so.

When the pressures to remarry had been balanced against the obstacles, it appeared that only a quarter of the mothers actually wanted to remarry. Another quarter would be prepared to consider remarriage, but the impediments appeared too large or the moment had not yet arrived; while the remainder did not want to remarry. Obviously, the mother's admission that she would like to remarry was to some extent based upon her judgement of whether she had much chance of doing so.

Relationships other than marriage

Marriage was only one of a number of possible ways in which the family's need for a man could be met. Although only a quarter actively wished to marry, a proportion approaching two thirds of the mothers had varying need for a man: for financial and social security, sexual satisfaction, companionship, a loving father or disciplinarian for the children. These needs were sometimes incompatible and they did not always point to marriage.

The younger unmarried mothers were most consistent in wanting to marry for security, and for a 'name' and someone to care for them. Among the younger mothers in the groups described as an 'underclass' there were very frequent engagements, although apparently not with much hope of their coming to fruition: the mothers knew that if they became pregnant their soldier friends would probably get a posting, or if the father was a West Indian he could easily move to another town. Nevertheless, the girls who slipped into and out of sexual relationships and cohabitation were still hoping for marriage. Younger oncemarried women were also rather more likely to think of marriage in the double sense of a sexual relationship and a father for their young children if they could overcome the fear that the children of the first marriage might get pushed out by any offspring of a new marriage.

Other women thought in terms of some isolated aspect or aspects of the husband/father relationship, rather than the whole. Few said directly that they wanted a fuller sex-life, perhaps because the topic was not easily discussed with a male interviewer; also, contrary to the popular stereotype, far from missing sex, probably for many of them sexual experiences in marriage had been distasteful. The majority of mothers tended to see the sexual relationship as decidedly secondary to companionship, if indeed sex entered their calculations at all. Older women thought of someone to talk to in their old age, but not a lover. If they were severely pressed by problems with children, they also wanted a disciplinarian. A divorced mother with three teenage sons said, 'I don't just want anybody. I want somebody who'll understand the boys and talk to them, reason with them.' With a husband it would be easy to make a permanent mistake. He might be financially unreliable, a bully, sexually demanding, and yet a poor disciplinarian or totally uninterested in the children. And he could not easily be discarded if he turned out badly. The older mother's requirements could best be met by a carefully chosen male lodger – preferably, one mother felt, a policeman.

A few younger women who wanted an exciting relationship with a man had despaired of finding a lover who would be also a father to their children. For them several courses seemed attractive. Possibly they could keep any sexual attachments distant, or at least away from the home and their children. They felt that time was on their side, and they could still hope for marriage in the future when the children were independent. A second possibility was trial marriage or even a prolonged common-law marriage. A separated wife said:

I think it's a lot better to live 'over t'brush'[11] because then if you've got your own house, the man doesn't own you, and if he doesn't turn out right and he starts bashing you about, you can put him out. But if you're married to a man, the police won't do anything. If he starts hitting you, they say it's just a husband and wife quarrel.

This sort of arrangement also proved attractive to women who had experienced difficulties in the past trying to keep up appearances when a marriage was going wrong.

Thus of the one in two mothers who would not consider remarriage, one third still wanted their husband and another third said they were simply afraid. But there was a further third who would actually prefer common-law marriage to remarriage. For them one taste of legal marriage had been enough.

A caution: the consequences of fatherlessness

We are now in a position to understand why, in flat contradiction of the widely held stereotype of the 'broken home', there is very little conclusive evidence that absence of the father *in itself* has an adverse effect on a child. Research has often been inconclusive because of the incompetence or naivety of the research workers. But basically fatherlessness is not one but many situations, and absence of the father cannot be isolated from a whole range of other causes and consequences of fatherlessness.

Thus, after a very careful examination[12] of 400 pieces of research on boys in fatherless families (which is essential reading for anyone interested in fatherlessness) Herzog and Sudia concluded that the studies had not demonstrated any adverse effects of father absence either upon the boys' school experience or their 'masculinity', and that although the boys *might* be somewhat more likely to engage in delinquent acts there were other influences leading towards delinquency which would dwarf the influence of father absence. Herzog and Sudia pointed out a number of areas of variation which preclude any clear-cut differences between 'fatherless' and 'complete' families, and which reveal the extreme difficulty of isolating the influence of the father's absence. Father absence differs in *type*, being socially stigmatized or honoured, short or long, isolated or recurrent, preceded by calm or stress. Its impact will probably depend on the *child's age*. Research has frequently neglected the *loss of income*, and its attendant problems and stress, which so often accompany the loss of the father. Children's problems may result from *the stress of the father's presence* (happy broken homes induce less delinquency than unhappy intact homes), either before his absence or upon his return.

And perhaps above all, as the present research has suggested, so much depends on what might be called the *family climate* or *family functioning* and on the behaviour of the *mother*: absence of the father makes its impact very often primarily through the mother's reactions and the way she and her children adapt together. The loss of the father bore most heavily on the mothers, who tended to suffer from depression, tiredness, ill-health, and a sense of guilt; yet a minority of the mothers felt released. To a large extent the children were cushioned from the immediate impact of fatherlessness by their youth, lack of understanding, and the mother's ability and willingness to help the child come to terms with the new situation. As a result the experience of fatherlessness could be vastly different, and might be shaped by an image of the father persisting after his loss but bearing only a distant relation to the truth. Whether or not delinquent behaviour would be the result of a mother's lack of control, there were immediate problems for her in day-to-day living, and the alternative trend towards clinging and over-protective behaviour also boded badly for the children's later development.

However, we cannot confidently say that such family relationships are peculiar to fatherless families: they may be merely exaggerations, perhaps not very great, of what happens in many 'normal' families.

To stress in this way the lack of evidence of the adverse effects of father absence is not to imply that a good husband and father is of little importance: where he is present there is obviously more likelihood of all his various functions being performed well. But the stereotype of the broken home needs countering because in itself it contributes to, and expresses, the stigma of fatherlessness. To put the point carefully, not having a father *need* not be as bad as having one is good.[13] There are various ways in which aspects of his role may be performed by other men, and we must therefore beware of generalizing too glibly about families where there is no father in the home.

In conclusion: what is fatherlessness?

The complexity and variety of the situations described in the last four chapters must mean that there is no simple set of answers to the question posed at the beginning of this survey: what is fatherlessness? Indeed, has 'fatherlessness', or any other collective term such as 'mothers alone', any real meaning and usefulness; or does the usage merely obscure differences and reinforce stereotypes?

A term like 'fatherless' has a use and purpose in helping to break down the present rigid conventional divisions between mothers of different marital status, which is the way we have tended to think of fatherless families in the past. The discussions of broken marriages and illegitimate births have illustrated how artificial and superficial marital status may be, as an indication of a mother's real social situation. For example, it looked as though some of the early influences which had led to hasty and broken marriages might be the same as those leading to unmarried motherhood, the difference resting on whether the father could be persuaded, or was able, to marry. There was considerable movement between different marital statuses: some of the separated, divorced, and widowed women had been unmarried mothers, and some of the unmarried mothers had later married or would marry. There were similarities of situation: illegitimate children were born to separated and divorced as well as to unmarried women, and might be their only dependants. Unmarried mothers may have been 'married' to their children's fathers in a much more real sense of a continuing supportive relationship and for much longer than some separated and divorced wives. Conversely, within a given marital status, the situations encountered could be widely different.

Further, the present community and emotional situations of these families revealed more cross-cutting similarities and distinctions. Community and kinship relations were thrown out of gear, and awkwardness and stigma were not confined to the unmarried. There were separated wives who behaved as though they had suffered a bereavement, and widows and divorcees who felt liberated by the loss of their husbands.

All this suggests that instead of identifying families in a number of categories according to the mother's marital status, we would be involved in fewer misleading assumptions about their social honour and likely morale if we could adopt some more general description such as 'fatherless families'. Not the least powerful recommendation for the change – as will be argued in the concluding chapter – is that such a shift may be essential for any advance in social security provision for these families.

But the adoption of a single description to counter the present spurious and invidious distinctions will not be easily achieved and must not be allowed to create a new stereotype or to reinforce the old one of the 'broken home'. For there are, as we have seen, very real differences among the families. Most obviously the mothers' relationships with the children's fathers were at different stages, the mothers were in different states of health, of different age, with different numbers of children, at different stages of the family cycle, more or less securely established financially and domestically. Less tangibly, the attitudes of the mothers and children towards the mother's remarriage, and the various ways in which the family had adjusted to the loss of the father, reveal that we might begin to think of father absence along a number of 'dimensions'. We might think of loss of a good husband and father as a lack – of economic support, companionship, a sexual relationship for the mother, an audience for her to play her role, a child-minder, a craftsman about the home, an authority figure or goal-achiever, a model as father and worker, a playmate for the children, an initiator of adult roles, a unit in the family and neighbourhood networks, and so on. The ideal father would provide all these family dimensions, and merely to list them in this way is to stress the deficiencies of many families where the father is present. But conversely where the father is absent, many of these dimensions of husband or father behaviour might be made up by some other man or even by a woman or child, although without actual marriage no male sexual partner of the mother can ever fill the father's slot in the kinship structure of the extended family.

Thus, while there may be very pressing reasons why we

should want to use a description like 'fatherless families' to describe families with no resident father, we must not lose the sense of the variety of human situations and needs which such a term can cover.

Finally it should be stressed, however, that although the mothers of the present survey had many problems in common, there was no evidence that they themselves were yet prepared to think of 'fatherless families' as a group. Rather, they used much narrower criteria. Thus, the younger unmarried mothers thought of themselves as 'young girls in trouble' or 'young girls with babies'. There was also some community of feeling among widows. And divorced and separated wives were brought together by their common problems of getting maintenance from their husbands. But between these groups there was hostility which would block any suggestion of a community of interest. Widows were felt by the others to receive preferential treatment with their pensions and the favourable earnings rule, and generally to be better off in terms of home-owning and the possession of furniture. Widows in their turn tended to share the view that separated and divorced women were loose and undeserving of state support. The separated and divorced mothers tended to distinguish among themselves between those who were 'innocent' and those who had 'done wrong'. Some of the unmarried, while admitting their own blameworthiness, pointed to their loyalty to their children and the children's gratitude as their expiation, and asserted that what they had done affected only their own lives, whereas separated and divorced women had sometimes broken up the homes of others as well as their own. Even among mothers in the underclass there were jealousies.

Apart from these feelings of mutual hostility, mothers applied different standards to those in a similar plight to themselves, according to their luck or toughness and how they faced up to the problems of fatherlessness. Thus one woman said,

Don't make me out to be too pathetic, it's not too serious, it's a bit depressing but I don't think about it much. Really I'm very lucky. I'm not like some of these little women who get left by their husband, they're so *defeated*.

So, with individual exceptions, in spite of their personal situation these mothers displayed little perception of the general problems of fatherlessness as I have described them, and surprisingly little sympathy for the plight of others. Lacking a wide acquaintance with the problems they drew on the community stereotypes which this study has questioned.

This account of the past and present personal and social situations of the fatherless families has been an attempt to provide the context which Part One had shown was essential for any discussion of living standards and deprivation. A major theme has been the informal influences of kin and community on the lives of these mothers and children. We now turn in Part Three to an exploration of the more formal help available to the families: the provision of local authority housing, legal assistance for actions against the children's fathers, and income from the National Assistance Board.

Part Three
Help from the Community

CHAPTER NINE

Local Authority Housing and Voluntary Schemes

The most pressing problem for a number of families had been where to live, and while kin helped with temporary accommodation this was far from satisfactory as a long-term solution. At the time of the interviews over half the families were living in council housing, and this might appear to indicate that the local authorities were providing an invaluable social service in supporting fatherless families who fell into difficulties. However, a closer look at mothers' past and present housing difficulties showed that provision for rehousing fell short of mothers' needs.

Only the widows had had few housing problems: they were already owner-occupiers or council tenants when their husbands died, several having been rehoused on account of the husband's terminal illness. Twelve widows had been council tenants at widowhood, and only two had transferred tenancies since.

The situation of divorced and separated mothers had been, and continued to be, more precarious. One third of them had been faced with the task of finding a new home when they parted from their children's father: twenty-one had actually left the marital home, but in addition five tenancies had ended with the marriage breakdown, and one middle-class mother had no longer been able to pay her mortgage. The mothers who had fared best among the separated and divorced had been lucky in that some of the home owners had had a joint share in the house when they were married, or they had been able to persuade their husbands to sell out to them, in five instances with money from relatives. The assistance of the local housing authority in bringing about a swift change of tenancy or eviction of the husband has already been mentioned.

Unmarried mothers tended to be in the worst plight, twelve,

or almost half, having to find new accommodation: this was not because kin had always turned out those who had left home, for in two instances there was overcrowding which prevented the mother from staying at home with her child. Nevertheless, only two mothers had had a secure tenancy when their child was conceived.

Homelessness

Families lacking help from kin had experienced the worst problems. Three mothers had taken 'housekeeping' jobs, which proved to be very hard work with little food and pay, or merely invitations to cohabit. Eight other families were split because the mother could not keep her children with her when she went into inadequate accommodation. Thus, a mother had taken one child with her when she left her husband in May one year, in July she took a second child and later took a third. But by November all three children were in care because she had been found sleeping in one double bed with them. This was not the end of her troubles, and she said, 'They've been in and out of homes till they're sick of it. It would break their hearts now if they hear about going into a home.'

The suddenness of the marriage breakdown, or the difficulty of finding accommodation with several small children and little money, had meant that eight families had become homeless in the past and were placed in local authority hostels (it will be recalled that this survey understates the incidence of homelessness by excluding those currently homeless from the sample).

An unmarried mother had first of all taken a housekeeping job, but becoming homeless she had gone to London to the Salvation Army hostel. She was turned away, but went from there to Newington Lodge. She stayed there and in another hostel for eighteen months, during the first four of which she and the children had to walk the streets because they were not allowed in the hostel in the day-time. The local authority struck her off the housing list in Seaston, because it was claimed she was no longer a resident or worker in the area, and only the intervention of the N.A.B. and welfare authorities got her a place in a temporary list from which she was rehoused after six months.

The mothers who had become homeless were appalled by the hostel population and lack of amenities there. Another unmarried mother said:

Oh, it's a terrible place is that, you're not allowed to put anything on the walls, and you've not allowed to have anything on the floors. And one winter the wind blew the glass out at one end and they wouldn't be bothered to repair it, so the glass blew out the other end and there was a howling gale blowing through. There was all sorts of people in there, swearing, and the language! People who'd been in prison. I got really down, I did get as though I didn't want to live. They thought I'd taken tablets to kill myself, but I hadn't. I just went to sleep one night, and I didn't wake up for two days, it was just that I'd lost the will to live.

There was a dreadful irony about some of these housing histories. Several mothers had tried desperately to have their children fostered or taken into care permanently or at least for a few weeks so that they could get a rest. But a mother who had twice been homeless (once when she left her husband, once when the house in which she was living was demolished) recalled,

They came to pull the house next door to ours down and they pulled one of the slates off the roof, and after that the rain came down the wall, so I went to see the cruelty man. But all he could do was take my babies away, and I said, 'Oh no, you won't take my babies away,' and I walked away. And I walked right on to St James's (the old workhouse) at the other end of town, to see if I could get accommodation there. But they said no, they could take my babies away, and I said, 'You will *not* take my babies away,' and I was really very ill myself, but I thought, 'I'm not giving up.' Anyway all they could do was to put me on the priority, get onto the Housing. The next morning the doctor came down to see me. Well, he looked at this, and he looked at the wet bed, and I was walking over, kind of bent, and he asked me what was the matter with me. I said I'd got rheumatism in my arm, and he said, 'Who sleeps in this bed?' Well, I'd pushed the babies over to the other side because I couldn't have them sleeping in the wet, and I slept in this damp bed. Well, he did swear, did that doctor. He said, 'What the bloody hell is this, trying to take your babies away, and you sleeping in a wet bed.' He said, 'If they gave

V.C.'s to mothers, you'd get one. You ought to have been a soldier, and all they can do is to take your babies away.'

Seaston used a county hostel, which meant that mothers becoming homeless in Seaston were passed over from the borough housing office to the county. There appears to have been a certain amount of evasion of the mother's problems by Seaston council officials, who referred mothers to the county office with the suggestion that they would be found accommodation, but failed to indicate that the only prospect was the hostel for the homeless.

Rehousing

Of the sixty-six families in council housing at the time of the interview, thirty-one, or almost half, had been rehoused while fatherless. The reasons given by the families for rehousing illustrate the extent of their past problems. Nine were top of the waiting list; but nine were rehoused when their previous house was condemned, nine because of serious overcrowding, six were homeless, and in four families the child's or mother's health was suffering (a few families gave several reasons). However, those among the mothers who had gained council houses did so only through exceptional backing from welfare authorities, doctors, or health pressure groups such as the Society for the Deaf or the Tuberculosis Fund. Thus while the rate of rehousing was high, perhaps it should have been higher. Mothers were almost powerless without some kind of official support for their case.

There was some evidence that the council housing authorities were reluctant to give fatherless families houses because they were a poor economic risk. One mother said, 'They said they couldn't give me a house, not in my financial condition. In my financial condition!'

She said she was helped by a councillor in getting her house. Whether discrimination also involved a mother's supposed moral status was more difficult to assess. The Northborough authorities maintained that there was no bar in gaining a house if the mothers had the requisite qualifications of hardship and residence. But this meant the larger families and the older mothers would more often qualify, and the younger unmarried mothers and mothers with illegitimate children would not. A few mothers said that only the poorest council housing was offered. In both areas of the survey the fatherless families were concentrated on certain estates well known to be the most inferior in terms of accommodation and status. The housing policy of both Northborough and Seaston was to place rougher and problem families together, and among these the fatherless families appeared to be classed. The exteriors of the houses were smoke-blackened or decayed and peeling pebbledash. The gardens were untended. Walking up the road to some of the interviews I found myself trying to estimate the proportion of broken windows. One woman, shortly after being rehoused from her old damp cottage, was bitterly regretting that she had ever moved, and feared that she and her family would be seriously injured during the period when the local children were testing out how far they could go with her.

The most insecure mothers – the underclass

The mothers of illegitimate children who had lost contact with kin and were living in a strange area were particularly vulnerable. They lacked a relative's house to stay in. They were without a large network of kin and friends who could search out and speak for cheap housing for them. They lacked a settled mode of existence which made them eligible for the normal procedures of rehousing. They moved frequently to try to find less expensive and more healthy surroundings, but with little success over the years.

One unmarried mother had lived with a friend on a caravan site, slept rough, lived with a mentally unstable woman, then with a friend, then in rooms alone, then moved back to the unstable woman's house, then to her present lodgings; all since arriving in the Seaston district. The movements of West Indian mothers were also frequent and almost unpredictable, as the mothers themselves said. Even moving so frequently, the mothers could not avoid exploitation, and time and again the name of one notorious landlady cropped up in their conversations. 'She gets all these places and they're dirty and scruffy, but she lets them to the Army and girls with children that she knows are desperate. She gets away with murder that woman!' Of all the mothers, the divorced and separated mothers of illegitimate children only had moved most frequently, averaging almost four moves each during the lifetime of their young children.

The sheer frequency of these moves defeated attempts to rehouse the mothers. After I had finally located an unmarried mother at her second change of address since the sample was drawn, she claimed to have been neglected by the housing authorities, but it turned out that she had been sent an offer of a house while she was in hospital, and letters simply were not passed on to her. Another mother had also applied for a house, but the correspondence had been lost because she had moved five times since then. She finally obtained a house by staying put in bad conditions until the council had time to work.

This group of the most vulnerable mothers were the 'under-class'. They had difficulties in obtaining council housing because of their small families and frequent moves. But in any case they were reluctant even to apply for a council tenancy, for they mistrusted authority, and in some ways preferred their present way of life. One unmarried mother was quite convinced. 'They don't give houses to the likes of me.' Without material and moral support from kin and friends they could not get together enough furniture and confidence to take a council house, and they did not know they might be eligible for furniture grants from the N.A.B. Fatherless families were regarded by furniture shops as a poor H.P. risk, and one mother of an illegitimate child described how lacking kin and friends she had been reduced to getting furniture off a rubbish tip.

I got my coal scuttle down there, and two washing-up bowls, and some little toys. I have a walk down there every day. And one time there was a nice man came up in a car and he was looking round a bit furtively, and he rolled a whole lot of stuff down. I thought, 'That looks nice stuff,' so I went to have a look and I said to him, 'Do you mind if I take some,' and he said, 'No, it's all right mate', he said, 'I'm just moving and we can't get rid of it. I'm bringing a mattress in a bit,' and it was a nice mattress. He brought some other stuff, shirts and jeans.

Mothers who occasionally lived with men felt that there would be too many rules and regulations, and too much interference from neighbours. But at a deeper level these mothers felt there was something too final about taking a council house and setting up a home alone. This would be an admission that the prospects of marriage and making a home with a husband had permanently receded.

Two studies of homelessness

Two recent reports on homelessness in London and in other areas of Britain[1] confirm the findings of the present survey and demonstrate on a wider scale the vulnerability of the fatherless family to homelessness and other housing difficulties. According to Professor Greve, 'Domestic friction was identified as the major cause of homelessness in 34 per cent of the sample of homeless families in the study of South Wales and the South West compared with 13 per cent of the London sample of admissions.'[2] Indeed Glastonbury suggested that for the South Wales study as many as one third to two thirds of homeless families were actually or potentially fatherless.[3] The studies underline the fact that fatherless families experience a number of different kinds of problems related to the mother's economic and legal dependency.

Thus Glastonbury observed that 'for the unsupported mother the experience of homelessness often stemmed from the straightforward reaction of the housing authority or the landlord . . . A woman at the head of the household was generally reckoned to be uncreditworthy and therefore at serious risk of getting into rent arrears. For this reason she might well have difficulty in getting the tenancy of a dwelling, whether from a private or council landlord.'[4] This is on top of the widespread discrimination against children by landlords.

Not only were landlords and councils reluctant to give women the tenancy of a house or flat, but as Greve says,

Most authorities were reluctant to give accommodation (in a hostel) in cases where marital disputes had resulted in the woman leaving home with her children, or her wanting to do so. Of 59 applications of this kind recorded in the survey, the 24 which were considered to warrant admission were mainly either night emergency cases or cases where the family had broken up some time previously. Admission was much less likely where the woman had left home very recently or where she was asking for accommodation to enable her to leave, the standard advice being that the woman should go back home or go to the Probation Officer to discuss a Separation Order.[5]

Glastonbury found,

In the survey there were accounts of wives admitted to temporary accommodation at their doctor's request to recover from quite severe beatings; there were husbands who threw their dinner at the wall or the furniture or out of the window; there was an attempted strangling and a knife fight in which the husband was stabbed in the stomach. This suggested the occasional need of a temporary refuge for families for a few days, but the problem was an unpopular one for official or police interference, and at least one authority responded to a growing demand by deciding that ill-treated wives no longer qualified for admission. They said that the wife in almost every case returned home voluntarily after one or two nights in hostel, and that therefore such women were not technically homeless.[6]

Thus among the reasons for refusing entry to a hostel in South Wales was 'the case was a marriage breakdown where the applicant was expected to return very soon to the family home.'[7] On the other hand, against the general trend of non-involvement, Glastonbury found that,

Two of the six local authorities covered by the survey openly used the hostel as a place in which the wife, often with the support of the social worker, could think through the marriage situation and decide what action should be taken in the best interests of herself and her children. If it was felt that separation should lead to divorce and an entirely different domestic arrangement, then that could be arranged from the hostel.[8]

These two surveys confirm the finding of an earlier chapter that the husband's possession of the tenancy meant that many marriage breakdowns were therefore sudden and created a crisis where the mother and children became homeless. Glastonbury says,

Under these circumstances it was quite normal for the first warning of the breakdown to come through the police. Although the police would bring in the welfare and housing authorities at the earliest possible time, it was usually too late to make any arrangement other than admitting the wife and children to a temporary accommodation hostel. It probably has to be accepted that there will always be a substantial number of families who become homeless so rapidly that no preventive action can be taken, and no emergency activity on the part of the police or any social worker could oblige the man to give up his tenancy. . . In fact landlords showed a good deal of reluctance in handing over tenancies to women, because they were reckoned to be less credit worthy and less liable to be regular payers of rent than men. The transfer of a tenancy to a wife tended therefore to be the result of prolonged negotiations between the landlord and the social agency.[9]

Both Greve and Glastonbury quote instances where, as a result of this tangle, men remained in large council houses because they were good tenants in the housing office's estimation, while their wives and six or seven children had to go into hostels for the homeless or even into care.[10] Evidently there will be occasional tricky problems where the father's rights have to be considered, but on the whole the balance of local housing authority activity seems against the rights of the mother and children.

Transferring tenancies can become very complex because it involves the state of the marriage, the rights of the father as opposed to the rights of the mother and children, and the interests of a number of agencies such as the housing authorities, the Children's Department, and the Supplementary Benefits Commission. Glastonbury says that the sincerity of the break between the couple might be questioned by the S.B.C. (who would now be called upon to pay the rent). There might be rent arrears in the husband's name, which made difficulties for the wife with the local authority. Probation Officers were concerned about 'the increasing number of husbands who sought advice because they were threatened with eviction by their wives.'[11] One development noted by Glastonbury was that some mothers had to enter into tenancy agreements which specifically excluded the husband as a cohabitee, while there were cases of women being evicted and penalized for their husbands' behaviour who could dissociate themselves from it only by a formal separation which was sometimes denied. Wives of convicted criminals were sometimes offered a transfer of tenancy if they would officially separate.[12] Glastonbury found that 'Encouragement to make separations permanent sometimes became quite strong. Mrs Willard, for example, was offered help with rehousing, virtually the promise of a house, if she would formalize the separation from her husband. More commonly the hostel was used following temporary marriage breakdowns, resulting in some kind of reconciliation.'[13]

We are seeing here the spasmodic, unsystematic, and often reluctant involvement of local authorities and various other groups in the control of marriage breakdown. In a situation of housing shortages, where there is discrimination against women and children and where women have scarce resources, those who control housing tenancies and the payment of rent are willy-nilly involved in deciding whether or not a marriage shall be permitted or even encouraged to break down. But unfortunately the strictly economic criteria which are often applied to promote the regular payment of rents seem hardly to take a broad enough view of what is in the best interests of the marriage and the family.

Greve concludes that in spite of the needs of fatherless families having been brought to the attention of local authorities in 1955 and 1959 and again in 1967, when it was recommended that in the interests of children local authorities should try to provide low-rent accommodation for them, little has been achieved on their behalf: 'Perhaps an association between husbandlessness and being an "unsatisfactory tenant" has had unfortunate effects on allocation of local authority tenancies to mothers and children only.'[14]

Housing schemes for fatherless families

It is clear from the figures of overcrowding and lack of amenities among fatherless families that such families are a disadvantaged group, in so far as they are forced into the poor accommodation of the privately rented sector. As we have seen, compared with complete families their needs can occur very suddenly, the families are disadvantaged economically and because they contain children, and they lack the social contacts and physical mobility which might enable them to find a reasonable house on the private market. They also lack the resources for key money and rent in advance. The description of local authority housing has shown inadequacies in the present community housing schemes. How can these deficiencies be mitigated?

Fatherless families should be recognized as a special need category. This would involve more systematic rent support schemes in conjunction with the Supplementary Benefits Commission (or under the proposed new schemes of rent-subsidy for private tenants)[15] and also the more generous provision of housing for this type of family. Merely to treat them by the same cumbersome housing points scheme as other families is effectively to discriminate against them.[16]

However, the ideal of rent support and positive discrimination in a public housing scheme may be running too far ahead of public opinion at this stage. Ordinary council housing must still fill the major needs, but as an alternative more voluntary housing schemes could be set up, and there seems to be increasing interest in this field. Holman has suggested the conversion of the increasingly unpopular Mother and Baby Homes to this use.[17] Here the experiences of two societies, Catholic Housing Aid[18] and the Family First Trust of Nottingham, will be useful.

The Catholic Housing Aid Scheme (now merged with Shelter into S.H.A.C.) recognizes, on the basis of its experience, some characteristic problems of fatherless families in the provision it makes. The Society buys houses, usually for conversion into two flatlets and never more than one house to a street, on 100 per cent mortgages from the L.C.C. The Supplementary

Benefits Commission after some demur now pays the full economic rent in the mother's allowance (this is essential because otherwise the mothers or the Society have a steady drain on their resources). The housing is permanent for as long as the mother wants it, and if she wishes to marry she will be found accommodation to move into. Welfare help from voluntary visitors is available *if the mother wants it*. In no sense is this surveillance, and any voluntary society, particularly a religious society, will have to come to terms with the fact that some of these mothers will have sexual relationships outside marriage. Special provision is made for West Indian families, where it is recognized that there will probably be more children and more space will be needed.

A major feature of the C.H.A.S. scheme is that it requires cash subsidies of about £1 a week per family, even though much built-in durable furniture is provided. The mothers are often unable to do repairs, and they have crises not covered by their supplementary benefit when shoes and clothing must be provided.

The only doubtful feature of this scheme is that families are selected. Mothers must be of proven stability and capability, and while C.H.A.S. argues that this is essential, such selection must be difficult to operate. There is a problem, too, that if mothers for reasons of privacy are dispersed geographically, there is less opportunity to provide the child-minding services which are essential if the mother is to go out to work. However, London is better provided than many areas in this respect.

Two features of the Nottingham scheme are interesting. The Family First Trust has a furniture store where mothers are able to buy good furniture, donated to the Trust, at reduced prices. This fulfils the mother's needs while preserving her self-respect, and it also pays the subsidy to the housing scheme. The policy here as in London is that the families deserve good standard accommodation and this is actually cheaper to maintain in the long run.

A revolutionary feature of the Family First scheme is that it has been used overtly to provide accommodation for mothers who wish to separate temporarily from their husbands so that the marriage relationship can be resumed on a more equal footing. Obviously there are legal complications here which the Trust has had to solve, to avoid the woman losing her grounds for maintenance. It is argued that this opportunity to leave gives the wife greater bargaining power, and can lead to an improvement in the marriage relationship.

Fatherless families will continue to need help with housing until their income needs and the regional shortages of houses are solved on a wider scale. Meanwhile these voluntary schemes are evidently important, but we must conclude that as yet they deal only inadequately with the housing problems of the fatherless. Above all there are nowhere near enough schemes and accommodation to cater for the needs of all the homeless or potentially homeless families. And, in particular, experiments are still required with different kinds of schemes and publicity before we can effectively reach and help the group I have called the 'underclass'. Also, as long as mothers and children remain at such a disadvantage in the housing market, there ought to be more explicit recognition of the constraints on the mother's freedom to end a marriage which is intolerable and harmful to herself and the children. In the last resort there is a need for accommodation for the wife to escape from a dead marriage, in contrast to the present arrangements which seem designed to keep wives subordinate to their husbands' domination.

CHAPTER TEN

Family Law for the Poor

Unless the father was prepared to support his family the mother had to take legal action against him to procure maintenance, alimony, or an affiliation order. The low level of support from living fathers was a major factor in the dependence of these fatherless families on assistance, and this chapter will explore what had gone wrong with legal procedures, or what in the situations of these mothers made them unsuccessful at law. It must be remembered that the mothers came on assistance precisely because they had procured so little support, and they therefore represent, say, the half of the mothers with the lowest incomes who meet the law at its most ineffectual. Although numbers are small, it is also hoped than an account of the mothers' experience with the former divorce law will make a useful contribution to assessing the likely human consequences of the reformed divorce law which came into effect in 1971. In this field of the law there is still a crippling lack of detailed and systematic 'consumer' studies.

Some unexplored areas of the law

Women's difficulties in obtaining support from their husbands after separation, or from the fathers of their illegitimate children, have a long history.[1] In the past a woman lost all legal rights in marriage – her legal existence was suspended – and children, too, had no rights on their father. The development of procedures and grounds for divorce, separation, maintenance, and affiliation exhibit a considerable reluctance and ambivalence on society's part concerning the provision of escape routes from marriage, or of maintenance for women and children outside the conventional family unit. Currently there is more emphasis on reconciliation procedures, and the probation service is statutorily involved in marriage counselling. But in the past society's ambivalence has emerged more characteristically in deterrence or denial: in a reluctance to extend the grounds for, or facilitate access to, divorce and separation, or to establish clearly the father's duty to maintain his dependants. Nevertheless, recurring fears that destitute fatherless families would become a burden on the 'parish' have produced a number of changes in the laws relating to the father's duty; and at the same time humanitarian and moral considerations have dictated that some escape route of matrimonial relief should be provided and made ever broader. More and more marriages which were ended in fact have been ended in law by contrived dissolution or separation – just how contrived some of the later discussion of grounds for divorce will make clear.

But avenues of matrimonial relief did not open up equally for all social classes. Since the beginning of the century there has been a shift in the pattern of legal actions, from separation to divorce. McGregor has traced out the change in the proportions of couples separating (before a magistrate) and divorcing (in the high court): in the past,

The well-off went to the high court and there received relief in the form of a licence to marry again and poor wives went with the petty criminals to the magistrates' courts which gave maintenance, licensed non-cohabitation, but kept the marriage bonds intact. At the beginning of this century some 93 per cent of all applications for matrimonial relief were heard by magistrates; a generation ago the figure was 76 per cent and is today 45 per cent.[2]

As a result the divorcing population is now a wider cross-section of the community and there are more working-class divorces.[3] Also, during the century from 1858 to 1957 there has been a fifty-fold increase in the number of divorce petitions, but as has been pointed out above because of the changing pattern this cannot be taken as an indication of a rise in broken marriages. Rowntree and Carrier have estimated[3] that a five-fold increase in divorce was due to the lowering of formal legal barriers so that divorce is now more accessible to the poor and to women petitioners. The remaining ten-fold increase they attribute to a growing acceptance, by society and individual couples, of divorce as a solution to marital problems (as we saw in Chapter Five, this acceptance may now have changed to a new trend of increased numbers of breakdowns). A major influence in recent years has been the Legal Aid and Advice Act of 1949, which provided that full financial help should be available for those who wanted divorce but had insufficient means to pay for a legal action.

The latest liberalization of the divorce law resulted from increasing concern over the operation of the law which was current at the time of the present survey, a concern which led to a compromise between the Church and the Law Commissioners in the Divorce Reform Act.[4] Prior to this reform, divorce law embodied the legal fiction that a marital 'offence' must have been committed by one spouse against the other. Only the injured party might be granted a divorce, and only if a wife was adjudged 'innocent' might she claim financial support for herself. Couples could not, and still cannot, legally get a divorce by mutual consent or through mutual agreement to furnish or simulate grounds, such agreement being classed as collusion. However, the fact that nine tenths of petitions are undefended exposes this particular fiction. Proportions of male and female petitioners have varied, but currently about three fifths are women, the most frequently used grounds for divorce being adultery and desertion, and, virtually by women only, cruelty.[5]

In practice, pressure of business in the law courts means that any new divorce law cannot move very far away from the old procedure which led to a very high proportion of quick, undefended petitions. Any alternative procedure requiring a thorough investigation of the state of the marriage relationship (whether or not such an investigation would be desirable and feasible) would take so much time that the backlog of work would soon choke the courts and effectively make divorce more, rather than less, difficult. The new Divorce Act has thus virtually retained the marital offences of cruelty, adultery, and desertion, while changing its wording to dub them causes or evidences of 'marital breakdown'.[6] However, this is a significant move away from the concept of the marital offence and the apportionment of 'guilt', and a separation of two years will be taken as evidence of breakdown from either petitioner, provided the other does not object, while a separation of five years may be evidence of breakdown even if one partner, for example a deserted wife, does object. In other words, spouses who would formerly have been adjudged guilty of a marital offence and therefore unable to petition for divorce are now permitted to do so.

This is the most controversial measure. In its support the changes should bring about the legitimation of up to 200,000 illegitimate children born in stable unions where one parent is prevented from divorcing by the present law.[7] Against the new measures, the plight of the 'innocent' wife is brought forward; the Act has been called a 'Casanova's Charter' and it is claimed that the wife stands to lose financially. Disagreement thus rests on the adequacy of provision for the support of wives who are divorced against their will, and on speculations about the justice of divorce in relation to the behaviour of the couple in marriage. It was undoubtedly true that up to the new Divorce Act, despite easier access to divorce and legal aid and the fact that grounds for separation and divorce overlap, many separated wives have not gone on to divorce.[8]

Interest therefore centres on whether the barrier to divorce has remained financial (people perhaps being unaware of legal aid provisions) or in the law itself (with the legal grounds not correctly or adequately affording divorce), or whether in fact there were a substantial number of women for whom there was no barrier to divorce save their sense of injustice or their reluctance. It is here that, hopefully, the present small survey will throw some light.

The procedures of separation require investigation even more urgently than those for divorce. Grounds for separation are similar to those which were current for divorce, but the action takes place in a magistrates' court and is almost exclusively directed by the wife against the husband for maintenance, and also, less frequently, for permission to live apart.[9] Also in contrast to divorce proceedings, the grounds of complaint are predominantly desertion and wilful neglect to maintain, with some allegations of cruelty but relatively few of adultery.[10] Action cannot be taken unless the husband can be found and served with a summons.

As with maintenance payments in divorce actions, if the husband is in arrears with payment he can be imprisoned, and in the magistrates' court the machinery for enforcement is less cumbersome and much more frequently used. In fact up to 1958 when provision was first made for the attachment of the husband's earnings (that is, automatic deduction of the maintenance order from the husband's wage), very large numbers of men were imprisoned, as many as a quarter of all husbands with maintenance orders being committed – some 3,000 men each year. Attachment of earnings brought some reduction in this figure but imprisonment for arrears of maintenance still continues, and rose again to 3,500 in 1965 from magistrates' courts, but only a handful from the high court.[11]

Affiliation proceedings, to obtain maintenance for illegitimate children, are also heard in magistrates' courts and involve a procedure of summons and the possibility of imprisonment for default in payment, although for various reasons only 3 per cent of fathers of illegitimate children with affiliation orders were imprisoned.[12]

According to the recent authoritative survey of magistrates' courts, by Bedford College, those who use the courts remain a different population from those who divorce.[13] They are, in fact, predominantly the wives of lower-paid manual workers. Possibly for this reason, legislation has focused attention on divorce, which is exclusively a matter for the higher courts, but the magistrates' courts, which cannot grant divorces but which deal with more than 30,000 applications for maintenance each year, have been left largely untouched by legal reforms. Prior to the Bedford survey, which rests mainly on documentary evidence and which was published four years after the completion of the fieldwork for the present survey, there existed no information about this system of handling broken marriages, apart from some inadequate statistics which appeared in the annual *Criminal Statistics*. In view of this dearth of evidence, here again was an area where the present survey could make a contribution. We now turn to the survey evidence.

The lack of legal protection for the mothers

The lack of legal protection for the mothers appeared in a number of ways. Not all the mothers had obtained maintenance from the fathers of their children. Of the separated and divorced women still with dependent legitimate children, two thirds had a maintenance order for both themselves and the children. But allowing for two voluntary payments, this still leaves ten women with no support, and ten with an award for the children only. Parallel information for mothers of illegitimate children shows a still lower rate of support: only twenty-two children, or less than a third, were covered by a court affiliation order. Allowing for eighteen voluntary payments by the fathers, this still means that almost half these illegitimate children received no support from the father.

Lack of any award or support for the divorced or separated mothers meant in eight instances that no court action for maintenance had been taken, usually because the father could not be found. A much higher proportion of mothers of illegitimate children had not taken court action. Of the thirty-nine mothers with no award, thirty-six had never taken court action: eighteen of these fathers could not be found.[14]

Possession of an award, even for the mother as well as the children, did not insure an adequate living standard, for compared with what could have been claimed the awards were small in size. This was not because the maximum permissible awards were low – although they were (and the limit has since been removed) – but because the courts made awards which seldom approached the then maximum.[15] In seventy-three instances where orders had been made the maximum possible total award would have been £720, but the awards totalled only £217: that is, on average they were only 30 per cent of the maximum, at £3 4s. per order. Only three orders were sufficient to maintain the family near assistance levels. In two instances, where the maximum award could have been £20, mothers were awarded as little as £4, and one mother with a possible maximum of £17 10s. was given only £1. Mothers of illegitimate children were never awarded more than £1 of the permissible £2 10s. It must be remembered, also, that these were only awards and not actual payments by the father, which were usually lower.

Lack of support from fathers who did not pay voluntarily could thus be initially attributed to the failure of the mother, particularly if she was unmarried, to take court action; to the partial failure from the mother's point of view of a small proportion of the actions which had been taken; but mainly to the low level of awards made by the courts.

Mothers' failure or reluctance to sue for maintenance

Mothers were unlikely to fail to take separation or affiliation proceedings for maintenance where these were at all feasible, because the National Assistance Board had a statutory duty to attempt to recoup from the father the amount of the allowance in payment to his dependants. N.A.B. officers devoted much time and effort to unravelling what were often delicate and complex cases, and pressed mothers to sue in person, since the mother could claim a larger amount than the national assistance allowance and possession of a court order was a step towards her independence. (A court order obtained by the mother herself would continue whether or not she was on assistance, whereas a court order obtained by the Board would lapse when the mother no longer drew an assistance allowance.) The N.A.B. was also concerned with some divorces: four fifths of the currently divorced women had been divorced without a previous separation, so that maintenance was first claimed during the divorce action. But the Board had no financial interest in helping the divorce of women who already had a court order, although should a separated wife apply for legal aid they were called upon to assess her resources. The N.A.B. proved to be the major (but unacknowledged) agency channelling legal advice to mothers, and, because of their intervention, failure to take court action was almost invariably attributable to the husband's disappearance or the mother's lack of grounds.[16]

However the N. A. B. gave advice only to women coming on to assistance, and there had been delays in taking legal action prior to this because of mothers' lack of knowledge of the law.[17] These mothers had needed legal advice much sooner, during their marriages, and if they had had such advice many of the marriages would have broken sooner, perhaps with a more satisfactory outcome for the mother financially. Only seven, or fewer than one in ten, of the working-class mothers had been to a solicitor themselves while the marriage was in being. Any direct approach had required some pushing from a Probation Officer or other official or professional worker, such as a doctor, the N.S.P.C.C. officer, a health visitor, or an almoner. Reluctance to go to law was overcome only in the most desperate straits. By contrast four, or half, of the middle-class mothers already had a family solicitor: however, two of these women paid for advice by selling jewellery because the lawyers omitted to inform them of legal aid.

Failing a direct approach to a lawyer, mothers probably gained most early help from the Probation Service, part of whose duties are marriage counselling. Even so, only one in ten mothers had been to the Probation Officer for advice on marriage problems.[18] These were instances where counselling had failed to reconcile the couple permanently, although the Probation Officer had the advantage, as an official, of being able to see both wife and husband, and several temporary reconciliations had been brought about. Although the same proportion of mothers, one in ten, had been to see a Marriage Guidance Counsellor, there seemed to be inherently less chance of success in these families. As with visits to the Probation Officer, advice was sought late and things had deteriorated too far. But also, where one of the spouses (in two instances a husband who may have been mentally ill) had been to see the counsellor, the other spouse was not willing and could not be forced to go.

Where marriages were violent or the family was very poor there were other ways that early advice could have come to mothers wishing to separate. Along with the group of professional workers already mentioned, the police sometimes had special knowledge of marital troubles. They were called round when wives had been assaulted or locked out. However, there were only two instances where the police had been helpful. A separated wife said, 'Somebody's told me since that the police don't like to be mixed up in divorce cases, they won't help you.' This ties in with many other incidents where the police had been called but had been unwilling, too overworked, or powerless to help.

The Citizens' Advice Bureaux in the two areas may not be typical, but their failure reveals how they might have been more useful. Seaston's Bureau at the time of this survey was merely a room in the public library, ill-advertised, and staffed only by a librarian equipped with a list of addresses of other local bodies. The advice received from Northborough's rather better-known Bureau was unhelpful and even downright eccentric. A wife whose mentally ill and alcoholic husband had beaten her up was told, '"Men are funny things you know. You've got to give in to them. You've got to humour them. You go back to him." I said to her, "I'm not so fussed for a man as you," and I walked out.' The general tenor of the 'advice' was much inferior to women's magazine level, and in the same direction – on no account must wives leave their husbands.

Several mothers wrote in desperation to newspaper legal advice columns in the *News of the World* and the *People*, and it seemed that this source of advice had been valuable in breaking the women's magazines' silence about existence of legal aid. At this time (although perhaps less so recently), women writing in desperation to such magazines as *Woman* and *Woman's Own* were told to make an effort to win back their husbands' love, or to talk things over with a Marriage Guidance Counsellor. But never were they given the basic information they needed: that they can get free legal help to obtain a divorce, and that if they divorce, the state will provide subsistence support for them and their children. One or two mothers had also turned to the Salvation Army tracing service for help in finding missing husbands.

The influence of lack of information about the law in causing delays could not be assessed, for there were other reasons why women were reluctant to take action. Some mothers have previously been identified as clinging, often unrealistically, to the possibility of a reconciliation with the children's father, and these women felt that legal action might worsen their relationship with him. Only one separated wife and six unmarried mothers finally refused to take court proceedings, in two instances because this would reveal the father's identity, but a larger proportion had been reluctant to act and had only succumbed to strong pressure from the N.A.B. A separated wife said,

I wouldn't have bothered taking out a court order only the Assistance Board practically forced me to. But I said to them, I said that if I had to stand up in court against him, I didn't think I could go through with it. It would put me in an early grave. If he was there in court I couldn't face him. Anyway it wouldn't do my relationship with him any good. So I said they could drop it altogether, even if they didn't want to give me assistance any more.

Mothers who were still emotionally attached to the children's father felt that the N.A.B. were inclined to ignore the fact that the relationship between mother and father might be in a delicate state of suspension. More would have refused to take a court action had they not felt that as dependants on assistance they must do as the Board wished.[19]

This reluctance to act against the father cannot be distinguished from a more general mistrust of the law as unsavoury or humiliating. Wives reluctant to go to court were more likely to find the proceedings repugnant. Nevertheless, there did seem to be some truth in what mothers said about the humiliations of the court.[20] They resented the arrangement that the petitioner had to stand in the witness box while the husband was in a less exposed position. A separated wife with one illegitimate and two legitimate children said,

In court they make you feel like a tramp, as though you're right soiled and dirty. I don't think they've any need to ask all them questions. I mean it's not as though I was claiming for Janice, I was only claiming for his own children. But they ask you all about it. I couldn't have gone through with it if it was in a public court, it's not open to the public. Those other courts, there's a friend of mine telling me how awful it was for the young girls who'd had babies. She said one young girl passed out. They were asking her all sorts of questions about who was the father, and she pointed to him, and they said, 'When did intimacy take place?' This girl got redder and redder, and they were asking where it took place and in the end she just collapsed. She passed out.

The humiliations of this exposure were partly responsible for the low numbers of actions for affiliation orders.

There were also fears among separated and divorced wives that a court action might end in the husband being granted custody or at least visiting rights to the children. Several women who had experienced violent marriages were hiding from their husbands, and in other families the scenes created by the husband in court had been sufficient to prevent the wife ever going back for divorce or a variation of the order.

In twelve instances a separated wife had been unable to take action for maintenance because she had no grounds in law, usually because she had left home. Also, establishing paternity of an illegitimate child was felt by mothers who associated with soldiers to be very difficult. These mothers said that the father's friends would allege in court that they too had had intercourse with the mother. It was felt that only if the parents had been living together could a mother hope to get an award.[21]

The failure of court actions

Court action usually failed to produce any significant award because the awards made seldom came near to the maximum. When the magistrate or judge fixed the level of the award, the father's circumstances were taken into account. Sometimes with another family to keep, or if he was living alone with additional rent payments to make, the father was not earning enough to be able to pay the maximum amounts it was open to the court to award. Even before separation wives had scarcely ever received as housekeeping for the whole family an amount approaching the maximum court awards, and the full court payment of £15 a week for a mother and three children would have been a princely sum by the standards of most of these marriages. Two wives, one with a voluntary payment of £8 for herself and two children, and one with £10 for herself and four children, considered they were not hardly done by.

According to wives it was comparatively easy for men either to lie about their earnings, to give only their flat-rate earnings, or only the earnings for their main job.[22] Alternatively, husbands were sometimes able to produce lists of H.P. commitments and purchases of a kind which the wife living on national assistance had not dared or been able to enter into. There were bitter stories of husbands buying new cars and radiograms while their children went hungry.

However, apart from the husband's real or pretended inability to pay, it looks as though, warned by previous experience, the magistrates took into account what the husband was likely to pay, and noted that a majority of the husbands had not supported their wives adequately in the past so that it was unlikely that much support could be expected now. Fixing an award high enough to match the wife's needs was only asking for future trouble over collection. The low awards to unmarried mothers, never more than £1, cannot be explained on the father's inability to pay, and must rest on calculations of his willingness to support, or other criteria. Perhaps they are fixed low to keep them in line with awards to 'innocent' married women with a number of children.

There were other factors behind these low awards. The Northborough Magistrates' Clerk asserted to me in an interview that even in those instances where a wife was legally innocent, 'Often the conduct of the wives has been such as to drive the husbands away. It doesn't always come out in the evidence, but we can tell.' So the law may not have been applied strictly on legal evidence in these instances. Perhaps similar feelings of the mother's guilt in the matter operated to reduce the awards to unmarried mothers, although affiliation awards are for the child's support only.

Five husbands had successfully defended the actions taken against them, and several of these wives complained that the case had suffered through the lack of interest or sheer inefficiency of the legal-aid lawyer.[23] One wife who had a complicated case said of her lawyer,

I wouldn't have him again. I tell you, my husband had him tied in knots. He did better for himself without a lawyer than I did with two solicitors for me. Mine hadn't tried. He hadn't asked me *one* question before I went in. Just, did I want to claim for myself.

Another said, 'If you want to *get* the money you've got to *have* money. With legal aid, it's just like the Army. You're just a number.' A woman who had lost all her furniture in the court action said,

I never knew I'd have to have witnesses. I just went there by myself. I think if I'd had witnesses I could have got it. The people where I work, afterwards they said they'd have gone for me. What they said in court was that I couldn't have earned enough money in that time to pay for all that furniture.

There were other signs that cases had been managed inefficiently or imprudently. Three mothers who had been working at the time did not sue for maintenance for themselves. Later, on assistance, they regretted their lack of forethought.

One important outcome of divorce was the division of property. Couples who in better times had not worried greatly whose name went on the household bills, found that it mattered a great deal when they parted. One woman who had never worked during her marriage said,

The furniture was in my name by chance, or perhaps it was the work of God. You see, we didn't believe in H.P., and it was a very good thing we didn't because we bought everything outright. Well, when we went to buy something, we'd choose it and he'd rush off and leave me to finish it off, and you know how they do in shops, they say, 'Sign here.' Well, naturally, they asked me to sign.

When her husband tried to get the furniture it was all legally hers. By contrast there were several mothers who had bought all the furniture in the marital home but who could lay no legal claim to it because their husbands happened to have signed the H P agreements, at the insistence of the shop-keepers.

Only in one instance did a wife suspect that the first court action had driven a wedge between her and her husband. In a number of cases the husband had deserted so that he could never be summonsed, or a direct confrontation in court was avoided in some other way. Where the couples did meet in court it was after the relationship had already soured.

The problems of collecting maintenance

In recognition of the difficulties of collecting maintenance, mothers were usually granted the facility of having their order collected by the N.A.B. while they themselves drew a fixed weekly allowance.[24] This meant that mothers only knew when the father was gaoled that he had not paid. However, the N.A.B. supplied information on payments for the 215 mothers originally contacted for the survey (Appendix Table 10). The Northborough and Seaston mothers on assistance shared the fate of the whole national assistance population. Half of the Northborough and Seaston orders were paid regularly, but just over one third were rarely or never paid. The national figures show the lack of court orders for mothers of illegitimate children: only one quarter of all such mothers on assistance in this country had an order.

In line with the N.A.B.'s national policy, the Seaston mothers were allowed to sign over their court orders to the N.A.B. for collection, and according to the N.A.B. thirty-seven out of fifty-three mothers with orders had done so. However, although the Northborough N.A.B. manager had frequently tried to get the local Magistrates' Clerk to allow the orders to be signed over, this had only been permitted in 7 out of 42 instances.[25] The Northborough Clerk told me that he did not see why wives on national assistance should be better off than others. He also said that making the women take out summonses against their husbands would cause them to retain an interest in their children's fathers and at the same time would engender a sense of responsibility in the men. For, he said, if the men knew that the state was going to support their wives there was no incentive for them to pay and public money was being wasted. He regarded collection of the money from the court as no more inconvenient for the mother than payments by the Board. However, what were the consequences of his refusal?

Numbers were small, but payments of court orders in Seaston were if anything slightly more regular than in Northborough, 28 out of 53 Seaston orders being classed by the N.A.B. as regularly paid, compared with 19 out of 42 Northborough orders. Certainly the Seaston proportion was not markedly lower.

There was inconvenience and humiliation for mothers trying to collect an irregularly paid order through the court. A divorced mother, whose child had been told his father was dead, described in detail the difficulties of collecting money from the North-borough court:

They don't seem a bit cooperative at this court. The number of times I've been down in the last few years and the money hasn't been there and it's been a wasted morning. And then I've got to take Geoffrey [her son] down, and you know what children are, he's always asking questions, and I have to try and explain to him. I told him it was my mother's pension I was collecting, but children get talking don't they, at school.

And then you'll be waiting in the same place, and some of them that go there, you can tell that they've done wrong, and you feel as though you're all classed together. You feel awful. The place where you wait there's only one bench, room for four to sit down, and the rest have to stand. You might have to wait half an hour, and they're all kiddies there, and you can't always keep them quiet all the time, and I suppose there's a court next door, and the policemen are always coming in and saying, 'Will you be quiet please, or you'll have to stand outside!' Where we go, it's like one of the entrances to the Town Hall, and one time there was a corset show on and we couldn't stop in there at all.

I go in on Monday sometimes, and the money's not there, so I go in on Tuesday, and if it isn't there on Tuesday I have to go to the Assistance Board on Wednesday morning. Well, many a time I've got to the Assistance Board, and they always ring up you know, to see if there's any money there, and when they've rung up they've found out the money was in, and you feel such a fool! You feel as though you're trying to make it up or something. And I've asked them to ask the girl at the court when it's been paid in, and often as not it's only just been paid in that day. Well, that way, you see, he's getting about a week at me, because he's meant to pay it in on the Saturday.

On Mondays the Court only pay out at 4.30. On Tuesdays they start paying out at three. Now you see, this week, we'll have to go down on Tuesday and if the money's not there, we'll have to go on to the Assistance, and they're not open next Wednesday, so I'll have to collect from there, and they close at four o'clock. We'll all be rushing on. If we don't get there in time, we're all going to miss a week.[16]

Alternatively, if there was any money left over from the court payment on Monday there was a rush from the court to the N.A.B. office to pay the money back on that day before the office closed at five o'clock and so avoid another journey into town. These stories of unpleasantness and inconvenience were echoed by ten of the Northborough mothers. They could have had the money sent to them fortnightly, but apart from the expense of registered post, they could not afford the two weeks' delay involved in postal collection. As the authors of the Bedford survey comment, 'it is certain that the convenience and feelings of litigants have hardly ever been considered in the administration of this branch of summary justice.'[27]

Women whose husbands did not pay regularly were inclined to wait, rather than claim the balance from the N.A.B. every week. Yet if they waited the arrears might mount, and when they eventually applied for an allowance the N.A.B. would not make up the arrears for them. Several mothers lost arrears of over £100 in this way when they were finally allowed to sign their court order over to the N.A.B. permanently.

An attachment of earnings order, where the money was deducted by the employer from the husband's wage, was only a partial solution to the mother's problem.[28] Men determined not to pay could easily leave their job, and it may be that an attachment order effectively reduced a man's chance of regular employment, since the clerical work involved was a charge on the employer and defaulting fathers were stigmatized.

The Clerk's wish to compel mothers to take an interest in their husbands was misconceived. Actions in court and frequent summonsing would not strengthen the bond between husband and wife where the husband had no desire to pay and the wife wanted only to forget. Nor did women who clung unrealistically to men who had gone need court orders as an encouragement to them to take an interest in their children's fathers. These mothers experienced uncertainty, which made worse the nervous strains they already laboured under. And their sense of impotence was only increased when, the husband having been found, the court's ultimate sanction of six weeks' gaol proved utterly ineffectual. As one wife said, 'He doesn't mind. He says it's as easy as sitting on a pot.'

Far from strengthening family bonds, the process of court action made the mothers extremely bitter. They were pushed to take legal action against their husband, only to find the sanctions useless and the police overworked and therefore uncooperative. The husband's employers would not reveal his address, and discovering his whereabouts was a greater inconvenience than having him disappear. There was a certain amount of passage of information about the husband between the Ministry of Pensions and the Northborough Magistrates' Clerk, but insufficient to make his insistence on the wife pursuing her husband any less impractical.

Whatever fundamental questions are raised by the N.A.B.'s facilities for signing over court orders and so assisting the mother to forget her children's father, these facilities are a humane practical recognition that it is not feasible to behave as if there were guilt and innocence in marriage, and as if all husbands can or will pay adequate maintenance to their wives. On one point only the Northborough Clerk was right. Many women who are not on assistance go through the same, or worse, problems in attempting to live on an irregularly paid court order.

The father's difficulties

Fathers were not interviewed for the present survey, but the Bedford survey has since emphasized how the inefficiency and inhumanity of magistrates' courts can involve considerable hardship and injustice for the fathers as well as the mothers. More fathers than mothers felt the courts to be unjust,[22] and the above strictures on the inconvenient administration of procedures for the payment of orders applies almost equally for the the fathers, since only three out of the fifty-two courts surveyed by the Bedford team stayed open late enough on one night a week to enable men to pay after work, and only seven stayed open for one or two hours on Saturday mornings.[26]

But above all there was the injustice of imprisonment for default. The inconvenience of payment procedures, the lack of clear information about the courts, and the distastefulness of court actions for the variation of orders meant that men who were off work for any reason or who were otherwise in financial trouble were likely to fall into arrears. There were wide differences in the courts' treatment of arrears and use of attachment of earnings orders and imprisonment, some magistrates reversing the intended sequence and attaching earnings only *after* imprisonment had failed (this, indeed, seemed to be the practice at Northborough). Only one quarter of attachment orders (which are little used in some courts) were successful.

The Bedford authors rightly ridicule the notion that the retention of the symbolic degradation and punishment of a very few defaulters has any significant impact on the stability of marriage as an institution. And they conclude, 'We find it hard to regard the retention of imprisonment for maintenance defaulters as other than a continuing discrimination between the very poor and the remainder of the population in the law which regulates family life.'[29]

Grounds for divorce and separation

The legal 'guilt' or 'innocence' of these wives which determined their entitlement to maintenance proved largely irrelevant in view of the low payments eventually made by their husbands. It was therefore ironical that legal problems often sprang precisely from the law's attempts to assess 'guilt' or 'innocence'. Our difficulties in discussing the working of present divorce law in relation to the mothers interviewed are precisely the same as were encountered in talking about broken marriages – the nature of 'offences' and the subjectivity of the spouses' accounts. But the law itself works with a similar handicap.

The situations of wives who were currently separated revealed that, with the law as it stands, very often a partner who wants divorce may not possess suitable grounds,[30] while a partner with grounds may not wish to divorce (Table 2). No fewer than sixteen of the separated wives, or over one third, were willing to divorce but had no grounds which they could prove in law: these were often women without maintenance orders for themselves or legitimate children. On the other hand, fourteen wives had grounds but were unwilling to take divorce action.

These groups corresponded to situations already described in the discussion of broken marriages.

Among those willing but unable to divorce, nine wives had deserted their husbands because of what they felt to be cruelty or non-support, but they could not prove the husbands' part in the desertion. Typically this was the aftermath of what wives described as an authoritarian relationship, and far from the husband having adopted a strategy to drive his wife away, he sometimes found her departure humiliating and refused to allow her freedom through divorce. He was, further, in a position to invite the wife to return to him, which was the last thing she wanted, and could thus easily place her in the wrong if she refused to go back to him. Perhaps the wives over-stressed the element of refusal to divorce, for where the husband had no wish to remarry it was easier for him to do nothing than start divorce proceedings which would involve him in some expense.

Table 2

Numbers of separated wives and husbands possessing demonstrable grounds for divorce compared with which partner wants divorce

Divorce pending or not yet considered	11
Wives with grounds who are unwilling to divorce	14
Wives without grounds, who were willing but unable to divorce	16

Total number of wives 41

Grounds of cruelty in such instances were difficult for the wife to prove. The doctor could play a key part in providing testimony of the cruelty, but he might be reluctant to become involved in court proceedings. One mother said her doctor, 'gave me to understand in a roundabout way that he'd go to court for nobody'. Even with the help of a doctor there were still difficulties of witnesses and evidence. Another woman said, 'I could get a psychiatrist and try to get him on grounds of cruelty, but my solicitor said that if I get a psychiatrist they'd bring a better psychiatrist into court and two experts never agree.'

Wives who considered their husband's behaviour to be sexually perverted were in an equally difficult position. As one deserting wife said cryptically, 'It is very difficult to prove what goes on in a private bedroom.'

Eight wives who lived apart from their husbands – including four wives who claimed they had been forced to desert – had later borne an illegitimate child. They thus technically committed a marital 'offence' against their husband, or, equally important from the angle of whether or not they took action, they felt they now had no grounds. It was possible that in some of these instances the court's discretion might have been exercised in their favour, but the mothers either did not realize this or were very pessimistic about their prospects. Ironically, four of them had previously been refusing their husband a divorce in the hope of a reconciliation or to keep some kind of hold over him.

The remaining three marriages of this group had ended in such a confused state that neither partner had grounds for divorce. Where there was no marital home to leave, for instance where the couple went their separate ways at the end of a tenancy, there was no desertion by either partner. A similar impasse could be reached if a husband successfully defended an action by offering to have his wife back.

Reluctance to take court action against the husband, which had not been strong enough to withstand pressures from the N.A.B. for maintenance actions, came much more to the fore in the matter of divorce. The fourteen wives reluctant to divorce their husbands had been deserted or in some other way the husband had ended the marriage prematurely, so that the emotional bond had not parted.[31] The wives failed to proceed to divorce for a variety of reasons, not the least being inertia. Where divorce was not a pressing issue, or even where it was, the easiest course was simply to do nothing. Allied to inertia may have been a distaste for the public exposure of court cases and occasionally the fear of extra expense. One woman, who had divorced her husband only after six years' separation, described how she had been finally pushed into divorce by a crisis.

I'd got no money at that time and so I was saying, 'Eeh, I'd better get down to the national assistance and see what they've got.' (I hate going to that place, I'd rather go anywhere than go there.) So anyway one of the lads said to the other, 'Shall we go and get him?', that were me husband like, so I thought I'd better put a stop to that because I knew if they went over and got him they'd do something to him. They might kill him and then I'd lose all parties, they'd be taken away from me. So that was how it was really, so I saved a bit of money like and went down and got a solicitor and after I'd paid a bit, he told me about legal aid. I didn't know about it before – I thought you had to pay yourself, so I got all my money back. But honestly that divorce, it's so degrading, it's like the national assistance.

Another woman had been advised by the N.S.P.C.C. that she could get her divorce paid for, but she said, 'I didn't think of it at the time. I've never thought of it really. I don't mind as long as he doesn't come bothering us like he used to.' These wives said they 'felt free' without a divorce. Another wife clung to her husband to protect herself. 'I hang on to my husband so that I can't rush into marriage again, because if I meet any-one it would take a time to get to know him, and it would take time to get a divorce and that will force me to take my time.'

Most of these wives were very far from thinking of themselves as possessing a hold over their husband. Among women who delayed or refused divorce there was a difference of opinion on whether divorce was seen by defaulting husbands as a reward or a punishment. A separated wife said,

I can't tell you what I think. I think I really would take him back. I've often sat here in this place; without him it's just a house, if he came back it would be a home. I've thought to myself, if I do put in for a divorce it might shake him. He might realize then that he'd never see his children again, and he might come back.

A woman who had divorced her husband said, 'When I found out this girl he was living with had had another baby I thought, "That's it. He's not getting away with that", and I divorced him'.

Only four of the separated wives fitted the stereotype of the vindictive wife who wishes to retain a hold over her husband simply in order that he may not marry again. One said she had 'made him wait because I didn't see why he should have it all his own way'. Two had started divorce proceedings only to drop them when they discovered their husbands welcomed divorce. Only one woman went so far as to obtain a judicial separation, the alternative in the high court to a full divorce and a procedure which lawyers characterize as the resort of the vindictive wife.

Three mothers felt they had an economic interest in remaining married. Two lived in houses owned by their husbands. And although the 1957 Act amended National Insurance regulations so that a divorced woman can claim a pension on her husband's contributions, a third, a middle-class wife, said that she stood to gain a much better pension if her husband should die while she was married to him. There was the feeling too, as she observed, that, 'If I don't get any money from him now when I'm his wife, I'd stand Sweet Fanny Adams' chance of getting anything from him when I'm divorced.'

These descriptions confirm what is already known, that under the old law the spouse with power to act gained no benefit from divorce unless he or she wished to remarry. Those women who choose to separate first are less likely to want to divorce, since their marriages have probably more often been ended prematurely by husbands to whom they are still emotionally attached; separation is seen by these wives as a maximum concession to obtain maintenance rather than a preliminary to divorce. But they do not often see themselves as keeping a hold over the husband.

However, the other side of the coin, *wives* held captive by the old divorce law, is less often stressed. These were women without maintenance for themselves, often with illegitimate children, unlikely to act because they felt powerless or guilty. Among them were women found to have the lowest incomes, sometimes members of the 'underclass'. They were unlikely to stay separated permanently, because their husbands would probably want to remarry. But until that time, and with relatively poor prospects of remarriage even then, the law reinforced their sense of imprisonment.

The difficulties of divorced mothers

The thirty-five women who were divorced had also had trouble because of the form of the law. In line with the national figures the wives had been the petitioners in a majority of cases, four fifths according to their own account. But there were marked discrepancies between the grounds on which divorces had been awarded and the husband's or wife's complaint (Appendix Table 11). Only in twenty out of thirty-five divorces, almost always violent marriages, did the wife feel the divorce was granted on appropriate grounds. In a further five marriages, the difficulty of establishing cruelty as grounds for divorce was demonstrated by the fact that although the wife said the husband had been guilty of cruelty, she obtained a divorce only after some time, usually on the grounds of her husband's adultery committed after the breakdown of the marriage. In another five marriages the husband had deserted but was later divorced also on grounds of his adultery which was totally irrelevant to the marriage situation.

In all five instances where the husband had divorced the wife, she maintained the grounds were unjust. In three of these instances, the wife had been divorced for adultery but said the adultery either came after the marriage breakdown or was a trumped-up charge. In the remaining two divorces, the wives said they had found marriage deadly dull, and emotionally and sexually frustrating, although they were not otherwise ill-treated and indeed were on the contrary well provided for materially. The two women deserted and were divorced some time later by husbands reluctant to take action, on the evidence of illegitimate births.

The reliability of adultery as grounds for divorce has important implications, for the possibility of proving adultery seems heavily weighted against the woman.[32] It was more likely that the wife would present her husband with grounds by having an illegitimate child than that she would be able to discover his adultery if he did not want her to. Thus it was likely that more of the deadlocked divorces would be resolved in the husbands' favour than the wives', and wives would tend to lose maintenance as the 'guilty' party. The odds against the woman establishing adultery were both biological and financial. One mother described how she was almost caught. Her husband had deserted her and had lived with another woman for some years, but the mother became pregnant. She said,

I didn't put in for a divorce, he did. I think somebody must have told him I was pregnant. Well, this bloke knocks at the door one day and I knows him and I says, 'Hello, what do you want?' and he says, 'Oh no, it's not you is it?' And he says, 'I'm a private investigator now.' He said they'd sent him to find out if I was pregnant or not. And I said, 'Right, I'm not then.' He said, 'You sure?' and I says, 'I don't know yet, I might be.' I thought to myself, 'I'll let him do the stewing now, poor devil!' So once a month, for three months after, he came. And then by that time I was five months gone and he didn't need to ask any more then; he could see. He said, 'Will you sign it?' So I felt, 'What's the use,' and I signed it and he said, 'Thank Christ for that.' Then he tried chatting me up, and he says, 'Well, you're pregnant anyway. Who's to know?'

But when it all came out in court my solicitor said, 'You're not going to take it so easily are you?' he said. 'We'll cross petition.' Because we knew my husband had been committing adultery for months, my solicitor said, 'We know, and you know.' So when we put it to my husband's solicitors they said, 'Oh no, it was a platonic friendship,' but I said, 'Don't give me that. I know my husband. He couldn't go that long. He must be going somewhere.' So I got the divorce in the end.

To establish adultery requires money which a lone working husband might have but a deserted wife with children on national assistance would not – detectives' fees cannot be paid by means of legal aid. With children to look after, the wife is less mobile and therefore less able to check on her husband's movements if he lives at a distance. Wives of servicemen were at a special disadvantage because it appeared that the service authorities gave no help to these mothers (nor in paternity cases), and indeed the mothers alleged they were prepared to post soldiers to a different area to prevent discovery of their whereabouts. Another biological disadvantage of the wife was that where, as in two tragi-comic episodes, the wife discovered a letter from her husband's mistress and attempted to hide it, when it came to a physical fight for possession of the evidence the man won.

If marriages were not ended by one or the other partner providing grounds by his or her actions, sometimes the only alternative to prolonged separation appeared to be a kind of legal charade or even straight collusion between husband and wife. In at least four marriages where the wife was technically the deserter, establishing grounds for divorce had required a kind of play-acting or bluff. Upon legal advice a mother in this situation attempted to establish constructive desertion by going back to her husband and trying to get him to tell her to go away. Such a course was only open to a woman who was not too scared to go near her husband, which many of these women were. Also the operation failed if the husband agreed to let his wife come back. Two mothers were successful in getting their husbands to turn them away. But two others were not. One described her dramatic failure.

We all got into the car and drove down, and my father came, and my sister and mother as well. When we got there my husband was out, and we had to break a window to get in. Well, what a dreadful day we had! I can't think now why we didn't take the children across the road to a friend's, but I didn't think at the time, and we argued and shouted and talked. Well, you can tell what it was like. It finished up with my husband pulling my sister by the nose, and she had a milk bottle in her hand, she hit him over the head with that and laid him out, and when he got up, he went mad! It took all of us to hold him down.

This trip had required considerable courage as well as family and legal backing, and even financial help, which many mothers could not command, even had they known their husbands' whereabouts.

Considering the way their marriages had broken down, the women interviewed on this survey were not the most likely to have been involved in collusion with their husbands to procure a divorce. Nevertheless, in no fewer than nine, or just over one tenth, of these separations and divorces mothers spoke of collusion. One middle-class mother said:

The lawyers were hopeless. First of all you'd get a letter one day and you'd be up in the air because we're winning. Next morning you've another letter and you're down under the table. The law's a hopeless mess. The only way I got my divorce was by us getting together and talking it over in a sensible manner. The solicitors, it's not the truth they tell, they just get one little bit and they put a story together out of that. We tried all ways. We tried cruelty and we tried desertion, but the only thing that could work was adultery. My solicitor said, 'There's nothing like a nice straight adultery.' So in the end my husband admitted it, and we got him to come round here with his girl friend, and I got a private inquiry agent here.

It is no accident that in common speech to 'give somebody grounds' for divorce is to furnish evidence of adultery. The dividing line between collusion and many of the undefended suits, where the husband had conveniently committed adultery after the marriage broke down, was very thinly drawn.

From 'marital offence' to 'marital breakdown'

This analysis of divorce and separation proceedings has been limited and one-sided, yet it confirms dissatisfaction with the old divorce law and bears out current dissatisfaction with the operation of magistrates' courts in relation to separation. According to the wife's account the fiction of the 'marital offence' was a misrepresentation in something approaching half the marriages, and had we the husband's version of divorce too, no doubt this proportion would rise. The 'marital offence' used in divorce actions was said to be often irrelevant; for example, as one lawyer said, 'a nice straight adultery', legally convenient but occurring after the marriage had broken down.

The change to viewing the 'offence' as evidence of breakdown will bring the law a little further into line with the truth. And, taking this change along with the other measures in the Divorce Reform Act, in so far as either husband or wife may now point to separation rather than adultery as evidence of breakdown the law will represent the true situation more accurately. It is likely that there will be a shift away from the use of spurious grounds of adultery towards real grounds of desertion or separation, since in the American experience couples tend to choose 'the legally most effective and morally least accusatory grounds'.[33]

Concerning the change that formerly 'guilty' partners are permitted to sue for divorce, these separations and divorces were also illuminating. Almost half the separated *wives*, and a similar number of separated husbands, may eventually take action now the change has come about, thus greatly reducing the number of long separations. And while a small proportion of the spouses tended to see the other or themselves as using their innocence in law to maintain a legal hold, a large number of these deadlocks under the old divorce law were the result mainly of inertia, of the person who had the grounds lacking any incentive, or indeed having an administrative disincentive, to divorce.

Whether a 'guilty' spouse should be allowed to benefit from his or her actions is a value judgement which no amount of argument from evidence can resolve. But legal opinion now seems agreed that 'if the marriage is dead, the object of the law should be to afford it a decent burial'.[34] And as the Bedford authors observe, 'private and public morality alike require a development in our matrimonial proceedings whereby *all* marriages which have ceased to exist in social reality should be legally interred.'[35] Prolonged separations seem undesirable and from the accounts presented in this chapter they seem often indefensible in terms of the 'guilt' or 'innocence' of the partners. Guilt was most difficult to apportion, even superficially, in desertions, which will be a large proportion of such cases. Wives who had deserted were quite sure they were not wholly or even mainly guilty, and if we could hear husbands who deserted tell their story they too would probably often prove less guilty in fact than they are at present held in law.

The divorce law has changed because lawyers have recognized that the procedures of a law court are incapable of determining guilt, and that the concept of guilt itself is often inappropriate and irrelevant.

However, while the magistrates' courts remain unreformed, there is still the possibility, although admittedly reduced, of prolonged separations. As the Bedford authors maintain, 'If dead marriages are to be decently buried and if the numbers of illicit unions and of illegitimate children are to be reduced, some method must be devised whereby the orders of magistrates' courts (or of any other preliminary procedure that may be adopted) cease to be a permanent alternative to the remedies available in the divorce court.' Accordingly they propose 'deliberately to convert the magistrates' courts' jurisdiction into a stepping stone of short duration to a higher court. If the complainant wishes to be in receipt of maintenance under a court order – private maintenance agreements would be left un-touched – he or she would be required to seek either a divorce or a judicial separation from the higher court within two years of making the maintenance order. In this way spouses would be forced to examine their matrimonial status after two years and plot the course of their lives. Thus a unified system of family law would serve as an active agent of social change, reducing the number of illicit unions and the incidence of illegitimacy.'[36]

A further proposal, which our research would support, is the creation of a special Family or Domestic Court, as an alternative to the magistrates' courts where, as the Bedford survey also found, 'the working class couples . . . feel they are treated like criminals in a court concerned with petty crime'.[37]

Family law and the poor law

Proposals for limiting the jurisdiction of magistrates' courts and for instituting an alternative preliminary Family Court would go a long way towards unifying family law. As the Bedford authors point out, it would help to destroy 'the difference bet-ween two jurisdictions, in which at present the limited legal remedies for matrimonial disaster available in magistrates' courts are used extensively for the poorest and least well-informed members of the community.'[38] However the unified system would still not provide one law for the rich and poor alike because of the continued involvement of the National Assistance Board, and now the Supplementary Benefits Commission, in the matrimonial breakdowns of couples with low incomes.

As Professor Kahn-Freund has stated 'ever since the Elizabethan Poor Relief Act, 1601, the English law of family maintenance has been closely linked with what may broadly be called the law of social welfare'.[39] The husband had a statutory obligation to reimburse the poor law authority for the cost of maintaining his wife if she fell upon the authority. This obliga-tion has continued in the National Assistance Act 1948,[40] and in the subsequent Ministry of Social Security Act 1966[41] which set up the Supplementary Benefits Commission. Moreover, as we have seen, the persistence of low wage levels for some men and the steady relative improvement of social security benefits have meant that the burden of supporting separated and divorced wives and the mothers of illegitimate children has passed more and more into the province of the new 'poor law' authorities.

The Bedford study has confirmed that in the present situation, in spite of the heavy involvement of the law in actions for maintenance, the real problem of defaulting husbands is not legal, it is not that they 'do not provide maintenance through regular court orders but that their incomes are too low for their lawful wives and for themselves, whether singly or with other women.' 'The husband's obligation to maintain is in many cases a fiction. Most wives go to the magistrates' court to obtain maintenance; in reality, many receive it in the form of supplementary benefit, and the courts simply duplicate the work which the Commission is better equipped to undertake.'[42]

Thus, as we have seen, the National Assistance Board was willy-nilly involved in separations and in giving legal advice. And the new proposals for limiting the jurisdiction of magistrates' court orders to two years would have the consequence that the Supplementary Benefits Commission would have to increase its activities to obtain court orders in what would now become *divorce* actions in the high court. The Bedford authors are undismayed by the prospect: 'The Supplementary Benefits Commission would be acting in the unfamiliar role of encouraging dissolution of marriage. This may be unwelcome to that body, but if it is public policy, as reflected in the new divorce law, that dead marriages should be legally buried then there is nothing untoward in a Department of State promoting that policy. The effect of such a proposal would be to raise the divorce rate (at least among the poor) to the point where divorce was most nearly an accurate index of broken marriages.'[43]

Yet, as the Bedford authors recognize, the continued involvement of the new 'poor law' authorities in the marital breakdowns of the poor means the continuation of a double system of family law. The next three chapters will describe the indignities of the new 'poor law' itself, national assistance. And in the last chapter it will be argued that we will never break the connection between the poor law and family law for the poor until we begin to think outside the poor law conventions of the authorities' duty to pursue the father through the courts for the cost of maintaining his dependants.

CHAPTER ELEVEN

Means-Tested Incomes: The Official Ideal of a Discretionary Service

This chapter, and the following two, will look at the experiences of unsupported mothers who were receiving means-tested national assistance allowances, to ask whether our society has yet found the best way of meeting the mothers' financial needs. The discussion will fall into three major sections. First, in this chapter, the problems of providing income for fatherless families, and the official 'ideal' solution in the form of a discretionary means-tested service, will be spelled out. This will provide criteria by which we can evaluate the mothers' experiences of national assistance. In the next chapter, the mothers will describe their experiences, to indicate whether, from their point of view, the official ideal was being approached at the time when these interviews were carried out. We can also draw on other evidence to support what the mothers said. And in Chapter 13, we will ask whether the current administration of supplementary benefits is likely to have improved or deteriorated as compared with national assistance in 1966, and what are the real obstacles to the achievement of the official ideal of a steady progression from needs to rights.

In 1942 Beveridge offered a partial solution to the problem, suggesting that legally 'innocent' wives as well as widows should be able to get a sort of contributory insurance benefit as of right, possibly on the production of a court order.[1] But in the event nothing was done about this proposal, and widows remained the only insured group.[2] The problems involved in supporting fatherless families were shelved; and indeed there was perhaps a case that administrative experience and information had to be gained before any more definite rights could be considered for fatherless families. In 1948 the families were handed over to the newly constituted National Assistance Board (N.A.B.), which Beveridge expected to remain a relatively little-used safety-net

beneath the bulk of the insured population. In effect the
N.A.B. and later the Supplementary Benefits Commission
(S.B.C.) have been asked to decide for the community how best
to deal with poverty and the problems of fatherlessness. But by
the time the present survey was carried out in 1965–6, the relative
improvements in national assistance rates and the deterioration
in legal awards and contributory benefits meant that the numbers
of fatherless families on assistance had increased six-fold,[3] and
today there are almost ten times the original numbers who drew
national assistance in 1948. It is obviously high time to see how
the system is working out, and whether we are ready to build on
the experiences of the national assistance administration to
devise new ways of providing income for fatherless families.

Although in providing income for fatherless families the
N.A.B. and its successor the S.B.C. have continued to perform
functions left over from the old poor law, there have been
attempts to remove the stigma of poverty and to confirm that the
poor have certain minimum rights to support. The National
Assistance Act of 1948 was heralded as the official ending of the
poor law, and it was thought that the legal entitlement to
assistance of unsupported mothers and their dependent children
was now unambiguous: the mothers were no longer required to
register for employment before they could receive assistance.[4]
It had already been enacted that relatives (other than the father)
were not liable to support those who became dependent on the
state. Further improvements were that those in receipt of
assistance could retain some savings, they were not required to
sell possessions, and they were given cash to spend as they
thought best rather than (as at one time) vouchers which could
be exchanged only for a restricted range of goods which the
authorities decided were 'necessities'. All these changes
represented a considerable potential and often real advance on
the old poor law. Together with the provision for the collection
of maintenance orders (described in the last chapter) they
established a reasonably secure and settled living, if at a not
very generous level, for a proportion of fatherless families.

However, the twenty years since the 1948 Act have tended to
cloud optimism about the rights of the poor to the support they

receive. There has been concern about the continued stigma of the means-tested service, and about the retention of wide powers of administrative 'discretion' which permit officers not only to raise but also to lower or completely withdraw the mothers' allowances in certain situations.

The official position is that discretion is necessary because of the complexities in dealing with groups like fatherless families. Thus, around the core of rights legalized in regulations passed by Parliament there is a halo of less specific administrative discretion in fixing allowances, and the professional exercise of this discretion is intended to be exploratory, humane, flexible, generous, just, comprehensible, and active in seeking out need. Within this area of official discretion there will therefore be embryo rights or rights-in-the-making which the system itself has detected, fostered, and helped to consolidate. By a process of evolution and adaptation in the fulness of time the needs of the poor will steadily become rights. From being Poor Law Guardians the Supplementary Benefits Commission will become 'guardians of the poor'.[5] This view of the role of the professional's discretionary powers in the redistribution of life-chances is, indeed, the same as that adopted by Max Weber who wrote the classic discussion of the workings of bureaucracy.

Nevertheless, critics argue that the continued existence of official powers of discretion seriously erodes the mothers' right to support, and that the administration alone cannot be trusted to protect claimants' rights. In many ways the controversies about means-tested benefits are a microcosm of the wider debate about the adequacy, progress, and security of the Welfare State itself, and of the even wider debates about whether the institutions of society 'evolve' to meet change or whether they must be forced to change by external political pressures.

The key questions are: Is the old poor law stigmatization of fatherless families really dead. What experience have we gained about 'fatherlessness' and 'poverty', and about the machinery of means-tested benefits? Should the S.B.C. be left to continue to solve the problems of fatherless families; or is it time the community stepped in to relieve them of this function, by providing the families with income through some system other than discretionary means-tests?

The official ideal as a yardstick

At the time when the present survey was first published, the rationale of national assistance had scarcely been opened up for public discussion. But recently the S.B.C., and in particular their Deputy Chairman Professor Titmuss,[6] have gone a considerable way towards describing and attempting to justify an ideal type of discretionary administration for means-tested benefits. With the publication of a *Supplementary Benefits Handbook*[7] and the discussion pamphlet *Cohabitation*,[8] and the freeing for research of some information on appeals by claimants,[9] the S.B.C. have shown a welcome and responsible desire to engage in debate with their critics. As a contribution to the debate I have revised the presentation of my survey material to give a more detailed description of the official position, and to draw attention to areas of controversy where evidence from the survey is still relevant.

There are a number of justifications for trying to evaluate national assistance in 1966 by the criteria of excellence set up for the supplementary benefits system today, and also for using the 1966 evidence to point the way to the likely current situation. Stressing that official claims for a system must be tested by evidence will underline a basic problem of legislation and administration: we cannot take intention for achievement. The importance of the ideals of the top administration and the individual members of the Commission must also be underlined, for the Commission members are lay specialists entrusted by the community with the task of setting the ideals, gathering information, and controlling the behaviour of the lower echelons of the administration to conform with those ideals.[10] Built into the present ideals must be the accumulated official wisdom and experience of the post-war period. And although we may highlight certain aspects of the supplementary benefits system and of the whole situation of means-tested services which have changed, it will be argued that the structure and administration of supplementary benefits remains substantially the same as that of national assistance.

It must be stressed very strongly that this chapter focuses on the discretionary system in relation to mothers alone, and the N.A.B.'s and S.B.C.'s achievements in the case of the old people, who form the bulk of recipients of benefit and whose rights to support are not publicly questioned, would have to be explored separately.[11]

Legalized rights and administrative discretion

We can most easily understand the official arguments and the best claims for a discretionary scheme if we look first at the complexities of investigating entitlement and meeting the needs of fatherless families. The circumstances in which fatherless families come on to assistance make the task of investigating entitlement and setting the level of allowances a very complex one. The accounts given previously of suddenly broken marriages, frequent informal separations, men-friends, health and legal problems have illustrated how quickly and unpredictably the mother's circumstances could change and what a great variety of need these families might reveal. On the one hand the investigation of means and circumstances, and on the other the need for individual justice in the assessment of need, might therefore require both a very thorough initial inquiry followed by a periodic review, and also a rather complex scheme of entitlements with the possibility of wide variation and swift action.

As we have seen, Parliament has legalized a number of basic rights for unsupported mothers.[12] But in addition, to meet the individual situations which arose, N.A.B. officers were given important powers, officially known as 'discretion'. When the officer had carried out the basic assessment of eligibility and of the size of the allowance according to the legal scale laid down he might then recommend a regular fixed addition to the weekly basic allowance, the increase being known as a 'discretionary allowance'. Or in what he decided were circumstances of 'exceptional need' he was officially empowered to make lump-sum grants, called 'exceptional needs' grants. On the other hand he also had power in certain circumstances to recommend the complete stoppage or reduction of the allowance. However, there is a general clause to the effect that the overriding concern in decisions should be the needs and well-being of the claimant.

This balance and distinction between claimants' rights and official powers of discretion over those rights is the key characteristic of the administration of national assistance and supplementary benefits. Professor Titmuss claims, 'In fact – and what is insufficiently recognized – the scheme does provide fully legalized basic rights, but it also provides for additional grants which allow flexible response to human needs and to an immense variety of complex circumstances.'[13] The recently published *Supplementary Benefits Handbook* takes identically the same line of argument in favour of the retention of flexible and generous administrative discretion, but insists that it is in the nature of discretion that 'not all the answers to particular questions that arise in a particular case can be listed in a book. If they could be discretion would have ceased to exist.'[14] However, while clinging to the emphasis of the indeterminate nature of discretion, the *Handbook* also stresses, 'When the Supplementary Benefits Scheme was introduced in 1966 emphasis was laid on the concept of benefit as of right.'[15] Accordingly, there has been a shift in the official description of people who apply for support, from 'applicants' through 'clients' to the present 'claimants', which was at one time reserved for insurance recipients. Publication of the *Handbook* was a response to demands for the publicizing of rights, but was also an attempt to promote cooperation between claimants and their advisers and the Commission: 'The Supplementary Benefits Scheme can only be fully effective if there is a cooperative effort between the Commission and its officers and those who are working in similar fields and with similar objectives. The concept of cooperation, in the Commission's view, goes to the heart of successful operation of the scheme.' The Commission further express the belief that both claimants and staff have a right to 'understanding relationships'.[16] In short, the means-tested scheme of mixed rights and discretion is officially seen as a 'service' to the client in the best traditions of English public administration, and it is hoped that in this way the stigma of charity can finally be dispelled.

Professor Titmuss stresses that the combination of administrative discretion with legalized rights is relatively widespread in the Welfare State, but sees the *degree* of discretion in the S.B.C. as potentially the most satisfactory way of striking a balance between a number of choices in administration which appear there in their most awkward form: between precision and flexibility, precedent and innovation, individualized justice and equity, complexity as against workability and intelligibility. Thus, the argument runs, while rules are precise they are inflexible and may therefore lead to injustice in the individual instance. The existence of a discretionary element is said to avoid the necessity of spelling out in complex detail a vast number of rules which would attempt to bind the behaviour of the officer but also would reduce the freedom of the claimant to spend his money as he wished. In Professor Titmuss's view, 'A definition of entitlement in precise material and itemized terms would deprive the recipient of choice, and by prohibiting flexibility would mean that whatever the level of provision it would become a maximum which no official *or* tribunal could exceed. A legalized itemized prescription of minimum entitlement would become a rigid ceiling against which cases crying out by any human standards for extra help – demanding individualized justice – would press in vain. Nor would such a system eliminate arbitrary decisions – "Your dustbin does not need renewing and your toothbrush is not worn out yet."'[17]

The most interesting and crucial claim for a discretionary system is the possibility of innovation of provision within an established structure of administration, a claim which is very relevant to the situation of fatherless families whose position was initially uncertain and ill-defined. In practical terms this would mean a continuous progression from the exercise of discretion to the legalization of rights. The ideal here is that in a changing society where new needs arise and where, indeed, needs are not immediately and clearly identifiable, the gradual and sensitive recognition of needs via individual exercises of official discretion will become consolidated into rights. The example quoted is the institution of a flat-rate increase in benefit for those who had been in receipt of an allowance for two years, which is said to have followed from the experiences of administering national assistance. Professor Titmuss has drawn the analogy here with the whole development of social policy in society: 'The central concept for progress under this head is the definition of contingencies which can be met, without discretion, either by flat-rate benefits, or benefits varying with precise conditions . . .'[18] In this sense the question of where to draw the line between rights and discretion is a constant challenge. And one way of assessing the achievements of the means-tested discretionary system would be to see how far it has facilitated the transfer of fatherless families to a non-discretionary, flat-rate benefit system.

The problems of investigating entitlement and preventing fraud and cohabitation

Unfortunately from the Commission's point of view, and at variance with the ideal of fostering cooperation, there has been an increasing tendency for criticism of the S. B. C. and for claimants to form unions to claim their rights which they assert are not adequately protected by existing arrangements.[19] Claimants' unions are disputing the right of professionals to administer the service, and are pushing the situation towards more open conflict with a view to more democratic participation. We can, in fact, identify a number of problems built into the investigation of entitlement and the exercise of discretion which might lead to the departure of officials from a professional ethic of impartiality and also to friction with claimants.

Problems arise because, for example, although the unsupported mother's position and rights appear clear in principle, in practice the N.A.B. and the S.B.C. have still been statutorily required to insure that her resources are below certain limits and that she really is unsupported by a man, before they pay an allowance. And in the investigation of these sometimes delicate matters, there is at least the possibility that the behaviour of officials may be such as to deny rights by making the claiming of those rights difficult, unpleasant, or humiliating.

The general problems of dealing with entitlement and checking on social circumstances and needs have been stated by the N.A.B. to be to guard, by a process of investigation which should not deter the genuinely needy, against the possibility of fraud:

A scheme which provides payments for anyone who can satisfy the Board's officer that he is in need and which aims at meeting need quickly and without too much formality necessarily offers some temptation to the morally weak as well as to the unscrupulous. The Board's aim has been to limit temptation as far as possible by getting their officers to ask the necessary questions carefully and patiently, but avoiding an inquisitorial approach which would deter people from applying.[10]

With fatherless families, apart from entitlement problems about means there also occurs the question of cohabitation. The difficulties raised by cohabitation have recently been discussed from the official viewpoint in the *Cohabitation* pamphlet. Briefly, the issue is presented as one of equity between married and cohabiting couples. A married woman may not draw benefit for herself if her husband is working, and the intention of cohabitation prohibitions is to insure that a woman who is cohabiting with a man shall not be in a more favourable position financially. The S.B.C. interpret the prohibition of cohabitation by withdrawing the benefit of women adjudged to be cohabiting. They also refuse in principle to pay supplementary benefit as a matter of course to the cohabiting mother for all children who are not of the current union; that is, a cohabiting man is normally required to support the mother's children by another man, even if that man is the mother's legal husband and is not paying for them.

Cohabitation is one of the areas where the administration has had to elaborate working rules of discretion, for cohabitation itself has never been defined legally, except in the Social Security Act 1966, Section 4, Schedule 2, para 3(1), which requires that,

Where a husband and wife are members of the same household their requirements and resources shall be aggregated and shall be treated as the husband's and similarly, unless there are exceptional circumstances, as regards two persons cohabiting as man and wife.

These exceptional circumstances have not been, and perhaps cannot be, very clearly spelled out. As the *Cohabitation* pamphlet illustrates, the administrative problems of producing a *working definition* of the phrase 'cohabiting as man and wife' are formidable, and they will be discussed in more detail below. Although the clause did not appear in the 1948 National Assistance Act, and was not debated when it appeared in the 1966 Act, the S.B.C. maintain that there is still considerable public support for the retention of this practice dating from poor law days:

the legislation merely gives formal shape to what remains the desire of society as a whole for fairness and equity in the distribution of the State's financial support to men and women and their families. It contains no element of moral judgement on, or penal sanctions against, informal unions which are not legalized.[11]

It will be asked, later in this chapter, in what way the co-habitation rule relates to 'society' and 'public opinion' – how far we are all involved in making discretionary rules – and whether the element of moral judgement can be kept out of the practical administration of such a rule. For the issue cannot be discussed entirely as a matter of the intention of the rule and the principle of equity, and account must be taken of the difficulties of administering the rule and its effects on the lives of claimants and their relations with officials. Most importantly the S.B.C. feel that the possibility of fraud makes necessary the use of special investigators:

These are ordinary members of the staff of the Department who conduct inquiries – not exclusively in relation to cohabitation – which any visiting officer of the Department could conduct but which it is more sensible for selected staff rather than local office staff to undertake because of their complex and time-consuming nature. They are specially selected only in the sense that some officers are clearly unsuitable, for example because of inexperience or by temperament, for a job involving at least embarrassment and at worst the risk of physical violence. In their training special care is taken to ensure that they always have in mind the overriding need to avoid intimidation or dishonourable dealing or any excess of zeal. They are well aware that they have no right of entry into private premises except by invitation of the occupier ... It is also unfortunate but equally unavoidable that, in attempting to detect concealment and dishonesty, special investigators have to cross check the accuracy of what they have been told by claimants. They may for example be prompted by an anonymous letter which may be spiteful and unfounded and they may have to make local inquiries without the knowledge of the claimant or to watch a house to see who lives there. This is distasteful work, to the investigator as well as to the claimant and others concerned. But it is the price that has to be paid for administering the cohabitation rule.[22]

The size of the N.A.B.'s and S.B.C.'s concern with cohabitation can be gauged from the official statistics. The N.A.B. stated in 1965,

These abuses ['false desertion' and cohabitation] continue to be prevalent and, *as a result of intensified efforts to deal with them,* there were considerably more prosecutions (525) than in the previous year (98). The 525 prosecutions resulted in 481 convictions. *In more cases, where it was not possible to obtain the evidence necessary for proceedings, the allowances were withdrawn or reduced. As in earlier years extremely few appeals were received against the decisions made in these circumstances.* Many persons who became aware that they were the subject of special inquiries voluntarily surrendered their allowances.[23] (My italics).

More recently the figures for alleged cases of cohabitation or 'false desertion' (not *prosecutions,* as in the above report) have been given as 6,173 cases in 1968, in which allowances were withdrawn or reduced for 3,194 families; and as 9,300 in 1970, with withdrawal or reduction of allowances in 4,388 instances.[24] This is out of a total of around 200,000 allowances.

Whether this rise represents a much greater frequency of cohabitation and false desertion, or increased public and official vigilance and severity, cannot be established. But the belief that there is a great deal of fraud is one of the persistent myths of the Welfare State, and constitutes pressure on the S.B.C. to increase the zeal of investigations to the point where there are counter-pressures from critics that methods of investigation are too tough and deterrent. The extent of the use of special investigators and their 'zeal' must bear some relationship to the degree of public suspicion of fraud, and is part of the balance to be struck between meeting need and preventing abuse. For example in 1969 there was a flare-up of accusations of fraud and official denials, provoked by newspaper articles. Mr Ennals, Minister of State at the Department of Health and Social Security, referred[25] to 'an almost hysterical attack on the work of the Supplementary Benefits Commission in some recent statements. People are being led to believe that there is fiddling on a mass scale. This is a gross distortion of the situation. It is the few who get the publicity and distort the picture of the magnificent work done by the staff of our Social Security Offices. Some of the attacks have been very unfair on our staff. On the one hand they are accused of handing out public money to those who are not entitled to it – and on the other of probing into people's lives as if they were the Gestapo. Both accusations are false.' He gave a further set of figures for the incidence of fraud: 'There is an obvious area of possible abuse among the 150,000 separated wives and divorced women and 63,000 mothers of illegitimate children who claim supplementary benefits. An article in a Sunday newspaper claimed that a study in 1965 had shown that one in four of these cases was fraudulent. This is absolutely untrue. The study in 1965 suggested that about 7 per cent of the 164,000 in this category had made fraudulent claims. More recent random surveys carried out in a cross-section of our offices have suggested that the proportion now is certainly no more, in spite of the increase in the number of women in this category.' This official statement catches very well the double-bind in which the S.B.C. finds itself with its critics.

It is clear from the above that officers make secret investigations of a claimant's means and social situation and reduce or totally withdraw an allowance, even where, according to the S.B.C., evidence necessary for proceedings in a court of law cannot be obtained. For the Commission the justification for such practices rests on their distinction between a legal right and official discretion:

Critics of the system sometimes complain that evidence obtained in this way is acted upon though it would not stand up in a court of law. This shows a fundamental misunderstanding of the object of special inquiries in the case of suspected cohabitation. They are not intended to be automatically a preliminary to prosecution, for which, in any case, the evidence must be such as to establish guilt beyond all reasonable doubt. They are intended to discover the acts on which to make a judgement about the case as a whole. This will include a decision as to whether, on the balance of probabilities, cohabitation is shown – a judgement which can be challenged forthwith in the informal appeal tribunal.[26]

But it is not that critics fundamentally misunderstand, so much as they do not share the official definition of the nature of discretion and do not believe that rights are adequately protected by the informal appeal tribunal. There is a gulf between the official insistence on the benevolence of professional discretions and external pressure for the protection of rights and effective participation in decision-making.

The problem of controlling the administration

The N.A.B. and S.B.C. have claimed to recognize the danger, which lie in a form of organization where power is vested in individuals who each perform their complex tasks independently in situations where direct supervision is difficult – even in the central office where claimants are interviewed officers will take many of their decisions alone, and a large proportion of individual officers' work consists of home visits.[27] The control of the exercise of discretion, and of officers' departure from the correct use of discretion, has been attempted in several ways.

First, discretionary powers have been minutely codified in the form of recommendations as to how officers should behave in particular sets of 'exceptional circumstances'. These codes provide at once a specification of a professional ethic and the ideals of the administration, and a guide of precedent, and they are constantly being added to. A second line of control has been that attempts have been made to see that officers acquire 'the skill and . . . insight and understanding of human behaviour called for by their often delicate duties, particularly with people whose personalities are in some way abnormal.'[28] Thus the N.A.B. and S.B.C. have had social work consultants, and provision has been made for officers to learn some theoretical knowledge of human relations to tie in with the practical day-to-day work of the administration of allowances.[29] Further, there are administrative checks by senior and regional officers, particularly and increasingly in the case of controversial and sensitive areas such as cohabitation.[30]

Yet in spite of such efforts there are difficulties, as the S.B.C. has recently acknowledged:

It must be apparent that mistakes and errors of judgement sometimes occur, in a service totalling some 18,000 staff, many of them reflecting the values of the local community in which they live, and all of them subject to the tensions inherent in the changing society of which they are a representative cross-section.[31]

However, in the Commission's view the proof of effective administration is to be found in the small proportion of claimants who ever appeal:

in view of the emotional problems involved we consider it just as noteworthy – and a tribute to the Commission's officers – that so very many investigations are carried out without complaint.[32]

Ultimately, then, the present S.B.C., like their predecessors the N.A.B., have rested their case on the efficacy of the appeals tribunals in picking up instances of maladministration. And indeed it is true that the appeal tribunals are relatively little used compared with those in other more or less comparable branches of social security.[33]

Areas of controversy between the administration and their critics

All these ideals and problem areas outlined above provide criteria by which the current and past means-tested systems can be evaluated. And controversies can be seen as arising from disagreements between the administration and their critics over the adequacy and scope of the system in meeting needs, the balance between economy and generosity, zeal and tact, and whether more attention is paid to critics of the poor or critics of the provision, the urgency with which the system publicizes existing services, the sensitivity in detecting new needs and reaching out to meet them, the speed with which discretionary provision for needs becomes consolidated into legalized rights, and the security of those rights once established in law.[34] The founding of claimants' unions has highlighted the question of what should be the relationship between administrators and claimants. Claimants assert that rights can never be adequately protected while a paternalistic service deals individually with suppliants. They see the official policy as one of 'divide and rule', and they look for an adequate protection of their rights only through the combination of claimants to exercise collective power, which will radically alter the officer-claimant relationship and improve the claimant's image of himself.

These disagreements follow a classical division between on the one hand those who see the institutions of society as 'evolving' through some inbuilt dynamic of structural change, and on the other those who lay more stress on the need for external political activity to overcome the rigidity, conservatism, and vested interest of institutions, bureaucracies, and society. The division can be overstressed[35] but it is a useful description of the controversy between the administration and those of their critics who push for greater rights for the poor.

Controversy has crystallized in issues such as the nature of the 'codes' of internal instructions to officials concerning discretion. The Acts embodying legislation have been relatively short and even ambiguous, so that the area of discretionary rule-making delegated by Parliament to the administration has been very large. Critics have claimed it is too large and too secret. They want the codes to be published entirely, since, it is argued, they form the basis of just that detailed specification of rights which the S.B.C. still deny is feasible. For a long time publication was refused on the grounds that the codes are essentially incomplete, too complex to be of use to outsiders (and indeed growing too complex for internal use), but in any case not legal specifications of rights, being instead merely internal and private recommendations and guidance on how officers should behave. Recently the

S.B.C. have been sufficiently pressured and impressed by some of the arguments in favour of *information* for claimants to publish a digest of the codes, and other information about procedures, in the *Handbook*. But the insistence on an indeterminate area of discretion remains, and the full codes have never been published. They are still protected, even from M.P.s, by the Official Secrets Act, although a number of copies are currently circulating unofficially, and extracts have been printed in the press.[36]

While the codes remained unpublished (or as now, somewhat incompletely and, it has been argued, inadequately and in some places erroneously or misleadingly digested in the *Handbook*)[37] both sides agree that they cannot be said to be legalized rights. And publication will not of itself transform paper rules into rights unless a knowledge of their existence is spread, unless they are applicable universally, and unless measures are taken to ensure official adherence to them. Accordingly, critics have brought pressure on all these points.

It has been argued that both in changing paper rules to rights and in protecting claimants from official meanness and malpractice or simply checking on the correct use of discretion, the informal appeals tribunals are not performing correctly or effectively; that the small number of appeals is not necessarily a justification for satisfaction, and may be an index of the inaccessibility and inefficacy of the appeals procedures.[38] Significantly there is a clash of definitions of the very function of the appeals tribunals. In line with the official view of the essential nature of a discretionary service, the complaints machinery is intended to be external to the administration, and informal and different from a court of law in a number of respects.[39] Crucially, the tribunals are lay bodies without lawyers, and their decisions set no legal precedent. Legal aid is not generally available for representation at these tribunals, and there is no court of appeal (although it has, perhaps, not been sufficiently emphasized that they are bound by the law of the land and by the laws of natural justice, and there could be appeals to law on these grounds).[40] Recently, also, a survey has drawn attention to the importance of the administrative machinery for the preliminary reviewing of appeals, which discourages or stops many appeals before ever they come to a tribunal.[41]

A very basic controversy in relation to rights *versus* discretion therefore exists over the extent to which the appeals machinery can and should be changed and lawyers introduced to tighten up the translation of discretionary rules into rights. Professor Titmuss has argued against the introduction of lawyers and the crystallization of discretionary powers into itemized rights on the grounds of the inflexibility and the incomprehensibility of legal proceedings: 'The risk here . . . is that responses to changing human wants may be inordinately slow because of their legal imprisonment in precedent and the cumbrous processes of gladiatorial combat.'[42] He fears the loss in human terms which might result from a move towards institutionalized 'adversary' relationships between claimants and the S.B.C., which he feels would actually generate hostility. On the other hand critics have not necessarily argued that tribunals should or could be completely taken over by lawyers, or that lawyers should be concerned solely in the process of consolidating rights into itemized entitlements. Rather they have argued that, *given the existing state of affairs* of the relative meanness and inflexibility of discretion and hostility between claimants and officers, access to legal advice and the more frequent intervention of lawyers may be necessary to improve the claimants' incomes, and beneficial in dispelling uncertainty and insecurity on the claimants' part.[43]

This description of the controversies has been taken far enough for the moment to indicate the official claims, the basis and range of the critics' disagreements, the sorts of evidence we need about the system, and the role of that evidence in resolving the disputes. Evidence cannot overcome the difference in value positions between those who believe in the perfectibility and desirability of a traditional 'paternalistic' professional service and those who would rather see a greater devolution of power in society, particularly a reduction in the power and secrecy of bureaucracies. But evidence can be useful in describing and gaining agreement on the virtues and defects of the system as it stands. Which direction we want to move in will depend on where we are now: how much of a 'service' is there, how accessible, flexible, and generous it is, how much cooperation or how much hostility and mutual misunderstanding now exist between officers and claimants.

In spite of the S.B.C.'s claims that there is a wind of change blowing through their corridors, and in spite of the establishment (in the Department of Health and Social Security) of a research unit upon whose services the S.B.C. can draw,[44] there is still remarkably little information published about the lives of claimants and their relationships with officials. To this extent, then, the evidence of the experiences with national assistance of mothers on the present survey remains relevant and even topical.

CHAPTER TWELVE

The Mothers' Experience of National Assistance

The evidence from the mothers' interviews showed that from their point of view the official ideal of a cooperative, flexible, generous, comprehensible, and just service was far from being attained. However, it would be unfortunate if, because the evidence was gained from the mothers only, this should make the problem appear too narrowly as one of mothers' rights *versus* officers' discretion. We must remember that the levels of allowance which the officers had to administer, and some of the tasks which the N.A.B. were trying to solve, were set for them by the community as a whole.

Some problems arise in interpreting the mothers' evidence because I was not permitted to interview the officers themselves. When interviewing began, it was not anticipated that dissatisfaction with national assistance would be quite so marked. But where mothers were critical of officers' behaviour I wanted to hear both sides of any dispute and I did attempt to get official permission from the N.A.B. to do so. However, the Board's correct concern for their clients' rights to confidentiality, mixed with an apparent reluctance to permit outsiders to study their internal procedures, meant that I was allowed neither to discuss with individual officers their overall viewpoint, nor to check their version of specific complaints from mothers, even though the safeguards of disguise and anonymity could, in my opinion, have been maintained. I interviewed only the managers of the local Northborough and Seaston offices in a rather preliminary way, and I was subsequently discouraged by the Board from having any further conversations with these local managers on any particular or general points raised by the interviews. A preliminary draft of my report sent to the then Chairman of the N.A.B. produced no comment. But one and a half years later, after a further request for advice, the S.B.C. produced some criticisms of a later draft, and I have tried to take account of those official criticisms which I considered valid.

In what follows, the clash between the mothers' views and the ideal of the authorities will raise questions at a number of levels. Are the mothers' stories representative and true for the situation in 1966? Are the mothers complaining about legalized statutory provisions and published regulations, or about the discretionary powers as elaborated and interpreted in the N.A.B.'s internal instructions and secret codes, or about officers' departures from the letter or spirit of the correct exercise of discretion? Because the codes and internal directives were secret we will not always be able to determine what was going wrong, but the distinction is important from the point of view of where the system needs improving. And if the mothers' stories are true for 1966, how relevant are they for the administration of supplementary benefits for fatherless families today?

The representativeness of the sample and the interpretation of what the mothers said have been discussed in the earlier parts of the book and in an appendix. From the mothers' responses to the survey (which I described in the Introduction) I believe the rather unfavourable view of the N.A.B. which emerges in this book probably comes from interviews with mothers who replied more readily and who mistrusted the N.A.B. relatively less. A full cross-section of mothers might have produced a more unfavourable picture, although hostile views are represented. Those aspects of the N.A.B.'s duties which might cause friction have been identified; and later I will argue that they must continue to do so under the very similar structure and financing of supplementary benefits administration today, in spite of tighter and more generous regulations and the administrative checks which have been introduced since 1966.

The inadequacy of alternatives to assistance

The experiences of the women interviewed were not solely of dependence, for among them were a proportion who had been alone yet independent of assistance. A study of the reasons why various families had eventually become dependent can tell us much about the problems of those who manage to remain independent, and also about the barriers and difficulty of access to national assistance.

The families had been dependent on assistance for widely different lengths of time. Of the 215 mothers for whom the N.A.B. supplied statistics, 38 per cent had been dependent *during the current spell* for less than a year, but 18 per cent had been dependent for over five years. Unmarried mothers and separated wives tended to have been on assistance for a shorter time than divorced and widowed women. These differences represent to a large extent the lengths of time the families had been fatherless. But for a substantial number of families there had been either a delay before coming on assistance or at least one spell of independence during the time they were fatherless.

Among the families visited for the survey, there had been a delay for forty, or one third. In nine instances the interval was only a month or two, but for fourteen families it was from three months to a year, for seven it was over a year, for a further five over two years, and for another five over five years. Another seventeen mothers had not received assistance continuously, but had experienced spells of independence. If these families are not untypical, this indicates that the numbers of fatherless families on assistance at any one time must considerably understate the proportion of such families who will be dependent at some time during fatherlessness, which may well rise to three quarters of those without pensions.

Because the mothers interviewed were dependent at the time they may have exaggerated the difficulties of gaining and maintaining independence in order to justify their position to themselves and me. Nevertheless, it has been shown that they would have a chance of rising substantially above assistance levels only if they had exceptional earning power or a stable income from some source. And the earning capacity of the mothers interviewed was low; only nine had any kind of education qualifications (including sub-G.C.E. qualifications such as R.S.A.), and only five had professional qualifications, four as nurses and one as a secretary. Approximately one third of the women had worked to achieve independence since the loss of the father, either before applying for assistance or later. Some also had income from a source other than work, but those who had not had been working very long hours as piece-work weavers, hospital auxiliaries, or in factories: in one canning factory, three of these women had worked double-shifts, sixty hours a week for £15. The value of such earnings was reduced if the father sought a variation of court order, as he was entitled to do when the mother's situation improved, and by deduction of tax, which must be paid at single person's rates by the divorced and the unmarried mothers, and also by separated wives whose husbands claimed a tax allowance on their maintenance.

Difficulties with child minding had proved the major stumbling-block to continuing or re-starting work. Altogether twenty-two mothers had come on to assistance at the birth of an illegitimate child which was not the mother's first child; that is, they had previously been without a man but self-supporting. Half the mothers gave as the major reason for dependence the fact that the children were too young,[1] and one third said they might work when the children grew older. But it was noticeable that these mothers, who urgently needed to work because they were not supported by their children's fathers, tended to be reluctant to leave their children for that very reason – they felt a child who saw neither parent for much of the day would be doubly handicapped. Relatives gave help with children; and day-nurseries might have helped but they were too few and remote, and moreover mothers complained (perhaps rationalizing their unwillingness to part with their children) that the children frequently became ill at the nursery, or were overfed.

Mothers with children of school age felt hardly more free. School holidays and children's illnesses were said to be insurmountable obstacles, and indeed some mothers complained that with children they had greater difficulty in getting taken on for work. One said, 'If you go for a job and they find out you've got children, they don't want to know.' Another said, 'If you're ill yourself, they understand it, but if someone else is ill and you've got to look after them, they don't.' Six mothers had come on to assistance only when a school-age child became ill, and four others had had to stop work when neighbours complained to them about the behaviour of children left unsupervised. However, 'latch-key' children were few. In one instance, a mother had been forced by the doctor to stop work and look after an ill seven-year-old whom she had been leaving unattended all day. In another, an unmarried mother had for many years left her child alone, giving him money for lunch and extra for the cinema on wet days to keep him dry, warm, and out of trouble. But on the whole these mothers had felt that they could avoid this kind of life for the children by going on assistance. Similarly, the present survey tells us little of mothers who had their children fostered, for this was another solution to their problems which mothers had been unwilling or unable to take.

Reasons for inability to work changed over time and with the age of the mother. For fifteen women who were older, illness was a major cause of dependence. Among them were widows who were old when they first came on assistance, but there were also other women who had been young when they first applied, and who had originally been dependent because of children now grown up. Ill-health and incapacity made these older mothers settle for a steady income on assistance rather than try to begin work again, sometimes after a gap of many years.

Incomes from sources other than work had also changed over time. At first, some mothers had been able to maintain their families either solely on their existing income or by working to supplement it. Often court orders had been paid sufficiently regularly for a short while to keep the family independent. Four separated wives of service personnel had automatically received the minimum allowance from their husbands' service pay until the husbands left the forces or the couples were divorced. Two women had had part of their husbands' sick benefit. A widow had had a small allowance from a local charity, and a separated wife had had an income from a charity at above the national assistance rate because her health had broken down when she was housekeeper to a rich family with strong church connections. Several mothers had had unemployment benefit which they had drawn, or maternity allowance. In eight families help from kin had been sufficient to make mothers independent of assistance, in some instances for over a year. Fourteen mothers with money saved had spent all, or nearly all, of it before applying for assistance. Usually the sums were under £100, but one unmarried mother had spent £300 since her pregnancy. Four mothers had sold belongings: a middle-class woman discovered for the first time what pawnshops were, and sold off or exchanged her best furniture and some of her jewellery, including her engagement ring, before she found out about assistance; while another woman had raised less than £60 by the sale of much of her furniture.

A woman who tried to maintain her independence might have to face at the same time a number of problems which hindered her efforts to work as well as declining fluctuating resources. A separated wife with a pre-school and a school child described her experiences after her husband deserted.

As soon as I got turned round, I went out to work. But I was travelling such a long way, I was spending 17/- or 18/- a week in bus fares. I had to get a bus to town first of all. Then I had to get a petrol bus to take Jane to the nursery. Then I had to walk up to work. To tell you the truth I was working and I was worse off than when I was on assistance, because I had to pay for the little girl at the nursery and I had to pay a neighbour to look after the children at tea-time if I worked over. But you could never tell what you were going to get on the weaving. It's a funny job. Some weeks you can earn a lot of money, other weeks you hardly get anything. And then with the maintenance you see, some weeks it would come through and some weeks it wouldn't. So I had to go down to the court and try to get that every week. There were other things as well. When I was working the children didn't get free dinners – they assumed I was getting maintenance. And many a time when I was poorly I forced myself to go on working because I knew if I'd stopped off work that week I'd have to stop off again next week to go and get the national assistance if I had a short week.

Eventually there was a crisis with her children, and her health broke down. Irregularity and fluctuation in size of incomes could force a family on to assistance just as surely as lack of resources.

Ideally, when a family's resources fell below assistance levels or when the continuation of work entailed too great hardship, the mother should have applied to the N.A.B. for an allowance.

However, there was some evidence that mothers had failed to apply or had continued working past the point when they would have begun to benefit from assistance.[2] In all, around one in ten mothers may have been living below assistance rates before applying for an allowance – the proportion may be larger owing to the difficulty of comparing incomes and assistance scales for some years back – and there were women who looked upon this interval as the most poverty-stricken period of their lives. Those most likely to be poor were families supported by their relatives or living off a court order irregularly paid; thus, when one woman finally applied for assistance her husband was £200 in arrears with a court order which was itself below the national assistance rate.

Delay might sometimes occur because a woman valued the self-esteem she gained from holding down a job. But much of the hardship through delay sprang from other causes, connected with the stigma of dependence and the difficulty of access to assistance.

Attitudes towards dependence on assistance

Fears of dependence may have played a large part in delaying applications for assistance, and in rendering mothers very touchy about the behaviour of N.A.B. officials towards them once they did apply. No fewer than three quarters of the mothers said they had felt very embarrassed at the initial application for assistance.[3] The old poor law cast a long shadow, and mothers had tended to fear that while they had other cash incomes of any size they would not be given assistance, and that they might be told to sell goods or spend savings. Those who were able-bodied had assumed that they would be expected to try to find suitable work.

A great deal of discomfort in social relationships stemmed from the mothers' sensitivity about their dependence on national assistance. How far their sensitivity was a result of actual disapproval from neighbours and friends we cannot say from the present survey. But it would appear that mothers' hardships and feelings about the inferior status accorded to fatherless families were deepened by the stress placed by neighbours and friends upon their dependence. Mothers were liable to be told, 'It's us that's keeping such as you.' A widow said uneasily, 'I feel I shouldn't be as tidy as I am in this front room. Whenever anybody comes in I think people take it for granted if you're on assistance you're dirty. If any of the neighbours come in I feel as though I daren't offer them a cup of tea.' A sense of being watched, of actually taking money out of the pockets of people living round about and their resenting it, pervaded a few interviews. If a mother was born overseas she was doubly persecuted: 'You foreigners coming here and taking all the national assistance and we keeping you.' Unhappily the status of dependence could marry with a shy nature to produce unbearable discomfort. A separated wife said,

I'm frightened to go out, me. I like to go out in the dark when nobody can see me, and then I won't meet nobody I know. Once when I was in the town centre I had me best clothes on and somebody was walking past and they said, 'Fancy her, dressed up like that on national assistance,' and ever since then I've felt awful. I suppose you're not entitled to go out or do owt. If I go to the pictures I feel guilty.

Feelings of dependence and the hostility of neighbours and friends were not as pronounced in the few middle-class families on this survey. A middle-class mother said of her friends, 'I wouldn't say they're intrigued by me, but I'm something of an oddity to them. They've learnt a lot from me since I've succumbed to N.A.' For these middle-class mothers assistance was seen as a welcome alternative to the real possibility of total dependence on family and friends. Generalizations from such small numbers are risky, but one aspect of the difference observed in this survey between middle-class and working-class attitudes to acquaintances on assistance appeared to stem from the social distance between the middle-class and the bulk of assistance recipients with whom they could in no way identify.[4]

At the time of the interview, a quarter of the mothers were able to preserve their self-respect by regarding assistance as benefits from contributions paid – if not their own then those of their husbands or other relatives: one woman liked to think the blood she gave as a donor was a repayment to the community for her assistance. A further quarter of the mothers had grown used to the idea of being on assistance. But the remaining half still felt acutely embarrassed, and some were secretive about assistance in various ways. Drawing the money presented problems for one in five mothers. A widow said,

I think if I'd had to go to the little post office here I wouldn't have had assistance at all, because it's a right little village is this: they all know your business. I take my book down to the General. Do you know there are seven widows on this road, and they're all on assistance because I see the woman (officer) go into their houses, the same one that comes here. But we never mention it to each other. We meet outside and we never say anything about it. That's the way you are with assistance.

Nine mothers said they went to the G.P.O. in this way to draw their money rather than collect it locally (the numbers may well be larger since no systematic questions were asked on this point). Seven said they were embarrassed by the colour of their allowance book which at that time was different from pension and family allowance books; they folded it so that the cover could not be seen, placed another book on top of it, or went to the length of getting a special holder for it. One or two widows said they made a point of prominently displaying their widows' pension book, 'to show I hadn't just the one book'. These mothers welcomed tact in the post office, preferring their money to be counted out of sight without the amount being spoken for others in the queue to hear. They tried to wait until the office was empty, and three never drew their money in person, but got an old neighbour or relative to do it for them. Those mothers who said they were no longer embarrassed at being on assistance gave the impression that they considered the admission to be not to their credit, almost a sign that they were becoming hard-faced. Seven mothers had not told relatives or friends, and one unmarried mother said of her daughter,

I worry about whether she'll find out it's so awful, keeping it from her, and it would be dreadful for the child. She's getting older and she asks. She knows I wasn't married, that's the worst thing. Thank goodness she knows that, but she doesn't know I'm on assistance, I try to keep that from her. I've still got a bit of pride left.

At least three mothers had not told children who would be old enough to understand. When they were interviewed several mothers had just left assistance by starting full-time work and they expressed very clearly their feelings of constraint. One said,

I used to feel so tied before. It's like a release now. Every penny that you spent, you felt as though you were spending their money. I felt as if I'd borrowed it and as though somebody would come along some day and ask for it back. It's a marvellous thing, but no.

It is clear from what these mothers said that they still regarded dependence on national assistance as a last resort only, to be avoided if at all possible. So it should be stressed that what mothers said about their experience of national assistance, and indeed the experience itself, was probably shaped by the emotional turmoil of their broken relationships, by their anxious hopes and painful needs, their preconceptions about the nature of 'public' assistance, their pride and their feelings about how the rest of the population looked at them.

Lack of information about assistance

Another major problem which effectively undermined the right to support had been lack of knowledge about the assistance provisions. The mothers' situations were often complex and changing so that they would have been baffled had they tried to work out their detailed entitlement. But they often lacked information at a much more elementary level. A quarter of the mothers, who had delayed applying, said the delay arose because they did not know about assistance. It seems likely that they all knew about 'public assistance' in a general sort of way, but they still had to be told that assistance was now intended to be more humane and available for women in their situation.

Mothers' difficulties in finding out about assistance were illustrated by the fact that only two had approached the N.A.B. in what was intended to be the normal way, by sending a form obtained from their local post office to the N.A.B. office requesting a home visit from an officer. Questioning the remaining mothers on how they had first heard of assistance provisions proved difficult because some had been on assistance many years, but rough proportions can be given for the different channels of information. About one fifth of the women had already received assistance before the spell of fatherlessness began: they had been married to men who had been unemployed, ill, or in prison. However, where the allowance had been paid to the husband, he had occasionally concealed from the wife that he was receiving money for her and the children. Thus, when the women needed to apply for assistance for themselves, they did not necessarily realize they could claim in their own right.

Almost two fifths of the women had found out about assistance from relatives, usually their parents – who were sometimes receiving assistance – or friends or neighbours. An advertising campaign and invitations to apply for assistance had been directed at the aged, and old people in particular were able to reassure mothers who were reluctant to apply. The fact that assistance had lost its terrors for at least a proportion of the aged indirectly helped fatherless families too. However, there was no advertising directed at the fatherless.

Another fifth of the mothers found out about assistance through contacts with the law – with the courts, solicitors, probation officers, or police. In seeking legal aid some mothers were automatically brought into contact with the N.A.B. In eight instances a solicitor had been involved, including three middle-class families where the solicitor himself had suggested that the mother should apply for assistance. One woman said,

I hadn't a clue what to do. I went to see my solicitor. He said to me, 'What the devil are you doing?' So I said I'd flogged my jewellery, and a few pieces of silver, but now there wasn't anything left. He said I couldn't go on doing that, so he told me about national assistance, and he arranged for them to come round and see me.

However, several Northborough mothers had failed for a long time to find out about assistance, although every week they went to the magistrates' court to try to collect their husband's maintenance payments. One woman said,

It was only accidental I found out about assistance. I used to go to the court and if there wasn't anything for me I just used to go home. And it was many and many a month before I found out that if he didn't pay, the assistance would make it up. Then I was just in court one time, and there was a woman in there, and she said, 'Hey well, I'll have to get on to the assistance, I suppose.' And I said to her, 'What do you mean?' She said, 'If they don't pay here, the assistance board will make it up.'

The Northborough court did not see its function as smoothing mothers' paths to obtaining assistance.

The remainder of the mothers gained their information in miscellaneous ways. Four doctors saw that individual mothers were pregnant, depressed by financial worry, or overworked, and told them to apply for assistance. Medical advice was not uniform, however: one unmarried mother's doctor had said, 'You should go out to work. Why should the state keep you?' Other women had learned of assistance via an almoner, a town councillor, the housing office (when they asked about rent rebate), the rates office (when they asked about rates rebate), or the Ministry of Pensions, when there was a query about a widow's pension (where the Ministry of Pensions had insisted on treating a broken family as one unit, paying sick pay to the husband for himself and his dependants, it had taken the intervention of the N.S.P.C.C. to convince the N.A.B. that the woman was unsupported).

Such a variety of channels of information about national assistance may seem reassuring But hardship was occurring because mothers found out too late about their eligibility for assistance. Their difficulties were often serious before they came to the attention of someone who could help or advise them. Scarcely any of them found out about the possibility of sending in a form from the post office.[5] And the variety of sources of information itself indicates that assistance was insufficiently publicized for mothers to discover their eligibility.

The initial reception at the office

The mothers' experiences during their first visit to the N.A.B. office also proved to be a deterrent to applying for assistance. All but seven first went to the office, and although afterwards they needed to go there only very occasionally or not at all, the office experience did much to colour their impressions of assistance as a whole. They were upset not only by the other applicants, but also by conditions there,[6] and the officers' behaviour at the counter.

In the office mothers had felt for the first time what it was to be labelled and treated as one of the needy. A middle-class mother rolled her eyes and threw up her hands at the memory: 'Oh my dear! There behind me were all these ghastly types, sitting at the back, really rough! The sort with knotted hand-kerchiefs tied round their necks. That's when it really hurt, terribly. I thought, "Have I come down to this?"' She walked out and went home to await an officer there. The lack of privacy in the office added to the shock. Mothers could request a private interview but were reluctant to draw more attention to themselves by doing so. A young separated wife said,

It was terrible then, it wasn't like it is now. There was only one little room, and one desk in it, no privacy at all. Everybody sat round this desk and they could hear what you were talking about. And I don't know whether I got a bad day or not, but the people that were in there! I've been since and they've been a bit better, but when I went that time they were real down-and-outs. So I looked at the type of people and you know what you're like, seventeen years old, I suppose it was a bit of pride. Now, I don't bother, but then I just turned round and walked straight out.

On this occasion she, too, did not apply for assistance but made arrangements to go out to work. It seemed that first reactions to the office, mingled as they were with the first realization of dependency, were likely to be exaggerated. But each time mothers went to the office again they were forced to consider afresh whether, in the public mind, they were classed along with other applicants whom they met in the office and felt to be undeserving: 'Some of them go past and they tell the people in the queue, "This is my beer money", and there are you sitting there with two kids and you've had no breakfast.'

The applicants likely to be seen in the office were probably untypical. Most assistance recipients are old-age pensioners, but many applicants in the office will be the unemployed. Also, people who had difficulty in budgeting, who had rent arrears, or whose claims might be fraudulent were asked to make frequent visits. And on these occasions some may have 'dressed down', wearing their oldest clothes to impress officials: one woman said, 'You see some of them outside in the street again, the same people, and they're normally dressed.' Thus, first and even later visits to the office were likely to give an inaccurate and unfavourable impression of the dependent population. Only if the mothers could keep away from the office were they likely to be able to preserve their self-esteem and come to terms with their dependent status.

According to what the mothers said, the N.A.B. officers were also affected adversely by the office situation. They had to deal with applicants whom they saw as members of a crowd, among whom would be a proportion intent on fraud. The problem outlined by the Board was here at its most acute, how to provide for the needy while singling out the dishonest applicants. In the office delays were frequent, and waiting their turn mothers, often freshly plunged into personal crisis, had witnessed arguments and even fights. 'The officer shouted at this old man, "I don't know how you've got the cheek to come in here" (and he was wearing pumps was this old man) "I'm not giving you any money," he said. And the old man had to go out again, and it was snowing outside.' Another time, 'There was one with crutches and a man behind the counter was shouting at him saying, "The doctor says you don't need crutches. Throw them away!"' Another mother said, 'I've seen women in there whose husbands had left them and they've thrown their children over the counter. They've brought them in, thrown one across and passed the other over and said, "Here, you won't give me any money, you can have them."' The picture mothers drew of their first encounter with the officers was of the Welfare State's overworked front-line defence against an army of potential scroungers.

According to the mothers, officers did not preserve the balance between wariness and tact, and their manner was in itself a deterrent to applicants. A separated wife recalled an early visit,

She was really nasty to me. She said, 'We'll get your false teeth and glasses, but don't expect us to keep your children.' False teeth! I didn't need false teeth, I've got me own teeth. I screamed at her. I threw the book in her face and told her she could keep it and went running out. But do you know, next day there was a cheque in the post for £17. They seem as though they have to get you to the point where you crack, where you turn round and hit back at them.

Other applicants felt that officers *always* behaved differently in the office from when they paid home visits. Another separated wife said,

On the counter they're pigs, they're more aggressive. They've got more protection around them and they're condescending. They don't take any time over you, they can't be bothered. If you ask them how they come to a ruling they say, 'That's the ruling and that's all we're going to tell you.' They never explain how they reach it. You're not supposed to know.

Officers at the counter appeared to become more impersonal, perhaps because the situation was less conducive to recognition and respect for the mother's personality than when she was seen alone in her home surroundings.

Large numbers of mothers may have been permanently deterred by their first experience of the office from drawing assistance, and may have gone out to work instead. The first visit to the office was probably the worst. Mothers had to swallow their pride and establish their eligibility for an allowance, but once this had been done they would receive an order book cashable at the local post office and a period of calm in the relationship might follow. Yet certain mothers were likely to find that two fundamental issues raised on their first application for assistance were never finally settled in their favour. They had to assert their legal right not to work, and they had to re-assure officers that they were not living with a man. From these two issues stemmed a great deal of the initial unpleasantness at the office and the continuing friction and discomfort which mothers experienced while on assistance.

The mothers' right not to work

Tension in the mother's relationship with the N.A.B. arose out of the pressures she felt were brought to bear upon her by officers to get a job, against which she had constantly to reassert her right not to work. It could be for her own good, both psychological and financial, if she worked part-time. But full-time work was another matter, involving a great deal of strain for little financial reward. In either case, the mother had the legal right – and she should have had sufficient information about her rights – to choose for herself the course she preferred. However, it appeared from what mothers said that those who worked part-time were regarded by N.A.B. officers as more worthy, while the same officers remained ambivalent about whether certain mothers should be allowed to draw assistance at all.

The first interview at the office tended to produce the worst conflict. A few mothers were asked if they had registered at the employment exchange for work, and they gained the impression they were obliged to register. In particular, some of the younger unmarried mothers said they had been under considerable pressure to work full-time. They found it difficult to distinguish between a formal direction to work and a very strong suggestion that they must find a job, but one unmarried mother said,

They've been right nasty with me. They're always trying to get me to get a job. They made me sign on twice a week at the Labour Exchange. They keep telling me, 'You've got to find a job,' and that used to make me nervous and insecure, because I used to think they might cut off my assistance and leave me with nothing.

Another unmarried mother said she had trouble with a home visitor and with Ministry of Labour officials:

They sent a visitor, but he was very nasty. He said the tax-payers didn't want to pay for me to have a baby, so I said I'd do without the money. Then they gave me some at the Employment Exchange. I went to sign on and there was a nasty old woman in there. She said, 'We're not going to sign you on,' she said.

She said she refused assistance after this for almost a year. Other unmarried mothers said they had been given a certain length of time to find a job, or had been told they must go out to work when their child went to school.

Altogether half the Seaston unmarried mothers said they had been pressed to work full-time in this way, and so did three of the divorced women with illegitimate children.[7] Northborough unmarried mothers also felt under pressure to work full-time, and the West Indians did not even seem to know they could remain on assistance while working part-time. The treatment of *young* widows, and other separated and divorced wives appeared less punitive, in that they had never been made to register or pressed so urgently to work full-time.

To some extent the greater pressure to work which officers brought to bear on unmarried mothers may have reflected the view that these mothers were young and fairly fit, with small families of young children who might conveniently be left if the mother wished; that is, these mothers were hardest pressed because they had the greatest chance to become independent. This may also partly account for the distinctive work-experience of these unmarried mothers, for all of those with more than one child had worked full-time until their families numbered two or three. Also there were other reasons why unmarried mothers might be pressed to get work. Their way of life tended to be less settled, and investigation of their resources presented greater problems. These were members of the underclass, and the suspicion that they were likely to have a man-friend somewhere, and even to be earning from prostitution, lay behind some of the N.A.B.'s nervousness. However, among the other mothers were some who were dating men, yet none of these women was made to register for work or directed to work full-time. For example, a divorced mother, with one child of school age and support from her family, said she was ready to work full-time and had anticipated being told to get a job, but, 'The man said when he filled in the form, from time to time they might get on to me to get a job, but they never have.' This does not mean that full-time work was never suggested to other women, but they were never strongly pressed or made to register at the employment exchange. Thus, the suspicion of discrimination against unmarried mothers by certain officers must stand.

There were further reasons why officers brought pressure on some mothers to work. When their children grew up and became independent, these mothers would no longer be eligible for assistance unless they were physically unfit or could show that there was no suitable work available for them. Thus, the older separated, divorced, and unmarried mothers might be faced with a complete loss of resources on the day their youngest child left school. The N.A.B. officers had the unpleasant duty of urging these older mothers to go back to full-time work, and after a long break from work some of the women experienced symptoms akin to those arising from institutionalization: even part-time work was difficult for them because it involved going out and meeting people. This problem was most acute with the older unmarried mothers, and although an excuse was advanced by one that her clothes were not fit to be seen, it seemed that she was really shy about her *person*. But all the older mothers except those with pensions feared the situation. One described the prospect of going back to work as like being on the edge of a precipice. Establishing that they were too ill to work full-time was difficult, and mothers said that officers' judgements of capacity to work differed. Some officers were said to be unconvinced even by a medical certificate. Here, as in other judgements, the N.A.B. managers appeared more liberal than some of the officers. Thus, a separated wife said, 'One of them said, "You only want to work a little bit and then you'll be off national assistance," but when the manager came round he said, "I don't think you look strong enough to work."' The need to prepare older mothers for independence does not explain the pressure on mothers who had patently no hope of earning an adequate wage, for example where a mother had three, four, or even five children.

Persistent pressures to work had a number of serious consequences. A separated wife said, 'That's the sort of thing that makes me think I shouldn't be here, I should be out working. Whenever I go to collect it I feel, "I shouldn't be doing this."' Women's dependence was emphasized, so that they were inhibited from asking for grants. Moreover, their feelings of insecurity and imprisonment were increased, for individual officers had approaches neither in line one with another nor with official policy, and this served to heighten mothers' sense of the arbitrariness of officers' powers over them.

In these circumstances the decision to take a full-time job was not a careful weighing of the advantages and disadvantages of work as compared with assistance. Several mothers who had just stopped receiving assistance or who were planning to work full-time were little better off, and might even be worse off, than if they had remained on assistance working part-time. But these mothers were so relieved at the prospect of being off assistance that they did not care if they were only a few shillings to the good. Mothers may have assumed that pressure to work meant full-time work, since at least four did not know that it was possible to work part-time while on assistance and retain earnings (I did not raise the point systematically because I had at first assumed that it would have been made clear to applicants). It may be argued that some mothers might benefit psychologically and socially from working, but in the circumstances mothers were being forced off assistance, rather than being allowed to take their own decision. And older mothers, who possibly needed a careful and gradual rehabilitation with trained social-work help if they were ever again to work, were instead being frightened by threats of withdrawal of assistance.

Pressure to work probably kept up the numbers of mothers who worked part-time, for otherwise resentment of the earnings limit of £2 was a strong deterrent. The fact that they could not improve their situation however hard they worked while on assistance did much to sap the mothers' morale and increase their sense of being trapped: 'They don't give you a chance to better yourself.' Twenty-nine mothers worked part-time, but the earnings limit and restrictions on the kind of work they were able to do meant that they frequently worked for very low rates of pay. One woman worked fifteen hours for a net gain of 21s. Another for 28s. did all a man's washing, ironing and house-work, cleaned his windows, washed his car and made his dinners on two days. Although the Board usually made adequate allowance for fares to work, the expense of having children minded was not offset against earnings, so that this ate into already minute profits. With part-time earnings also there was a failure of communication at the most elementary level, where several mothers thought the earnings rule was even less than £2: this occurred because the instruction in the book specified that the mother should tell the Board if her earnings rose *above their present amount*, which was written in the book, with the result that mothers took this rather than £2 to be the earnings limit.

Because mothers' needs and their resentment against the earnings rule were great, the temptation not to declare earnings was strong. Six mothers were retaining more than they were supposed to at the time of these interviews, and altogether one in five mothers admitted to doing so in the past. Two were still repaying for previously undeclared earnings. Often mothers in a temporary crisis had taken a job in the hope of getting quick money, knowing that it was certain to be discovered before long. The N.A.B. frequently decided not to prosecute, but the warnings given to mothers who had earned a few shillings extra were awesome, with threats of prison.

The N.A.B. itself had no adequate detective branch (although this was being expanded) and officers were too over-worked to be able to devote much time to policing individual families. As a result, often the N.A.B.'s only hope of detecting undeclared earnings was an anonymous letter. The source of such letters might be the neighbours, but could also be other assistance recipients who resented someone else on assistance getting away with illegal work. As one mother observed, 'You have to watch it when you're apple picking, because if somebody gets jealous, if they think you're really making something, they'll split on you.'

Thus in a literal sense, assistance recipients were kept under surveillance, and a limit set to illegal earnings, by the surrounding community. It was only the attention given by the Board to these anonymous letters which made the system of checking workable.

Cohabitation

The second major, and larger and more sensitive, problem of investigating means and establishing entitlement was the N.A.B.'s concern that the mother should not be cohabiting. An officer finding evidence of cohabitation or even strongly suspecting cohabitation could stop the mother's allowance, and, as the Board said, many women who were suspected of cohabiting voluntarily surrendered their allowances, although for a successful prosecution evidence of financial support from the man would have had to be obtained.

The S.B.C. have only recently published their administrative practices and changed and revised instructions to staff in relation to cohabitation, so we have no clear idea what were the instructions and official directives to officers at the time when the present survey was carried out. Perhaps reading between the lines we can now take the areas which receive particular stress in the *Cohabitation* pamphlet as those where more uncertainty and difficulty were experienced by the N.A.B. and the S.B.C. with their officers in the past. The new instructions are now very definite that cohabitation should not depend solely on any single factor. Obviously economic support from the man is of vital interest, but, failing direct evidence of total support, common residence or irregular sexual intercourse are not now in themselves regarded officially as sufficient evidence of cohabitation:

The first step should be to ascertain evidence of any form of public acknowledgement. If public acknowledgement is lacking, further enquiries into possible cohabitation are to be made only on the authority of a senior officer and where there is some actual evidence justifying further investigations. Such evidence might be, for example, the birth of a child of the union; information that the couple are known as a married couple in the neighbourhood; indications, for example, from their going on holidays together, that their relationship might be other than the usual landlady/lodger one; or the obvious unsuitability of the accommodation for a lodger. The instructions also provide that if a woman denies cohabitation or says that the man living in her household is a lodger, and there is no public acknowledgement, a decision that the couple are cohabiting may only be taken with the authority of a senior officer. The Commission have also given instructions that, in reaching decisions, considerable emphasis should be placed on the stability of a union as evidence of cohabitation and that, conversely, the fact that a woman receives an occasional visitor, whether he sleeps with her or not, does not of itself justify a decision that there is cohabitation. They accept that adherence to this instruction will frequently lead to criticism, especially in the case of a woman who has a number of men visitors who stay overnight or a woman who receives frequent visits from the same man. [8]

Here, then, is a definite attempt to stand out against any illiberal community pressures. There is also a tightening-up of instructions and checks on officers' behaviour, although it will be apparent that there is still room for ambiguity to arise in particular cases. It looks as if the invoking of senior authority for proceeding with cases and the instructions in relation to evidence, continuity, and sex are new, or have received new emphasis. But we must postpone judgement on how far these measures will be effective until we have seen what the practical difficulties are.

At the time of this survey an immediate result of officers' concern with cohabitation was that on the first visit to the office the mother's word that she was alone was likely to be disbelieved or doubted. This partly explains the eagerness of some of the officers that the mother should take the father to court. Possession of a court order was a valuable aid towards independence should the mother wish to work, and the mother's court order would not lapse if she became independent of assistance in the way that an order taken out by the Board would do. But a court order was also the most convenient proof that the father had gone and was not merely feigning desertion. So, as one N.A.B. manager admitted to me, some mothers were 'bullied' into taking the father to court against their wishes. In two instances, unmarried mothers said they were specifically told in the office that this was a condition of their receiving an allowance, and one had to go to the reference library to discover for herself that it was not. Thus here, as in the field of housing, maintenance orders were being used as credentials of a mother's entitlement to help.

Mothers could not always obtain a separation order (if the

husband or father had disappeared for instance) and they might then have to go to the office, weekly or more often, for a period of a month or until such time as their very persistence proved the separation to be of sufficient permanence for a permanent allowance to be granted to them. Once a mother had convinced the N.A.B. that the father had gone, her relationship with the Board usually entered a more tranquil period. If she had no wish or opportunity for courtship and remarriage, possible support from a man might never again be in question.

If, however, the mother had a man-friend and the relationship became at all close, the suspicions of an officer were likely to be aroused. A separated wife said that one day an officer had called when her friend was visiting and had asked,

'Is this man cohabiting with you?' and I said, 'You what? If that means is he living with me, the answer is no.' And I said, 'If you want to check up there's plenty round here that can tell you, because who-ever you are, you've got enemies, haven't you?' And he said, 'Nay, we don't do things like that.'

Suspicion of cohabitation fell upon mothers unevenly, depending on their age, marital status, and mode of life. Unmarried mothers who had more than one illegitimate child by the same father in a 'visiting marriage' were suspected, and also the mothers who have been described as belonging to an 'underclass' were frequently harried. A young separated wife was suspected of cohabiting with a man of fifty; but a separated wife of over forty cohabiting with a lodger aged twenty-seven, a widow with a lodger aged fifty, and a forty-five-year-old woman cohabiting with her brother-in-law were not suspected (I think the informa-tion given to me in these instances was probably of similar status to that available to the N.A.B.). Whether a woman fell under suspicion partly depended on how suspicious-natured an officer might be: thus one mother – who probably was having sexual intercourse with her lodger – did not fall under suspicion until a new officer came to see her.

Numbers were small, but the pattern of officers' suspicions which emerged might look something like this: unmarried mothers and young women generally were thought more likely to cohabit than older women, including most of the widows. Women were thought more likely to have sexual relations with men older than themselves. And women living in certain types of housing or areas of the town were thought more likely to be cohabiting.

As with illegal earnings, and for similar reasons, the basic evidence for these suspicions appeared usually to be anonymous letters, whose source was difficult to establish. They were more frequent for mothers living on council estates then elsewhere. Mothers pointed to ex-husbands, erstwhile friends who were now enemies or rivals for a man's affections, and other assistance recipients or working neighbours who were jealous of what they regarded as unfair income. It is unfortunately impossible to be more precise, although an analysis of these letters and their influence on the Board's work is of prime importance.

In several instances mothers claimed that their allowance had been cut off after an anonymous letter following one overnight stay by a man. In other instances where officers became suspicious, their attempts to establish evidence revealed that cohabitation was being defined for practical purposes on a very narrow basis: whatever the intentions of the N.A.B., the stress of questioning and investigation by officers appears to have lain in establishing the existence of sexual relationship, however unstable and infrequent. Moreover, because officers had no special powers to question or obtain entrance to houses to gain evidence of fraud, according to mothers they were forced to adopt questionable and even illegal practices, which had a sinister and often bizarre quality.

Officers would make unexpected visits, sometimes as many as three a week, in the hope that the man would be caught or frightened away. A mythology had grown up about the subject and mothers told stories of officers taking assessments while men hid in wardrobes or underneath the very settee on which they were sitting. One mother, although she was enthusiastic about some home visitors, described a particular officer with distaste:

That B—, he's a nasty sod he is. He's like a detective. He knocks at your door and he's looking at your line at the same time to see you're not doing any men's washing, and all the time he's in here he's looking under the sofas to see there's nothing there, no men's shoes or nothing.

Other women claimed that officers, in their eagerness for confirmation of their suspicions, had entered houses without permission:

We wondered whatever he was doing. He came in, and he didn't knock until he got to that door (an inner door of the house). Then he came in, and all of a sudden he walked across, and the kitchen door was closed, and we wondered wherever he was going. And he went right through and caught Jackie's father in the pantry.

If it could be established that the mother was concealing the fact that a man was living in the house she apparently stood self-convicted, and this was sufficient to warrant stopping the allowance. However, if the mother took a lodger openly, went to live at a house where the tenant was a man, or stood her ground when a man was discovered in her house, claiming that he was a genuine lodger, the procedure of establishing cohabitation was more complex. The officer asked the customary questions about financial arrangements, but apparently he was also, and even mainly, interested in the possibility of the couple having sexual relations. One mother said,

They were really horrible. First one man came round, then another, saying, 'Do you sleep with Mr Barnes? Are you committing adultery with him?' And I told him it's my own private business, but the man says, 'You *can't* tell me that a man and a woman living in the same house don't go to bed together,' and I told him that's dirty talk and I don't like it at all.

According to another,

The N.A.B. say I am getting housekeeping from Mr Johns, but that is not true. He doesn't give me a thing. And they say I must get some money, and do we have separate beds, do we have intercourse, all these questions they ask, but they cannot prove anything, and it is not so.

It seemed clear from these encounters that it is not only the degree of financial support which is at issue, but chiefly the nature of the sexual relationship between the couple.[9]

In practice it was often doubtful whether there was any financial support from men with whom the mothers were living.

A separated wife described her difficulties when she was accused of cohabiting with a separated man who was not the father of any of her children. Because they were very attached to one another, and the mother in particular derived a great deal of support from the relationship, she fought the Board, and was still fighting at the time of the interview.

They took my book away and said he can keep me now, but for that week I was nearly living there. They wouldn't give me my book back, but they gave me bits and pieces till the officer came to see me, two days' money and three days' money ... [She lost her appeal.] They gave me £1 each for the children and only 13/- for me. At first they weren't going to give me nothing, but I got onto the Welfare and Probation Officer and they rang up the national assistance. They said, 'You can't expect another man to keep them children.' I told them if they don't give me no money, they'll have to go back into homes.

Only when the lodger was off work sick did she get her full allowance, since then he could not claim dependants' allowance for her. At the time of the interview she was apparently being stopped almost £5 more than if the man had been treated as a lodger and assessed on what he actually paid her.

The S.B.C. has said that 'in the last resort' only will the children be supported in cohabitation cases. On this evidence 'the last resort' seems likely to take some reaching and to be a desperate case indeed.

Where intercourse between a couple was suspected but was not admitted and could not be established or presumed beyond doubt, in several instances the Board had stopped about £3 from the mother's allowance. One mother was told that this was 'in lieu of earnings as a housekeeper', although she specifically denied that she was earning. Two other families who had money stopped had had visiting West Indian fathers. But in one instance the father had now disappeared. In the other the N.A.B. may have decided that the father's declared voluntary payment understated the extent of his financial help to the mother.

The N. A. B practices with regard to cohabitation discouraged the mother from starting any new relationships with men, and helped to break up any relationships which she had formed.

One divorced woman described the difficulties she had experienced when the father of her illegitimate child (who was himself separated, with two children, who lived with his wife, to maintain) came to live with her and her four other children, and she voluntarily surrendered her national assistance allowance.

If the assistance would have kept only two children we could have managed. He was finding it difficult with his two children and at the same time trying to keep this lot going. The problems we had. There were so many children involved. I kept thinking about mine, and he kept thinking about his. And I thought why should mine suffer, and I realized I was going to be better off on national assistance. You see he didn't get a very big wage, he only had £10, and I suppose it was difficult for Mr Gunn, he must have known that I'd been used to a weekly allowance and men don't like you to have independence. And he liked to smoke and drink, and I suppose it was difficult to go without for a man who wasn't going to keep his own children.

After a short time, to the woman's regret, this relationship fell through, and several years afterwards she still felt that through shortage of money it had never been given a chance.

It is important to stress that these mothers' allegations in relation to officers' interpretation of the cohabitation rule are not unsupported. In an account of his experiences in another N.A.B. office between the years 1960 and 1963, Hill both describes similar practices in that office and suggests reasons why officers behave in this way. The reasons make it likely that such behaviour was widespread. He identified the most prevalent form of the misuse of officers' powers as the manipulation of *access* to support for mothers and the unemployed. He also suggests that cutting off the allowance and filing away the case papers in instances where cohabitation was only suspected but not proven could be 'an avoidance of the ponderous and long-winded procedure for dealing with fraud' and also, presumably, an avoidance of some unsavoury probing into the mother's private life. Hill says,

This tactic (described as 'mucking applicants around') was particularly used with unmarried mothers or deserted wives where they were suspected of continuing a relationship with a man, the aim being to make it more difficult for the woman to get money from the N.A.B. than from the man . . . In this type of case inevitably the woman often comes back for more Assistance, hence 'mucking around' consisted of giving small payments, after a long wait in the office, the inadequacy of which forced her continually to re-apply for Assistance. The official doctrine [Hill does not say in what sense this was 'official'] on this kind of case was (a) not to make large payments when marital reconciliation seemed imminent, and (b) in case of suspected fraud to secure regular written statements from the person which might subsequently be produced as false statements in court . . . Such cases tended to involve a great deal of frustration for Executive Officers arising from their inability to provide the kind of evidence that would satisfy the lawyers that court action was justifiable.[10]

Thus, whatever the rationale, the intention and the aim of the cohabitation rule, its existence and practical administration by the N.A.B. officers entailed a number of highly unfortunate consequences. Relationships between the officers and a large proportion of the mothers were soured. And the more malicious or ill-disposed members of the community were given an unsavoury hold over the mother's social life and livelihood. The net effect of the rule was thus to discourage those relationships with men upon which the mothers depended for companionship and help and indeed for any possibility of remarriage and independence. The rule was a source of official malpractice and even illegal behaviour, and whatever the spirit of the codes of discretion, the interpretation by officers appears narrow and biassed by community prejudices against illegitimacy, separation, and divorce. The ambiguity in the official ruling that only in the last resort will the children be supported in cohabitation cases seems likely to insure the recurrence of tension and conflict; and the insecurity will be particularly harmful to the children over whom the wrangling takes place, a wrangling which sometimes becomes physical.

Discretionary allowances and grants

We will now go on to examine the other claims for discretionary schemes, that discretion operates flexibly to meet need and generously to benefit the client, so that too close a specification and publication of discretionary rules would be against the clients' interests. As a research worker attempting an external investigation of discretion, I experienced some of the mothers' bafflement with a system where information was so inadequate. The *Handbook* had not yet been published. I had the advantage of knowing the published regulations which most of the mothers had not seen or even heard of, and I had also a range of comparable cases from which some aspects of the N.A.B.'s discretionary practices could at least be inferred.[11] But although in theory the mothers could obtain a written statement of how their allowance had been calculated, none of them had done so.[12] I therefore had to carry out my own 'assessments' of the mothers' basic entitlements, and from these infer whether, and in what direction, discretion had been exercised. Inevitably, this will not permit any very close discussion of individual discretionary rules, although we can comment on some of the more striking anomalies in the overall pattern.

For the 115 mothers whose incomes I assessed, in 48 instances my assessment (which did not initially allow for any discretion) agreed with the actual allowances paid; 22 of the allowances were higher than my assessment, but 45 were lower (Appendix Table 12). All the discrepancies noted were of 5s. a week or more. Of the 67 instances where the mother's allowance differed from my assessment of her basic scale allowance, all but 9 could be explained as exercises of officers' discretion, but in a small number of cases it appeared that the full facts of the mother's situation were not known to the Board. In practice the distinction between a regular weekly increment for special need, i.e. a 'discretionary allowance' or addition, and the exercise of discretion in the mother's favour is blurred, and they will be discussed together.

(a) *Discretionary Additions*

These mothers had extra expense with H.P. spent on getting a home together, pregnancy, children's illnesses, and so on. Yet there was little evidence of encouragement being given to officers to make discretionary additions. The number of discretionary allowances for special needs, nine, was low. One unmarried mother said that when her baby was born, in February, 'I asked for some coal to keep the baby warm, but they said no, I couldn't have any, that was only for old people.' At the time of the interview another mother with a very young baby had no discretionary addition to her allowance. Two mothers said they had been persuaded to draw their maternity allowance only (that is, the weekly allowance paid for working contributions) *instead* of assistance when their babies were born, and this allowance was not equivalent to the national assistance basic scale rate plus the discretionary addition which the birth merited. Pregnancy and the time immediately after would appear to be a situation where mothers clearly need extra and a standard ruling is possible, but discretion was not being exercised uniformly.

Of the remaining thirteen mothers who were receiving an allowance at more than the basic scale rate, in six instances the officer had not deducted from the mother's allowance the full share of the rent payable by a non-dependant living in the household although that non-dependant's contribution to household expenses warranted the deduction. Thus a mother whose son gave her £4 had only 5s. stopped, and another woman whose brother gave her as much as £4 10s. some weeks had only 10s. taken off. In a further two families a mother who already benefited substantially through living with parents was given the maximum allowance towards the rent, although less would have been justified; and one widow had no deduction for cash savings in the bank over the then Regulation limit of £125. Four high payments could not be accounted for by the mothers' circumstances as revealed to me.

In general it would appear that, unlike old people, fatherless families are not yet accepted by N.A.B. officers as a group likely to have needs meriting discretionary allowances.

(b) *Allowances below the Scale Rate*

More frequently allowances appeared to be paid below scale rates. In eighteen instances there may be a case for altering the existing written Regulations of the N.A.B., or checking on officers' interpretation of them. Home-owners receive only the interest

repayments and a small amount for repairs, and must find the
capital repayments out of their allowance. Thus, ten home-
owners, nine of whom were still paying for their houses, received allowances which were on average 15s. below their true
housing costs, that is 15s. below what they would have received
had their accommodation been rented. Also five mothers aged
below twenty-one were being paid at juvenile rates. The two
youngest had been specifically told that they could not receive
more than a child's rate, which was over £1 lower than that for
an adult, and that mothers under eighteen could not even receive
a rent allowance. As a result a sixteen-year-old girl with a six-
month-old baby received only £3 7s. a week. It might have been
possible for officers to have paid young mothers at adult rates,
for the manager of one N.A.B. office thought this was being done.
Finally among these instances where written Regulations need
overhauling, three families may have been rent-stopped; in other
words the N.A.B. officer concerned may have refused to pay their
high rents. This was one of the more difficult inferences to make
from the data, but these families had allowances more than 5s.
below, and in one instance 10s. below, the assessment I calculated, and each mother said that an officer had frequently
complained about the rents. The rents were all over £3 10s.,
high but not unreasonable for Seaston, where all the families
lived, and there were other instances where the Board paid equally
high rents in full. The rent-stopped families all lived in inferior
accommodation, and two contained pre-school children. The
proportion of rent-stopped fatherless families may be higher
than the national figure of 1 per cent of cases where housing
costs are not fully met by the N.A.B.[13]

In eight instances where the allowance paid was below my
assessment the mother shared a household with others not
dependent on assistance. The N.A.B. applied a rigid ruling to
such shared households, but, precisely because this took no
account of the actual financial situation, there were anomalies.
As we have seen some mothers were able to benefit substantially
by living with relatives. But in four families mothers were inter-
mittently supporting young sons who worked irregularly, but
who would not or could not apply for unemployment benefit and

did not receive national assitance in their own right. Only in one of these families was the deduction from the mother's allowance (in lieu of the son's share of the rent) reduced because he did not pay her anything. In another instance the mother had not told the N.A.B. what was happening, but in the remaining two families officers had said that the sons' work record was none of their business. The N.A.B. managers, when I spoke to them, took a sympathetic line but offered no solution to this problem. There were also complaints from mothers that the N.A.B. did not pay sufficient attention to the transition period when a child began work. Although the child's allowance was not completely stopped immediately, sometimes the child's initial low earnings did not cover the purchase of the new clothing for work and the books for evening classes, and the burden fell on the mother. In two families the deduction for the rent share of a non-dependent child was found to be larger than the child's actual payment. In two other instances deductions were made for lodgers upon whom the mother made a loss: thus a woman who charged her lodger only £1, in the misunderstanding (fostered by the lodger) that the N.A.B. would take away any further money, had £1 deducted from her allowance as a rent contribution. Such a misunderstanding was possible because the woman did not know the scale rates and the Regulations governing deductions, and she was too frightened to question the N.A.B. officers.

Where a mother was living with parents for whom she cooked the N.A.B. officers had sometimes suggested she was acting as housekeeper and the parents should support her. Whether this view prevailed appeared to depend on the family's resources and on how strongly the mother was prepared to resist. One mother allowed the N.A.B. to stop £3 from her allowance, but another had had nothing stopped, and a third, who did housekeep for her relatives and gained a substantial benefit from it, was assessed as a lodger and given a rent allowance of 10s. Deducting money in such circumstances appears to come perilously close to the old poor law again.

In eight further instances, the mother's allowance was low apparently because the N.A.B. suspected she had undeclared income from a man. In six families deductions for contributions from the children's father were larger than his actual payments. The mothers were unaware of the excess deductions. Sometimes this appears to have been a deliberate over-estimation by the officer, but in at least one instance where a court order was paid only in part and irregularly the mother was not prepared to tell the Board each time the payment was short and so lost by the amount the husband had underpaid. In two families already discussed, mothers made a very substantial financial loss on men with whom they were suspected of cohabiting.

Apart from several instances already mentioned, four mothers had low allowances possibly because the N.A.B. possessed insufficient information for a correct assessment. In two instances expenses incurred in travel to work were not fully allowed; it may be that the N.A.B. knew but thought them excessive or inaccurate. One mother had been advised – as was the N.A.B. practice – to draw unemployment benefit when she stopped her job. Although she had previously been drawing assistance to supplement her earnings she was at the time of interview being refused assistance on the grounds that her unemployment benefit should be adequate, but it was not and over three weeks she had lost £9. Another woman's allowance was low because she was too frightened to tell the Board she had had another illegitimate child.

Lastly two women were still paying fines for undeclared earnings. There were four instances of low payments where I could in no way account for the reduction, unless it was for some supposed income from relatives or friends.

It was evident that there were possibilities of misunderstandings or failure to inform the Board of all the relevant facts, which could lead to a loss of money to which the mother was entitled. It was also clear that although scales were laid down for allowances, there were many ways in which officers could choose to exercise their discretionary powers. And, unfortunately, this discretion appeared not to be exercised consistently, and more often seemed to be exerted *against* raising the allowance where a rise could have been justified.

Yet the most disturbing feature of the situation was not the variation in level shown by these assessments, although some of the Regulations should be rethought, but the fact that the mothers themselves could not tell me how their allowances were arrived at, and some whose allowances were subject to deductions were unaware of their loss.

Mothers could not readily compare their situation with others because allowances include rent, and certain differing resources are deducted. They had no written assessment from the N.A.B., or oral explanation, and few had seen the Post Office leaflet setting out scale rates. As a result, there were confusions of the most elementary kind as to what national assistance payments were meant to cover, with virtually no likelihood of the mother checking her own allowance.

(c) *Exceptional Needs Grants*

Officers could also exercise their discretion to give 'exceptional needs grants', and again the provision of such grants was low. The N.A.B. supplied figures of grants, and of the 215 mothers originally contacted only 67, or one third, had ever had one. A blockage in thinking about fatherless families appears clearly in respect of the special £4 grant which was made at Christmas 1964, supposedly to tide assistance recipients over the delay at that time in raising national assistance rates. All old age pensioners received the grant, but of the 215 fatherless families only 40, or 19 per cent received it. These mothers must in some way have been judged the most needy, but from my own interviews I could not establish any consistent criteria by which the N.A.B. might have selected families for payment.

The system of exceptional needs grants was inadequate to cope with the needs of mothers who started to build up a home with no possessions apart from the clothes they stood up in. By contrast with mothers who had complete homes all paid for, their needs were huge, yet nowhere were really large grants paid by the N.A.B. From what mothers said, very rarely, if at all, did it seem that the N.A.B. officer concerned had exercised his powers to give even a £20 grant. Nor did the larger grants always go to mothers in the greatest need, or to those who had been on assistance a long time. For example, one unmarried mother had been twelve years on assistance and had had no exceptional needs grant, without suspecting that there were such grants. A separated wife had been receiving assistance for seven years and had also received no special grant. A mother of six, having been refused a grant by the Board, was given £30 from a local charity which she discovered only through the good will of the Probation Officer. A woman who had to furnish a house completely for her large family at a cost of over £200 had received from the N.A.B. only £9 for some curtains. Mothers who had babies but no maternity grant did not always receive a grant.

The pattern which emerged from inadequate data was that three quarters of the grants were for clothing, shoes, and bedding, mainly for the larger families, some of whom had come to regard them as a regular if too infrequent addition to the basic national assistance allowance. There were few grants for lino and deposits on cookers, and very little money for furniture, which was one of the mothers' chief needs.

Considering the very small contribution of these grants towards mothers' living standards, and the much greater importance of the use of officers' discretion in weekly allowances, it was surprising to find that exceptional needs grants were responsible for many of the criticisms of unfairness levelled at the N.A.B. By their nature exceptional needs grants were made to some families and not to others, so that there were bound to be disappointed applicants. But the chief problem was that the mothers did not know the criteria of need on which grants were being awarded.

Different officers might give different judgements. One mother grew quite enthusiastic about some of the home visitors: 'There's three or four of them as soon as you see them you think, "Oh lovely!"' And occasionally the officer became well enough known to be asked advice on personal problems unconnected with finance. But all officers were not the same. Three mothers said they had a request refused by one officer but granted by another. The behaviour of the officer, B—, has already been mentioned in connection with cohabitation: in the office he appears to have been equally vigilant in guarding the public purse. 'The rest of them are nice, but if B— is on when you go in everybody moans and says, "Oh Christ, B— is on, let's hope he's not seeing me." It's as if he's paying you out of his own pocket.' Here again the N.A.B. managers' interpretation of the Regulations appeared as more liberal, and one manager spoke of his difficulties in getting the older officers to be more imaginative in seeking out need.[14]

The bias in giving grants to larger families may have resulted because they had greater problems, but also because they tended to be found on corporation estates where information about grants circulated more readily. Certain groups such as prisoners' wives, when backed by social workers, may also have been more successful in getting grants. Other women had waited in vain to have their manifest needs officially noticed, and the longer they were on assistance the less inclined they felt to ask for grants themselves: 'They'll say, "You must have been managing before."' 'It's a case of if you will you must, and the poorer you profess to be, the more they'll help you, I suppose.'

From his experience Hill says that in officers' behaviour, 'It was again possible to discern with regard to these grants the pattern of reluctant yielding to pressure, the . . . tendency for the demanding to get more than the meek.'[15]

There was thus evidence that the system of exceptional needs grants, apart from being obscure to recipients, did not operate generously and equitably to relieve need. There was a basic dilemma for mothers. If they were proud they would keep their children clean and the house tidy and try to manage. Yet obtaining a grant depends on being needy, and if mothers didn't *look* needy enough and were too proud to ask insistently they might never get help.

Another undesirable side effect of discretion, and one which lends some support to allegations that discretionary policies are ones of divide and rule, is that the irregular distribution of grants seemed to exacerbate jealousies between the claimants themselves. Discretion thus militates against the claimants making a common cause together.

The relationship of the N.A.B. with other bodies

The process of obtaining grants for special needs was made much more complex for mothers by the number of sources of help potentially available to them. In addition to the N.A.B., Local Education Authorities were permitted to relieve need. Furniture could sometimes be obtained from Housing Welfare Departments, and there were also several voluntary and charitable organizations in the field, of which the W.V.S. and N.S.P.C.C. were the most conspicuous. Rotary, the Round Table, Cinderella societies, the Red Cross, private charities, and the Mayor's Fund were also mentioned. In the context of an interview about national assistance, many mothers were really complaining about the deficiences of these other bodies, or about the sheer confusion which ensued from so many different channels of help with no clear information about any one.

The main overlap occurred with the Local Education Authority, and in Northborough and Seaston two different arrangements had been reached. At a confrontation in Northborough (described for me by the Youth Employment Officer who had been an eye-witness) the N.A.B. manager had been outmanoeuvred – or so it was expressed to me – by the Chief Education Officer when it had been pointed out to him from the Parliamentary Acts that his duty to relieve need was *mandatory*, whereas the L.E.A.'s was *permissive*. As a result, for a family on assistance, the Northborough L.E.A. would relieve need only if the N.A.B. had specifically refused to do so. In fact, the situation was further complicated for mothers by the Northborough N.A.B. office's practice of referring some applicants to the W.V.S., and the equally doubtful practice of the Education Office in keeping a set of old clothes which some mothers were pressed to take before they were considered for the grant to which they were entitled. The Northborough N.A.B. also had under its wing a private charity which it revealed only to mothers considered especially needy, but to whom the Board itself did not feel inclined to make a large grant.[16] In Seaston, on the other hand, the N.A.B. had – in one sense – finally won a running battle by getting the L.E.A. to agree that grants for school-children's clothing should be the sole responsibility of the local authority. In Seaston the Board appeared to make less use of the W.V.S., although mothers were referred there by social workers.

In practice, the Northborough situation was very bad indeed. Instead of one application for grants, mothers might have to make two, and the criteria of need were unknown for either. Up till quite recently the local authority means test for free school meals was more stringent than the national assistance scales, and probably remains more stringent with regard to clothing grants. One mother said:

I did try to get some shoes. It was just after I started work (part-time) and all the kiddies wanted shoes at the same time, so I went down to see them, and they said they couldn't help me. The trouble I had with that. First I went down to the Education Office, and they said, well, they couldn't do anything because I was working. And they stopped the school meals as well – I had to fill in a form about whether I was earning thirty shillings a week. They wrote me a note saying from next week the meals wouldn't be free any more. And they sent me on to the Assistance, and they said because I was on the Assistance they should do something. Well the Assistance wouldn't do anything, and they sent me back to the Education Office. So I went back down there, and the Education Office filled in a form and I took that back to the Assistance, but they still wouldn't do anything. So I went back to the Education Office and told them. That was three times to the Education Office and two to the Assistance and I didn't get anything, so after that I gave up and didn't bother. I was dizzy going backwards and forwards.

Perhaps the system worked better in instances where mothers had a clear-cut case. But several other women said they had been sent backwards and forwards in this way. Even if the outcome of the application was favourable, there was always delay and fatigue. Perhaps the only good things to be said for the Northborough situation were that a mother who had, for no clear reason, failed with one set of officials might succeed with the others; and also the Education Office might be slightly more generous in respect of school uniform for grammar school children. Thus one mother had been told by an N.A.B. officer when she applied for a uniform grant, 'Why did you send him to that school if you knew you couldn't afford it?' But she got a grant from the Education Office.

The unified arrangements made between the N.A.B. and the Education Office in Seaston were no better for the mother. Indeed, they appeared to reduce the mother's chance of obtaining a grant, because the only source open to her was the relatively less liberal Education Office. It might seem that N.A.B. officers would recommend grants more readily if the Board did not have to meet the costs, but this did not happen. When approached, some Seaston officers appear to have confined themselves to the misleading statement that, 'We don't do grants for school clothes,' and there the application had ended. Other officers were evidently not clear how people should apply to the Education Office and recommended applying to the school, but this had seemed to the mother to involve the child too directly. One mother was told about grants but was discouraged because the officer felt the Education Office was 'cutting down or something'. Mothers who went further discovered that the Education Officers' procedure involved getting their employers to testify to earnings, and, 'They said they weren't there to fill forms in,' or the mother had not wished to let her employer know she was in need. Moreover, the local authority means test appears to have been more stringent, or more stringently applied, than the Board's. The only way to be sure of getting shoes or clothing, according to the regular recipients, was to keep the child off school until the Attendance Officer came round. The procedure for obtaining an education grant was also more embarrassing than the N.A.B. system, since any education clothing purchases made were supervised in the shop. One woman said, 'They were always degraded by it, my three. The oldest wouldn't go. He said, "I'm not going to meet him, they all know him in the shop."'

Neither the N.A.B. nor the Education Office appeared to be sufficiently sensitive to the growing pressures for school uniform in primary and secondary modern schools, and mothers who wished their children to be like others in this respect had to pay the price themselves. Even more serious, it seemed incredible but true that three mothers with children at school after the statutory school leaving age knew nothing about maintenance allowances (equivalent to over £1 a week) because it appeared to be nobody's duty to ensure they had early information about such grants.[17] The decision to leave school early was being taken without the knowledge that grants were available.

The arrangement between the Board and the W.V.S. was obscure, the W.V.S. declining to comment. But it appeared that applicants – some of whom were eligible for cash grants – were referred by the N.A.B. to the W.V.S., possibly as the 'less deserving'. The W.V.S. then applied further rough screening by appearance alone to reject a few. Also there was some kind of obligation placed by the N.A.B. on applicants to visit the W.V.S. and see that nothing was suitable before the Board would help further. A very few mothers approved of W.V.S. clothing, but most of them resented going to the W.V.S. more than any other N.A.B. arrangements involving outside bodies. A criticism of W.V.S. clothes was that they were for old women. One woman said, 'You never saw such a load of old muck that they gave me. I took it like, but I'd never go there again. There was a coat down to my ankles. Army boots for the kids. To tell you the truth in the end I gave it to the rag man.' Another said, 'The stuff they gave us were as black as a fire back. We took it along to the National Assistance and we threw it back at them and said, "What the hell do you think we are?"' Again, some mothers were put off by the transfer from one source of help to another. In Northborough one mother who had thought about applying for a grant was told by an officer, misleadingly, that, 'You could get chits for clothes but he wouldn't advise me to try, because I might be too fussy.' And there was the impression in some parts of Northborough that the Board never gave cash grants for clothes, although they might for shoes. One woman complained that having once received a grant from a church charity the Board pressed her to apply again first to this charity, rather than giving her a grant themselves.

There were other ways in which mothers lost money or benefits through inadequate liaison between different bodies. Mothers visiting children in local authority homes or in hospitals had difficulty in getting refunds of fares. Allowances were sometimes reduced for a child who was taken into care or who went to boarding school, although the mother still had calls on her income for clothing or spending money. The N.A.B. appeared not always to inform mothers about their rights to free dentures and spectacles, free prescriptions, or free orange juice. Nor apparently were they always prompt in issuing the booklets for these welfare foods and free milk: several mothers had obtained one book but never obtained a further one after the first ran out.

A disturbing aspect of this situation was that the various Northborough bodies were combining not to seek out and relieve need but – as in the days of the Charity Organization Society – primarily to guard against the possibility that a family might obtain help from two sources at the same time. To frustrate this, information – which we had been refused because it was highly confidential – was freely circulating between national, local government, and voluntary bodies. Yet this questionable circulation does not seem to have relieved some mothers from making the walk between the offices several times.

Arrangements between the N.A.B. and other bodies therefore appear to have been unsystematic and even inimical to the mothers' interests. And the presence of these various other bodies, with their different criteria of need, engendered in the mothers a greater sense of deprivation than the N.A.B. alone would have created. Indeed, had there been no possibility of help from any other source, it seems likely that mothers would have been less dissatisfied than they were with the existing confusion and uncertainty.

The right of appeal

There was the right of appeal to an Independent Appeal Tribunal against any officer's decision, and when disputes arose the officers appear to have been scrupulous in informing the mothers of this right. The procedure was that the mother must give written notice of her appeal, and then she would be called before the Tribunal. The N.A.B.'s official comments gave the impression that the small number of appeals was a sign that the system of discretion was working well, but this survey points to different conclusions. In several instances a mother's declared intention to appeal had caused the officer to change his decision. Also, it was a deterrent that the mother must make a written appeal, and moreover the appeal was against an N.A.B. officer who might still have dealings with her after the case was over. But mothers seldom decided to appeal because, as we have seen, they had no standards for checking their entitlement and often doubted that there were fixed criteria against which they might appeal. In addition they doubted the independence of the Appeal Tribunals. One appeal, that of a mother who was cohabiting, partially succeeded only after the official hearing was over, when a number of social workers protested strongly. In another a sixteen-year-old mother who received only £3 7s. had possibly missed a £1 a week discretionary allowance at the birth of her child because the officer had not suggested she might claim until the baby was two months old:

They said I couldn't have it because I'd got no good reason for not claiming it [at the time]. So they said I could go in front of a Board [Appeals Tribunal], only when the time came I was poorly and I didn't go. I knew they wouldn't let me have it. They didn't intend me to have it, so it was a waste of time.

The hopeless and impotent tone caught here was characteristic. In spite of all the grumbling and possible grounds for appeal revealed by the disputes of this chapter, very few mothers had ever appealed. Like these two mothers they said when the time came for the appeal to be heard they were ill or had no friend to go with so they merely sent a letter. Mothers had little confidence in the power of their word against that of the Board.

In summary: the failures of national assistance

These mothers' accounts of their experiences of national assistance seem to me good evidence that the system of administration was falling far short of the official ideal which is now set for a means-tested service. Although the number of mothers interviewed was not large, and they lived in only two areas of the country, there are reasons both for placing reliance on the truth of much of what they said, and for regarding their experiences as representative of a larger group of fatherless families who were assistance recipients. I was able to cross-reference different accounts, and even descriptions of the behaviour of individual officers, drawn from individual mothers who did not know one another, and their impressions and complaints formed a strikingly consistent pattern. But, above all, as we shall see in the next chapter, we can identify the *structural* factors and problems which were built into the administration of national assistance and which inevitably led to friction and failures of communication.

At the time of this survey, national assistance was still stigmatized and very inadequately publicized for fatherless families. The establishment of the right not to work could be humiliating, and the pattern of mothers' reports of widespread pressures to work and bias against unmarried mothers in this respect points to the intention if not the letter of the code being fairly consistently distorted or ignored. At the very least officers seemed insufficiently aware that, coming from someone in their position of authority, what they might regard as 'advice' to work could actually become for the client pressure to work. The application of the cohabitation rule was also in practice a source of stigma and emotional insecurity for the mothers and a constant irritant in their relationship with officials. The practical implications of the legislation on cohabitation had not been thought through, since it put the N.A.B. and the officers into a difficult situation because the relationship of 'man and wife' is virtually impossible to specify in the form of a set of checking procedures which can be used to police relationships non-punitively, especially with the lack of staff and very limited powers of investigation. Without adequate time or powers to check the clients' credentials, officers could not but suspect that some proportion of the claims they passed were fraudulent and this suspicion provoked increased severity. Indeed, the policing of national assistance was probably only possible because of anonymous letters from the public. Mothers agreed in describing what seemed to them rudeness, curtness, and insensitivity in the pressure to produce court orders or to name their child's father, and the suggestion of pressure was confirmed, with what he felt were justifications, by one of the N.A.B. managers. The mothers' complaints of the way officers manipulated access to benefit by deliberate delays and the promotion of inconvenience in the issue of allowance books have been backed up by Hill's independent account. Entry without warrant, which some mothers alleged had occurred in cohabitation searches, was actually illegal.

Thus, in spite of the official claim that the rules are morally neutral, in the operation of the means-test and cohabitation rules, the N.A.B. officers were in effect acting as agencies of social control in supporting conventional sexual morality and the institution of marriage. This is a major reason why the position of mothers alone on national assistance might differ from that of old people, whose sexual activities were not in question.

Rather than their needs being sought out and generously, flexibly, and comprehensibly met by official discretion, mothers were in the humiliating position of having to urge their needs upon reluctant or insensitive officials, and the exercise of discretion was felt to be ungenerous, arbitrary, and obscure. Discretionary allowances were not always given in apparently identical circumstances of need, for the birth of a child, for example. Fewer exceptional needs grants were given to these groups, as the N.A.B.'s own figures show, and the grants were given and withheld unpredictably: the grants never approached the maximum of £20 which could and should have been given without permission of the officers' superiors, for example even when a family had lost their home and all their possessions, or when they had been dependent for many years. It was also evident from the mothers' identification of the same officers, such as B——, that some officers were always more reluctant to exercise discretion in favour of the client. This reluctance was mentioned by both the N.A.B. managers as a problem of the system, particularly with older officers who had operated under the previous, less liberal regulations. In short, contrary to official hopes that discretion would provide generously and would be flexible in crying cases of need, in practice the discretionary rules appear to have been distant maxima, seldom approached. The Board's agency function for other welfare benefits was inadequately exercised, and relationships with other bodies seemed designed to minimize, rather than increase, the help reaching the mothers.

The relatively small number of appeals appears to be an indication of the remoteness and lack of manifest impartiality of the appeals machinery rather than of the satisfaction of claimants or the satisfactory control of official discretion.

Thus, if we are to take access to support and the treatment of claimants by officials and the general public as criteria for the death of the old poor law, in 1966 the heralding of that death was premature. Rights which were so inadequately publicized, so difficult of access, and which could entail such humiliation and uncertainty could scarcely be classed as rights at all. The combined influences of official and public fears concerning fraud, the obscurity and parsimony of discretion, and the inaccessibility of the appeals machinery all militated against the ideal of co-operation and a professional, impartial service.

Hill has stressed, from his personal experience as a national assistance officer, that the experiences of different groups on national assistance reflect community prejudices. 'The prevalent attitude was a combination of . . . two positions in which most officers sought to do as much as possible for the old and undeniably sick, but few had much time for the long-term unemployed or for women whose family life was of an unstable kind. In as much as these were the common attitudes it is unreasonable to represent the N.A.B. officer as anything other than typical of the society from which he is drawn.'[18] Thus, probably the most striking feature of the discretionary means-tested system was this permeation of a public service by the stereotypes and low public esteem attached to groups like fatherless families whose behaviour was in some way different from the rest of society.

CHAPTER THIRTEEN

The Continuing Failures of Means-Tested Benefits

This discussion of means-tested benefits opened by making the best possible case that can be advanced for the handing over of fatherless families to a discretionary means-tested service. Perhaps a period of time was needed because the problems of administration were still unexplored; and claims have since been elaborated that a discretionary means-tested system is capable of discovering and consolidating rights for the poor. And it is true that over the years the administration has built up a large body of experience, some recently published in the *Supplementary Benefits Handbook* and the *Cohabitation* pamphlet, but much remaining unpublished in the secret codes. Yet manifestly in 1966 the gains in administrative experience were overshadowed by the continuing failures of a discretionary means-tested service to meet need adequately and without stigma. The problems of 'fatherlessness' and 'poverty' were not being solved, as the winding-up of the National Assistance Board in 1966 seemed to acknowledge.

Nevertheless the founding of the Supplementary Benefits Commission in 1966 was heralded as yet another fresh start. New rights to benefit were officially stressed, some discretionary power was converted into rights, and attempts were made to improve the flow of information about the workings of the system and to tighten up internal administrative checks and instructions to officers.

We must therefore still ask whether the discretionary means-tested system can be made to work for fatherless families. Is there any indication that the practical administration of supplementary benefits is moving any closer to the official ideal? And to what extent does the evidence for fatherless families substantiate the wider claim of the Supplementary Benefits

Commission to stand out impartially as 'guardians of the poor' and creators of rights?

The origins and function of discretion: an alternative description and its implications[1]

From the 1970s we can now see that hopes for the N.A.B. and S.B.C. have run up against two major obstacles. There has been the sheer and increasing difficulty and ambiguity of the dilemmas which our society has left these bodies to try to solve. And as part of these dilemmas there has been a consistent failure to provide adequate resources for the poor and those services which deal with them. In fact the origins and functions of discretion in the means-tested sector are much more convincingly described as attempts to *shelve* rather than solve the problems of fatherlessness and poverty.

The traditional view in English public life has been that the ultimate safeguard of administration lay in the professionalism and impartiality of the civil servant, and attempts have been made to build barriers to 'protect' the administration from political 'interference'. The N.A.B. and the S.B.C. were given lay supervisory policy committees with this in mind, their task being to gather information and give impartial advice on difficult policy questions.[2]

But, as Professor Titmuss points out, the S.B.C. is being called upon to resolve an increasing number of moral dilemmas upon which society as a whole is divided, and upon which it is therefore difficult, within the sphere of supplementary benefits, to take a clear line. 'Because, in recent years, the definition of "subsistence" or "poverty" has in relative terms been substantially raised, and for many other reasons besides, the Commission has attracted more and more clients, more and more duties, and more and more victims of the "diswelfares" and moral confusions of society today.'[3] Thus, when society could not agree on Beveridge's proposals for the support of fatherless families they went to the N.A.B., and their numbers drawing allowances have since expanded enormously. And the S.B.C. now has to deal also with: the payment of benefit below the scale rate to those whose last work was inadequately paid, in order to 'encourage' them to seek work (the 'wage stop'); the question of benefits for the dependants of strikers; the question of how much rent a family should pay in the uncontrolled housing market; the question of support for single, unemployed men in areas where unemployment is high, arguably as a result of national policies; the question of support for young people who want to take a course of study while they are unemployed but for whom society has not yet provided adequate education maintenance allowances; the payment of rents of council tenants who are s.b. claimants but who are withholding payment in a rent-strike, and so on.

In the case of fatherless families, for example, there have grown up anomalies in the application of the cohabitation rule as between different branches of social security: for national insurance purposes the woman and children are not counted as the man's dependants, nor for tax purposes, yet if the couple are adjudged by the S.B.C. to be living as man and wife, the man is held more liable to maintain the children than is their own father. This anomaly amounts to recognition of common-law marriage by one part of the social security system (where public money can be saved) but not by another (where it would have to be spent). The problem that adequate subsistence payments for fatherless children would constitute a financial disincentive to marriage, if those payments are to be withdrawn upon marriage, would disappear either if *all* children were suitably endowed with income in the form of an adequate family allowance at subsistence level,[4] or if the fatherless children could receive a sort of fatherless child's allowance which continued into the mother's subsequent remarriage. *In effect, for the S.B.C. to agree to the support of children in cohabitation cases as a matter of principle would be the beginning of the introduction of a fatherless child's allowance*. Thus the problems to be solved in relation to fatherlessness now lie outside the scope of the scheme of means-tested benefits, if indeed they ever lay within it.

A basic dilemma which has been handed over to the N.A.B. and the S.B.C. has been the very definition of poverty. True, basic scale rates have been legislated by Parliament, but, as

Hill in particular has made clear,[5] the *degree* of discretion in the N.A.B. and the S.B.C. administrations can be seen as expressing the community's unwillingness to support the poor at such a level that their needs can be met adequately out of the flat-rate allowance. In consequence, second thoughts of humanity force the grudging specification of numerous and increasing circumstances of what are euphemistically called 'exceptional' need, the secret codes being a sample of such second thoughts. Thus, in spite of the claims made for discretion, the overall low level of allowances has meant that the small margin of generosity offered by discretion has remained insignificant.

The grudging attitudes of society, which place means-tested benefits in an embattled double-bind position, have continued to be all too clearly expressed in Ministerial speeches, which persistently couple news of any rise of benefits and drive for greater uptake with promises of tighter measures to detect and deter 'scrounging'.[6] Although allowances may rise relative to levels of living in the surrounding community, calls for increased official zeal will rise at the same time. A basic meanness and ambivalence also appears in the continuing failure to publicize adequately the provision of income for the poor, especially for those of the poor whose behaviour is in any way deviant. It is extremely doubtful whether publicity for the support for fatherless families (and indeed others apart from old people) has improved very much since the time of this survey; and the inadequacy of publicity campaigns, and of post offices as agencies for the dissemination of leaflets and information, continues to be demonstrated.[7]

Along with inferior allowances, the N.A.B. inherited from the old poor law days a back-log and tradition of inferior buildings and salaries. Stowe discussed the staffing problems in 1961,[8] and there is still a high proportion of temporary staff. Training courses, while staff turnover remains high, must necessarily be short and therefore not very effective in dealing with community stereotypes. The salaries of some junior staff have been lower than the allowances which they handed out over the counter, a fact not calculated to improve their understanding of the claimants' rights.[9] Professor Titmuss has commented in 1966[10] and again in 1970 on the poor conditions in some S.B.C. offices: 'few objectives are as difficult to attain, without massive public support, as compensating in full for the long years of public assistance neglect.' He sees resources as the crucial issue in training and quality control: 'In this area of the Commission's responsibilities as in others – as well as the personal social services – our society is failing to invest enough resources in manpower, staff development and training programmes.' He concludes, 'With no immediate prospect of being relieved, it is in danger of being overwhelmed. Already it has too many claimants, too many callers, too many clients, too large a case-load. For the consequence of this its staff is unjustly criticized. The more this happens the harder will it become to avoid "the stigmatizing process"...'[11]

Limits to the control of officers' behaviour by internal checks and rules

On this analysis, our society's failure to resolve the moral dilemmas about the levels of poverty and whether to provide income for certain groups who behave in problematical ways continues to be an increasing burden for the members of the Supplementary Benefits Commission and for the senior administrators. The decisions which are delegated are precisely those where the administrators themselves will have most difficulty in making up their minds and avoiding the influence of community prejudices. Yet in sorting out the 'deserving' from the 'undeserving' poor, they must set a liberal line, and control the behaviour of the inadequately selected, poorly trained, and sometimes uncommitted staff who are underpaid and work in poor conditions, as a result of society's parsimony towards the poor.

The S.B.C. have argued, however, that improved administrative checks and clearer rules have to some extent helped to protect the rights of claimants, for example in cohabitation cases. But there are strong indications from studies of other organizations, as well as from the structure of the S.B.C. itself, that internal checks can be successful only up to a point in the control of discretion.

Beyond the difficulties inherent in the moral ambiguities with which the instructions must attempt to deal, there are problems in the feed-back of information on how instructions are being carried out, and how officers' interpretations of rules are affecting claimants. Knowledge of what is happening at the lowest level of an organization may filter back to the top only with some difficulty and in a distorted form. That this was the case under the N.A.B. seems to be confirmed by an early move of the S.B.C. in setting up a Policy Inspectorate, and in insuring that the Commission meet regularly rank-and-file members of staff from area offices, and some claimants.[12]

Yet, even if the top administration does take a liberal line and is in close contact with what is happening, the difficulties of maintaining a quality control are increased by the administrative structure adopted for discretion, which provides only relatively loose supervision. The structure is one where initiative (that is, discretion) is vested in what have been called 'front-line' offices and individuals, each performing tasks with a fair measure of independence.[13] Other organizations with similar structures have found problems in the supervision of 'front-line' individuals performing tasks which are not closely specified. Staff may act in such a way as to subvert or at least distort the aims of the organization. For example, closely parallel to the S.B.C., Blau's pioneering study of an American job-placement agency has shown how officers' behaviour is regulated and distorted, sometimes to the disadvantage of the clients, by the influence of relationships between colleagues and by the measures which superiors apply to evaluate officers' performances of their tasks.[14] Other instances of distortion of the aims of an organization are the inhumanity and remoteness of staff in some mental hospitals[15] and old people's homes,[16] who reduce these institutions to a merely custodial or even destructive role. And there is the behaviour of teachers, some of whom persist in 'streaming' behaviour and formal teaching within schools and classes which are unstreamed and intended to be informal, a clash which has been shown to have unfortunate consequences for the average and below-average child.[17]

A number of organizational studies show how officials tend to work in layers, each insulated from the layer above.[18] In the N.A.B., Hill pointed out,[19] this may lead officers to learn the norms of behaviour in their jobs from older colleagues whose attitudes were more appropriate to a previous generation of legislation. It is difficult to see how, within a loose discretionary structure, the S.B.C. could solve this problem of leadership. The very stress on autonomy in a discretionary system is in opposition to supervision and teaching by superiors, yet it is a source of work satisfaction for officers which might to some extent compensate for the more distasteful aspects of the job and its poor rewards. Cutting down the area of discretion might therefore be resisted by the staff. The tasks of tighter supervision through more closely specified instructions and closer contact with superiors is therefore inherently difficult; and if attempts are made to specify and control discretion too tightly, beyond a certain point it is all too likely that official discretion will be replaced in personal relationships between officers and claimants by unofficial behaviour which to all intents and purposes has the same appearance and consequences for the claimant.[20]

Thus, in a discretionary service relying on complex officer/claimant encounters, the humane and liberal operation of administration still rests to a large extent on the quality and attitudes of the staff, whatever the intentions and attitudes of the top administration. The conclusion must therefore be that in most respects at the 'front line' the system of supplementary benefits must look very similar in operation to national assistance. It is the shortage of cash, leading to the permeation of the staff by community stereotypes, which restricts the S.B.C. to the traditional role of an agent of social control over both the numbers and behaviour of the poor whom the state supports. Like the N.A.B. before it, the S.B.C. must remain in effect the ultimate sanction against too easy separation and divorce, illegitimacy, and so-called 'voluntary' unemployment.

The appeals tribunals

Potentially, then, the appeals tribunals still retain a key position both as a control on the administration and a possible instrument for preserving and consolidating rights. But a recent study of the tribunals, and of the administrative review of administrative action on appeals before they reach the tribunals, has demonstrated that the experience of the mothers on the present survey was not untypical and is not yet out of date.[21]

Coleman, reviewing information provided by the S.B.C. concerning 26,096 appeals received in the year from November 1968 to October 1969, when there were 6,081,000 claims for benefits, commented that the supplementary benefits appeals tribunals are under-used, considering the complex and controversial nature of the decisions and compared with similar appeals machinery in other spheres of social security. He points out that, even of the appeals made and recorded, 23.2 per cent were resolved by an administrative decision within the service (which, however, may not have been to the claimant's maximum advantage), while 11.2 per cent were resolved by the claimant withdrawing his appeal altogether. 'In all, then, in the region of one third of all appeals notified were resolved, not by a quasi-judicial hearing before an appeal tribunal, but by the administrative pre-hearing process. This is a considerable proportion.' Coleman concludes, 'the low appeal rate and the high success rate when an appeal is undertaken, taken together, suggest perhaps that the Supplementary Benefits Commission may be protected by the passive attitude of many claimants from extensive questioning of low-quality initial decision-making.'

Coleman's conclusion is that this passive attitude probably stems from the unrealistic assumptions of the Commission that relationships between officers and claimants are essentially cooperative. To counter this, 'greater recognition should be given to the adversary aspects of the relationship between claimants and the Commission, and steps taken to protect the interests of claimants.' This was the impression gained from the present survey also.

One improvement in the claimants' position is the publication of the *Supplementary Benefits Handbook*, although whether this information will reach the claimants themselves will still depend on the quality and range of advisory services for the poor. And it has been pointed out that in some respects the *Handbook* has been criticized as incomplete, misleading, or even erroneous. There is thus still a need for the complete publication of the codes for reference purposes for tribunal members as well as claimants. Also, until society decides it can afford to furnish each claimant with a written statement of how his or her assessment has been made, the claimant will still be at a marked disadvantage as compared with the administration.

Improvements to supplementary benefits

If a means-tested discretionary system like that of supplementary benefits is to be retained for a proportion of fatherless families, then some improvements are possible even within existing budgetary constraints. We can recommend a closer scrutiny of some of the rules of discretion. There is the rule in relation to the disregard of earnings: mothers with more children might be given a disregarded income in proportion to family size, so that more of those who wanted could go out to work. Indeed the earnings rule as a whole might be reviewed for fatherless families, where a strong case can be made for the benefits not only to the economy but to mothers' self-esteem and peace of mind if they can take a part-time job. There is the rule in relation to young mothers: those with full household responsibilities should receive full payments at adult rates, and mothers under sixteen should be allowed to claim benefit in their own right. There is the rule on mortgage repayments: house-buyers could conceivably be paid in full, or at any rate be loaned the money for capital repayments. There are the unrealistic ceilings for 'fair' rents: it needs to be recognized that fatherless families have to pay more for housing because they are discriminated against. There is the requirement that older mothers who have been supported by the state for many years should still go out to work when their children cease to be dependent: these mothers might be allowed the choice of remaining on supplementary benefit.

Above all the cohabitation rule needs much more discussion, as the S.B.C.'s publication of the *Cohabitation* pamphlet explicitly recognizes. The S.B.C.'s intentions of recognizing that mothers may enter into a number of levels and types of relationship with a man which yet fall short of common-law marriage would be a valuable advance if they could be attained in practice. And there have been reports of instances where women having sexual relations with a man with whom they are living have been allowed, on appeal, to retain their allowance on the grounds that inadequate financial support was involved. But unfortunately these cases set no firm precedent. As an interim measure, pending more adequate and responsible public discussion of cohabitation, the evidence of the present survey strongly supports the view that the issues of cohabitation are so complex and the room for malpractice is so great that *all* cohabitation cases should be referred to a satisfactory appeals tribunal, and the mother's allowance should not be withdrawn until the appeal has been heard. The ambiguities and very drastic action involved in decisions to withdraw benefits would justify such a move. Even so, we might still doubt whether mothers could be adequately protected from tactics of discouragement from applying for benefit or from appealing.

How tribunals are to be made more satisfactory is beyond the scope of this discussion.[22] In fact there has, as yet, been no systematic study of the effects of the introduction of lawyers into the tribunals. They might be involved in key cases where whole categories of rights are involved, or in key issues such as cohabitation. But there is a shortage of lawyers with a knowledge of the system and an interest in the poor. The setting-up of legal advice centres for poor people seems the most promising development at the moment. From the present survey it appears that improving the status of the appeals machinery could actually improve officer–claimant relationships, for undoubtedly much of the hostility and uncertainty noted in the interviews stemmed from the obscurity of the discretionary system and the indefinite status and remoteness of the appeals machinery.

The rise of the claimants' unions

It is too early to say whether the formation of claimants' unions will constitute a major force for change in the structure of supplementary benefits or whether the unions will remain merely an uncoordinated set of fringe vigilantes. Locally a claimants' union may help to provide an external check on some of the grosser inequities in treatment and other administrative abuses. And there seems to be strong evidence from a number of branches of the social services that *without* more participation by 'consumers', rights cannot be effectively protected.[23] However, it is not clear that, short of revolution, the unions have a distinctly different structural solution to offer at a national level.

There are now said to be ninety or more unions, whose members distribute leaflets to claimants as they wait in the offices of the S.B.C. and labour exchanges, accompany claimants as they are interviewed at the counter, and help claimants to conduct appeals. The unions would probably see their main task as an attempt to politicize the situation and to arouse the political consciousness of claimants so that they will form local and national movements to demand rights for the poor.

So far the official S.B.C. view has been that claimants' unions are unnecessary if not undesirable, and official reactions have varied from frosty thanks to the unions for improving the detection of 'administrative error' to a more open hostility which has emerged in refusal of access to premises, refusal of more than one union member at appeals, and strikes by counter-staff. The claimants' unions say they have won thousands of pounds for their members. What has been lost depends on whether the former officer–claimant relationship could be viewed as cooperation rather than the apathy which this study and others have indicated. But undoubtedly the presence of a union increases and focuses conflict between front-line staff and claimants.

Predicting developments from this stage of local skirmishing is difficult for a number of reasons. Argument from American precedent seems treacherous. There is controversy about whether American civil rights activity on behalf of the poor has won rights and created a national system of support, or whether Nixon's parsimonious national schemes can more realistically be seen as a backlash against the too-articulate and too-demanding poor.[24] In any case the American legal system is a much better weapon for defining and extending citizenship rights, especially since Britain's obscure and complex legal system is faced by an equally obscure discretionary system which acts as a 'rubbery defence against the possibility that the need can be generalized into a right'.[25]

Preliminary and unsystematic reports of the claimants' unions also suggest that their ideology and mode of operation are, initially at any rate, handicapping them as a force for change. The unions often seem to insist on a grass-roots democracy where policy is jointly discussed and decided by all members, a process which is itself educative. Yet whatever its virtues, this democratic process has made 'getting it together' at local level difficult, and regional and national conferences are even more difficult to handle. An 'anti-leadership ethic' makes confrontations with conventional political machines and bureaucracies difficult. The unions are also suspicious of setting up bureaucracies, probably rightly in the light of historical and American experience. Yet as a result they apparently still remain vulnerable to being taken over by 'ego-trippers'. And a lack of bureaucratic records perhaps inhibits the production of case law with which pressure could be maintained on the S.B.C.

Pending (or failing) more widespread structural changes brought about by claimant action, there is still, therefore, a case for discussing how best to protect fatherless families from the stigma which operates through administrative discretion. Indeed, the question now arises whether fatherless families should be left on supplementary benefits while the administration continues in its present form.

Guardians of the poor?

Can we now say anything about the claims of the S.B.C. that they can transform the traditional role of Poor Law Guardians into that of Guardians of the Poor? The Commission's members had the task of gathering information and giving impartial advice on broad policy issues. But, as we have seen, claims for the responsiveness of the organization have been challenged by external charges of conservatism and by political pressures for change. Does the fate of fatherless families under the discretionary means-tested scheme throw any light on this debate?

It seems characteristic of the discretionary system hitherto that we should find a shortage of published information when we try to discuss its achievements or official position. Indeed, whatever information may have been gathered, the S.B.C. have actually *published* less information about the service they offer and the workings of discretion than did the old N.A.B. In the S.B.C. Reports certain tables disappeared, and we have had, for instance, no information on regional variations in the exercise of discretion as between different geographical areas. On the subject of the present survey, the Commission have made no statement about the rights of fatherless families as a group, and we are unable to assess how far individual Commission members have been able to influence national policies behind the scenes.[26] In fact, what we know or what we can read of the Commission's work falls short of the more ambitious claims made for it.

To gather information the S.B.C. set up a Policy Inspectorate and they were also able to use the D.H.S.S. research unit. But although some research has been carried out, at any rate by the Inspectorate, nothing useful has been published on fatherless families.[27] No unfettered facilities have been offered for outsiders to do research on the Commission's relations with these families. We have therefore been left with the situation that while the Commission has a function of information-gathering, and they have asserted that they welcome 'constructive criticism',[28] so far no information has been published by the S.B.C. themselves, nor has there been any way in which outsiders could obtain evidence for close criticism. When the government's White Paper on social security[29] was published in 1969, after twenty years during which many thousands of fatherless families had been closely supervised by the N.A.B. and then the S.B.C., it was stated that further research would be needed before the situation of fatherless families could be discussed. This statement might be seen as a failure either of successive administrations, for whatever reasons, or for lack of resources, to collect adequate evidence, or of the government to accept the Commission's evidence. We do not know which, but in either case the S.B.C.'s influence appears too weak.

It is also difficult to see the Commission as impartial. They have the task of supervising a large, loosely structured and under-budgeted service, where the morale of the officers is constantly under attack from critics on both sides. The net result of attempting to maintain the fiction of the impartiality of the S.B.C. administration is that political pressures and responses operate more subtly, secretly, and obscurely.

The recent publications of the Commission are an attempt to throw open the rule-making to public discussion. But while greater openness is obviously a step in the right direction, the guarded defence of existing administrative practice hardly seems adequate to achieve the correct balance between discretionary rules and responsible public discussion.

The *Cohabitation* pamphlet may be taken as one small test of the strengths and weaknesses of the Commission's public position. This is the Commission's only major statement on fatherless families, and for that reason what it says and fails to say are significant. Above all, it is unfortunate that it should deal only with an issue which stresses the differences, rather than the common needs, among fatherless families. Too sharp a criticism of a pamphlet concerned with a small, if important, area of policy would clearly be unfair. The pamphlet is obviously based on a wealth of experience, and there is evidence that the Commission have to some extent taken a stand against more illiberal public condemnation of mothers' relationships with men. As a departmental document it is unusually frank and even revealing in parts. But it *is* a departmental document, to a great extent designed to argue the case for continuing the practice of the poor law, rather than changing it.

Cohabitation has never been adequately debated by Parliament: indeed the rule only appeared in legislation for the first time in 1966. Yet the pamphlet defends the retention of the cohabitation rule, as interpreted by the Commission and their officers, as being the wish of 'society as a whole' and 'public opinion'. The pamphlet explicitly sets out to reply to critics who have attacked individual officers on the grounds that the cohabitation rule has a disastrous effect on some mothers' lives; and while there is some acknowledgement that administration of the rule can have adverse effects, on the whole the pamphlet is inadequate in failing to stress in sufficient detail the influence of the rule on the social lives of mothers who wish to have friendships with men or to remarry. Perhaps the most telling indication of the narrowness of the S.B.C.'s position in relation to policy-making for fatherless families is the Commission's failure to institute (through the support of children in cohabitation cases) and the pamphlet's omission to argue the potential benefits for claimants *and officers* of a fatherless families' allowance, or at least a fatherless child's allowance, which would fundamentally ease the Commission's task.[30]

In short, the Commission cannot really be seen as championing the cause of fatherless families by any of its public actions to date. And because the problems with which the Commission deal are so broad and resources so inadequate, we must still question whether they can gain enough information for their decisions, whether they can be impartial, and whether their policy-making influence ranges widely enough to make them 'guardians of the poor'.

In summary: the permeability of a discretionary service to stigma[31]

We are now in a position to describe more generally how an under-budgeted discretionary service must remain permeable by community stereotypes of the low status and deserts of certain groups in the population. The situation can be summarized in the form of a model of the inception of social policy and its translation into administrative practice.

Social security measures begin life with goals which may be ill-expressed or not expressed at all. They may be aimed at social groups whose identity is only dimly or even falsely perceived; and they may attempt to deal with problems, like poverty and cohabitation, which have no neat and equitable solution, or at least none whose scope lies solely within legislation in one isolated field. Underlying the measures are often crude, ill-founded, and possibly conflicting or self-contradictory beliefs about 'human nature' and about the institutions and processes of society, for example what a normal family is, what supports or erodes marriage, and what makes people work. Already at the drafting stage the legislation will have been moulded to some extent by precedent, for example from the poor law, and by the organizational demands and constraints of the administration, such as the N.A.B. and S.B.C., whose principal civil servants will have had a major (some would argue *the* major) hand in the drafting. In passing through Parliament the legislation is pummelled by opposing ideologies and trimmed by the Treasury. And again the process is subject to sometimes not-too-well founded assumptions about what 'society' wants or should want, will tolerate, and can afford. Hitherto, the outcome of the Parliamentary process has been a set of means-tested and contributory benefits which are too low.

Because Parliament is ill-suited to resolving value dilemmas, and because the mystique of the impartial professional civil servant still holds sway, legislation is 'delegated' to the social security organizations which had a hand in the drafting and these organizations are given discretionary power to take care of the ambiguities, inadequacies, and confusions in the main legislation. Discretion is wider in proportion to the dilemmas to be solved, and is used by the top administration to elaborate a set of procedures, instructions, and checks for translating the legislation into practice. But the elaboration of these rules, which form the ideal of the service, is difficult to carry out impartially because at this stage the top members of the administrative hierarchy are themselves subject to the moral pressures in the community, they are constrained by the administrative weaknesses of their organization, and they are caught in a cross-fire of political attack from both sides.

The discretionary rules and instructions pass down the administrative hierarchy to individual officials who must find ways to operate them, or to change and bend them if they prove in practice to be uncongenial or inoperable. The officers themselves may share the community stereotypes of the social identity of groups like fatherless families, depending on how far their training has proceeded and upon its orientation. Officers' behaviour will be influenced to some extent by guidance from superiors and by the discretionary rules, but there is still room for the officers' own values to influence their behaviour because supervision cannot be complete. Officers evolve their operation of discretion under pressures from a number of directions, and in relationships with different groups – colleagues, members of the public, and the clients themselves.

The various stages in the moulding of social security may be interdependent: legislators, administrators, front-line officers, and the bulk of society may share a common view of the group at whom policy is aimed and of how much money should be spent on programmes for them. And upon the priority given to the programmes will depend not only the funds paid out to clients but also the wages, training, and work conditions of the officers – and hence the quality of service to the client. Thus, parallel to the stratification of society into different income levels, with the lowest level corresponding to the 'undeserving' poor, there is a stratification of social services, buildings, working conditions, and job opportunities, with services for the poor coming at the bottom of the pile. The stigma of the client attaches to the service itself. And even if an attempt is being made by the top administration to impose a new view of the deserts of a particular group like fatherless families, in an under-budgeted discretionary system there will be sufficient slack for the organization to remain permeable to community stereotypes which will re-emerge in the front-line administration.

The overall conclusion of this chapter must therefore be that fatherless families have been left within the discretionary means-tested sector for too long. What may initially have been a way of discovering how to solve their problems has become with the passage of time an avoidance of pressing decisions about the families' rights. The shift of mothers onto benefits as of right (like widowed mothers' pensions and allowances, for example) would protect them to some extent from community stigmatization; and the move would also help to reverse what Professor Titmuss has called the 'deteriorating' imbalance between discretion and rights, between means-tested and universal services. Hopefully, the setting-up of the Finer Committee to review the whole situation of single-parent families was a recognition that the rights of these families can no longer be ignored. Only when fatherless families are removed from the limbo of the discretionary system will they escape the long shadow of the poor law.

Part Four *Conclusion*

CHAPTER FOURTEEN

A Summary of the Survey Findings

This study began with two questions which our society has not asked sufficiently clearly and persistently: what is poverty and who are the fatherless? The study explored the situation of 116 fatherless families through interviews with unmarried, separated, divorced, and widowed mothers with children, who were dependent on national assistance. First an attempt was made to measure and describe their standard of living at the statutory level of poverty in this country. And second, this standard of living was related to the past and present social relationships in the families. Primary aims of the study were to assess the range of problems faced in common by the families as a consequence of their low income and lack of a father, to discover as far as possible why the families were poor and fatherless, and to check on the effectiveness of any help received from the community.

It must be stressed that the families studied were relatively few and taken from two areas only, although they still out-number those in the best government survey on the fatherless. They cannot, therefore, be fully representative of either 'the poor' or 'the fatherless', for at the time of the survey over half of all fatherless families were not dependent on state support. Moreover the evidence describes the situation in 1966 when the interviews were carried out. On the other hand, rather more fatherless families will have been dependent at some time, and the proportion of fatherless families drawing means-tested benefits has continued to rise so that now the majority are dependent on the state at any moment in time. More recent evidence has been quoted, but there has been no substantial work covering the same field as the present survey.

This cross-section of mothers of different marital status drawn from the national assistance population expressed a relevant distinction in social situation, that mothers of different marital status tend to be of different ages and to have families at different stages of development. This has important implications for comparisons of the economic fortunes of the different groups of mothers. There were few widows so that little new can be said about the detail of their situation, but nevertheless they provided a valuable reference group against whose standard of living those of the mothers could be compared.

The book began with a description of the incomes of the families. The National Assistance Board provided a cash allowance on the basis of a means-test of the mother's cash resources. The level of the allowance (for a two-child family paying £2 a week rent) was equivalent to only half the income of the average couple with two children in the general population. Nevertheless, it was only a little below the income an unsupported mother could achieve by working. The average total income of the families (including cash equivalents for incomes in kind or lump sums) was slightly above the national assistance basic weekly allowance scale, at 123 per cent. However, the incomes varied widely, so that national assistance was by no means a uniform level of living, nor was it a minimum below which none could sink. Widows were found to be least poor among the families, while the mothers who had only illegitimate dependants had the smallest incomes of all. Widows also drew the least proportion of their income from national assistance, and in that sense were less dependent. A major cause of dependence was lack of support from the children's fathers. On the evidence of this survey, undeclared income, whether from the fathers or from work, was negligible. So also was help from charities.

The variations in mothers' incomes could be attributed to several main factors or influences. First, widowed mothers received formally, in the National Assistance Regulations, slightly preferential treatment of their pensions, as compared with other women who had support from their husbands. Second, it was found that informally, through the exercise of N.A.B. officers' 'discretionary' powers, certain of the other women were given low allowances. Third, because the mothers of differential marital status were at different stages of family life, proportionately more of the widows had support from non-dependent children and could work part-time. Fourth, to some extent independently of marital status, help from the extended family was more frequently given to *young* mothers who had been 'readopted', usually by their parents.

The standards of the homes of these families showed similar variations. The average standard was buttressed by the very high proportion of mothers in council dwellings, 57 per cent. None of the widows, but two thirds of the unmarried mothers and half the separated and divorced women lived in poor housing which was privately rented from non-relatives. Half the families were overcrowded, one fifth of them had no furniture, and compared with the average in the country they lacked household appliances. And again in these comparisons the unmarried mothers came off worst and the widows least badly.

The conclusion is that fatherless families are disadvantaged in housing to the extent that they are forced into the poor accommodation in the privately rented sector.

In a host of large and small ways there was evidence that incomes were inadequate, and that as a consequence the families were deprived. Mothers were going short of food, and although the children of school age usually had school meals, their diets were likely to suffer at weekends and during the school holidays. For clothing, mothers relied largely, and children also to a great extent, on gifts from the family, and where these were not forthcoming deprivation was apparent. This reliance on gifts meant that problems of clothing were greater for older children, and the clothes worn by the families tended to be unfashionable.

The families' current needs sprang at least in part from the style of life to which they had been accustomed and with which they were still to some extent in contact. Patterns of consumption were moulded by what the mother felt the community demanded of her, by the need for psychological well-being as well as material comfort, and by the standards set by the rest of the community. And items not conventionally regarded as 'necessities' were nonetheless regarded as necessities by the mothers and children. It mattered that clothes were unfashionable, that the children could not have school uniform, and that the families could very seldom have a holiday unless helped by relatives or a charity. The same proportion of the mothers smoked as among women of their age generally, and a number also kept pets, which cost money. Social life was restricted, and the normal tenor of neighbourly relations was strained by lack of money.

The children were going to academically inferior schools, and children's lack of success was partly due to their being marked off from their schoolmates in many small ways through lack of money. Mothers found themselves unable to keep up with the rising demands of schools, whose requests for money from the home were geared to average levels of living in society. There was evidence that this had adversely affected educational aspirations in some families. Mothers feared the expense of grammar school education. Children were eager to start work and leave behind the embarrassment of school. However, it must not be forgotten that, for a minority, poverty and fatherlessness manifestly provided a challenge to succeed in the eyes of the community.

The distinction between 'good' and 'bad' housekeeping was inappropriate, for these families lived in a society of convenience foods and planned obsolescence where domestic skills were little prized. 'Bad' housekeeping was very often a normal pattern of housekeeping persisting in a situation where the mother no longer had adequate resources.

The mother's overall subjective feeling of deprivation was assessed, in an attempt to estimate the build-up of many individual deprivations. Two thirds of the mothers said they felt poor some or all of the time, this despite the fact that mothers, as dependants of the state and members of society in which children's welfare has a high priority, were reluctant to say they were going short. To a limited extent feelings of deprivation tied in with level of income. However, the overriding influence upon how mothers felt – as with the distribution of incomes and the standards of the mothers' homes – appeared to derive from outside their immediate material situation.

Poverty and fatherlessness were intermeshed. The mothers' main point of reference proved to be memories of their living standards in the past, or aspirations for the future. Feelings of material deprivation for certain mothers became intermingled with longing for the husband; but hopes for the children could mitigate present hardships. However, in a host of small ways the mothers continually felt deprivation, principally through their children. These mothers still felt very strongly the pressures to conform with the surrounding community – for instance in the weekly cycle of expenditure with its generous outlay at weekends, and in seasonal expenditure, particularly at Christmas and Whitsuntide. But their own social contacts had been reduced, partly to avoid painful comparisons with the standard of living of others and in response to embarrassment about receiving national assistance. Their already troubled relationships with their children were sometimes further distorted by poverty, which also tended to increase the social isolation imposed by fatherlessness. Poverty was often felt to be a personal failure, and mothers would usually have been insulted by the suggestion that they were in poverty.

Deprivation could therefore be understood only in the fuller context of the families' social relationships and past lives. This kind of study could not pretend to uncover the causes of broken marriages or illegitimate births, but from what the mothers said certain distinctive life patterns or 'careers' could be picked out, and important changes in social relationships could be mapped.

The patterns of these mainly working-class marriages were more easy to follow because the breakdown proceeded very often by physical acts rather than discussion. Underlying these break-downs were psychological tensions, but marital tension does not always lead to separation or divorce, and the present survey therefore asked how the marriages broke down, what external factors were influential, and what were the economic consequences.

According to the wives, in twenty-one marriages the wife left her husband; in twenty-two she forced her husband to leave, by evicting him or obtaining a separation or divorce; while in the remaining thirty-three marriages the husband deserted. The wives who had left or evicted their husbands blamed them for offensive or intolerable behaviour, but wives who had been deserted blamed their husbands much less. There were problems of interpreting the validity of what mothers said, but two material discoveries appear important. First, in over half the marriages the wife claimed she had not been adequately supported by her husband even during marriage, so that the chances of support after marriage breakdown looked poor: one third of the wives said they were better off on assistance, and a further one in six said they were no worse off. And second, wives who left their husbands were more likely to have housing problems and to lack goods from the marital home.

The marriages where the husband's behaviour was found most offensive had lasted because the wife was often not free to leave. With children, she was dependent for a home and an income (of a sort) upon her husband. Community disapproval of broken marriage had also been influential in keeping unhappy couples together. As a result, according to the wives, almost always such marriages ended with a crisis or an opportunity. The wife's family played a key part in ending some of these marriages by providing moral support and temporary shelter, and the local housing authority had also intervened in a few instances to secure the marital home for the wife.

Less was known about marriages where the husband had deserted. Some of the desertions had seemed sudden. All were, for the wife, difficult or painful to explain, and her emotional involvement with her husband persisted long after he had gone, in some instances for years.

Almost half the mothers interviewed had had one or more illegitimate children. The unmarried mothers appeared more likely to be temporarily dependent than any other group of mothers on assistance. For this reason, four older mothers who had only one child but who had been on assistance many years were of special interest: they had had their children late in life, after the age of thirty, and had apparently suffered a great emotional shock which had led to their withdrawal from social relationships with neighbours and workmates.

Five West Indian mothers contrasted in circumstances with the English-born unmarried mothers, having an average family of four children frequently born of a stable relationship with the child's father who had subsequently deserted. Their situation provided the only evidence from the present survey of a culture leading to fatherlessness. But there was no firm evidence of the extent to which these West Indians were a minority in special difficulties or the forerunners of a developing pattern (which would pose a problem for social security designed for a different cultural situation). My guess is the former.

As with broken marriages it was possible to see among these unmarried mothers a number of distinct 'careers'. A few were married in all respects but the ceremony. Depending on how late in life the child was born, the mothers could have considerable savings. The mothers' fortunes also differed depending on whether they could remain at home after they had the baby.

Separated, divorced, or widowed women who had had an illegitimate child often compared closely in their present or past situation with the unmarried mothers. Either they had been unmarried mothers themselves, or they now resembled unmarried mothers because their only dependent child was illegitimate. The mothers claimed that scarcely ever had the child been born of a relationship which had caused their marriage to break down; rather, they said, the birth came as a response to the loneliness of life without the husband.

Fatherlessness brought a change in the families' relationships with kin and community. A quarter of the families, usually with younger mothers, received considerable help from the mother's parents. But 'readoption' by the parents could create tensions. The mother's and father's kin took sides over marital breakdowns and illegitimate births, with the result that the father's kin were later seldom seen. Mothers without husbands no longer fitted in with their own kin, and in varying degrees the mothers also felt stigmatized and ostracized by the community. These social strains led to isolation from kin and community. Some women, turning to one another and to soldiers or young West Indians for comfort and companionship, had become a kind of 'underclass' cut off from normal society. These were often the mothers of illegitimate children, who had the lowest incomes.

Within the nuclear family fatherlessness also brought changes in relationships. For some mothers the absence of the husband was primarily a relief from an intolerable situation. For others, however, and not only if the man had been a good father and useful about the house, the problems of supporting and running the household and bringing up the children alone were daunting. They found a conflict in trying to be the centre both of authority and affection for the children. According to their accounts over a quarter of the mothers had had nervous breakdowns, and one in nine mothers had made suicide attempts, mostly following the loss of the father, but also later, in connection with the problems of bringing up the children on a low income.

No generalizations can be made about the effects of fatherlessness on children. To a large extent the children were cushioned from its impact by their youth and lack of understanding. Stigmatization by the community and discrimination in housing seem sufficient to explain some of the delinquency found among fatherless children. However, for the children the family became, at one extreme, overpoweringly close or, at the other extreme, disintegrated into a kind of anarchy; and, either way, the family environment seemed likely to be harmful for some.

Marriage or remarriage was contemplated as a solution to their problems by only a small proportion of mothers. For in one or more respects up to one third of the families were not totally fatherless – there was the father himself still visiting, or a male relative, or a lover who was effectively a father to the children or husband to the woman. The mothers' social situation was usually such that they seldom met any marriageable men. There were economic disincentives to remarriage, for the mothers must forfeit their assistance allowance. Partly as a result, there was a significant move towards relationships with men other than marriage, a search for a lodger or a willingness to consider cohabitation rather than be committed again to a legal tie with a man who might prove unreliable. Mothers' prospects and approach to remarriage were often governed by their age and the size of their families.

How did the various organizations of society which had dealings with these fatherless families help them to resolve their problems? The provision of housing by local authorities, of legal aid, and of income by the National Assistance Board, were all studied.

One third of the families had to find a new home when they became fatherless. The situation of the unmarried mothers was worst, but the group of separated and divorced wives who had left their husbands also had serious difficulties. Although over one third of the mothers had lived with kin at some time after the family became fatherless, this was only a temporary, and often inconvenient, expedient. Almost half the sixty-six mothers in council housing at the time of the interview had been rehoused during fatherlessness. However, rehousing had been too slow to protect these families from poor housing conditions, and there was some evidence of reluctance of the authorities to rehouse fatherless families. Such families were thought a bad financial risk, and tended to be rehoused on the poorest and roughest estates. Families without help from kin had had the worst problems. They had become homeless, or had been split up. And the mothers in the worst housing at the time of the interviews were the mothers of the underclass. They did not want permanence, and they valued the anonymity and freedom from surveillance which went with their poor housing.

The legal dealings of the families interviewed for this survey represented the law at its most ineffectual, since lack of maintenance from the husband was a major factor in their dependence on assistance. Lack of support from the father was partially attributable to the inability or failure of the mother to take court action, particularly if she was unmarried. But the main factor was the low value of awards made by the courts, on average only 30 per cent of the maximum permissible awards.

Pressure to take court action was brought to bear by the N.A.B., sometimes a little prematurely or against the mother's judgement. There was a failure to publicize the existence of legal aid for mothers wishing to divorce. The N.A.B. was the main agency channelling legal advice to the mothers, but such advice concerned only actions involving maintenance, and came after marriage breakdown. With better and earlier legal advice, many of these marriages might have ended sooner and with an outcome more favourable to the mother, in terms of her legal 'innocence'. Unmarried mothers were more often unable and reluctant to take action against the father because of the difficulty of proving paternity and the humiliation of court proceedings.

Court awards were reduced on a pessimistic estimate of what the father could and would pay, and even these low awards were paid inadequately and irregularly. The fathers probably had too low an income to support their wives at the levels which the court was permitted to set, and many never had supported their wives adequately in the past. In addition mothers found the court proceedings humiliating, and arrangements for collection were inefficient and inconvenient. The N.A.B.'s underwriting of court orders was a humane recognition of the court's impotence to enforce payment. The father's 'liability to maintain' had become a legal charade.

Considering the financial outcome, it was ironical that the reason why divorce law caused so much trouble was that it attempted to apportion 'innocence' and 'guilt' in marriage breakdown as a criterion for the payment of maintenance. Over the years access to the law has been improved, and at best husband and wife were allowed to part with a reasonable respect being paid to the overt facts of the marriage breakdown. But at worst the law was producing deadlock or wrongly stigmatizing one partner as 'guilty'. In many of the separations the partner who had grounds for action would not benefit by divorce. Women who had deserted found difficulty in proving their husband's cruelty, while women who had been deserted were more likely to remain separated because they were still emotionally attached to their husbands. A feature of the situation not previously stressed was that, at least among this group, more women than men were held captive by the law, including women in the underclass. Among the divorcees an irrelevant adultery had often proved the key to unlock the marriage. Changes in divorce law have brought it nearer to, although not into line with, the marital situation. And many of those wishing to divorce will now have grounds to act.

As in the findings of the recent large Bedford College study of separated wives and unmarried mothers, the overall conclusion of this review of legal actions was that, owing to the continued involvement of the N.A.B. in maintenance proceedings, the magistrates' courts, where many of these cases were heard, remain a distinctly second-class and 'criminalizing' process of separate family law for the poor.

In the mothers' relationships with the National Assistance Board it was evident that the old poor law cast a long shadow. (It should be pointed out that this survey dealt only with the fatherless and therefore the Board's problems in dealing with fraud may be understressed, since we are not discussing men eligible for employment; and also the Board's achievements in the field of the elderly cannot be assessed.) The women's approach to receiving assistance and the attitudes of officers interpreting the regulations often did not fulfil the aims of the 1948 National Assistance Act, which was heralded as the end of the poor law. National Assistance was little publicized. Mothers had discovered assistance only when they fell into difficulties, and sometimes after suffering hardships. When applying for assistance they found the reception in the office cold, and the interview humiliating and depressing, for conditions of privacy were poor and officials were concerned to make sure that the woman was not living with her husband or another man. The officers' application of the cohabitation rule discouraged mothers from applying for assistance, and later tended to prevent friendships with men and possible remarriage. There was some evidence too that in spite of statutory provisions for assistance for these families, officials had not fully accepted that the mothers were entitled not to work. Because of the lack of publicity and initially unwelcoming reception in the N.A.B. office it seemed likely that many mothers entitled to assistance would not apply for or receive help. Mothers on assistance felt they were stigmatized by society, and, failing adequate staff-training and powers, some officers were found to be applying society's distinctions of desert. The N.A.B. relied on anonymous letters from the community to police mothers' activities. Officers tended to bring pressure on mothers, particularly the mothers of illegitimate children in the underclass, to look for work; and in various other ways, most drastically when cohabitation was suspected, allowances were reduced or not paid in full. Out of 115 allowances checked, twenty-two were above the basic scales, but no fewer than forty-five were being paid at less than basic scale. Also two thirds of the mothers had never received any kind of exceptional needs grant. The existence of other bodies empowered to relieve need, such as the local education authorities, confused mothers further, because of the different means tests. And arrangements between these bodies and the N.A.B. served to cut down help to the mothers rather than increase it. Against lowering of the allowance or refusal of a grant, these mothers seldom appealed. They neither knew the criteria upon which allowances and grants were paid, nor did they accept that Appeal Tribunals were independent of the N.A.B.

The best case to be made out for leaving fatherless families on public assistance in 1948 was that time was needed to gain administrative experience of the problems, and under the means-tested system the innovation of new rights would be possible. But the conclusions of this survey, and of an analysis of changes under the new Supplementary Benefits Commission, must be that these hopes have not been borne out. Leaving the families on supplementary benefit can now only be seen as a way of shelving their problems, and it is to be hoped that the establishment of the Finer Committee to review the situation of single-parent families was a recognition that the rights of fatherless families can no longer be ignored. Discretionary means-tested systems of benefit, because they are chronically under-budgeted, will continue to lead to discrimination against fatherless families. Only by giving the families, as far as possible, benefits as of right, can they be allowed to escape from the stigma of the poor law.

CHAPTER FIFTEEN

The Needs and Rights of Fatherless Families

With all the qualifications which must be made concerning the interviews and the passage of time since the field-work, this survey nonetheless raises important questions about society's attitudes towards women, marriage, and the poor, as expressed in policies for fatherless families. Here are mothers alone and their children with common needs, yet hitherto there has been a persistent failure on society's part to match those needs with rights. Hopefully, the recommendations of the Finer Committee on One-Parent Families will, when they are published and acted upon, go a long way towards rectifying this situation. But even if these recommendations render obsolete my previous criticisms of existing provisions for fatherless families, there are permanent lessons to be gained from the record of our slow and hesitant steps towards recognizing the needs of this varied and stigmatized group, and towards providing them with an adequate system of social security. There is no 'evolutionary' process of societal development by which the needs which arise in society are quickly and adequately met by policies.

We may place the legal and social security provisions, which will be the main subject of this last chapter, in a more general context. The larger national survey of incomes and resources (of which this small survey of fatherless families is a part) discovered that the situation of individuals and families could most meaningfully be described in relation to their access to a number of systems through which our society distributes resources, social security schemes being only one of these (see Peter Townsend's *Poverty in the United Kingdom*, to be published). The findings of the fatherless families survey may be summarized by saying that it has demonstrated how *the social situation and social dishonour of fatherless families, their*

*stigma and lack of good credentials, mean that they have only a
limited access to all the various systems of rewards and resource
distribution in our society*, such as: social and legal security
schemes of many kinds (pensions, maintenance, supplementary
benefits, but also education and health); the labour market and
wages; the possibility of home ownership, a tenancy in good
council housing, or a good private tenancy; the capital market
for borrowing to buy goods; and private income in cash and
kind informally received from the family, the neighbourhood,
and other local sources.

The present survey has underlined the gross defects in
provision for mothers alone, in housing policy, in the law, and
above all in financial support. Other surveys have emphasized
the lack of day-care and job-training facilities to assist these
mothers to earn a living. But these gaps in provision are not
new: the poverty of fatherless families has continued throughout
the last four centuries of policy development under the poor
law. It will therefore help us to discover the general obstacles to
policy formation, and to point to the direction for advance
and the principles which should underlie improved support for
fatherless families, if we can account for the sheer persistence
of poverty among this group. In fact, right up to the present
day we can see the influence of social prejudice leading to,
but being in turn moulded by, the development of punitive,
fragmented, and incomplete policies for the families.

The poverty of fatherless families and the support of marriage

A historical survey of legal provisions for fatherless families
(such as that undertaken by McGregor and his Bedford colleagues[1] and sketched out in Chapter 10 of this book) reveals
that mothers alone and their children have never been viewed
as having *in their own right* needs which deserve to be met.
Support for these families – by the children's father through
family law, by the state through the poor law, or more recently
through social security – has followed upon moral judgements
of the mother's relationship with the father, or a legal view of the

property relationships involved. There have always been covert or overt fears that to provide adequate financial support for women to live apart from their husbands, or to maintain illegitimate children, would effectively condone immorality or blameworthy behaviour in marriage, and so erode marriage as an institution. Considerations of humanity have forced the recognition of some needs at rather a low level of subsistence. But there has been only a piecemeal and fragmented development of policies each embodying differing conceptions of desert and degrees of social esteem.

Illegitimate children and their mothers are the only group for whom the interaction of social policy and social esteem has been mapped in any detail. The status of illegitimate children and their mothers has changed markedly over time and has differed between different social classes. According to Dr Pinchbeck, 'It was not until the sixteenth century that social stigma attached to illegitimacy in any marked degree, and even then only upon a class basis. The cause of this change would appear to be twofold: first dependency caused by providing for illegitimate children through the poor law, and secondly, the rise of Puritanism, which was largely responsible for the obsession with moral guilt which characterized the early bastardy laws.'[2] In the middle class, illegitimacy represented a serious threat to the property of legitimate heirs. There were calls that the poor law should be administered so as to make the bearing of illegitimate children 'burthensome and disgraceful'. And McGregor and his colleagues concluded from their survey of the changing legal position of illegitimate children that 'it is likely that much of the stigma which attached to illegitimacy in the nineteenth century resulted from the inevitable involvement of poor mothers and their children with the poor law which put its thumb-print of degradation on all who fell within its care'.[3] A parallel example may be drawn from America today, where vastly different social esteem and treatment are accorded to white as opposed to black mothers of illegitimate children, the better treatment of white mothers being partly attributable to their greater earning power and family resources which render them much less likely to become dependent on public assistance.[4] The status of illegitimacy also probably interrelates in a complex way with the market for adopted babies (white babies more readily finding adoption), and with mothers' willingness to place their children for adoption.[5]

McGregor and his colleagues have also shown that the husband's liability to maintain a wife who lives apart from him has only been granted with great reluctance by the law.[6] Divorce law has been slow to change and has changed through pressures from the upper and middle classes, which have brought reforms mainly for their benefit. But the continued entanglement of the poor law with the matrimonial, as well as affiliation, proceedings of the poor has meant that legislative reforms have by-passed the magistrates' courts, leaving them as a separate 'criminalizing' system of family law for poor, separated wives as well as the mothers of illegitimate children.

Widowhood, however, cannot be seen as constituting a threat to the institution of marriage, and while widows might be pitied or even shunned it is patently to the encouragement of child-bearing in wedlock that the financial risks of widowed mother-hood should be reduced. Hence we have had the arrival of occupational and state pensions for widows, in 1925 – late, but as yet the only contributory social security scheme for the support of any mothers alone.[7] Even for widows, however, pension rights have been linked to the husband's occupation, the manner of his death, and his thriftiness. Margaret Wynn has documented the anomalies between different widows, whose pensions and widowed mother's allowances vary according to whether their husbands had paid sufficient contributions, died in the war (as officers, or as other ranks), died in industry, or died in other ways.[8] Right up to today, although their situation still leaves something to be desired, widows remain *relatively* a favoured group. A *New Society* poll in 1967 showed that widows were bracketed with old age pensioners in public esteem, as deserving more state support.[9] Widows receive a 'disregarded' income from the widowed mother's allowance if they draw supplementary benefit.[10] There have been outcries in Parliament when the cohabitation rule on widows' pensions has been too plainly spelled out in leaflets. The earnings rule has been lifted from their pensions, so that at the time of the present survey a widow with full pension and the average woman's wage would have an income equivalent in living standard to the average married couple.[11] The 1967 Budget gave only widows special tax concessions, and as recently as 1969 only widows were exempted from tax on increased family allowances. The present Conservative government, in a time of cutbacks in some areas of the Welfare State which had been thought secure, has extended the age range of widows' pensions down to forty.

The most striking indication of the difference in financial position between widows and other groups of mothers alone is in the relative numbers of mothers drawing national assistance or supplementary benefit (Figure 3). Margaret Wynn comments: 'The lower line shows the number of widowed mothers who, year by year, over more than a decade, received a supplement to widowed mothers' allowance. It will be seen that though this fluctuates a little it is about a straight line; in other words the *proportion* of widowed mothers who needed this help has been steady at about 12 per cent of the total, or around 16,000 to 18,000. In sharp contrast the line showing the number of "other mothers" (that is those who are divorced, separated, deserted, or unmarried) has gone up from 61,000 in 1958 to 176,000 in 1969. The census figures suggest that the *total number* of such mothers has risen very little. What has happened is that an *increasing proportion* of them have to depend on supplementary benefit. There were about 247,000 "other than widowed" mothers in 1966, so that at least 64 per cent of them depend on supplementary benefit. The difference between the two lines on the diagram is due to the different work possibility open to widowed and other mothers.'[12] Even allowing for possible differences in family size and the age of the children (widows' children probably being fewer and older), the greater financial independence of the widowed mother, drawing a benefit as of right which is not means-tested, is striking.

It is significant that the different policies towards families are expressed in official statistics, where fatherless families have appeared, if at all, broken down into groups according to the mother's marital status, or to society's provision for her support.

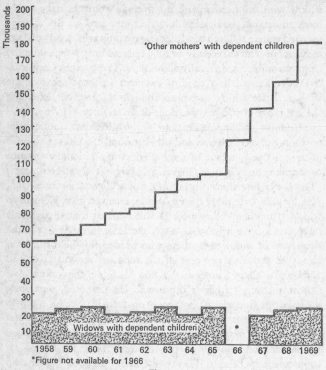

Figure 3
Fatherless families receiving national assistance supplementary benefits 1958–69.
(Reproduced from Poverty, 16/17.)

We have noted how some statistics on illegitimacy and separations appeared in the *Criminal Statistics*.[13] And up to its demise in 1966, although the N.A.B. was virtually treating unsupported mothers as one group, there was no easy way of estimating how many unsupported mothers and their children were receiving national assistance: statistics were presented with widows in a separate category and dependants mixed between different columns. In this context the calculations in the notes to the Introduction of this book,[14] and Margaret Wynn's very complex calculations[15] to find out the total numbers of unsupported mothers and children in different situations in 1964, show how statistics on fatherless families appear in a variety of incomplete forms in various publications of different government departments.

Distinctions of type and worth of fatherless families are expressed in the very pressure groups which have been formed in the twentieth century to fight for their rights, but to fight on a series of separate fronts. The National Council for the Unmarried Mother and Her Child (a name which in itself reveals the problem that unmarried mothers themselves do not attract much support) was early in the field, in 1918, and has done marvellous work. But when the N.C.U.M.C. was first founded, the suggestion that widowed mothers too might be covered by the council had to be rejected, partly so as to concentrate on the unmarried mothers who most needed help, but also because it was feared that widows would object to being bracketed with unmarried mothers.[16] The widows, for their part, have more recently had a pressure group which is reputed to have a press officer one of whose duties is to keep the image of widows clear of association with other groups of unsupported mothers. In the 1960s there have appeared groups for separated and divorced women, and for prisoners' wives. But sketchy information seems to point to these groups very seldom covering the whole range of unsupported mothers. Divisions follow the divisions in mothers' consciousness which the present survey noted.

This description of the ways in which policies for fatherless families have developed historically, and been embodied in the public consciousness, in the statistics, and in the very pressure groups formed to fight for the mothers' rights, may be summarized by saying: in terms of policy the fatherless family has had no 'social identity'; or rather there have been a large number of separate policies relating to, and expressing, different and fragmented social identities.

Beveridge and after – a case of social myopia

Over time, the fragmented social identity of the fatherless family, from being an expression of prejudice, has itself become a constraint on the development of policies adequate to meet the families' needs. There has been a failure to recognize the true social identity of the fatherless family – a case of social myopia, where society has not been able to see the needs of the families which stem from their common economic position. This failure can be traced by looking at society's reluctance to develop policies which treat mothers of a different marital status in the same way, and by tracing the painfully slow official acceptance of the description 'fatherless families'.

Beveridge's proposals for the partial extension of widows' rights to some other mothers provide an interesting example of the complex intertwining of principles of morality and insurance with practical expediency. Significantly his vision did not embrace all fatherless families. The relevant paragraphs from the Beveridge Report are worth quoting in full.

347. *End of Marriage otherwise than by Widowhood:* Divorce, legal separation, desertion and voluntary separation may cause needs similar to those caused by widowhood. They differ from widowhood in two respects: that they may occur through the fault or with the consent of the wife, and that except where they occur through the fault of the wife they leave the husband's liability for maintenance unchanged. If they are regarded from the point of view of the husband, they may not appear to be insurable risks; a man cannot insure against events which occur only through his fault or with his consent, and if they occur through the fault or with the consent of the wife she should not have a claim to benefit. But from the point of view of the woman, loss of her maintenance as housewife without her consent and not through her fault, is one of the risks of marriage against which she should be insured; she should not depend on assistance. Recognition of housewives as a distinct insurance class, performing necessary service not for pay, implies that, if the marriage ends otherwise than by widowhood, she is entitled to the same provision as for widowhood, unless the marriage maintenance has ended through her fault or voluntary action without just cause. That is to say, subject to the practical considerations mentioned in the note below she should get

temporary separation benefit (on the same lines as widow's benefit), and guardian or training benefit where appropriate.

NOTE: The principle that a married woman who without fault of her own loses the maintenance to which she is entitled from her husband should get benefit is clear. It is obvious, however, that except where the maintenance has ended through divorce or other form of legal separation establishing that the default is not that of the wife, considerable practical difficulties may arise in determining whether a claim to benefit, as distinct from assistance, has arisen. There will often be difficulty in determining responsibility for the break-up of the marriage. There will in cases of desertion be difficulty in establishing the fact or the permanence of the desertion. There will in all cases be the problem of alternative remedies open to the wife. The point to which the principle of compensating a housewife for the loss of her maintenance otherwise than by widowhood can be carried in practice calls for further examination. It may for practical reasons be found necessary to limit the widow's insurance benefit to cases of formal separation, while making it clear that she can in all cases at need get assistance and that the Ministry of Social Security will then proceed against the husband for recoupment of its expenditure.[17]

As we saw in the chapters on means-tested benefits Beveridge's note of reservation foreshadowed the way in which the value problems of moral worth and entitlement to support were handed over unsolved to the N.A.B., which intervened on an ever-increasing scale to mitigate the failures of the legal system to secure support for the mothers from men who could not afford to pay. Even in the 1970s the implementing of Beveridge's proposals would represent an advance on the existing arrangements.

But that advance would be a limited one, for it is now clear that Beveridge's appreciation of the problems of fatherlessness and his reasoning were narrowed by the context in which the Report was produced and by his own, traditional values. The Beveridge Report was produced in a nationalistic phase during wartime, after a period of fears about the low and falling birthrate. Great stress was laid on insurance for 'the housewife', and as Beveridge himself said, 'The Report emphasizes the vital task which housewives as mothers have to undertake in the next thirty years in ensuring the adequate continuance of the British race'.[18] Accordingly, the proposals 'put a premium on marriage in place of penalizing it'. For Beveridge insurance was a strong moral principle, and insurance benefits were intended to cover the vast bulk of subsistence needs, so that the proportion of the population on means-tested benefits should be small and dwindling. Beveridge's emphasis on marriage and the housewife meant that he could not view all unsupported mothers in the same way, nor could he use a single term to describe them. Although he conceded elsewhere in the Report that in the interests of the *child* certain benefits intended for married women, for example maternity benefit, ought to be extended to unmarried mothers, he omitted these mothers from his discussion of needs which were like those of the widow. And he raised the question whether 'the interest of the State is not in getting children born, but in getting them born in conditions which secure to them the proper domestic environment and care.'[19] Beveridge also discriminated between wives according to their responsibility in law for the marriage breakdown. The legal fiction of the marital offence combined with Beveridge's focus on insurance principles to make him see the problems of marriage breakdown and mothers' deserts in too simple a way: he equated breakdown with an uncomplicated purposive non-insurable action on the part of one or other marriage partner. Under Beveridge's proposed scheme, the problem of motivation in insurance terms would have been congruent with the moral issue of marital guilt or innocence in the courts.

In the 1970s, however, the urgency and feasibility of apportioning marital guilt for the administrative purpose of deciding entitlement to a contributory benefit have been much reduced. Changing societal and legal views of marital breakdown have questioned the pinning of all the 'guilt' on one or other partner. Indeed the whole climate of public discussion of individual sexual morality has become more openly polarized in challenging traditional assumptions. Compared with Beveridge, we are less certain about the supremacy of the Western two-parent nuclear family as a child-rearing unit, about the complementarity of roles of the sexes in marriage and the social esteem of the 'housewife' role, about women's dependence on men, and about the possibility of thrift in a society where massive structural inequalities and economic uncertainties have persisted in spite of a long spell of full employment and two periods of Labour government with an overt commitment to improving the life chances of the disadvantaged groups in the community.

But above all 'guilt' in marriage breakdown has become irrelevant because of the ineffectuality of the legal machinery, and the massive growth of state support for fatherless families through non-contributory benefits which are larger than the contributory benefits of the widows' pension. This has turned the father's 'liability to maintain' into a legal fiction, as both the Graham Hall Report,[20] and the Bedford survey have made clear. Further, the setting-up of the Supplementary Benefits Commission in 1966 marked the beginning of an official attempt to blur the distinction between contributory and non-contributory benefits for old people, an attempt which may now influence the position of fatherless families.

Yet it was not until 1967 that government publications began to feel their way towards using the one term 'fatherless families'. The survey *Circumstances of Families* and the Plowden Report both used the description and presented statistics combining unsupported mothers of different marital status. But there have been signs of official ambivalence about taking any further action. In the winter of 1968 the late Mr Swingler, Minister of State in charge of Social Security, informed a *Times* reporter that the new White Paper on social security would contain '"novel points" on groups like the disabled and fatherless families, previously excluded because of their lack of contributions'.[21] However, when the White Paper appeared two months later there were only small proposals for the disabled and nothing for fatherless families beyond the setting-up of the Finer Committee to review the whole issue of one-parent families. Although the climate was favourable for a discussion of common provision, as in the S.B.C.'s later *Cohabitation* pamphlet, the official emphasis was on the complexity of the issues and the differences between the families:

It is often suggested that the national insurance scheme should go further and cover either all 'fatherless families' or at least the children in such households: this would mean an insurance benefit for divorced, separated and unmarried mothers. 'Fatherless families' as a whole, however, not only divide into obvious groups but also show wide variations of need and circumstance within each group. There is a great difference between the needs of an unmarried mother who supports her child alone, and those of another girl who has a stable relationship with her child's father; and there are many possible gradations between these two extremes. Similarly it is often very difficult to distinguish between temporary separations and marriages that have finally broken down. Again, the father of the children is normally liable to contribute towards their maintenance, while he may not be liable for the maintenance of the mother. Whatever the extent of his liability, he may or may not be honouring his obligation. The available information about the numbers, structure and needs of these families is very inadequate.[22]

The use of quotation marks around 'fatherless families' and the suggestion that the families fall into 'obvious groups' (unspecified), the raising of the issues of cohabitation and the father's liability to support his family, and the contention that information is inadequate, taken together form a passage which is remarkable for its ill-informed and possibly calculated opacity and confusion. In the thirty years since the Beveridge Report highlighted the needs of some fatherless families and indicated the urgency of further discussion and research, literally hundreds of thousands of fatherless families have spent many years on public assistance under its various names. These mothers have been intensively interviewed and visited in their own homes, and many have been the subject of special investigations. Official research has been carried out, but not published, and there are indications that the *Cohabitation* pamphlet, with its wealth of administrative experience, must have been available to the writers of the White Paper. If it was claimed that we still needed further research and discussion before we could decide how best to provide for the needs of fatherless families, then our ignorance owed less to the complexity of the moral issues and social situations involved than to our unwillingness to recognize and look squarely at the problems at all.

Although the decision to set up the Finer Committee can only be warmly welcomed, it is difficult to see it as anything but a symbol of society's continuing neglect and shelving of the problems of fatherless families.

A social policy identity for the fatherless family

The gaps in policy-making goals, and the ambiguities which pervade and subvert the administration's relationship with fatherless families, thus stem from our society's failure to see and recognize the fatherless families because of worries about meeting needs without condoning immorality and eroding marriage. Yet a major lesson of the present survey[23] has been that even though the mothers did not see themselves and their children as members of a group, they were in fact sufficiently alike even in social situation to make one term, 'fatherless families', 'unsupported mothers', or 'mothers alone', a more accurate and relevant description than the various degrees of matrimonial status by which they were known and thought of themselves.

For example, mothers of similar marital status could be in vastly different social and emotional states, while women of different marital status could be in remarkably similar situations. The use of the term 'fatherless families' emphasizes that the families have needs in common while preventing the intrusion of irrelevant stereotypes of a mother's social worth (based on suppositions about her behaviour) associated with marital status. On the other hand the use of one term must not be taken to imply that all fatherless families are alike. Obviously mothers are of different ages, with different numbers of children, of differing degrees of dependency. The father, another man, a relative (even one of the children), may still perform some aspects of the role of father – bread-winner, companion, model of masculinity, authority figure, sexual companion, friend, and so on. And the mother's emotional attitude to her situation, which also appears crucial for the happy development of her children, may depend on this support and may range from grief and despair, through indifference to positive relief and happiness.

We should think of fatherlessness as a state having complex 'dimensions' and cycles of development which are not, however, integrally or meaningfully related to past marital status. With some of these dimensions of fatherlessness, social policy could not be expected to deal, but we can find examples and precedents for dealing with other variations on a universal basis.

Once we recognize the common, if complex, social identity of the fatherless family, the problems of policy-making may be seen as two-fold. We must protect the fatherless families as far as possible from the adverse effects of their present fragmented and stigmatizing social identity: as we saw in the chapters on means-tested benefits this entails removing the fatherless families, as far as possible, from dependence on an under-budgeted discretionary means-tested service. But at the same time policy should not merely be reactive, and the creation of a set of common policies in a number of spheres such as income, housing, and child-care would in itself help the public and fatherless families themselves to break out of their present stereotypes. Essentially, to aim a set of policies specifically at the rights of the fatherless family would be to create for the families a new social identity; they would become a new social policy category, in much the same way as widows have been a category hitherto.

As with the widows the new category should not be seen as permanent, and we must always be sensitive to the problem that such categories may imprison groups as well as represent opportunities for them. But at the present moment in the development of society, with women so far disadvantaged, the advances of the widow are impressive, and the immediate goal should be to achieve for all mothers alone the policy recognition which has been given to widows.

The goal (intentional or unstated) of drawing distinctions of worth between fatherless families according to unverifiable suppositions about the mother's past motivations and behaviour is misguided, virtually unattainable, and inhumane. It should be explicitly rejected, whether on the grounds of a supposed defence of marriage or of insurance principles. It is probably true that the more adequate we make the provision for fatherless families, the larger will be the number of families who become and remain fatherless. With each easing of divorce law a larger proportion of the married population has taken the opportunity to divorce (although, as a previous chapter has shown, the relationship between rates of divorce and grounds for divorce is more complex than this); and the lower marriage rate of young widows is possibly more attributable to the economic security provided by their pensions than is commonly appreciated. But it is arguable that the rate of marriage breakdown – as opposed to the rate at which already broken marriages are formally ended – is unaffected by financial provision. And marriage as an institution can remain unimpaired by a high rate of formal breakdown: the previous situation of little divorce was a sham, the cause of a great deal of unhappiness and deception, and now only the most unsuccessful marriages will be terminated. To attempt to reinforce marriage by deterrent measures, whether in poverty for wives or imprisonment for husbands, is quite to mistake the nature of the forces which have led marriage to become more and more popular in our society. Such policy sanctions are not only distasteful; they are deeply irrelevant and even immoral.

At the time of writing one of the structural reasons why it has been difficult in the past to advocate larger allowances for fatherless families has been diminished, at least temporarily, by the Conservative government's attempt to introduce the Family Income Supplement (F.I.S.). The greatest amount of family poverty occurs in households where the father is in full-time work, so that supplementary benefit levels and, in particular, benefits for fatherless families have crept ahead of wages and ahead of the housekeeping allowances received by very large numbers of married women. The blockages to improving benefits for fatherless families (in that they might be seen as creating an economic incentive to marriage breakdown) have therefore been the absence of adequate minimum wage legislation, and the setting of family allowances at below the subsistence cost of a child. But now in principle F.I.S. has potentially raised the income of families where the father is in work to a level comparable with supplementary benefits, so that, whatever drawbacks there might have been *in principle* against the raising of allowances for fatherless families, these have now been reduced.[24]

Income security for fatherless families

A scheme of social security for fatherless families should be sensitive to the range of *needs* which the families might possess in common, whatever the mother's marital status, and the time is now right for such a scheme.

What mothers share is a common economic position. Essentially the fatherless families' problems stem from the structure of our society, where an increasingly large majority of the population marry, and women's work is still regarded as secondary to marriage. Men are the bread-winners and women often work for wages which are virtually pocket money. The average wage for a woman remains fairly steadily around half the average man's wage: a report for the Ministry of Labour at the time of the present survey showed that more than half Britain's eight million working women earned less than 5s. an hour, while only about 4 per cent of them could expect to earn as much as 10s. an hour. Equal pay for women would by no means close this gap, for in many instances women do not do the same type of work as men. The fact that the average woman's wage is so low is the end product of a complex chain of low occupational and educational choices and aspirations, both by and for women, coupled with various forms of discrimination by society. Divorce and property laws are only the most glaring examples of society's reluctance to grant, and women's reluctance to seek, full equality of status.

Thus in any proposals the long-term goal of advancement of women to equality of social status and pay must be pursued, and this demands wide-ranging measures in education, the law, tax arrangements, work conditions and opportunities, and the provision of ancillary services such as day-care and nursery school facilities. Mothers are at a disadvantage in the labour market because they are expected, and they themselves usually expect, to care for their children full-time while the children are young, and at least part of the time when they are older. Thus even legally 'guilty' mothers are frequently granted custody of their children, and up to now one hears of few unmarried *fathers* rearing their offspring alone (although this has been known).[25] The motherless child, that is the child who has no mother figure, is a comparatively rare phenomenon in our society – a father without a wife can usually call on female kin to bring up his children, or he can advertise with community approval for a woman housekeeper. But the fatherless child, who truly has no father figure, is comparatively common.

It may be that true economic equality of the sexes will not be achieved unless we get a radical redefinition of the masculine role in relation to caring for children, or alternatively until we get a redefinition of the feminine role which places much less emphasis on constant maternal care in the early years.

If the disadvantaged economic position of the fatherless, compared with the complete, family stems from the mother's low earning power and ties to her children, then measures taken to provide social security should have as their main aim the alleviation of this disadvantage, the mother's reduced earning power. On this basis any allowance should be geared in some way to the income of a married couple. And the income should go to the mother, rather than to both her and the child or to the child only.

A suggestion which combines income to the child in the form of a children's allowance, as in other insurance benefits, and income to the mother, in the form of a child care allowance, has already been made to the Finer Committee.[26] Such an arrangement has obvious analogies with the Guardian's and Children's Special Allowances, and it seems only right that a mother should be paid as much to bring up her own child as we would give a foster-mother to do the same job if the child were taken into care.[27] Alternatively, to support a fatherless child without singling him out from other children, increased family allowances could be paid to all families,[28] while mothers alone could receive compensation for the loss of income which results from their inability to work.

But having identified the underlying goal of common provision, whether to the mother or children or to both, there still remain formidable problems of financing and eligibility which will only be overcome, if at all, by considerable administrative ingenuity. The complete design of a fatherless families allowance is beyond the scope of this book, but some of the practical problems must be discussed since, as we have already seen, it is impossible to separate out the principles of a scheme from the practical details of its administration.

Financing the allowance – the father's liability to maintain

For example the question of who should pay for allowances to the fatherless families raises a number of ethical problems which interlock with administrative detail. At present the sources and manner of payment of allowances are major determinants or expressions of differences of economic status among the fatherless. Widows' pensions are paid from an insurance fund to which the husband must have contributed. Other women receive payments directly or via the court from the living fathers of their children; or out of general taxation.

In line with the shift of emphasis from the mother's marital status to her current needs, the question of the father's liability to support his family should in principle be treated and assessed on the basis of his capacity to pay, as far as possible separately from the issue of his family's needs. Either the fatherless families allowance could be a non-contributory benefit financed out of taxes (like family allowances), or it could have the character of the widow's pension, fatherlessness becoming an insurable risk. This would mean that the father's liability to maintain his family would be transformed from a legal obligation to a social security contract.

In practice which of these two courses is chosen could have very different results. The adoption of a flat-rate allowance would run counter to the view that fathers ought to support their children, and sometimes their wives, directly by cash contributions. It would also conflict with some fathers' desire to take financial responsibility for their family's future, and the fact that with richer fathers a legal agreement would give more generous support than a social security benefit. Direct support would, however, still be possible on an informal, private legal, or voluntary basis, and presumably richer families would still negotiate support at the time of the breakdown of the marriage.

With the alternative of a scheme based on insurance contributions, if we can overcome the question of insuring 'purposive' actions in marriage breakdown or giving birth to an illegitimate child, we run up against the problem that contributory schemes (even for widows) tend to reflect the economic fortunes or thriftiness of the husband or of the mother herself if she has worked. And these problems increase with the growth of wage-relation of benefits. Thus, the contributory benefits could be related to the previous family income, and this would compensate the unsupported mother for her low earning power. At the same time, wage-related benefits would insure that the family of the richer man does not suffer such a drastic fall in income. However, a contributory scheme would effectively discriminate between the bulk of the once-married mothers and the unmarried, because the contribution record of the unmarried mother would be based on a woman's rather than a man's wage. A contributory scheme would also penalize further the wives of those men who would not or could not work. Some of these difficulties might be overcome in practice by the administrative device of 'crediting' women in certain categories with contributions which their husbands or the children's fathers have not paid or cannot be shown to have paid.

The best way for a father to pay according to his means appears to be through his tax coding. Attachment of earnings (or a payment through the man's insurance stamp) suffer from the problem that the man is identifiable to an employer as being apart from his wife, and attachment of earnings actually costs the employer money to collect. Payment through the tax code would be equitable, administratively simple, and would save the state cash, since there are seperated fathers who obtain money for dependants whom they do not in fact support. On a less ambitious scale than a full fatherless families allowance, the state could at least underwrite maintenance orders up to a certain limit, and undertake collection from the father through his tax code (it has recently been pointed out, however, that tax codes in themselves can convey considerable information to wages clerks and employers).

There is growing pressure that along with the re-examination of the father's duty to support his children there should be a re-appraisal of his rights in relation to the children. In the past the rights of the fathers of illegitimate children have been neglected in the attempts to obtain maintenance for the child.[29] And large numbers of poor men are still being imprisoned under society's mistaken impression that their example will force others into more responsible behaviour towards their families. There is growing evidence that the fathers of illegitimate children might take a more responsible attitude towards their children if the state would let them by recognizing that they have certain rights. And with regard to imprisonment, as McGregor and his colleagues have pointed out, this distinction constitutes another aspect of a separate family law for the poor and it is, besides, ineffective. There are alternative methods of debt collection, such as distraint, which would serve to enforce maintenance in a less discriminatory and more effective way.[30]

Problems of eligibility

Supposing we could agree and solve more or less satisfactorily the goal of a common allowance and the principles of financing the scheme, and that we could decide that the mothers will be best protected from stigmatization if they could be dealt with by a non-discretionary service, we would still be left with the problems of determining eligibility, which proved such a formidable obstacle to the discretionary system. Problems of eligibility have to do on the one hand with the mother's own income and ability to support herself by work (if the allowance is means-tested) and with the question of cohabitation (whether the allowance is means-tested or not).

If the allowance is to compensate a woman for her loss of earning power, logically the allowance should be means-tested, the limit being the fairly high one of the woman's deficiency in earning power, that is, half the average man's wage. Although widows have no earnings rule it would seem that women's earning power is relatively so low that an earnings rule is not worth the problems and stigma entailed in enforcement and policing. The psychological and social value to these mothers of holding down a job should be the major consideration here, and the lesson of Figure 3 is quite clear: the allowance should not be means-tested, so that it may be a springboard beneath the mothers' feet to enable them to move towards independence, rather than a ceiling, like supplementary benefits, against which they constantly bang their heads.

Depending on the form chosen for the allowance, much of the problem of cohabitation could disappear. For example with a fatherless child's allowance which the child retained while under working age, or with raised family allowances, much lower sums of money, for the support of the mother only, would be involved in cohabitation cases (also rent shares in some instances). Unfortunately the government's current proposals for a tax credit scheme contain the appallingly retrograde and sexist argument that family allowance income should pass from the mother to the father's tax credit. This would seriously exacerbate the cohabitation issue. If the sting does not go out of the cohabitation issue in some way, we must insist that in a changing and pluralistic society the matters of principle associated with cohabitation can never be settled finally and must be kept under constant review. Even in existing legislative and administrative practice it is not true, as is sometimes officially asserted, that financial arrangements which make marriage a less favoured state are against some basic principles of public finance. There occurs a point in higher taxation where it is advantageous for a couple with separate incomes who conceive a child not to marry.[31] And any number of maintenance payments to ex-wives may be offset against income tax, making serial divorce financially quite a painless process for high tax-payers.[32] In some situations students who marry may be penalized financially.

We should constantly question the interpretation, intention, and effect of cohabitation provisions in particular pieces of legislation, laying more stress on the problems created for unsupported mothers. Where fatherless children have no income of their own, and, where a mother has several children, the mother's prospects of remarriage are in any case very poor. Therefore to suggest that a major reason for not supporting these women or their children would be that such support constitutes a major disincentive to men to marry and assume the responsibilities of fatherhood seems short-sighted and a false interpretation of the mother's position. The crucial question is whether the relationship of a man with a woman who has several children in previous relationships ever can or should be regarded as entailing quite the same financial responsibilities as legal marriage. While the answer for the mother herself might be a carefully qualified yes, the S.B.C.'s current policy of making, or attempting to make, the man support the children is plainly wrong in intention and can lead to great hardship in practice.

The present trend towards the finer specification of a number of different degrees of relationship implying differing obligations to support seems to be the correct one, and could be further elaborated in terms of legal rights for men who assume the responsibilities of support; for example rights to draw unemployment and sickness benefits for those of the family who count as dependants.

Legal arrangements for family law are at present the subject of much discussion in the profession, and there are strong advocates that matrimonial and affiliation proceedings should be transferred to a 'Family Court'. If this happens, then the qualification for eligibility for a fatherless families allowance could be some kind of certificate, perhaps a sworn affidavit that the couple were separated, obtained from such a court. This would be the equivalent of the death certificate which the widow must produce at present for her pension.

But a difficult problem arises in some instances where a couple frequently separate, or where it cannot be confidently asserted that the couple will be separated for a long time. Here it may be better to think of two stages or two tiers in providing an allowance. A mother initially draws a temporary allowance on a short-term basis, but, when the separation has been shown to be a lasting one, she moves to a permanent allowance. One way of getting round the problem of temporary separations is that if a woman is living in an unstable situation she should be given an allowance permanently, and the money recouped from her husband, fully if he lives with her, thus giving her some security. Obviously the actual workings of such a scheme would need to be scrutinized, before it could be placed on a permanent footing. It is similar to other proposals for a 'mothers' wage' and 'family endowment' combined.

The role of policy-oriented research

The fate of the fatherless family holds important lessons about the role of independent research in policy-making. Our society has developed a number of policies which impinge on fatherless families in various ways, mainly to demonstrate exemplary punishment and to try to limit any growth in their numbers. Yet for the next generation the most effective preventive measures against insecure relationships in adult life probably lie in adequate support for today's fatherless families. While for the present generation of adults, the sanctions and preventive measures controlling fatherlessness lie – and should be seen to lie – elsewhere in the social fabric than in the adequacy or otherwise of policy provisions for the needs of fatherlessness.

But the needs of mothers and children in their own right have remained invisible to the policy-makers and society in general. Implicitly, therefore, this book has been making the case for policy-oriented research which will look outside current definitions of need as expressed in existing policies. Apparently we cannot rely on such research from the policy-making bodies themselves, and one focus of interest has been this continuing failure of official research, a failure which is mirrored in other policy fields.[33] Independent research is still needed to make up for deficiencies in the administration, both by urging new definitions of need and by helping to generate and feed external political pressures for change.

At the time when this survey was carried out, the policy achievements for the category of widowed mothers had been impressive: they were the only unsupported mothers receiving allowances as of right, free of a means-test. The interests of other unsupported mothers seemed best served by a study of the extent to which they shared needs in common, so that parallels with widowed mothers might be drawn where appropriate. The use of the labels 'poverty' and 'fatherless family' in the title of this book may have appeared to some readers to prejudge the research, but my decision to use these descriptions is, in fact, an outcome of the research rather than an initial bias. When I was asked to begin the study I had no experience of the groups involved, and inevitably to some extent I shared community stereotypes about them. If anything, one of my qualifications for the job was a more than usual ignorance of the subject matter; and while this can hardly be recommended as a general principle, my initial ignorance has meant that the writing of this book became a personal attempt to assess the validity of labels, 'poverty' and 'the fatherless family', which were only just becoming current.

The use of the labels in the title is thus a deliberate, political, statement. I have been conscious in writing that the dangers in labelling are great. Individuals may be insulted and alienated, even stigmatized, by the labels we try to apply – for example, those mothers to whom I suggested the word 'poverty' were sometimes offended, and not all the mothers whom I have described as heads of 'fatherless' families would feel the description was appropriate or that they had much in common. Social groups and social needs change, and, as in the past, labels may come to obscure needs and imprison individuals. We should have the wisdom and courage to abandon labels when they are no longer valid, as well as to search for new ones.

Yet it seems to me inevitable in research that we work with labels, if not new ones then old ones, and if not explicit ones then ones which we have not made explicit. The very act of research is a labelling of problems, a political statement about what we think of the policies which society is pursuing and what we feel ought to be done. It is as well then to be explicit.

If I was ignorant at the beginning of this research, by the end I was personally convinced that only the use of a common description was appropriate for the social situations of the mothers of different marital status whom I had interviewed. And only the word 'poverty' adequately conveyed the kinds of deprivation which the mothers were experiencing. The survey demonstrated to me, and I hope the reader, that mothers of different marital status have needs and deserts which are not fundamentally different. And the research also made clear, I believe, that poverty is not just a lack of purely physical necessities, and that those in poverty are not poor through their own fault.

Above all, the survey has provided a case study to show how we as a society have a way of tidying awkward social problems out of sight, losing them in the machinery of administrative discretion. But it should be our public concern continually to scrutinize who are the poor and to re-draw the poverty line. For as long as those supported by the state remain as far below the general standard of living as these fatherless families they are in poverty, and they are our responsibility.

Appendix One

Extracts from N.A.B. Explanatory Leaflet A.L. 18 (Supplements to Pension and Other Assistance Grants)

(These Regulations and Scale Rates have been revised and the extracts printed here apply only to 1965–6. Current Scale Rates (1971) are printed for comparison, but anyone requiring up-to-date guidance should get leaflet S.1 from the post office, and consult the Supplementary Benefits Handbook.*)*

2. *How to apply*
Persons who are under pensionable age and available for work should apply through their local Employment Exchange. Others should get a form of application (form O.1) from the post office, fill it in and either post it or, if the need is urgent, take it direct to the local office of the Board. An Officer of the Board will then call to obtain particulars of the applicant's circumstances.

4. *How payment is made*
Where appropriate (but not of course in the case of sick, aged, or infirm persons),* the Board may make the grant conditional on registration for employment at the Employment Exchange, and in that case payment is made at the Employment Exchange. Payment to other persons is made by means of a book of orders cashable weekly at the post office, or by postal draft.

5. *Appeals*
Any person who is not satisfied with the result of his application may appeal, within twenty-one days of the decision, to an independent Appeals Tribunal.

6. *The assessment of needs*
A person's need of help from the Board includes the need to provide for his wife and children under 16 living with him and is calculated by

*Note this does not specify unsupported mothers of young children.

taking the appropriate figure or figures from the table below, adding an allowance for rent (see para. 7) and deducting such amount of any resources he may have as the Regulations say is to be taken into account (paras. 8–12). The result may be adjusted as described in paras. 13 and 14.

Scale of allowances (1965–6)

Ordinary Scale – The following table sets out the amounts which the Regulations allow for needs other than rent:

(a) for a married couple	£6 5s. 6d. a week.
(b) where the above rate does not apply –	
(i) for a person who is living alone or is a householder and as such is directly responsible for rent and household necessaries	£3 16s. 0d. a week.
(ii) for any other person	
aged 21 years or over	£3 7s. 6d. a week.
aged 18 years or over but less than 21 years	£2 11s. 6d. a week.
aged 16 years or over but less than 18 years	£2 4s. 6d. a week.
aged 11 years or over but less than 16 years	£1 13s. 6d. a week.
aged 5 years or over but less than 11 years	£1 7s. 0d. a week.
under 5 years	£1 2s. 6d. a week.

Main increased supplementary benefit rates (1971)

	Weekly Rate £
Ordinary scale	
Husband and wife	9·45
Person living alone	5·80
Any other person aged	
Not less than 21	4·60
Less than 21 but not less than 18	4·05
Less than 18 but not less than 16	3·60
Less than 16 but not less than 13	3·00
Less than 13 but not less than 11	2·45
Less than 11 but not less than 5	2·00
Less than 5	1·70

7. Rent allowances

Where the applicant is living alone or is a householder the amount to be added for rent is usually the net amount of rent he pays if this is reasonable in the circumstances.

The term 'rent' includes rates and similar outgoings. If the applicant is living in his own or his wife's house and there is a mortgage, the interest payments are treated as rent but not the capital repayments.

Where the applicant is not the householder but is living as a member of someone else's household the amount to be added for rent is normally a reasonable share (depending on the number of people in the household) of the rent payable by the person with whom he is living, but the amount added will not be less than 2s. 6d. nor more than 15s. No rent allowance is given to applicants under 18 years old.

8. *What resources are taken into account*

When the applicant's needs have been calculated, the next step is to see whether there are any resources to be taken into account. The term 'resources' means money coming in from any source, savings and property (except, of course, furniture and similar personal belongings) of the applicant, wife or husband, and dependants, but certain resources are disregarded either wholly or in part as explained below (see paras. 9–11). Unemployment, sickness and injury benefit, retirement and non-contributory old age pensions, widows' benefit, and family allowances are taken fully into account. (See also para. 12.)

9. *Resources which are disregarded*

The following are disregarded – except that where the applicant, wife or husband, and dependants have more than one resource (apart from earnings – see para. 10), the total amount which can be disregarded is limited to 30s.

(d) Additions for children in National Insurance widows' benefits – from 7s. 6d. upwards according to number of children.

Maternity and death grants are disregarded altogether. [So also are education maintenance allowances, D.M.]

10. *Treatment of other income*

Earnings – Where the earner is required to register at the Employment Exchange or is under 16 years of age the first 15s. of any net earnings is disregarded; in other cases the amount disregarded is the first 30s. plus half of the next 20s. Net earnings means the amount payable after deduction of statutory insurance contribution and income tax, less any travelling or other expenses necessarily incurred in connection with the wage-earner's employment.

11. *Capital assets*

The term capital assets means all money, bank balances, investments, and house property owned by the applicant, wife or husband, and dependants. The following are disregarded –

(a) the capital value of the house in which the applicant lives ... Other capital belonging to the applicant, wife or husband, and dependants is aggregated and if the value is less than £125 in all, this too is disregarded; but where the value is £125 or more up to £600 it is taken into account at the rate of 6d. a week for first £125 plus a further 6d. for each further complete £25; for example, if the applicant has £160 in the bank, 1s. a week is taken into account in respect of it. Where there is capital not disregarded under (a) and (b) above which is worth more than £600, no grant can usually be made.

12. *Contributions from non-dependent members*

The Regulations provide that the resources of a householder (unless he is a blind person) are regarded as including a reasonable contribution towards the household expenses from any member of the household who is not a dependant of his. The contribution is not to exceed the member's proportionate share of the rent payable by the householder, and no contribution is assumed where the member is earning no more than £3 a week.

13. *Special circumstances or exceptional needs*

If there are any special circumstances or exceptional needs which have come to the notice of the Board's officer, they will be taken into consideration and where necessary the weekly grant will be adjusted to meet them. A grant can also be made in case of real urgency even though the person would otherwise be disqualified.

15. *National Health Service charges*

Grants may also be made to persons (whether or not in full-time work) who are in need on the basis of the standard laid down in the National Assistance Regulations to enable them to meet certain charges under the National Health Service for new supplies of glasses, dentures, and for dental treatment.

Appendix Two
The Sample

Sampling procedure

The N.A.B. rightly wished to preserve the confidentiality of their dealings with individual applicants, and they would neither pass on the names of applicants to us, nor did they wish to know who had responded or failed to respond to our request for an interview. Accordingly, we supplied a set of duplicated letters explaining the purpose of the survey, and the Board addressed and despatched them to the mothers for us; using our 'University of Essex' envelopes, with a postage stamp, to dissociate our request from official communications (these arrive in buff-coloured, franked envelopes, with the N.A.B. crest). The letter began,

Dear [Marital status and name typed in by the N.A.B.],

There has been hardly any discussion about families like yours in which the mother is bringing up children without a father. Probably if something was known about their problems more could be done to help fatherless families.

Then followed details of who I was, instructions as to how to reply, a statement of the intention to publish a report, an assurance of confidentiality, and a further assurance, signed by me, that I have no connection with the N.A.B. With this letter each mother also received a reply envelope, addressed to me at the university, again marked 'University of Essex', and stamped with a postage stamp (to encourage response). There was also a post-card on which was printed her name and address, with a request that any mother interested should place the card in the reply envelope and post it back to me, after which I would call and explain the survey. In this way, only I need see who had replied.

Names and addresses were drawn from the N.A.B.'s current files by officers experienced in the field. Only addresses within the borough boundaries were selected, every third one in North-borough and all those in Seaston. The N.A.B.'s files were arranged chronologically and identified by colour tags for individual groups, and care was taken to ensure that all current cases were in the files at the time the sample was drawn.

The Survey Response	North-borough	Seaston	Total
Names originally selected by the N.A.B.	100	115	215*
Prisoners' wives who did not respond and were excluded (number known from statistics supplied by N.A.B.)	5	2	7
Mothers with no child still dependent: no response: mother was excluded:	0	1	1
mother responded and was interviewed, but income data was not used	(1)		(1)
Effective sample	95	112	207
Replies to first letter	37	47	84
Replies to reminder	7	15	22
Mothers who did not reply, but who were subsequently traced through acquaintances also on the sample	1	14	15
Thus, total who replied or were contacted	45	76	121
Emigrated after replying	1	0	1
Refused interview after replying	0	2	2
No contact, probably a refusal	0	2	2
Interviewed mothers: total number	44	72	116†
percentage	46	64	56

*These were the mothers for whom the N.A.B. subsequently supplied statistics.
†115 for the purposes of income data.

Letters were sent out first in Northborough, in March 1965, and later in Seaston, in September 1965. In Northborough, 100 letters brought initially thirty-seven replies, and very near the later response in Seaston. When we could produce this definite evidence that one letter was insufficient, the N.A.B. agreed to send reminders. To preserve confidentiality, *every* mother was again circularized, these reminders stressing that the Board did not know who had replied. After a gap of four months these reminders were late, but still brought in seven replies. The

Board felt a further reminder would bring too great pressure on mothers to participate.

In Seaston, after a similar response to the first wave, reminders were sent out after a fortnight and brought fifteen replies. In addition I now discovered that because the Seaston sample included a very large proportion of all the fatherless families in the area, some of whom knew each other, I was able to trace more of the *original sample* through their acquaintances whom I had interviewed. I visited these other mothers who had not returned our card and explained the purpose of the survey, not telling them who had given me their name, but stressing that the N.A.B. were not responsible for my tracing them. Several were glad to take an opportunity they thought they had missed by dilatoriness; only one refused (motives for responding are discussed more fully in the Introduction).

The two groups of interviews were added together to produce the final sample. Although this means that the picture is slightly weighted towards Seaston, in view of the overall deficiencies of the sample compensatory weightings were inappropriate.

High and low response rates of sub-groups

Because the N.A.B. supplied overall statistics for the 215 Northborough and Seaston mothers to whom letters were originally sent, I was able to identify high and low response rates among sub-groups of the sample. Seven prisoners' wives, none of whom replied to our letters, were excluded from the survey.

	Interviews	N.A.B. total
High response		
Widows	15	18
Divorcees	36	40*
Mothers with three or more dependent children	18	22
Mothers with five or more dependent children	6	6
Low response		
Separated wives	42	98*
Prisoners' wives	0	7
(Separated wives with one child only	6	31*)

*The N.A.B.'s divorce figures are not up to date, so they understate the number of divorcees and overstate the number of separated wives.

Widows had the highest response rate. Next came divorcees,

although the N.A.B.'s low figure for divorcees will mean that their apparent response rate is inflated while that of separated wives is reduced (thus I interviewed more Seaston divorcees than the N.A.B. had on their records). Unmarried mothers also had a low response. Among the separated, mothers with only one child appeared less likely to reply. The N.A.B. told me that six separated wives had later been reunited with their husbands, yet in none of the interviews had this appeared at all likely: the survey may therefore under-represent relationships which are in a delicate state of balance, where mothers did not welcome the interference of an interviewer.

The mothers interviewed had families slightly larger than the average family contacted, most of the mothers with three or more dependent children, and all those with five or more dependent children, replying. As a result the average number of dependent children of the mothers interviewed was 2.5, compared with 2.1 for mothers contacted. Those interviewed had also been on assistance slightly longer during the current spell than those contacted.

It therefore appears that a high response rate was promoted perhaps by consciousness of desert (the widows), while a low response rate might stem from a fear of condemnation (prisoners' wives, the unmarried and separated), or the likelihood that the present spell on assistance would soon end through the return of the mother to her husband or to work (those with smaller families).

Mothers did not respond differently because of their country of origin, or their residence with kin. There was no reliable information on the social class composition of the original group of mothers contacted.

Methods of sampling

My experience with this sample indicates that postal sampling, however carefully the letters explain the purpose of the survey, is likely to be misunderstood and to produce a poor response. Failure or reluctance to respond usually stemmed, as far as I was able to check, not from any disagreement with the aims and methods of the survey, but from a variety of extraneous factors such as misunderstanding, misapprehension of the source of the letters, or sheer inertia. A personal explanation on the doorstep almost invariably brought cooperation from women who were anxious for someone to talk to. Seen in this light, perhaps the Board's refusal of alternative methods of approach – divulging names, or sending letters out, to be returned if the person did not wish to cooperate – appears over-cautious. However, there may be a moral in the case of the American poor, where ready access to public assistance records for survey work appears to be symptomatic of the inferior status of those supported by the state.

Appendix Three
Statistical Tables Referred To in the Text

Table 1

Some characteristics of dependent fatherless families,
by the mother's marital status
(215 families contacted by the N.A.B.)

Mothers	Unmarried*	Separated†	Divorced	Widowed	All mothers
Most often aged between‡	21 and 30	21 and 40	31 and 40	41 and 50	21 and 40
Average number of dependent children	1·7	2·4	2·2	1·6	2·1
Percentage currently in receipt of assistance for more than two years§	40	40	60	60	45
Percentage with dependent children over 5 years old	30	60	80	90	58
Percentage with non-dependent children	10	20	30	50	21
Percentage living away from parents	70	70	70	100	70
Percentage of mothers of given marital status	24	49	19	8	100
Total number of mothers	52	105	40	18	215

*Includes 14 West Indians, all in Northborough.

†Includes informally as well as legally separated, among them seven wives of men in prison.

‡By inspection from a table supplied by the N.A.B. (a median could not be calculated).

§Where numbers are compared with a total of less than 100 percentages have been rounded to the nearest 10 per cent.

Table 2

Percentage of 115 fatherless families with incomes received in cash,
and total incomes, above and below national assistance scales†*

Percentage of N.A.B. scale rates plus rents	Percentage of families whose income comes into each bracket	
	income received as cash‡	total income from all sources including income in kind
Under 90	8	4
90–99	13	2
100–109	39	17
110–119	10	17
120–129	16	18
130–139	10	17
140–149	1	10
150 or over	3	15

*Of the 116 originally interviewed, one mother, excluded from the income information, had no dependent children when the sample was drawn.

†The table does not show that the scale used for ten owner-occupiers allowed only for interest repayments on the mortgage, so that their disposable income was effectively lower by the amount of the capital repayments they had to make on their houses. (See also footnote on p. 353)

‡Includes a rough assessment of the value of housekeeping exchanges of cash and goods between dependent and non-dependent members of the household (see note 2, p. 359).

Table 3

Average current incomes of mothers of different marital status

Mothers	Income received in cash		Total income from all sources checked (including income in kind)	
	average p.a.	as percentage of N.A.B. scale rate	average p.a.	as percentage of N.A.B. scale rate
Unmarried	£270	98	£325	118
Separated	£395	100	£485	123
Divorced	£490	106	£570	123
Widowed	£550	117	£600	127
All	£415	105	£485	123

Table 4

Incomes of fatherless families, grouped into six categories by type or method of receipt (averaged over time and expressed as a percentage of national assistance scale rate, taking the median* income of each type)

Type of income or method of receipt	Income as a percentage of N.A. scale rate (median* income)
Regular cash income — regular and dependable amounts from assistance, pensions, family allowances, money from husbands, part-time earnings, education maintenance allowances, and income (not always cash) accruing to the mother from other non-dependants in a household she shares as a householder or boarder.	104
Regular state benefits in kind — regular benefits to which the mother has a statutory right, such as *free school* meals, and free welfare foods and free milk for the pre-school child.	4
Private cash receipts — occasional or marginal income to the nuclear family (mother and dependent children) from dis-saving, sale of possessions, school children's earnings given to the mother. Plus cash gifts from relatives or non-relatives outside the household: amounts usually disregarded by the N.A.B.	4
Private incomes in kind or 'tied' income — e.g. gifts of clothing, food, or a holiday. But also money given to the family for a specific purpose (payment of TV, etc.), or money not going to the mother herself yet raising the family's standard of living (e.g. school children's earnings, retained and spent by them).	9
Occasional state or local authority payments — including maternity benefit, and the N.A.B.'s 'exceptional needs grant', i.e. lump sum payments for the purchase of specific items (for which proof of purchase is required). Also school uniform grants from the local education authority.	2
Undeclared income — (which would have been deductible from the national assistance allowance) including earnings over the £2 limit, cash from the father of a child, or cash in excess of board from a man with whom the mother was cohabiting.	1
Total income from all sources checked	124

*The median income is such that as many incomes lie above it as lie below.

Table 5

*Numbers of mothers requiring different amounts of earnings to achieve independence
of assistance at the maximum attainable assistance level (scale rate plus £2),
in shillings per week*

Earnings in shillings per week	Unmarried	Separated	Divorced	Widowed	All number	All percentage
80 or less	1	0	3	8	12	10
81–120	2	5	5	3	15	13
121–160	8	9	8	1	26	23
161–200	13	15	7	2	37	32
200 or more	2	12	11	0	25	22
Total number of mothers	26	41	34	14	115	100

Table 6

Number and percentage of fatherless families and of all households having different articles

Article		Marital status of mother				All fatherless families (percentage)	Large and small urban areas* (percentage)
		unmarried (26)	separated (41)	divorced (35)	widowed (14)		
TV	access	20	34	31	31	84	81†
	owner	1	2	7	4	12	–
Washing machine		3	15	19	8	39	55
Refrigerator		1	6	6	5	15	30
Telephone			5	5	5	4	16
Furniture		10	38	30	12	78	–

*Source: *Family Expenditure Survey, 1964.* H.M.S.O., 1966. This was the only year in which breakdowns of possession of these items for large and small urban areas were given.

†The figures are not strictly comparable, since the *Family Expenditure Survey* figure is for *licences* rather than sets. Here again fatherless families probably had fewer appliances.

Table 7

Numbers and percentages of mothers* who felt hard up

Feeling hard up	Marital status			All mothers	
	unmarried	separated and divorced	widowed	number	per-centage
Always	8	17	1	26	36
Sometimes	4	16	2	22	31
Not	3	15	6	24	33
Total	15	48	9	72	100

*Only the Seaston mothers were asked the question systematically.

Table 8

Numbers of marriages where wives complained that certain behaviour of the husband was the immediate major cause of marriage breakdown, and the total numbers of marriages where the behaviour was mentioned, compared with how the marriages ended.

Wife's complaint of her husband's behaviour:	wife left husband (21)		wife divorced or evicted husband (22)		husband deserted (33)		Total (76)	
	behaviour caused breakdown	behaviour mentioned	behaviour caused breakdown	behaviour mentioned	behaviour caused breakdown	behaviour mentioned	behaviour caused breakdown	behaviour mentioned
Non-support	6	13	8	17	6	10	20	40
Physical violence	5	11	8	13	2	2	15	28
Other women	2	8	4	9	2	8	8	26
Excessive sex or perversion	4	5	1	3	0	0	5	8
No objectionable behaviour	4	–	1	–	23	–	28	–
Husband's temporary desertions	–	6	–	10	–	20	–	36
Wife deserted during marriage	–	9	–	8	–	3	–	20

A Note on Classifying Marriage Complaints

Table 8 includes only behaviour of the husband which was given by at least one wife as the *major* reason why her marriage ended. In the second columns are the totals of the marriages where this sort of behaviour was mentioned at all. Judgements of the *major* complaint are the mothers' own.

Not included as complaints are:

(a) *descriptions* of how the marriage ended, e.g. 'he deserted', or 'he went off with another woman', where the wife absolves her husband from blame.

(b) 'Second-order' explanations which express sophistication, or which are in some ways alternative descriptions, e.g. 'a clash of values', 'personality defect' or 'mental illness'.

(c) behaviour complained of in only a minor way, which the mother believes was not the major cause, in that it was tolerable, or which she believes she could have overcome, e.g. impotence or insufficient sex, lack of affection, irresponsibility with money, temporary desertions.

(d) behaviour causing the major complaint, e.g. drinking leading to *violence* or *non-support* (either of which would themselves be the major complaint).

This classification attempts to allow for the fact that some women make a major complaint, while others have really no complaint. It is more subjective than Goode's classification (W. J. Goode, *Women in Divorce,* op. cit., p. 113 ff.), which, however, confuses the various levels of complaint, descriptions and second-order explanations, and thus assumes that all wives make complaints.

Table 9

The origins and ages of unmarried mothers on assistance, together with the numbers and ages of their illegitimate children

Mothers born in England:	
Young mothers (aged 16 to 30) with one baby (under one year)	7
Young mothers with several children (under 5 years)	7
Other mothers (aged 36 or more) with several older children (10 years or over)	2
Older mothers with one older child	4
Mothers born in the West Indies:	
Young mothers with one baby	1
Young mothers with several young children (average family size four)	5
	26

Table 10

Numbers and regularity of payment of court orders for 215 Northborough and Seaston mothers,* and for all fatherless families on national assistance†

Type and regularity of payment	Northborough and Seaston mothers		All separated wives on assistance		All mothers of illegitimate children on assistance	
	number	per-centage	number	per-centage	number	per-centage
Court order, regularly paid‡	47	22	21,000	20	6,000	16
Court order, irregularly paid	13	6	7,000	7	1,000	3
Court order, rarely or never paid	35	16	15,000	14	2,000	6
No court order	120	56	61,000	59	27,000	75
Total number of mothers	215	100	104,000	100	36,000	100

*Figures supplied by the N.A.B. for all mothers contacted for our survey.

†Figures from *N.A.B. Report for 1965*, op. cit., pp. 27–8. Figures of regularity of payments to divorced mothers were not given.

‡There is some doubt whether the criteria for regularity (3 to 4 weeks' money, 1 to 2 weeks' money, and less than one week's money per four-week period) are exactly the same in the survey and national figures, but they are near enough for our purposes.

Table 12

Numbers of mothers receiving an allowance at, or more or less than the basic scale rate of assistance (my calculations)

Mothers with an allowance at the basic rate		48
Mothers with an allowance less than the basic rate		45
(a) *Where N.A.B. Regulations provide less than the adult maximum rate* (18)		
Home owners who did not receive the full cost of housing*	10	
Mothers aged under 21 years who were paid at children's rates*	5	
Mothers whose rent was not met in full by the N.A.B.	3	
(b) *Where the mother was in a household with others not on assistance* (9)		
Deductions made for children who were intermittently off work and dependent on the mother*	4	
Deduction for the rent share of a non-dependent child exceeded his payment	2	
Deduction for a contribution by a lodger exceeded the lodger's payment	2	
Mother living with parents had deduction 'in lieu of earnings'	1	
(c) *Where income to the mother from a man was imputed* (8)		
Deduction for contribution from the children's father exceeded his payment	6	
Deduction 'in lieu of earnings as housekeeper' where cohabitation was suspected	2	
(d) *Where the N.A.B. possibly had insufficient information* (4)		
Expenses incurred in travel to work not fully allowed	2	
Mother should have received an allowance to supplement inadequate unemployment benefit, but was refused assistance	1	
No allowance for a child whose birth was unknown to the N.A.B.	1	
(e) *Other*		
Fines incurred for undeclared earnings	2	
(f) *Not accounted for*		
Possibly deduction for regular income from friends	4	
Mothers with an allowance higher than the basic rates:		22
'Discretionary allowance' for special needs	9	
Deduction of boarder's rent share not enforced in full, where deduction would have been justified by Regulations	6	
Generous rent share for mother living with relatives	2	
No deduction for declared resources of cash in the bank, where deduction would have been justified by Regulations	1	
Not accounted for: discretion for some aspect of the mother's situation not perceived in the interview, or a clerical error	4	115

*In Table 2 the scale rates used were: for home owners the housing cost *excluding* capital repayments: for mothers under 21 the juvenile rates: and for mothers with unemployed children to support the rate excluding those children, although discretion could have been exercised in favour of the mothers. As a result the incomes in Table 2 expressed as percentages of reduced scale rates appear relatively higher for these families than they in fact were.

Table II

Numbers of divorced wives giving accounts corresponding and not corresponding with grounds on which the divorce was given

Wife Divorced Husband	
Wife thought the legal grounds did not misrepresent the breakdown	20
Husband guilty of cruelty: divorce for adultery	5
Husband deserted: divorce for adultery	5
	30
Husband Divorced Wife	
Husband deserted: divorce on grounds of wife's adultery	3
Wife deserted: divorce on grounds of wife's adultery	2
	5
Total number of divorces	35

Notes

Introduction

1. The National Assistance Board was subsumed under the Ministry of Social Security as the Supplementary Benefits Commission from the autumn of 1966 (and the Commission has again been subsumed within the Department of Health and Social Security, but this time retaining its name). The information gathered in this survey comes from the period autumn 1965 and spring 1966, so where I discuss the survey data I refer to 'national assistance' and 'the National Assistance Board (N.A.B.)', rather than the current terms which are 'supplementary benefits' and 'the Supplementary Benefits Commission (S.B.C.)'. Later in the book, in discussing policy changes and the current situation I use the current terms.

2. *The income af a fatherless family with two children compared with the average income of a married couple with two children (1966 values)*

Type of family and income (with family allowance)	Weekly income	As a percentage of national assistance allowance‡
Fatherless family, with two children, and income from		
(i) average woman's wage (net of national insurance*)	£9 14s. 6d.	115
(ii) basic national assistance allowance	£8 10s. 0d.	100
(iii) national assistance plus £2 maximum part-time earnings	£10 10s. 0d.	123
Average income of a married couple with two children (net of tax and national insurance)†	£22 3s. 6d.	202

Ministry of Labour Gazette, August 1966, H.M.S.O., Vol. LXXIV, No. 8 (figure for April 1966).

†Ministry of Labour, *Family Expenditure Survey for 1965*, H.M.S.O., 1966, pp. 83, 87.

‡The national assistance allowance includes an amount for each person in the household, according to status and age, and an allowance for rent (see Appendix One for the full rates). For the purpose of this calculation the children are assumed to be aged between 5 and 9, and the rent to be £2.

The above table gives the situation at 1966 values. For the purpose of comparing families of different compositions it may be taken that families with the same percentage of the national assistance allowance will be living at the same level. Appendix One gives the scales of payment current at the time of the survey, and extracts from the National Assistance Regulations governing the payment of allowances. The rates of allowances were increased slightly and the Regulations amended in October 1967, and there have since been further increases which may have slightly altered the position of poor families relative to the rising levels of the rest of the community. The 1971 rates also appear in Appendix One. (But see note 2, p.365.)

For a subtle and detailed discussion of the relative economic positions and needs of families of various kinds, see M. Wynn, *Family Policy*, Michael Joseph, 1970. And throughout that book information will be found which is relevant background reading for the present survey.

3. General Register Office, *Sample Census 1966, Household Composition Tables, England and Wales*, H.M.S.O., 19, Table 23, p. 256. And *Annual Report of the National Assistance Board for 1965*, Cmnd 3042, H.M.S.O., pp. 6, 8, 11, 62. Figures for national assistance recipients in 1965 are taken because the sample from cases was not taken by the S.B.C. in 1966 owing to pressure of work. The Report does not clearly state how many fatherless families were dependent. There were 18,000 widows, with 27,000 children, receiving supplements to pensions. 108,000 women aged under 60 with dependent children and not receiving national insurance benefit were described as 'mostly separated and divorced wives and unmarried mothers'. In addition there would be a few mothers receiving supplement to sickness and unemployment benefit. Figures for children of the 108,000 are derived from the fact that the women are drawn from the 110,000 persons under pension age who have approximately 225,000 children in all. An estimate of approximately 200,000 children was therefore used for the 108,000 mothers.

The Seebohm Report estimated that the numbers of children under 16 who are 'at risk' are 672,000 illegitimate children and 1,390,000 children in families broken by death, divorce, or separation. These children, of course, are not all currently fatherless. *Report of the Committee on Local Authority and Allied Personal Social Services* (The Seebohm Report), H.M.S.O., Cmnd 3703, 1968.

4. I am indebted to Margaret Wynn for this calculation in a draft report, as yet unpublished, of evidence to the Finer Committee.

5. For a discussion of poverty surveys and measures, see P. Townsend, 'The Meaning of Poverty', *British Journal of Sociology*, September 1962, Vol. XIII, No. 3, pp. 210–25. Also P. Townsend (ed.), *The Concept of Poverty*, Heinemann, 1970.

6. See B. Abel-Smith, and P. Townsend, *The Poor and the Poorest*, Bell, 1965, pp. 17–20.

7. The difficulties of using the Ministry of Labour's *Family Expenditure Surveys*, op. cit., are discussed in B. Abel-Smith, and P. Townsend, op. cit. The Ministry of Social Security's survey, *Circumstances of Families*, H.M.S.O., 1967, published after the present research had been undertaken, included only 96 fatherless families, all with two or more children. There must be some doubts about the accuracy of the survey data, collected by N.A.B. officers, because no mention is made of inaccurate payments of supplementary benefit, although we know that something like 25 per cent are in error.

8. The other studies are *Unemployed in Shields* by Adrian Sinfield (to be published in the series of L.S.E. Occasional Papers in Social Administration), *Large Families in London* by Hilary Land, Bell, 1969, and a study of the chronic sick by John Veit Wilson.

9. This is not to say, of course, that they are not good in their field. Among the better studies are Peter Marris's moving (but neglected) book on widows, *Widows and Their Families*, Routledge and Kegan Paul, 1958. He wrote, 'Poverty accentuates all the morbid tendencies of grief – the isolation, bitterness, apathy; the sense of being rejected, a drag on the happiness of others – while to secure a comfortable living standard would ... encourage (the widow) to master them.' In 1965 Pauline Morris wrote, 'The great majority of prisoners' wives live in conditions of grinding poverty.' Her book, *Prisoners and Their Families*, Allen and Unwin for P.E.P., contains much that is parallel with the present research, since the prisoners' 'wives' were often unmarried or separated. Some studies of unmarried mothers are summarized in V. Wimperis, *The Unmarried Mother and her Child*, Allen and Unwin, 1960. Margaret Wynn's book *Fatherless Families* was a pioneering work in using the term, and gathers together some survey evidence and a mass of contradictory administrative provisions (Michael Joseph, 1969).

In a survey of the (largely unmarried) members of Mothers in Action, an association for unsupported mothers, Holman pays close attention to *Mothers Alone*, providing useful confirmatory evidence and opening up issues neglected by the present research, notably day-care. R. Holman, *Unsupported Mothers*, published in 1970 by Mothers in Action, 25 Milton Rd, London, N6.

10. Thus, *Circumstances of Families*, op. cit., p. 27, showed 46 per cent of families being assisted at the survey date, but 61 per cent at some time in the previous year.

11. That is, I was able to interview 56 per cent of the mothers whom the N.A.B. had originally contacted by letter. Full details of the sampling procedures and a discussion of the representativeness of the interviewed mothers are given in Appendix Two.

12. See Table 1, Appendix Three, for some characteristics of the dependent fatherless families, arranged by the mother's marital status, which show the links with the age and child-bearing cycles.

13. Appendix Two.

14. Peter Townsend discussed recent trends in inequality in *The Times*, 8, 9, 10, 11 March 1971. For a discussion of the relative movements of wages and social security benefits, with particular reference to the introduction of wage-related benefits, see F. Lafitte, 'Income Deprivation', in R. Holman (ed.), *Socially Deprived Families in Britain*, Bedford Square Press, 1970. Although Lafitte argues that the volume of poverty as measured by the yardstick of late 1966 (*Circumstances of Families*, op. cit.) must have been reduced, he cannot discuss the actual standards of living of poor families whose spending patterns will differ from the national average in ways which make the use of one price index inappropriate. He concludes that, 'Without a fresh survey the present dimensions of child poverty, applying present poverty standards, cannot be precisely delineated.' Lafitte's calculations for 'single-handed' mothers show that pensioned widows are considerably better protected now than other unsupported mothers, and that without assistance other single-handed mothers are always likely to be in poverty if they cannot work because maintenance payments from the children's fathers are generally at sub-poverty rates.

1: The Incomes of Fatherless Families

1. Only large gifts (£5 or over) or small regular gifts were taken into account. Lump sums were averaged over the year. Items like cigarettes and coal were priced, and some meals received from relatives were priced on the same basis as boarder incomes (see note 3). Of other gifts, only a narrow range of large, new, recent items could be at all reliably priced and averaged weekly. Attempts to price second-hand

goods were defeated by the fluctuations in the value of such goods depending on their utility to the recipient, or the route travelled, via jumble sale, chain of friends, or shop. Holidays were a significant item and a token 1s. a week was added per individual who received a free holiday (equivalent to £2 12s. in a year).

2. Comparisons of different families, based on these percentages, assume that the national assistance scales correctly allow for family size and composition. But in fact there is some evidence to show that fatherless families and complete families of different sizes on national assistance are not given equivalent incomes. The allowances for a single person and a married couple, and the allowances for extra children, have varied slightly in proportion to each other over the years. They are not in line with the proportionate allowances given in other social security scales in Britain and other countries. It will be seen from Appendix One that the proportions for children of different ages were, at the time of the survey, simply arithmetical ratios. The scale rates derive indirectly from the approach used by Seebohm Rowntree, but no official explanation has ever been given of how they are arrived at; see M. Wynn, *Family Policy*, op. cit., Chapter 6, and C. Bagley, *The Cost of a Child*, copies from the author, Institute of Psychiatry, London, SE5. Also, C. Bagley and B. Abel-Smith, in P. Townsend (ed.), *The Concept of Poverty*, op. cit.

3. This cash income includes where appropriate an assessment of the value to the dependent family accruing from the housekeeping arrangements with non-dependent members of the household. In households where the mother *boarded*, her food was estimated to cost 30s. per week (5s. less than the average in the population as a whole), and food consumed by the children was estimated at fractions of this 30s. in accordance with the equivalence ratios expressed in the N.A.B. scale (Appendix One). On reflection these figures for the children are undoubtedly low. From comparisons with mothers living as householders, the boarder mothers saved in gas, electricity, etc., something like 30s. a week. In fact, 20s. is the amount given to boarder families in lieu of these expenses. The benefit to boarders is then caclulated as the cost of mother's and children's food plus 20s., unless the finances were known more accurately in other ways.

Mothers who were *householders* had a variety of arrangements with boarders. In general, the food of boarders was costed at 30s. a week, where appropriate split into 5s. for breakfasts, 15s. for the main meal, and 10s. for the other meal taken at home. If the householder's mother helped with clothing, 5s. was allowed, and if she bought all the child's clothing, 10s. For a lodger who was not a child, a further 10s. was added, for what would probably be extra expenses incurred by the mother in providing separate facilities or slightly more elaborate meals.

Other transactions, e.g. gifts, pocket money, payments for TV, were costed separately.

4. See, for example, the gift exchanges in middle-class families described in C. Bell, *Middle Class Families*, Routledge and Kegan Paul, 1969, pp. 92–5.

5. For a full discussion of the matrimonial jurisdiction and workings of magistrates' courts, see O. R. McGregor, L. Blom-Cooper, and C. Gibson, *Separated Spouses*, Duckworth, 1970. There was some doubt from the interviews as to the type of court in which the maintenance order was made. Therefore the lower figure of possible maximum awards in a magistrates' court has been taken. This limit has now been removed (see Chapter 10).

6. Figures for all fatherless families on national assistance are: yearly rate of assistance expenditure approximately £45 million; yearly payments received from fathers by applicants approximately £4 million. (The fact that this also is around one tenth is something of a coincidence, although national assistance scales are comparable with maximum court awards.) *N.A.B. Report for 1965*, Cmnd 3042, H.M.S.O., Table 13, p. 27. See also Table 17, p. 156; and O. R. McGregor et al., op. cit., pp. 149–63.

7. For the limits, see Appendix One. The chapter on national assistance has a more detailed discussion of how allowances are arrived at.

8. See note 3.

9. Evidence on the take-up of welfare benefits and rights is published in some issues of *Poverty*, the magazine of the Child Poverty Action Group. See also Chapter 11.

10. The point could not be pursued without a more detailed knowledge of the mothers' and fathers' contribution records. But, very roughly, mothers who had worked, and widows and separated wives whose husbands had enough contributions, could get benefit. But unmarried mothers and divorced women, and separated wives whose husbands had not worked, could not get anything. They were thus dependent on exceptional needs grants, and these did not always approach full benefit rates.

2: The Home

1. Two recent reports on homelessness reveal how vulnerable the fatherless family is. Greve and Glastonbury both noted a high proportion of the homeless were fatherless families, about a third, mainly separated wives. Greve stresses the low incomes of fatherless families as a cause. (J. Greve, *Homelessness in London*, Scottish Academic Press, 1971, pp. 90 and 94.) Glastonbury describes his sample as follows: 'The overall picture emerges that two thirds of the entire sample were either actually or at risk of becoming fatherless at the time they went into the hostel ... Homelessness, which may happen once or several times, appeared very much as an integral part of the course of a marriage breakdown.' (B. Glastonbury, *Homeless near a Thousand Homes*, National Institute for Social Work Training Series, no. 21, Allen and Unwin, 1971.)

2. That is, 40 per cent, compared with 32 per cent for the regions and 31 per cent for the country as a whole. General Register Office, *Census 1961, England and Wales, Housing Tables. Part II. Tenure and Household Arrangements*, H.M.S.O., 1965. However, for evidence of rather worse housing standards among fatherless families, see Ministry of Social Security, *Circumstances of Families*, H.M.S.O., 1965, pp. 58–9, where it is stated, 'The housing of fatherless families ... was worse, in structural condition, lack of amenities and overcrowding, than that of families of other types.' This report also notes that bad housing among the fatherless was not restricted to poorer families, a finding echoed by R. Holman, *Unsupported Mothers*, op. cit., Chapter 6.

3. Of the 215 mothers originally contacted 107 or 50 per cent were in council property. For Northborough and Seaston districts as a whole the figures were: council tenants 23.3 per cent, private tenants 28.3 per cent, and owner-occupiers 48.4 per cent.

4. These forty-two include flats, houses, rooms, and caravans (some rented from relatives), together with several condemned dwellings awaiting demolition but recently taken over by the council.

5. Full data supplied by the N.A.B. for all 215 mothers in the original sample (to whom letters were sent) show the proportions of mothers living in council or owner-occupied property as: unmarried 40 per cent, separated 40 per cent, divorced 72 per cent, and widowed 94 per cent. For further evidence on accommodation for unsupported mothers, see R. Holman, *Unsupported Mothers*, op. cit., p. 47 and Chapter 6.

6. The index used was the bedroom deficiency index devised by P. G. Gray of the Government Social Survey (P. G. Gray and R. Russell, *Social Survey Report SS319: The Housing Situation in 1960*). The number of bedrooms possessed by the household was compared with the standard:

(i) Each couple or mother was given a bedroom.

(ii) Any other persons aged 21 or over were each given a bedroom.

(iii) Persons aged 10–20 years, inclusive, of the same sex were paired off and a bedroom given to each pair.

(iv) Any person aged 10–20 years left over after this pairing was paired with a child under 10 of the same sex. If no pairing of this kind was possible, such a person was given a separate bedroom.

(v) Any remaining children under 10 were paired and a bedroom given to each pair. Any remaining child was given an additional room.

(*Children and Their Primary Schools*, H.M.S.O., 1967, Vol. 2, Appendix 3, p. 112.)

It was thought that for fatherless families this index might be too stringent, and the data were re-worked to allow children up to two years to share with the mother. However, the use of this index produced virtually no change in the overall proportion of families overcrowded.

7. *Children and Their Primary Schools*, op. cit., p. 124.

3: Spending on 'Necessities' and 'Luxuries'

1. A report by the Office of Health Economics, reviewing available data and present nutrition surveys, states that these are patchy, 'since the methods of assessing nutrition in the main are new and still relatively undeveloped'. The report also says, 'In the area between chronic deficiency and optimum health, more is known about animals than about man.' Any investigation of nutrition requires the collection and assessment of several types of evidence. 'Information is required on the food consumption and nutrient intake of the population. Details of clinical examinations are needed to indicate the extent to which health has been affected by differing diets. The results of biochemical tests may be used to indicate the level of nutrient reserves within the body. The study of vital statistics and anthropometric data demonstrate the impact of dietary variations. . . . Only after an examination of all these areas and their interrelationships can an adequate assessment of nutritional status be made.' (*Malnutrition in the 1960s?*, Office of Health Economics, 1967.) See also the chapter on nutrition by R. McKenzie in P. Townsend (ed.), *The Concept of Poverty*, op. cit.

2. Professor Yudkin of Queen Elizabeth College advised that there was no satisfactory way of detecting malnutrition by means of ordinary interviewing, but that anyone consuming half a pint of milk or more a day was very unlikely to be suffering from malnutrition. We therefore used the milk consumption as a *broad* criterion of adequate nutrition. But because the children tended to get the food the mother's diet may still be at risk, even though the family as a whole is above the half pint of milk per head standard. Below that standard, there may be a good case for probing for further evidence of malnutrition.

3. *Circumstances of Families* gave a lower proportion, 7 per cent, of children not receiving school meals, but the families all had two children; 16 per cent paid. (Op. cit., p. 29, Table III, 10.) The continued importance of school meals and milk has been underlined by further surveys done by Queen Elizabeth College, which have shown that by B.M.A. standards one third of children have a poor diet. See G. Lynch and S. de la Paz, 'The Politics of School Milk', *New Scientist and Science Journal*, 1 July 1971, pp. 32–3.

4. The recent price rises in school meals have once again brought reports that some authorities and schools issue tickets of a different colour and line up children in a separate queue for free meals, or otherwise identify children in a way which may attract stigma. See the exposures by C.P.A.G. in Manchester, in November 1969, of continuing segregation (Hansard, Vol. 793, 11 December 1969, col. 617); and also the survey by the Newcastle branch of C.A.S.E. in 1970.

5. All figures for national expenditures in this chapter come from the *Family Expenditure Survey for 1965*, H.M.S.O., 1966.

6. 50.3 per cent of women aged 25–34, and 51 per cent of women aged 35–39 are smokers. *Statistics of Smoking in the U.K.*, No. 1, Ed. 4, Tobacco Research Council, 1966.

7. Half of a sample of young working-class wives never went out in the evening. H. Gavron, *The Captive Wife*, Routledge and Kegan Paul, 1965.

8. R. Hoggart, *The Uses of Literacy*, Chatto and Windus, 1957, p. 116.

9. One of the justifications which used to be advanced for not publishing the 'A' Code which guides officers in the exercise of discretion in the giving of state subsistence allowances and discretionary grants (see Chapters 11 and 12) was that the code contains provisions for the payment of arrears in certain circumstances and that publication would encourage clients to run up arrears. In fact the evidence of this survey

pointed to discretion being very seldom, if ever, exercised in this matter.

4: On Feeling Poor: The Social Context of Poverty

1. As Runciman has pointed out, if we think of different kinds of comparisons, of which one kind is where a person measures himself against the standards of a group, called a 'reference group', 'The term [reference group] can be used not only to mean the group with which the person compares himself; it can also be used to mean either the group from which he derives his standards of comparison or the group from which the comparison is extended and to which he feels he belongs ... the reference "group" need not be a group at all; it may be a single person or even an abstract idea.' Runciman also suggests that 'in hard times comparative reference groups [i.e. in the instance of fatherless families, groups with whom the mother compares herself] will be more restricted than in good.' (W. G. Runciman, *Relative Deprivation and Social Justice*, Routledge and Kegan Paul, 1966, pp. 10–12, and p. 21.)

2. Pauline Morris noted this desire but did not relate it to the customary activities of working-class families. 'The less intelligent wives really believed that if the N.A.B. money was paid on a Friday instead of a Monday they would have no financial problems.' (P. Morris, op. cit., p. 154.) One might suggest that the wives, in this, were more 'intelligent' than the N.A.B. authorities. The need for payments or collections by official authorities to fit in with the weekly cycle of expenditure, on estates in particular, has been underlined by the discovery that, for example, rent arrears can be cut simply by arranging for the rent collector to call at a more sensible time than every alternate Wednesday, and that rent arrears rise if fortnightly rather than weekly collections are instituted.

3. Germany does give extra seasonal grants to the poor. See M. Wynn, *Family Policy*, op. cit. p. 202. The book has a whole section on seasonal needs which is highly relevant to this discussion of feelings of deprivation.

4. Figures from Public Attitude Surveys Limited.

5. Department of Education and Science, *List 69 (1964)*, H.M.S.O. 1965. Figures are for the proportions of thirteen-year-olds with selective places, excluding comprehensives.

6. D. Marsden, 'Poverty – the Fate of One in Six', *Where*, No. 31, Advisory Centre for Education.

7. The findings about the influence of fatherlessness *per se* on educational performance are not conclusive. The problem is to separate out the associated factors of poverty and a poor material environment from fatherlessness. Thus, Herzog and Sudia concluded after a review of 400 mostly American studies of fatherless families, 'it seems unlikely that father absence in itself would show significant relation to poorer school achievement, if relevant variables (including type of father absence and socio-economic status) were adequately controlled.' (Children's Bureau, Office of Child Development, U.S. Dept of Health, Education and Welfare, 1970; also to be published in *Review of Child Development Research*, Vol. 3, under the auspices of the Society for Research in Child Development.) See also *Boys in Fatherless Families*, U.S. Department of Health, Education and Welfare, Office of Child Development, Children's Bureau, 1970; 'Fatherless Homes: a Review of Research', in *Children*, September–October 1968, pp. 177–82; 'Family Structure and Composition: Research Considerations', in *Race, Research and Reason*; all by the same authors. Coleman's massive American study of education concluded that, 'Absence of a father in the home did not have the anticipated effect on ability scores. Overall, pupils without fathers performed at approximately the same level as those with fathers.' (J. S. Coleman et al., *Equality of Educational Opportunity*, U.S. Dept of Health and Welfare, 1966.) A similar conclusion is reported by Wilson: 'Neither our own data nor the preponderance of evidence from other research studies indicate that father absence *per se* is related to school achievement. While broken homes reflect the existence of social and personal problems, and have some consequences for the development of personality, broken homes do not have any systematic effect on the overall level of school success.' (A. B. Wilson, 'Educational Consequences of Segregation in a California Community', in *Racial Isolation in the Public Schools*, Appendices, Vol. 2 or a report by the U.S. Commission on Civil Rights, Washington D.C., U.S. Government Printing Office, 1967.) Blau and Duncan, in their (much criticized) work on American social mobility, say: 'Apparently we must conclude that a background of living in a broken family or with parents with disrupted marriages has some adverse effect on educational attainment. partially because of its association with socioeconomic background factors but partially for other reasons . . . The educational handicap is, in turn, translated into poorer than average occupational achievement, but there is little or

no direct effect of rearing in a broken family on occupational success apart from this.' (*The American Occupational Structure*, Wiley, 1967, p. 336.)

In England, Dr Douglas, in his large longitudinal study of a cohort of children born in 1946 (which, however, excluded illegitimate children), discovered that, 'insecurity in the family, whether from the father's absence, unemployment, illness or death is associated with poorer performance at school and early leaving. It is prolonged insecurity that seems to be important; the sudden death of a father whether early or late in the life of his child, has no apparent effect on school work.' (*All Our Future*, Peter Davies, 1968, p. 188.) But it is not clear whether Douglas has controlled for the factor of *economic* insecurity in fatherlessness: widows probably have a greater security of income than other women after the father has gone. *The Plowden Report*, op. cit., failed completely to appreciate that while income *level* might not have much influence on a child's school performance, as compared with 'parental aspirations', those aspirations might be intimately bound up with the parents' position in relation to the economic structure, through factors of income such as source, predictability, rate of change, shape of trends over time, etc.

The second longitudinal study of British children born in 1958 has included illegitimate children, and shows that by the age of seven 'time and again the illegitimate were at the bottom of the league table, be it for general knowledge, oral ability, creativity, perceptual development, reading attainment or arithmetical skills.' The children were initially not markedly different in social class, but there were more very young mothers, and mothers who decided to keep their children sunk in the social scale, so that by the age of seven less than half the original proportion were living in middle-class homes. A high proportion of the illegitimate children (three times the average) were placed in day care. Relationships in the homes of illegitimate children were disturbed, and material conditions were very poor. Even children staying in middle-class homes did less well than legitimate middle-class children from such homes. Adopted illegitimate children performed much better. See E. Crellin, M. L. Kelmer Pringle, and P. West, *Born Illegitimate, Social and Educational Implications*, National Children's Bureau, National Foundation for Educational Research, 1971.

8. See, for example, B. Jackson, *Streaming: an Educational System in Miniature*, Routledge and Kegan Paul, 1964, and J. B. Lunn, *Stream-*

ing, N.F.E.R., 1969, for evidence of the disadvantages of working-class children and children from broken homes.

9. See M. Wynn, *Family Policy*, op. cit., Chapters 3 and 6, for a very detailed discussion of needs in relation to the family cycle.

5: Broken Marriages

1. These seventy-six broken marriages are the broken *first* marriages of the divorced and separated, or the first divorce or separation of a widow. Thus there are thirty-seven divorces, comprising the dissolved first marriages of thirty-four currently divorced women, one widow and two separated wives; and there are thirty-nine separations, comprising the remainder of the forty-one separated wives after subtraction of the two previously divorced. The chapter does not include information on four divorces and two separations in second marriages.

2. For a discussion of divorce and separation statistics, see O. R. McGregor, *Divorce in England*, Heinemann, 1957; O. R. McGregor, L. Blom-Cooper, and C. Gibson, *Separated Spouses*, Duckworth, 1970; and G. Rowntree and N. H. Carrier, 'The Resort to Divorce in England and Wales, 1858–1957', *Population Studies*, March 1958, Vol. XI, No. 3. The divorce rate began to rise again in 1959, after seeming about to level off. For a comparative study of divorce rates in different countries, see W. J. Goode, 'Marital Satisfaction and Instability: A Cross-Cultural Analysis of Divorce Rates', *International Social Science Journal*, 1962, Vol. 14, pp. 507–26.

3. R. Chester, *Journal of Biosocial Science* (1971), 3, pp. 389–402. Chester comments on the key works in note 2 (above), and provides a different and slightly more up to date analysis of the data.

4. For example, in very detailed American studies of marriage the scales predictive of 'adjustment' include items on sharing decisions and activities and the enjoyment of sex. For a summary of the scale findings see H. Locke, *Predicting Happiness or Divorce in Marriage* New York, Holt 1951, and for criticisms of the principles and methods of scaling, see C. Kirkpatrick, 'Measuring Marital Adjustment', in *Selected Studies in Marriage and the Family* (ed. R. F. Winch et al.), New York, Holt, 1962, pp. 745–51. Locke mistakenly proposed as a working hypothesis for divorce research: 'Marital adjustment ranges along a continuum from very great to very little adjustment. Happiness in marriage, as judged by an outsider,

represents adjustment, and divorce represents maladjustment' (op. cit., p. 358).

5. See, for example, E. Bott, *Family and Social Network*, Tavistock, 1957, for a picture of different patterns of marriage in Britain. Bott's attempt to relate these patterns to the social networks of the couples has been criticized as providing a less satisfactory explanation of behaviour than does the couple's definition of sex role behaviour.

6. M. Hunt, *The World of the Formerly Married*, Allen Lane The Penguin Press, 1968, p. 36.

7. E. Slater and M. Woodside, *Patterns of Marriage*, Cassell, 1951.

8. H. Locke, op. cit., p. 27.

9. H. Locke, op. cit., and W. J. Goode, *Women in Divorce*, New York, Free Press, 1956, pp. 25–6.

10. The discussion of 'divorce strategy' and the classification of complaints are in W. J. Goode, *Women in Divorce*, op. cit., Chapters 10 and 11.

11. L. Pincus, *Marriage: Studies in Emotional Conflict and Growth*, Methuen, 1960, and H. V. Dicks, *Marital Tensions*, Routledge and Kegan Paul, 1967.

12. This compares closely with the only other figures for *de facto* and *de jure* lengths of marriage, in R. Chester, 'The Duration of Marriage to Divorce', *British Journal of Sociology*, XXII, No. 2, June 1971, p. 175. This article contains an interesting discussion of how the lack of knowledge of the *de facto* lengths of marriage, and our consequent use of the *de jure* figures, may conceal information about changing patterns and differential behaviour. In particular observers have been led to underestimate the speed at which marriages break up (op. cit., p. 178).

13. For a fuller discussion of the role of local authorities in marriage breakdown, see Chapter 9.

14. See Chapter 9.

15. There are 85,000 women who cannot trace their husbands. Anthony writes, 'Curiously enough there is a constantly recurring pattern: the man is about 40 years of age, without any outside hobbies or interests, he belongs to no church or club and once home from work

has his supper and then watches television until bedtime. In the morning he gets up at the same time and goes off to work. He has no social contacts, almost never entertains people at his home and seldom accepts invitations to other people's homes. He doesn't know his neighbours and they don't know him. The wife is usually under the impression that she has a steady husband and that she herself is a devoted wife and mother; in her view she is happily married. She is not aware that her husband has been nursing a grievance for many years ... Talking to the men who conform to the above pattern reveals a strikingly similar story. They were bored with their wives but stayed with them for the sake of the children. By middle age the children have grown up, the vital need to stay has lessened, and off they go.' Perhaps the men in the present research could not wait. See E. Anthony, 'Where Has He Gone?', *Justice of the Peace and Local Government Review*, 6 May 1970, p. 391.

6: Illegitimate Births

1. *The Registrar General's Statistical Review of England and Wales for 1964, Part III: Commentary*, H.M.S.O., 1967, pp. 63–4, reports a special follow-up study of married women based on the 1961 census.

2. A key example is L. Young, *Out of Wedlock*, McGraw-Hill, which looks like a predictive model until you try to see whether in a particular case adoption or retention of the child can be predicted from particular types of family relationships.

3. In a cross-national study reported by Christiansen, in 'Cultural Relativism and Premarital Sex Norms', *American Sociological Review*, Vol. XXV, 1, February 1960, pp. 31–9; also in W. Roberts (ed.), *The Unwed Mother*, New York, Harper and Row, 1966. This is an invaluable book of readings, with a useful discussion of causation theories by the editor in Chapter 1.

4. W. J. Goode, 'Illegitimacy in the Caribbean Social Structure', reprinted in *The Unwed Mother* (ed. W. Roberts), op. cit.

5. See, for example, *The Unwed Mother*, op. cit.

6. C. E. Vincent, *Unmarried Mothers*, Illinois, Free Press 1964. This study found no difference in psychological traits and background between a group of American mothers and a control group. Also, Anderson, Hamilton, and McKenna, after a small study of illegitimate pregnancy in girls under sixteen concluded that 'simple operation of chance sexual impulse in biologically ready individuals can account

for a large number of cases' (*Psychiatrica et Neurologia*, 133, 4, 1957). R. Bernstein has pointed out a source of bias in surveys of unmarried mothers, since *all* pregnant women have some neurotic traits, and unmarried mothers are often interviewed during pregnancy and at a time of great stress. ('Are We Still Stereotyping the Unmarried Mother?', reprinted in *The Unwed Mother*, op. cit.).

7. See R. Illsley, 'New Fashions in Illegitimacy', *New Society*, No. 320, 14 November 1968; and R. Illsley and D. G. Gill, 'Changing Trends in Illegitimacy', in *Social Science and Medicine: an International Journal*, Vol. 2, November 1967. The finding concerning the social descent of unmarried middle-class mothers comes from the recently published longitudinal study of a cohort of children born in 1958. See E. Crellin, M. L. Kellmer Pringle, and P. West, *Born Illegitimate, Social and Educational Implications*, National Children's Bureau, National Foundation for Educational Research, 1971.

8. There is a thorough assessment, as far as this can be done at the moment, in M. Simms, 'The Abortion Act after Three Years', *The Political Quarterly*, Vol. 42, No. 3, July–September 1971, pp. 269–86.

9. C. E. Vincent, op. cit.

10. Examples of studies reporting absence of family support as a distinguishing characteristic of families dependent on social work agencies are H. R. and E. B. Schaffer, *Child Care and the Family*, Bell, 1968; K. Kammeyer and C. D. Bolton, 'Community and Family Factors Related to the Use of a Family Service Agency', *Journal of Marriage and the Family*, 1968, 30, pp. 493–4; J. E. Mayer and N. Timms, *The Client Speaks*, Routledge and Kegan Paul, 1970.

11. See Christiansen, op. cit.

12. Herzog suggests that we can classify American unmarried mothers into two populations: one educated, middle-class, white and largely self-supporting, the other lower-class, non-white, and likely to become dependent on welfare because of low education and skills. The first group are secretive and are likely to receive psychotherapeutic and rehabilitative help. The other group receives more punitive and occupationally oriented advice. See E. Herzog, *Clinical Pediatrics*, Vol. 5, No. 2, February 1966, pp. 130–35.

13. W. J. Goode, 'Illegitimacy in the Caribbean Social Structure', op. cit., p. 54.

7: New Relationships with Kin and Community

1. This area of kinship appears not to have been explored systematic-ally, but for a note on the changing nature of roles when key members of the family are dead, see P. Townsend, *The Family Life of Old People*, Penguin Books, 1963, postscript. Interestingly, Holman gives two case studies of 'readoption' problems almost identical with those sketched in Figure 2. (R. Holman, *Unsupported Mothers*, op. cit., pp. 26–8.)

2. P. Marris, *Widows and Their Families*, op. cit.

3. The Registrar General noted that at the census there is understate-ment of divorce and overstatement of widowhood. See *Registrar General's Statistical Review of England and Wales, Part III*, 1963, pp. 21–7, for a discussion of the question of statements about marital status.

8: The Meaning of Fatherlessness to Mother and Children

1. This was a major finding of Goode's survey (although his methods tend to obscure its importance among a mass of more trivial correla-tions): the women who experienced a one-sided separation or divorce had a higher trauma index and were slower to re-enter courtship. By 'trauma index' is meant an indication of distress such as sleeplessness, more smoking, etc. (W. J. Goode, *Women in Divorce*, op. cit., p. 178.) Anthony also writes of the wife whose husband disappears suddenly: 'The psychic shock to the woman and her children is far worse than after a divorce and many of these women have to have intensive psychotherapy. She has been totally unprepared for the shock and suffers from a deep sense of humiliation.' (E. Anthony, 'Where Has He Gone?' *Justice of the Peace and Local Government Review*, 6 May 1970, p. 391.)

2. P. Marris, *Widows and Their Families*, op. cit.

3. See Chapter 4, note 7.

4. P. Glasser and E. Navarre point out that the absence of a man can severely disrupt the structural organization of the family, so that normal patterns of communication, power, affection, and task allotment are all dislocated. The mother can become the sole focus of power in the family with a resultant shift in the mother-child relationship. 'Structural Problems of the One-Parent Family', *Journal of Social Issues*, January 1965, XXI, pp. 98–109.

5. Cicourel says, 'It is the probation officer's use of the layman's or the sociologist's theories (broken homes and disorganized neighbourhoods produce delinquency) that accounts for the preliminary findings. Any imputed history of "disorganization" influences the probation officer's decision to accept the application for petition. Juveniles with similar offence records become singled out for "treatment" and court hearings because of lay theories of delinquency causation. Thus commonsense or lay theories are transformed into semiprofessional interpretation.' (A. V. Cicourel, *The Social Organization of Juvenile Justice* Wiley, pp. 34–6.)

6. For a comment on the disruptive effects of the conjunction of the children's adolescence with maximum economic stress on the family, see M. Wynn, *Family Policy*, op. cit., pp. 139–40.

7. Margaret Wynn gives evidence that the risk of a fatherless child going into care is eighteen times as great as for a child in a complete family. (*Fatherless Families*, op. cit. p. 125.)

8. For a discussion of remarriage rates, see *The Registrar General's Review of England and Wales, 1964; Part III*, H.M.S.O., 1965, pp. 23–8.

9. W. J. Goode, *Women in Divorce*, op. cit., Chapter 15.

10. P. Marris, op. cit.

11. In one form of common-law marriage ceremony a couple were deemed married if they stepped over a brush handle.

12. E. Herzog and C. E. Sudia, *Boys in Fatherless Families*, op. cit.

13. The sentence is drawn from an inversion of a Yiddish proverb, 'Money is not so good as lack of money is bad', by Kadushin, quoted in E. Herzog and C. E. Sudia, *Boys in Fatherless Families*, op. cit.

9: Local Authority Housing and Voluntary Schemes

1. J. Greve, *Homelessness in London*, Scottish Academic Press, 1971; and B. Glastonbury, *Homelessness Near a Thousand Homes*, National Institute for Social Work Training Series, No. 21, Allen and Unwin, 1971.

2. J. Greve, op. cit., p. 112n.

3. B. Glastonbury, op. cit., p. 49.

4. ibid., p. 68.

5. J. Greve, op. cit., p. 140.

6. B. Glastonbury, op. cit., pp. 212–13.

7. ibid., p. 223

8. ibid., p. 70.

9. ibid., p. 127.

10. ibid., p. 213, and J. Greve, op. cit., pp. 209.

11. B. Glastonbury, op. cit., p. 213.

12. ibid., p. 213.

13. ibid., p. 70.

14. J. Greve, op. cit., p. 229.

15. At the time of writing both political parties have tabled schemes for subsidizing *tenants* rather than types of property, and if these are generous enough and access is easy (two large ifs) fatherless families should be helped in the housing market.

16. A notorious example of this is the Birmingham Corporation's points system for council housing, which with its qualifications of residence and war service had the appearance of a fair scheme but which very effectively excluded immigrants from council housing. J. Rex and R. Moore, *Race, Community, and Conflict*, Oxford University Press, p. 167.

17. R. Holman, *Unsupported Mothers*, op. cit., p. 47.

18. Greve devotes a chapter to a description of this society's work in London. (*Homelessness in London*, op. cit.)

10: Family Law for the Poor

1. For a very scholarly and full discussion of the evolution of the law in relation to separation, divorce, maintenance, and especially the duty of the husband to maintain his dependants living apart, see O. R. McGregor, L. Blom-Cooper and C. Gibson, *Separated Spouses: A Study of the Matrimonial Jurisdiction of Magistrates' Courts*, Duckworth, 1970, Chapter 1. There is a briefer discussion and a comment on the current situation in *The Report of the Committee on Statutory Maintenance Limits* (The Graham Hall Report), Cmnd 3587, H.M.S.O., 1968, Chapters 1 to 3. For a sociological discussion of the whole of Family Law, see J. Ekelaar, *Family Security and Family*

Breakdown, Penguin Books, 1971. Ekelaar, from comparative studies of changes of divorce law and divorce rates in other countries, argues that changes in the law have apparently no effect on trends in family breakdown, that is, legal changes follow, or proceed outside, changes in social patterns.

2. O. R. McGregor, 'Towards Divorce Law Reform', *British Journal of Sociology*, Vol. XVIII, No. 1, March 1967, p. 92. See also O. R. McGregor et al., *Separated Spouses*, op. cit., Chapter 2, and O. R. McGregor, *Divorce in England*, Heinemann, 1957.

3. G. Rowntree and N. H. Carrier, 'The Resort to Divorce in England and Wales, 1858–1957', *Population Studies*, March 1958, Vol. XI, No. 3.

4. For two different reassessments of divorce law see the report of the Archbishop of Canterbury's study group, *Putting Asunder: A Divorce Law for Contemporary Society*, S.P.C.K., 1966, and the Law Reform Commission's *Reform of the Grounds of Divorce: The Field of Choice*, Cmnd 3123, H.M.S.O., 1966. These are reviewed in McGregor, 'Towards Divorce Law Reform', op. cit., pp. 91–9, where there is an account of the change in divorce law grounds and access to the law by different sections of the community. A compromise between the two views was reached in the Divorce Reform Act passed by Parliament in 1969. See also J. Ekelaar, op. cit., Chapter 9.

5. For a detailed discussion of the incidence of grounds used in divorce petitions, see R. Chester, 'Sex Difference in Divorce Behaviour', *Journal of Biosocial Science*, Supplement 2, 1970, pp. 121–8. Chester shows clearly that up to 1923 divorce legislation was sexually discriminatory against women, and that the proportion of women petitioners is still increasing. Over the past decade there has been a shift towards the use of grounds of adultery, for both sexes, and also cruelty, for women. But Chester says that much of the value of court records as data 'can only be realized when this information is supplemented by the results of a field inquiry'. See also the Graham Hall Report, op. cit., p. 37.

6. For a detailed discussion of grounds see J. Ekelaar, op. cit., Introduction and Chapter 9.

The original Bill, a Private Member's measure sponsored by Mr William Wilson (Lab., Coventry S.) was to enable a petition for divorce to be presented only on the ground that the marriage had irretrievably broken down. Breakdown of the marriage would be established by satisfying the court of one or more of five points:

that the respondent had committed adultery and the petitioner finds it intolerable to live with him or her;

that the respondent has behaved in such a way that the petitioner cannot reasonably be expected to live with him or her;

that the respondent has deserted the petitioner for at least two years immediately before the petition is presented;

that the parties have lived apart for at least two years immediately before the petition and that the respondent does not object to a decree;

that the parties have lived apart for at least five years immediately before the petition.

There was a revealing discussion, on the way adultery has not changed in nature from an 'offence', in the Standing Committee on the Divorce Reform Bill, 3 April 1968.

7. *Reform of the Grounds of Divorce: The Field of Choice*, op. cit., pp. 18–19.

8. See, for a discussion of this question, *Separated Spouses*, op. cit., Chapter 9.

9. O. R. McGregor et al., *Separated Spouses*, op. cit., Chapters 1 and 4.

10. ibid., p. 59. See also the Graham Hall Report, op. cit., p. 37.

11. O. R. McGregor et al., *Separated Spouses*, op. cit., pp. 23–4, 97–114, and 205.

12. ibid., pp. 177–87.

13. ibid., Chapter 5.

14. This proportion compares fairly closely with the Bedford College finding that only 13 per cent of mothers of illegitimate children even apply for a court order. O. R. McGregor et al., *Separated Spouses*, op. cit., p. 177.

15. O. R. McGregor et al., reviewing their own evidence and that of the Home Office's survey for the Graham Hall Committee (op. cit), noted a similar finding, with less than 2 per cent of the wives and one fifth to two fifths of the children receiving the maximum, the amount awarded per child showing a steady decrease as family size increases so that average amounts for children 'fell far short' of the then statutory maximum. Less than one in five awards exceeded supplementary benefit levels. The Home Office's figure for the average award was £2 18s. The Graham Hall Committee's recommendation for the

removal of the limits as having no perceptible rationale and as serving no useful purpose, was accepted by the government.

16. It was for this reason, the N.A.B.'s involvement in the law mainly where low-income couples were separating, that McGregor et al. suggested that there *may* be large number of informally separated middle-class couples where financial arrangements have not gone through the courts and whose marriages, consequently, do not appear in legal statistics as broken. (*Separated Spouses*, op. cit., p. 147.)

17. For a discussion of the sources of legal advice (which unfortunately neglects the role of the N.A.B.) see McGregor et al., *Separated Spouses*, op. cit., pp. 124–6. Interestingly, 'rather more than half the wives and husbands who did not have legal aid said that they were ignorant of the possible availability,' and men more often lacked information than women. Both the Graham Hall Report, op. cit., p. 68, and McGregor et al. comment on the lack of information on court procedures, and the Graham Hall Report advocates the issue of explanatory leaflets. McGregor et al. found that out of sixty-nine spouses whom they interviewed, three quarters went to court with no understanding of the procedures. (*Separated Spouses*, op. cit., p. 127.)

18. The proportion is similar to that found by McGregor et al., *Separated Spouses*, op. cit., p. 125. These authors quote some startling variations in the 'success' rate for applications for maintenance, from 97 per cent in Liverpool to 34 per cent in Birmingham. In view of Birmingham's reputation on abortion (another area for the 'defence' of the family) this variation is not unexpected, and it may stem from the Birmingham court in question using much stronger attempts to reconcile the spouses or at least to deter them from separating. See *Separated Spouses*, op. cit., pp. 56–7.

19. Pauline Morris noted a similar failure of relationship between the mothers and the N.A.B. over this matter of court orders. See *Prisoners and Their Families*, op. cit., p. 269.

20. Similar observations are made by the Graham Hall Report, op. cit., p. 35, para. 112; and McGregor et al. found that out of 52 courts only 14 made any special arrangements, by setting aside a special time for hearing marriage cases. Out of a sample of over 400 users of the courts 'nearly a third of the husbands and more than one fifth of the wives felt they were being treated like criminals'. (*Separated Spouses*, op. cit., pp. 128–9, 134, and 208.)

21. The legal and practical difficulties of affiliation procedures are

described in McGregor et al., *Separated Spouses*, op. cit., pp. 177–8.

22. McGregor et al. found that no fewer than three quarters of a group of 274 separated wives who were interviewed felt that the maintenance award was unfair, but strikingly an even higher proportion of husbands felt the same, an indication both that justice is not seen to be done and that there is probably insufficient money to support both spouses. The authors speculate on a change in the whole style of matrimonial courts, to a more inquisitorial role. (*Separated Spouses*, op. cit., p. 129.) The Graham Hall Report also comments on difficulties in assessing the husband's means (op. cit., pp. 69–71).

23. See note 17. McGregor et al. were worried by the speed of magistrates' court actions, which they felt was incompatible with a fair hearing: thus for a group of 79 couples they interviewed, 16 per cent of the hearings were over in less than a quarter of an hour and 26 per cent in less than half an hour.

24. 'It is now a regular practice for the Board to collect the money from the Court, arrangements to do so having been made with the woman's consent and the cooperation of the Justices' Clerk ... This procedure ensures that the woman has a regular weekly income at the national assistance standard and saves her the inconvenience of frequent visits to the office of her Magistrates' Clerk to collect any money paid into the Court.' (*N.A.B. Report for 1965*, Cmnd 3042, H.M.S.O., p. 27.)

25. The Graham Hall Report, op. cit., p. 33, comments approvingly on the arrangement for signing-over and says that in 1965 the practice was extended so as to be 'now almost universal', so Northborough must have been, or have become, very unusual in this respect.

26. Regrettably this mother's experiences are all too typical for those who continue to collect from the courts. Thus McGregor et al. found that out of fifty-two courts only a minority had a separate office for the collection and payment of maintenance, while 'for the rest husbands and wives waited in the queue with those paying fines for criminal offences and the like.' Of the fifty-two collecting offices, sixteen opened daily, the rest ranging from four day opening to eleven which opened for seven hours or less a week. Only three of the fifty-two court offices stayed open on one evening a week for collection. Four very large courts would send money by post only to women outside the city, and seven, including two very large courts refused to accept or strongly discouraged telephone calls. (*Separated*

Spouses, op. cit., pp. 121–2 and p. 208.) The government has now (1971) decided that all mothers should have the facility of receiving their maintenance by postal cheque.

27. O. R. McGregor et al., *Separated Spouses*, op. cit., p. 122.

28. The history and failure of attachment of earnings are well documented in O. R. McGregor et al., *Separated Spouses*, op. cit., Chapter 7.

29. O. R. McGregor et al., *Separated Spouses*, op. cit., p. 206.

30. McGregor et al. came to the conclusion that probably many separated wives were robbed of desertion grounds for divorce because the magistrates' courts made excessive use of non-cohabitation clauses merely through incompetence, the failure to strike out the relevant words in a standard order. (*Separated Spouses*, op. cit., Chapter 4, p. 67.)

31. Chester's data show that the median interval from separation to final divorce is 2.9 years, with one third extending beyond four years. Half of those divorcing had been separated for three years or more, even though the actual legal process takes seven months only. Although the time length to the break-up of the marriage did not differ according to grounds used for divorce, delays in taking court proceedings where the husband had deserted were on average eight years, that is far longer than the legal three-year minimum and also substantially longer than where the petition was for cruelty or adultery. This fits the earlier suggestion, and Goode's findings, that desertion by the husband is most likely to be associated with the wife's longing for his return. (R. Chester, 'The Duration of Marriage to Divorce', op. cit., p. 176.)

32. R. Chester, op. cit., found that adultery accounted for 67 per cent of grounds for men, and as much as 88 per cent for husbands aged 20–24, but only 45 per cent for women.

33. W. J. Goode, *Women in Divorce*, op. cit., p. 114. That this may be a consequence of divorce law is suggested by the recent *contrary* movements of petitions in America and Britain; see R. Chester, op. cit., p. 126.

34. *Reform of the Grounds of Divorce: The Field of Choice*, op. cit., para. 17.

35. O. R. McGregor et al., op. cit., p. 213.

36. ibid., pp. 211–12.

37. ibid., p. 208.

38. ibid., p. 212.

39. Quoted in McGregor et al., op. cit., p. 28.

40. National Assistance Act, 1948, s.42 and s.43.

41. Ministry of Social Security Act, 1966, s.22 and s.23.

42. McGregor et al., op. cit., p. 215.

43. ibid., pp. 213–14.

11: Means-Tested Incomes: The Official Ideal of a Discretionary Service

1. W. Beveridge, *Social Insurance and Allied Services* (The Beveridge Report), Cmnd 6404, H.M.S.O., 1942, p. 134, para. 347, and note. These are quoted in Chapter 15.

2. Widows received state pensions rather like old age pensions under the Widows', Orphans' and Old Age Contributory Pensions Act of 1925.

3. See *Reports of the National Assistance Board* for the relevant years, and Chapter 15, Figure 3. Professor Titmuss has described the setting up of the N.A.B. and the S.B.C., and the changing nature and size of the population served in R. M. Titmuss, 'New Guardians of the Poor in Britain', in S. Jenkins (ed.), *Social Security in International Perspective*, Columbia University, 1969.

4. This right was reasserted in Parliament during discussions of the setting-up of the Supplementary Benefits Commission. The Minister of Pensions stated in reply to Lena Jeger in a debate on Clause 11 of the Social Security Bill, '... it is envisaged that the Commission, as the (National Assistance) Board does at present, will only require the registration of persons who are in the unemployment field. Persons like those mentioned by my Hon. Friend, who are unfit or who are the mothers of children of school age, will not be required to register. (*Hansard*, Vol. 1729, No. 35, Friday, 17 June 1966, paras. 1897–1906.)

5. See R. M. Titmuss, 'New Guardians of the Poor', op. cit., for a full discussion of the official intentions and hopes surrounding the transition from the old Poor Law to the N.A.B. and then the S.B.C.

6. R. M. Titmuss, 'Welfare "Rights", Law and Discretion', *The Political Quarterly*, Vol. 42, April–June 1971, pp. 113–32.

7. Supplementary Benefits Commission, Department of Health and Social Security, *Supplementary Benefits Handbook*, H.M.S.O., 1970.

8. Report by the Supplementary Benefits Commission to the Secretary of State for Social Services, *Cohabitation* (*The Administration of the Relevant Provisions of the Ministry of Social Security Act 1966*), H.M.S.O., 1971.

9. R. J. Coleman, *Supplementary Benefits and the Administrative Review of Administrative Action*, Poverty Pamphlet 7, Child Poverty Action Group, 1 Macklin St, London W C 2.

10. See the speech by the Minister of Social Security, in *Hansard*, House of Commons, 24 May 1966, col. 339 (quoted by R. M. Titmuss, in 'New Guardians of the Poor', op. cit., p. 165). The Minister says, 'it is a deliberate step to establish within the Ministry independence in adjudication of the new benefit and wisdom in guiding its administration through that group of knowledgeable people ... The second thing I stress is that we intend that the members of the Commission shall cover a wide variety of interests, that they will be a source of advice to the Minister on many social problems, and that, in particular, they will assist the Minister's programme of research into those problems.'

11. For example Professor Titmuss underlined the reduction in preventable blindness which had occurred as a result of referrals by N.A.B. officials in the course of their work with old people. (*Commitment to Welfare*, Allen and Unwin, 1968, pp. 69–71.) On the other hand there has been controversy about the scope of coverage of means-tested benefits, and the setting-up of the S.B.C. was partly an acknowledgement that the N.A.B. was still not reaching a large proportion of old people. Owing to pressure of work the S.B.C. has had to cut back on visits to old people, probably at the expense of welfare activities.

12. The basic scale rates and some regulations are printed in Appendix Two, together with the scale rates current in 1971.

13. R. Titmuss, 'Welfare "Rights", Law and Discretion', op. cit., p. 127.

14. S.B.C., *Supplementary Benefits Handbook*, op. cit., p. 1, asserts, 'An exclusively legal approach to a non-contributory benefits scheme can only lead to a narrower not a broader concept of the "rights" of claimants, since those rights are or should be social as well as legal. It will also tend to a more restrictive rather than a more generous or

adaptable range of entitlement ... By definition no one can claim as a "right" that a particular discretionary power should be exercised in his favour. But for the individual claimant the existence of these discretionary powers may be more valuable than a precisely prescribed right because they give the scheme a flexibility of response to varying situations of human need.'

15. ibid., p. 1.

16. ibid., p. 1.

17. R. M. Titmuss, 'Welfare "Rights", Law and Discretion', op. cit., pp. 126–7.

18. ibid., p. 127.

19. For example, the Birmingham Claimants Union, which has become the centre for a National Federation of Claimants Unions.

20. *N.A.B. Report for 1965*, Cmnd 3042, H.M.S.O., p. ix.

21. S.B.C., *Cohabitation*, op. cit., p. 4, para. 9.

22. ibid., p. 8, para. 22.

23. *N.A.B. Report for 1965*, op. cit., p. 40.

24. Communication from the S.B.C. to Mr Frank Field, Secretary of the Child Poverty Action Group.

25. Report in the *Guardian*, 10 December 1969.

26. S.B.C., *Cohabitation*, op. cit., p. 8, para. 23.

27. There is a description of the workings of an N.A.B. office (which Professor Titmuss has called 'an illuminating and balanced essay': 'Welfare "Rights", Law and Discretion', op. cit., p. 130) in M. J. Hill, 'The Exercise of Discretion in the National Assistance Board', *Public Administration*, 1969, Vol 47.

28. K. R. Stowe, 'Staff Training and the National Assistance Board: Problems and Policies,' *Public Administration*, Winter 1961.

29. *N.A.B. Report for 1964*, Cmnd 2674, H.M.S.O., pp. 57–8, describes the Board's efforts in this field.

30. R. M. Titmuss, 'Welfare "Rights", Law and Discretion', op. cit., p. 128 and S.B.C., *Cohabitation*, pp. 9–10.

31. S.B.C., *Cohabitation*, p. 6, para. 17.

32. ibid.

33. R. J. Coleman gives the figures for rates of appeal as Supplementary Benefits, 0.26 per cent; National Insurance, 0.06 per cent; unemployment benefit, 0.65 per cent; Industrial injuries, 1.82 per cent. He points out the trades unions are heavily involved in unemployment and disability cases (op. cit., p. 11, Table C).

34. See, for example, *Poverty*, the journal of the Child Poverty Action Group.

35. The very words 'evolution' and 'dynamic' beg the question of how change takes place in institutions; individuals in such institutions are not immune from political pressures; the internal processes and external pressures may be complementary. In any case we are very seldom in possession of enough information about a particular change to say the process was 'adaptation' rather than 'coercion'.

36. For example, *Sunday Times*, 8 August 1971; see also the *Guardian*, 9 August 1971.

37. The *Supplementary Benefits Handbook* is discussed in *Poverty*, 15, 1970.

38. See R. J. Coleman, op. cit., pp. 12–13.

39. See, for example, the article by C. Glasser, in *Poverty*, No. 15; also R. J. Coleman, op. cit.; R. M. Titmuss, 'Welfare "Rights", Law and Discretion', op. cit., and Child Poverty Action Group, *A Policy to Establish the Legal Rights of Low Income Families*, 1969.

40. See C. Glasser, article in *Poverty*, No. 15.

41. R. J. Coleman, op. cit.

42. R. M. Titmuss, 'Welfare "Rights", Law and Discretion', op. cit., p. 129.

43. Child Poverty Action Group, *A Policy to Establish the Legal Rights of Low Income Families*, and T. Lynes, in *The Fifth Social Service*, Fabian Essays, 1970.

44. The setting up of the S.B.C. and new arrangements are described in R. M. Titmuss, 'New Guardians of the Poor in Britain', op. cit., pp. 164–5: 'The Policy Inspectorate [are] a group of able civil servants, whose main responsibility is to operate as the "eyes and ears" for the Commission. They undertake pilot and prepilot surveys.'

12: The Mothers' Experience of National Assistance

1. Even in Bermondsey, where there is a tradition of women working, convenient shift-work is available, and there is an extensive network of kin available for minding children, only one in five mothers of preschool children work. P. Jephcott, *Married Women Working*, Allen and Unwin, 1962. See also R. Holman, *Unsupported Mothers*, op. cit., Chapters 3, 4, 5, and 7, and pp. 47–50, for a discussion of work and day-care.

2. R. Holman, *Unsupported Mothers*, op. cit., p. 10, found that fifteen out of ninety-five mainly unmarried mothers were working for incomes below supplementary benefit level. The Ministry of Social Security Survey, *Circumstances of Families*, op. cit., p. 25, found a smaller proportion of families below the poverty level, 7 per cent, but is probably unreliable on this point since numbers are small. But in any case the problem is not the proportions who remain below the poverty line, but the proportion who, for their own social good, would be better off working part-time or not at all, but who fail to claim state support.

3. See S. Kaye, in D. Bull (ed.), *Family Poverty*, Duckworth, 1971, Chapter 3, for a discussion of feelings of stigma.

4. There are analogies here with Runciman's study, where certain more remote income groups were not seen as competitors. (W. G. Runciman, op. cit.)

5. See D. Bull, 'Current Research', *Poverty*, No. 11, Summer 1969, p. 14, for an investigation of the inefficiency of post offices as a means of disseminating leaflets.

6. Professor Titmuss has commented on the poor state of the offices in *Unequal Rights*, London Cooperative Society, 1966, and also in 'Welfare "Rights", Law and Discretion', op. cit., pp. 131–2.

7. *Hansard* for 13 March 1967 had an exchange about unmarried mothers, between Dr Hugh Gray, M.P., and Mr Norman Pentland, Parliamentary Secretary. Dr Gray said that some unmarried mothers had complained of a display of moral attitudes and pressure to divulge the name of the father by the Ministry of Social Security officials. It was also alleged that officials tried to persuade unmarried mothers to return to work while their children were still young. Mr Pentland said that if he produced the facts he would look into them. It was quite untrue that claims for supplementary benefits by unmarried mothers

were discouraged. In this context there was also an interesting correspondence in the *Guardian*, 17 and 18 November 1970, describing
the unpleasantness experienced by a young unmarried mother when
she applied for supplementary benefits.

8. S.B.C., *Cohabitation*, op. cit., p. 10, paras. 28 and 29.

9. In this context, see the letter from 'Cohabitant', *New Statesman*,
15 March 1968, p. 334.

10. M. J. Hill, op. cit., p. 82.

11. For example, where my assessments involved only one 'unknown'
quantity (as far as I could judge) such as an officer's deduction from
an allowance because a lodger was liable for part of the rent, I was
able to infer from the regulations and my calculations what had been
done. Where, however, there were additional unknown quantities
such as a repairs allowance or a discretionary allowance for diet, the
value of individual items could only be inferred by analogy with
similar but more simple situations containing only one unknown. In
this way the uncertainty could be reduced but not entirely eliminated.

12. At the request of the administration, written statements are not
issued for reasons of cost in time and money to the S.B.C. See *Hansard*,
Vol. 729, No. 35, Friday, 17 June 1966, paras 1897–1906, for a discussion of this and related points.

13. *Report of the N.A.B. for 1965*, Cmnd 3402, H.M.S.O., p. 16,
shows a 'rent-stop' figure of 1.1 per cent.

14. Hill says that in the office where he worked, 'Reputations for
harshness or generosity were well known throughout the office, and
Clerical Officers who did much of the revisiting, would – if recom-
mending the upward revision of some allowances - seek to avoid
submitting their cases to known harsh officers for approval, a practice
that involved evading the formal channels in many cases' (op. cit.,
p. 81).

15. M. J. Hill, op. cit., p. 81. For another comment on the apparent
arbitrariness of discretion from the clients' viewpoint, see J. Owtram,
The Right to Help?, D.I.G. paper No. 10.

16. Other charities, too, could easily have become dependent on or at
least partially controlled by the N.A.B., such as the Seaston charity
which approached the N.A.B. for names of needy families to take a
holiday in its caravan, although the N.A.B. fair-mindedly allowed the
charity to select its own families.

17. The form for local authority grants and maintenance allowances may require to know both parents' incomes, and 'any special circumstances' must be explained in a covering letter. A correspondent writes that she is hiding from her husband and does not want someone from the education department to start trying to trace him in case he should find her whereabouts. She dare not apply for a uniform grant, and is extremely worried about the time when her child will enter the sixth form and she will need a maintenance grant.

18. M. J. Hill, op. cit., p. 87.

13: The Continuing Failures of Means-Tested Benefits

1. I am grateful to Mr Michael Hill for a chance to see his discussion of the origins and control of discretion, which was very useful in writing this chapter. See M. J. Hill, *The Sociology of Public Administration* (to be published), Chapter 4.

2. There is a very close parallel here with the failures of educational policy since 1944, where the really difficult decisions of educational redistribution have been evaded in Parliament and handed over unsolved to the Ministry of Education and the D.E.S., whose civil servants have played a consistently conservative role in first blocking comprehensives and then completely failing to provide guidance and information to ensure that local authority schemes became truly comprehensive. As with supplementary benefits, the ultimate result has been that the value dilemmas have devolved to local level, and to individual teachers. See D. Marsden, *Politicians, Equality, and Comprehensives*, Fabian Tract 411, 1971. The S.B.C. differs from the D.E.S. in having an explicitly lay committee.

3. R. M. Titmuss, 'Welfare "Rights", Law and Discretion', op. cit., p. 131.

4. The case for more generous family allowances has been argued by Sir John Walley in *Poverty*, No. 10, and by Peter Townsend and Tony Atkinson in *Poverty*, No. 16/17, 1971.

5. M. J. Hill, 'The Exercise of Discretion in the National Assistance Board', op. cit., p. 87.

6. See, for example, D. Bull, *Action for Welfare Rights*, Fabian Research Series, 286, 1970.

7. D. G. Bull, 'Out-of-Form Post Offices', *Poverty*, No. 12/13, 1969.

8. K. R. Stowe, op. cit.

9. A. J. Baker, 'The Men Behind the Counter', *Poverty*, No. 8, 1968.

10. See Chapter 12, note 6.

11. R. M. Titmuss, 'Welfare "Rights", Law and Discretion', op. cit., p. 131.

12. R. M. Titmuss, 'The New Guardians of the Poor in Britain', op. cit., pp. 165–6.

13. See D. E. Smith, 'Front Line Organisation of the State Mental Hospital', *Administrative Science Quarterly*, Vol. 10, No. 3, December 1965, pp. 381–99.

14. P. Blau, *The Dynamics of Bureaucracy (A Study of Interpersonal Relations in Two Government Agencies)*, University of Chicago Press, 1965.

15. E. Goffman, *Asylums*, Penguin Books, 1969.

16. P. Townsend, *The Last Refuge*, Routledge and Kegan Paul, 1962.

17. J. Barker Lunn, *Streaming in Primary Schools*, N.F.E.R., 1969.

18. M. Crozier, *The Bureaucratic Phenomenon*, Tavistock, 1964.

19. M. J. Hill, 'The Exercise of Discretion in the National Assistance Board', op. cit., p. 87.

20. M. J. Hill, *The Sociology of Public Administration*, Chapter 4 (to be published). R. M. Titmuss, 'Welfare "Rights", Law and Discretion', op. cit., pp. 126–7.

21. R. J. Coleman, op. cit.

22. See Chapter 11, note 39, for discussions of the introduction of more legal assistance.

23. The claimants' unions are understandably suspicious of social researchers and bar membership to those who are not themselves claimants, although with admirable wit the Birmingham Claimants Union raises money by offering would-be researchers a 'research membership' whereby, for payment of a substantial fee, the social investigator may receive a suitable assortment of union documents upon which to exercise his curiosity. Hilary Rose, to whom I am indebted for some of the information in this short section, is currently engaged in research on claimants' unions and welfare rights move-

ments. She has published an interesting preliminary comment on the shift to militant action in the social services in *Rights, Participation and Conflict*, Poverty pamphlet five, Child Poverty Action Group, 1 Macklin Street, London WC2.

24. See, for example, H. Rose, op. cit.

25. H. Rose, op. cit., p. 5.

26. Professor Titmuss is at present a member of the Finer Committee on One-Parent Families.

27. The first Research Report was a curiously wrong-headed comparison of two unrepresentative but matched groups of fatherless and complete families drawing supplementary benefit. Unfortunately the Report arrives too late for detailed comment here. It seems to confirm (although without acknowledgement) some of the research findings of the present survey, notably on the distribution of living standards and accommodation between the groups of different marital status. But a misplaced academicism in matching the two sets of families renders the Report virtually useless as an indicator of how the average fatherless family on supplementary benefit is faring. (*Families Receiving Supplementary Benefit*, Statistical and Research Report Series No. 1, D.H.S.S., H.M.S.O., 1972.)

28. S.B.C., *Cohabitation*, p. 8, para. 24, and p. 6, para. 17.

29. D.H.S.S., *National Superannuation and Social Insurance, Proposals for Earnings-Related Social Security*, Cmnd 3883, 1969.

30. Just before we go to press, Sir Keith Joseph announced that children in cohabitation cases would be supported for a month only to tide the mother over the period after the withdrawal of her allowance. A small concession, but perhaps the thin end of the wedge of a fatherless families allowance.

31. There is an interesting discussion of the problems of discretion in services for the 'undeserving' poor, which points to the same conclusion as the analysis in this chapter, in F. H. Handler, and E. J. Hollingsworth, 'Reforming Welfare: The Constraints of the Bureaucracy and the Clients', University of Pennsylvania *Law Review*, Vol. 118, No. 8, July 1970 (reprinted by Institute for Research on Poverty of Wisconsin-Madison, Reprint 66).

15: The Needs and Rights of Fatherless Families

1. O. R. McGregor et al., *Separated Spouses*, op. cit., Chapters 1 and 11.

2. I. Pinchbeck, 'Social Attitudes Towards Illegitimacy', *British Journal of Sociology*, Vol. 5, No. 4, 1954.

3. O. R. McGregor et al., *Separated Spouses*, op. cit., p. 168.

4. E. Herzog, *Clinical Pediatrics*, Vol. 5, No. 2, February 1966, pp. 130–35.

5. C. Vincent, *Unmarried Mothers*, Illinois, Free Press.

6. O. R. McGregor et al., *Separated Spouses*, Chapter 1.

7. See, for example, V. N. George, *Social Security: Beveridge and After*, Routledge and Kegan Paul, 1968, Chapter 7, for an account of death benefits.

8. M. Wynn, *Fatherless Families*, op. cit., p. 28.

9. *New Society*, 12 October 1967, No. 265, p. 514.

10. See N.A.B. Regulations, Appendix 1, paragraph 9(d).

11. That is, calculated for a two child family as in note 2 of the Introduction. The figure is almost exactly 200 per cent of scale rate.

12. M. Wynn, 'F.I.S. and Fatherless Families', *Poverty*, Child Poverty Action Group, No. 16/17, p. 23.

13. See Chapter 10.

14. Introduction, note 3.

15. M. Wynn, *Fatherless Families*, op. cit., Chapter 2.

16. The Council is currently negotiating with the Charity Commissioners to have its articles changed to cover all fatherless families.

17. *Social Insurance and Allied Services* (The Beveridge Report), Cmnd 6404, 1942, para. 347.

18. Sir W. Beveridge, *Pillars of Security*, Allen and Unwin, 1942, p. 68.

19. *Social Insurance and Allied Services*, op. cit., p. 135, para. 348 (iii).

20. *Committee on Statutory Maintenance Limits* (The Graham Hall Report), Cmnd 3587 (1968), para. 215. See also *Separated Spouses*, op. cit., pp. 214–15.

21. See Pat Healey, 'Fatherless Family in Security Plans', *The Times*, 11 December 1968, p. 8.

22. *National Superannuation and Social Insurance, Proposals for Earnings-Related Social Security*, Cmnd 3883, 1969, para. 41.

23. See Part Three, especially Chapter 8, conclusion.

24. However, F.I.S., while it should reach a number of fatherless families (perhaps at a maximum 54,000 where the mother is working full-time), cannot be seen as offering to the 176,000 mothers on supplementary benefit a real choice of going out to work. The principle of F.I.S. is that for the working poor the Government has laid down minimum income levels, and the amount of F.I.S. paid will be equivalent to one half of the amount by which the family income falls short of the relevant 'make-up' level. The levels are £15 for a one-child family, £17 for two children, £19 for three children and so on, adding £2 per child. The maximum F.I.S. will be £3. The mothers who will benefit are therefore those who have a low rent, or who are working in spite of the fact that they are worse off than they would be on supplementary benefit. But F.I.S. offers nothing to mothers who already receive a large rent allowance through supplementary benefit, and who are allowed to work part-time. F.I.S. also takes no account of the cost of children of different ages. See M. Wynn, 'F.I.S. and Fatherless Families', *Poverty*, 16/17 op. cit., for a discussion of F.I.S. See also D. Barker, in D. Bull (ed.), *Family Poverty*, op. cit., p. 74. Barker too, concludes that the value of F.I.S. depends closely on the fees for child care.

25. A book, *Motherless Families*, by Paul Wilding and Victor George, will be the first systematic evidence we have about such families (to be published).

26. *Forward for the Fatherless*, N.C.U.M.C. evidence for the Finer Committee, 1971. For a summary and comment see 'Finer and Families', *New Society*, 475, 4 November 1971, p. 860.

27. R. Holman in *Unsupported Mothers*, op. cit., gives the following comparative figures for supplementary benefit and fostering: child 0–5 years, £1 5s. as against fostering, £2 0s. 8d.

28. See Sir J. Walley, *Poverty*, No. 10.

29. See the proposals for improving fathers' rights in *Forward for the Fatherless*, N.C.U.M.C., 1971.

30. O. R. McGregor et al., *Separated Spouses*, op. cit., pp. 200–206.

31. See, for example, the interview with Miss Priscilla Chapman in the *Sunday Times*, 30 November 1969.

32. See R. M. Titmuss, *Income Distribution and Social Change*, George Allen and Unwin, 1962, pp. 77–9.

33. The fate of poverty research on old people, for example, or the fate of Glastonbury and Greve's housing research.

Index

Penguinews *and*
Penguins in Print

Every month we issue an illustrated magazine,
Penguinews. It's a lively guide to all the latest Penguins,
Pelicans and Puffins, and always contains an article on
a major Penguin author, plus other features of
contemporary interest.

Penguinews is supplemented by *Penguins in Print*, a
complete list of all the available Penguin titles – there
are now over four thousand!

The cost is no more than the postage; so why not write
for a free copy of this month's *Penguinews*? And if
you'd like both publications sent for a year, just send us
a cheque or a postal order for 30p (if you live in the United
Kingdom) or 60p (if you live elsewhere), and we'll put
you on our mailing list.

Dept EP, Penguin Books Ltd, Harmondsworth,
Middlesex

Note: *Penguinews* and *Penguins in Print* are not available
in the U.S.A. or Canada.

Working Class Community

Brian Jackson

It is only slowly being appreciated (partly through such books as *The Uses of Literacy* and *The Making of the English Working Class* and the work of such bodies as the Institute of Community Studies) that a rich vein of culture and tradition runs 'on the wrong side of the tracks'. Brian Jackson was born in Huddersfield where he made this lively, yet objective, survey of the thriving world of working-men's clubs, brass bands, mills and bowling-greens which flourishes north of the Trent. The more youthful and modern outlook of the town is reflected in a chapter (largely written by schoolgirls) on 'Growing up in Huddersfield', in another on the Jazz Club, and in a report of a series of Saturday night riots.

'His theme is that working-class life is not a problem mutation of the middle-class norm but that it has a richness, a vitality and a social complexity of its own completely beyond the grasp of the housing authorities, the bosses and the well-meaning middle classes in general. He brings the novelist's as well as the sociologist's eye to his subject' – Keith Waterhouse in the *Sunday Times*

Education and the Working Class

Brian Jackson and Dennis Marsden

'The way our parents do things and look at things, the way they set about living – that's altogether foreign to us. We look at it from the outside, and it seems strange.'

The effects, in human terms, of the slow revolution being brought about by education are examined in this absorbing survey made under the auspices of the Institute of Community Studies. Eighty-eight working-class children (now grown up) who have passed through the grammar schools of Huddersfield since the Education Act of 1944 were selected as a sample (typical, at any rate, of a North Country 'Boom' town) for this study.

From interviews with them and their parents the authors have composed a revealing, and often surprising, record of the ambitions and frustrations, the pressures and anxieties, the successes and failures, and the changing loyalties of young people who are on their way to the 'high places'.

Not for sale in the U.S.A.